Philosophical Perspectives on Punishment

Philosophical Perspectives on Punishment

Edited, with an introduction, by Gertrude Ezorsky

State University of New York Press Albany 1972

Gertrude Ezorsky is Professor of Philosophy
at Brooklyn College of The City University of New York

Published by the State University of New York Press
99 Washington Avenue, Albany, New York 12210
Copyright © 1972 by State University of New York
All rights reserved
Printed in the United States
Designed by Richard Hendel

Library of Congress Cataloging in Publication Data

Ezorsky, Gertrude, 1926- comp.
   Philosophical perspectives on punishment.

   Bibliography: p.
   1. Punishment—Addresses, essays, lectures.
I. Title.
HV8675.E9   365   72-37999
ISBN 0-87395-212-X
ISBN 0-87395-213-8 (pbk.)

Acknowledgment

My thanks to the
City University of
New York for a
Faculty Research grant

Contents

Chapter I. Concepts of Punishment

Chapter II. The Justification of Punishment

1. TELEOLOGICAL THEORIES

2. RETRIBUTIVISM

Chapter III. Strict Liability

Chapter IV. The Death Penalty

Chapter V. Alternatives to Punishment

Gertrude Ezorsky

The Ethics of Punishment

"Punishment," writes McTaggart, "is pain and to inflict pain on any person obviously needs justification." But if the need to justify punishment is obvious, the manner of so doing is not. Philosophers have advanced an array of diverse and conflicting arguments to justify punitive institutions. I shall sort their claims into three varieties: teleological, retributivist, and teleological retributivist.

What are the distinctive claims of our three kinds of philosophers?

Teleologists believe that punishment should yield, in fact, some further effect, which is desirable. Thus Bentham, a utilitarian, held that while the suffering of punishment is itself evil, nevertheless the threat of punishment, strengthened by enforcement, may serve a good purpose, e.g., deterrence of aspiring criminals and a consequent reduction in the misery wrought by crime. Notice that this sort of view may be empirically confirmed, or refuted, by a factual investigation, for punishment is conceived as a causal means which, given our laws of nature, will yield the effect of crime prevention.

Retributivists, however, take a different view of the matter. They claim that necessarily the distribution of deserved suffering for wrong doing is either just or intrinsically valuable, irrespective of any further good consequence, e.g., crime prevention. Some philosophers might put the matter in this fashion: punishment for immorality would exemplify justice or have worth not merely in our familiar world, but in any possible world.

Teleological retributivists pay their respects to a plurality of principles. Thus, they share with utilitarians the notion that penal laws should yield some demonstrable beneficial consequences. Justice is not served by the infliction of deserved suffering for its own sake. But they derive the following view from retributivism: justice is served if teleological aims are held in check by principles of justice, e.g., that the suffering of punishment should not exceed the offender's desert.

Let us consider the merits—and the demerits—of these three perspectives on punishment.

Teleology

Teleologists view punishment as desirable either primarily for the guilty man, i.e., making him a better person, or primarily for the world, e.g., by isolating and reforming criminals or deterring potential offenders, punishment makes the world a better place.

Early better man thinkers, like Plato and Aristotle, conceived crime as a spiritual disease, curable by the bitter medicine of punishment. For Hegel, (as interpreted by McTaggart) the pain of punishment yields repentance, whereby the criminal recognizes his sin. He does not merely change his ways. Fear of future punishment might yield this superficial reform. He really becomes a better man; thus, Hegel declares, realizes his true nature.

It is tempting to challenge curative theories by pointing to the sparsity of supporting evidence. (Do hardened criminals really mend their ways, either superficially or in depth, when punished?) But there are more fundamental objections at hand. Let us assume that in some cases punishment really does produce the effects claimed by these philosophers. It would not follow then that punishment is justified. Suppose the social costs of producing the punitive cure required were very burdensome? Or suppose that symptoms of a propensity to commit crime appeared before crimes were committed? Should preventive punishment—if effective—be imposed as we might impose preventive medicine against communicable disease? Imagine that a very severe punishment cured someone guilty of a petty offense. Would not such a punishment be undeserved, hence unjust?

The same sort of problems arise for those who see treatment, e.g., psychoanalytic therapy or drugs, as an alternative to punishment. Should preventive treatment be imposed on persons who will most likely commit crimes? Should the bill for slightly successful, but very costly, treatment be imposed on society? Remember, too, that cures can be more painful than punishments. According to a 1966 experiment performed in a Canadian mental hospital, treatment can, to some extent, reduce the amount of liquor ingested by alcoholics. The treatment? Intravenous injection of 20 mgs. of succinylcholine chloride which induces paralysis and suppression of respiration, that is, a *drowning to death* experience. Surely no reasonable person would suggest treating alcoholic petty offenders in this fashion. The treatment would, of course, not be imposed as a punishment. Yet who would hesitate to call it undeserved? The moral problems raised by curative theories of punishment (or treatment) require, not merely an account of beneficial effects on the criminal, but a comprehensive moral perspective. Utilitarians claim to have it.

Utilitarians are better world teleologists. They evaluate punishment as follows. A moral agent ought to choose that act which of all feasible alternatives, has maximum utility. (The utility of an act is measured by its efficacy in producing happiness or reducing suffering, for everyone.) How does the suffering of punishment fit into this scheme? Bentham puts the matter in this fashion:

The general object which all laws have, or ought to have in common, is to augment the total happiness of the community: and therefore, in the first place, to exclude, as far as may be, every thing that tends to subtract from that happiness; in other words, to exclude mischief . . . .But all punishment is mischief; all punishment is in itself evil. Upon the principle of utility, if it ought at all to be admitted, it ought only to be admitted in as far as it promises to exclude some greater evil. (Principles of Morals and Legislation, Ch. XII).

Punishment serves to "exclude some greater evil" when by the workings of isolation, reform, and deterrence, the misery and insecurity created by crime is reduced.

It may be objected that the reform and deterrence effects of punishment have been exaggerated. Nevertheless, it is reasonable to suppose that some criminals, when punished, do not repeat an offense and that the threat of punishment stays the hands of some persons tempted to crime. In such cases, if punishment, as compared to other alternatives, e.g., psychiatric treatment, has maximum utility, the utilitarian is obligated by his views to endorse punishment.

Critics of utilitarianism claim that punishment which passes utilitarian standards may be undeserved, hence unjust. Indeed, as they see the matter, utilitarians are committed to undeserved punishment of two sorts, legal and illegal.

Let us consider the legal variety first. A legal punishment is undeserved when the offender is not morally responsible for the offense or if his prescribed punishment is excessive. An offender is not morally responsible when the following conditions obtain: he is punished either retroactively (by ex post facto law), or vicariously (for the act of another), or he has a valid excuse for committing the offense, i.e., insanity, ignorance or mistake of fact, necessity, incompetence, or automatism. When such excuses are not accepted, the offender is being held *strictly liable*.

How could retroactive sanctions, vicarious punishment, or strict liability serve utilitarian purposes?

Consider the following sort of situation. Suppose death and injury due to shooting were very much on the upgrade because too many people had guns. In that case there may be a utilitarian rationale for the following laws prescribing undeserved punishment.

Retail gun sellers are held strictly liable if any of their guns are found on a person without a permit. Sellers of guns would become extra careful in scrutinizing permits and protecting their stocks from theft. The iron clad rule, No excuses, toughens the deterrent threat of punishment.

Vicarious punishment is prescribed by law for parents if any of their children under twenty-one is discovered in possession of a gun. Parents, consequently, would make a greater effort to ensure that their children have no guns.

An ex post facto law prohibits the use of guns by individuals against unarmed persons trespassing on their property. As a consequence of this law, shootings by persons *not* covered by the law, e.g., armed guards, decline because they fear future ex post facto laws under which they would be retroactively punished.

It is perfectly possible that laws prescribing these three sorts of undeserved punishment would maximize utility by reducing deaths and injuries due to shootings. But consider the injustices that might be perpetrated under such laws.

Suppose gun sellers were held strictly liable if one of their guns were found in the possession of an individual without a permit. F, a scrupulously honest retailer, sells a gun to G, who has a permit. G plants the gun on H, who has no permit. Discovery of the gun on H sends faultless F to prison.

Imagine that parents are vicariously liable if a gun is discovered on the person of any of their children. An eight-year-old girl on a treasure hurt with her classmates finds a package which she brings back to school as her "treasure." The child's parents, ardent pacifists, are convicted and serve a prison sentence.

Suppose an ex post facto law makes it a criminal offense to shoot unarmed trespassers on one's property for any reason whatsoever. Before enactment of this law, the following incident occurred. Gangsters threatened to kidnap Jones' children. Jones saw three of them on his property making off with his child. He fired at one who is unarmed. Note that at the time Jones's act was not only morally defensible, it was perfectly legal. But when the ex post facto law is enacted, Jones is convicted and punished, retroactively.

Laws prescribing excessive punishment, i.e., undeserved in light of the offense, may also satisfy utilitarian standards. Imagine a community where loitering is so widespread as to be a public nuisance. A law is enacted prescribing one year in prison for loitering. It might very well be the case that only one person would be punished under this law. The threat of such severe punishment, reinforced by infliction on one offender, is sufficient to deter all other potential offenders. The good utilitarian effects of the law may very well outweigh the bad ones. But a one year jail sentence for loitering is certainly undeserved, hence unjust.

Finally, we may note that the guilt of an offender is usually held to decrease with extenuating circumstances, e.g., that the crime was committed in a state of passion. But, as Bentham noted, where the temptation to commit an offense is greater, the threat of more severe punishment is required to overcome the temptation. Thus to secure effective deterrence, crimes committed in extenuating circumstances should be punished more severely. However, these are precisely the circumstances where the offender, being less responsible, deserves a lighter penalty.

In all cases just described, punishment while either wholly or partially undeserved would, by hypothesis, be perfectly legal. But utilitarians, it may be argued, are also committed to undeserved punishment which is illegal.

Let us suppose there has been a wave of vicious crimes, and the police are unable to find the culprit. Since no one is punished for these offenses, the deterrent threat of punishment becomes increasingly ineffective, and more persons are tempted into committing the crime. To frame and punish an innocent for these offenses may reinforce the deterrent threat of punishment. A few such scapegoat punishments might avert great harm and be worth while utility-wise.

It may be objected that those who hold a revised form of utilitarianism, namely, rule utilitarianism, are not committed to such illegal punishment of the innocent. A rule utilitarian believes that our conduct should be guided by estimating the utility not of any single, particular action, but of the general practice of that kind of act. Rule utilitarians may argue that they are not committed to what Professor Rawls calls "telishment," the illegal punishment of innocent scapegoats. Such punishment might, in a particular case, maximize utility, but it is doubtful that the general practice of "telishment" would meet utilitarian standards. Consider that the deterrence effect of the general practice of "telishment" depends on the success of systematic deception. Unless the general public believes the innocent scapegoat is guilty, the desired deterrence effect would not be achieved. But it is extremely difficult to imagine that such systematic deception could be maintained successfully. Hence the practice of "telishment" cannot be justified on rule utilitarian grounds.

Notice, however, that the rule utilitarian argument against illegal punishment has no application to legal undeserved sanctions. Excessive penalties, strict liability, retroactive and vicarious punishment are perfectly compatible with rule utilitarian principles. No deception is required to sustain the practice of these undeserved punishments. Provision for such punishments can and has been incorporated into public law.

Moreover, it seems false that the rule utilitarian is *never* committed to "telishment."

Suppose that D, the sovereign of a powerful nation, has a grievance against Smith, a citizen of a small nation. D demands that E, the sovereign of Smith's country, ensure that Smith be convicted and imprisoned for some particularly disgraceful offense of which Smith is innocent, e.g., sexual assault on a child. Unless innocent Smith is convicted and punished, D will launch an attack on E's country and massacre the whole population. E can with the aid of a few trusted security police manufacture evidence which would convict Smith in a court of law. The massacre of a whole nation would surely have more disutility than the harmful effect of Smith's illegal punishment. Thus it seems that for rule utilitarianism, in this rare kind of case where averting a catastrophe depends on an innocent's being "telished," the rule should be, "telish" him.[1]

It may be objected that in this kind of case the rule utilitarian's violation of justice is warranted. We might reluctantly agree to the punishment of one innocent in order to prevent the massacre of a whole nation. But as Hart notes "we should do so with the sense of sacrificing an important principle." However, the rule utilitarian is not sacrificing any of his principles. On the contrary, punishing innocent Smith satisfies his principles.

Retributivism

Pure retributivists claim that deserved punishment is necessarily either just or of some moral worth. Undeserved punishment is always either unjust or of negative moral worth. As Kant sees the matter, to perpetrate undeserved punishment for any purpose whatsoever is to use a person as a means only, rather than as an end in himself.

For some retributivists punishment for wrong doing is just because it restores the moral balance disturbed by crime. What is a state of moral balance? One version derives from Kant. A moral balance is exemplified by "a proportion between welfare and well-doing." The good are happy and the wicked suffer for their misdeeds. Thus an imbalance obtains when a criminal fails to suffer for his crime. Punishing him sets matters right, with respect to the criminal. Full moral balance is achieved, however, when the criminal is punished and the victim is compensated. Then a proper proportion between welfare and well-doing is achieved.

1. This sort of case is suggested by Alan Donagan. See "Is There a Credible Form of Utilitarianism? in *Contemporary Utilitarianism*, ed. M. Bayles, Anchor Books, 1968.

The trouble with this moral balance view is that if it justifies punishment it can also justify crime. Suppose a moral disproportion obtains in M's case. He has been made to suffer excessively for his crimes. However, a moral disproportion also obtains in N's case. Given N's conduct his happiness is excessive. (N is good, but not *that* good.) Suppose M commits a crime against N. It is possible that M's crime against N may achieve a state of moral balance for both M and N. Thus if obtaining a moral balance justifies punishment, it can do the same service for crime.

For all retributivists punishment has moral worth independently of any further desirable effects. *Ceteris paribus*, the world is better, morally speaking, when the vicious suffer. Thus it is not surprising that retributivism is sometimes characterized as the vindictive theory of punishment.

We may test this position by imagining a world in which punishing criminals has no further effects worth achieving. Thus the criminal, punished, is perfectly ready to go out and commit his crime all over again. Ordinary men are not deterred in the slightest from crime by the threat of punishment. Victims of crime have no desire for retaliation, and the pleasure of vengeance is unknown. According to retributivists, individuals in this world are still obliged to bear the burden of maintaining institutions of punishment. Indeed, they have an obligation to sacrifice so that punishment is kept going. But what sort of sacrifice is anyone obligated to make for the sake of utterly useless punishment? I suggest that in this case there is no obligation whatsoever to punish wrongdoing.

Retributivists believe, presumably, that their views should find expression in actual systems of law. Is this possible? Remember these philosophers emphasize that only the guilty may be punished. But no infallible method for determining guilt has ever been devised. Indeed, it is a virtual certainty that honest, reasonable jurors have convicted defendants who appeared guilty but were, in fact, innocent. Thus, as it turns out, the price of a system which punishes the guilty is sacrifice of some innocents. Unless retributivists avoid punishing the guilty, they will be unable to avoid punishing the innocent.

Moreover, it is possible that more innocents would be punished in a society governed by retributivist, rather than utilitarian, principles. Here is why: for utilitarians, punishment is justified only if, by comparison with other alternatives, e.g., treatment, punishment would maximize utility. Suppose a painless but expensive pill were devised which cured any propensity to crime. The pill's utility surpassed that of other alternatives to punishment and slightly exceeded that of punishment itself. In that case utilitarians should endorse adoption of the crime cure pill and abolition of punishment. But retributivists believe that punishment of the guilty is either necessarily just or has some intrinsic value. In that case retributivists might refuse to substitute the crime cure pill for punishment. But juries would most likely remain fallible. Thus some innocents would be punished along with the guilty. Hence if retributivist principles held sway, some innocents would, as a consequence, be punished. While if utilitarians had their way, not a single innocent would suffer punishment.

Teleological Retributivism

Teleological retributivists, whom I shall call TR philosophers, are pluralists. They mediate between a teleological principle, i.e., utilitarianism, and principles of justice held by retributivists. Let us contrast utilitarianism and retributivism with one plausible version of TR pluralism. I shall refer to a philosopher who holds this version as TR, to the retributivist as R, and to the utilitarian as U.

Consider (A1).

(A1) *If X deserves to suffer, then the amount of suffering in the world ought to be increased by X's suffering, as much as he deserves.*

(A1), a claim about the *amount* of suffering in the world, is an aggregative desert principle. R believes (A1). However, both TR and U deny that (A1) is true. TR and U believe a different aggregative principle, (A2).

(A2) *The total amount of suffering in the world ought not be increased by anyone's suffering.*

Consider now (D).

> (D) *If either X or Y is to suffer, and X but not Y deserves to suffer, then X not Y ought to suffer (but not more than he deserves).*

(D) is a distributive principle, since (D) is a claim about how suffering ought to be distributed. Both TR and R believe (D). However, U denies that (D) is true. Only the amount of suffering matters to the utilitarian. Who does the suffering is morally indifferent. Thus TR shares a distributive desert principle, (D), with R and an aggregative utilitarian principle, (A2), with U.

The different views of TR, R, and U may be illustrated in the following cases.

Suppose three men know they will die within 24 hours. The first, a philosopher, is not in pain, but the other two—a sadistic ex-SS criminal and his former victim—are suffering and to an equal degree. The philosopher has two pain killing capsules, each totally effective for 24 hours. If the philosopher were TR or U, he would, following (A2), give each sufferer a tablet. However, if he were R, he would, following (A1), refuse to give the Nazi criminal a tablet.

Imagine now that the philosopher had only one such indivisible pill. If he were R or TR, then he would, in accord with (D), give the pill to the innocent man, not the criminal. However, if the philosopher were U, he would have no reason to alleviate the innocent's pain rather than the criminal's. After all (A2) would be satisfied by either choice.

How would our TR philosopher justify punishment?

Consider the case of C who has committed a crime. If he were punished, as he deserves, then, and only then, would he be deterred from committing a further crime against some innocent person. Hence, punishing C, a criminal, would prevent the suffering of an innocent. Our TR philosopher, following (D), would claim that C ought to be punished.

Notice, however, that (D) is an affirmative principle indicating when the guilty should be punished. But TR philosophers, like retributivists, also hold some negative principle of justice, e.g., Kant's principle of humanity, which implies that undeserved punishment is wrong.

Kant, we recall, urged that a person ought not be treated as a means only, but always as an end-in-himself. Suppose that an undeserved punishment would serve utility. Then, as Raphael, a TR philosopher, puts the matter:

The claim of social utility is opposed by the claims of the individual to be treated as an "end-in-himself" and not merely as a means to the ends of society.

(HP) is an application of Kant's principle of punishment.

(HP) Never treat a person as a means by punishing him undeservedly in order to benefit others.

Both TR and R would endorse (HP). Thus TR is committed to three principles: (HP), (D), and (A2). [R adheres to (HP), (D), and (A1), while U is committed to (A2)].

Are TR's three principles really compatible? Remember innocent Smith. Unless Smith's sovereign punishes him for a disgraceful offense of which Smith is innocent, the head of a powerful nation will have the entire population of Smith's country massacred. Suppose Smith's sovereign were TR. He could not adhere to both (HP) and (A2). By punishing Smith he violates (HP). But by not punishing Smith he violates (A2). [If Smith's sovereign were R or U, he would have no problem. R is committed to (HP) but not to (A2). Hence R would refuse to punish Smith and allow the nation to be massacred. U is committed to (A2) but not to (HP). Hence U would punish Smith to prevent the massacre.]

Some TR philosophers, e.g., Ross, hold that an innocent should be punished "that the whole nation perish not."

If our TR sovereign took this view he would sacrifice a principle of justice, (HP), in favor of a utilitarian principle, (A2). But TR's view of undeserved punishment would still be quite different from the utilitarian's. Remember U is not committed to (HP). Hence U would endorse undeserved punishment to achieve a slight gain in utility. But TR would abandon (HP) and opt for undeserved punishment only to avert a catastrophe. In that case TR would avowedly be sacrificing one of his principles, (HP), in favor of another, (A2). But in punishing innocent Smith, U sacrifices no principle whatsoever. TR's position is, I believe, closer to our common morality.

A complete TR view of punishment would incorporate two types of principles. The first may be dubbed a *recognized first order* principle, e.g., (A2), (D), or (HP). However, such principles may, as we have seen, conflict. Hence, some *absolute, second order* principle is required to referee the outcome. Thus our TR sovereign would, by punishing Smith, be following some absolute, second order principle which implies that in catastrophe cases, (A2) takes priority over (HP).

Criminal Desert

R believes that deserved punishment, *in toto*, should be inflicted on the criminal. While for TR the deserved penalty merely sets the upper limit of permissible punishment. But the notion of a deserved penalty is not easy to explicate.

Note first that the deserved penalty may differ from the penalty a state is legally entitled to impose. A government is legally entitled to inflict any punishment whatsoever—no matter how undeserved—if law permits. Thus, should cutting off an offender's hand be the legal penalty for petty thievery, then a judge is legally entitled to impose such sentence. But plainly the penalty is undeserved. Legal entitlement is not a moral concept. We ascertain legal entitlement by consulting a legal code. But a legal code cannot suffice to determine what a criminal deserves to suffer as a penalty. The misery he deserves depends on the moral wrong he has committed. Thus desert is a moral, not a legal notion. Suppose that torture of children were perfectly legal and shoplifting were illegal. It would be true, nevertheless, that those who torture children deserve to suffer more than shoplifters.

To determine the deserved penalty, one must decide how much misery an offender deserves for his wrongdoing. In such assessment, two kinds of questions may arise, one of degree and one of scope.

Let us look at the degree problem first. Consider the following kinds of offenses.

A: *blackmail, kidnapping, rape, murder*
B: *loitering, shoplifting, tax evasion, petty theft.*

Type A offenses are usually more grave, morally speaking, than type B. Hence it is usually reasonable to claim that a type B offender deserves a lesser degree of suffering as punishment. But such a comparative claim is crucially incomplete. We should like to know just how much misery a blackmailer or petty thief deserves.

Suppose we ranked offenses in an ascending order of moral gravity and penalties in a parallel order of severity. Could we then match offense to deserved punishment? What would constitute deserved punishment for the most serious moral wrongs?

Hobbes describes the punishment for high treason in 17th century England as follows:

To be drawn upon a Hurdle from the Prison to the Gallows, and there be hanged by the Neck, and laid upon the ground alive, and have his Bowels taken out, and burnt, whilst he is yet living; to have his Head cut off, his Body to be divided into four parts, and his Head, and Quarters to be placed as the King shall assign.

By comparison a one year prison sentence seems mild indeed. But would we not consider a one year sentence too severe for a mild offense (e.g., loitering)?

Note again that plausible comparative rankings of offenses by their degree of moral seriousness and penalties by their degree of severity seem possible. But such rankings cannot determine the noncomparative degree of suffering deserved for a specific offense.

The difficulty may arise in part because desert is a moral, not a legal, notion. Yet our intuitions of criminal desert are moored to our legal code, i.e., what seems mild or severe by that code.

Some philosophers suggest that a punishment is deserved if it fits the crime. But a criterion of fittingness is notoriously difficult to explicate. Consider one plausible formulation of such a criterion:

A punishment is fitting if and only if the degree of suffering inflicted on the criminal equals the degree of suffering imposed by the criminal on his victim.

Is it? Compare a criminal who assaults a helpless invalid with one who assaults a healthy adult. Suppose both victims endured an equal degree of suffering. The first criminal would still deserve a more severe penalty. His offense is, after all, much worse morally speaking.

A fitting penalty should match the moral evil of the offense. But how does one know when the match is made? For example, how many years in prison does the first criminal deserve for his crime?

I turn now to the problem of scope.

Suppose one could match deserved misery to moral evil. Let us assume then that (α) is true.

(α) A penalty of Z' and no more than Z' is deserved for the offense of Z, of Y' and no more than Y' for the offense of Y, of X' and no more than X' for the offense of X. . . .

Consider Jones, who committed the offense of X, a performance which ended at time t_1. Since (α) is true, so is (I).

(I) Jones deserves to suffer X' and no more than X' for committing X.

But can we assume that (II) is also true?

(II) Jones deserves to suffer X' and no more than X' at t_1.

If Jones had committed other offenses before t_1, (II) might be false. Let us assume however that, in fact, X is the only offense Jones committed in his whole life. Can we now assume that (II) is true?

Suppose that before committing X at t_1, Jones had suffered X' at time t_0 in a natural disaster, e.g., a flood. Then, one might claim—and not incredibly—that Jones had paid his desert debt in advance. His preoffense ordeal of X' at t_0, nullifies his post-X desert debt of X' at t_1. Hence while he deserves to suffer X' for committing X, he does not deserve to suffer X' at t_1. Although (I) is true, (II) is false.

Let us call this perspective on criminal desert, the whole life view. It may be objected that this view seems plainly misguided. Jones' flood ordeal was both prior to his crime, and nonpenal, i.e., came about through natural causes. Hence that ordeal has no bearing on the penalty Jones deserves at t_1, after he committed his crime. If this objection is sound, then criminal desert at a given time should be unaffected by two items:

                (1) suffering prior to an offense
                (2) nonpenal suffering

Let us consider the first item. Suppose that an immoral government penalized Jones by X' at t_0 for an offense he did not commit.

Jones served an undeserved prison sentence of one year. A new and idealistic regime is installed and Jones proceeds to commit X at t_1. Jones might inform these idealists that he deserves compensation for the undeserved penalty he suffered. But the standard to which compensation should, where possible, conform is *restitution*, i.e., restoring the equivalent of what was taken. At t_0 Jones was undeservedly deprived of his freedom from incarceration for one year. Deserved restitution at t_1 can only be made by giving Jones one year of freedom from incarceration, i.e., suspending his deserved one year prison sentence for committing X. Hence what Jones deserves at t_1 is that he not endure his deserved X' penalty for committing X. Thus he does not deserve X' at t_1.

To so compensate Jones would of course be moral madness. As a consequence any person punished undeservedly would earn the right to commit a crime. But remember that *what* reason forbids is treating Jones *as he deserves* at t_1.

I conclude that criminal desert, at a given time, may be altered by item (1), i.e., suffering prior to the offense. But can such desert be affected by item (2), nonpenal suffering, e.g., an ordeal caused by some natural disaster.

Imagine a world W, quite different from our own. Only one sort of evil obtains in W. A class of persons, dubbed Fists, occasionally feels sadistic impulses which they vent on others. How? Fists have very powerful right fists which they use when so inclined to pummel others. Moreover, Fists are so strong and so swift that they can neither be controlled nor deterred in the slightest. A potential victim can only try to stay away from these Fists. But once assaulted the victim feels no desire for vengeance. Indeed, Fists aside, inhabitants of W are (by our standards) remarkably pacific and reasonable. They know that even if punishment of Fists were possible, no good would come of it. A Fist would not be affected in the slightest by punishment.

However when a Fist attacks, then as a causal consequence, he feels severe pain—just the degree he deserves—in his right hand. Thus in W, there are only two sorts of misery, undeserved pain inflicted by Fists and deserved pain which these Fists endure as a consequence. Since Fists receive their full measure of deserved pain through natural causes they deserve to suffer no more. Hence, both R and TR would agree that there are no occasions in W for penal intervention. (A1) as well as (D) are superfluous principles in W.

Reflection on W should serve to remind us that, from the perspective of criminal desert, punishment intervenes to accomplish what, in fact, could come about through perfectly natural causes. Hence, it is false that such nonpenal suffering cannot affect criminal desert.

If the whole life view of criminal desert is correct, then R and TR are in serious difficulty. Assessment of a criminal's desert after an offense would require that one balance all of his moral wrongs against the suffering of his entire life. But such reckoning is usually beyond ordinary mortals. An omniscient deity could of course know all the wrongs a person has committed as well as the tribulations he has endured. However those who determine legal penalties are not omniscient. To rely on them for such life-spanning estimates of desert is plainly out of the question. In that case how can we be certain that when an offender is penalized, he does in fact deserve to be so treated?

Moreover, we may, I believe, safely assume the following: first, a large number of legal offenders have led miserable, deprived lives. Secondly, at least some, and possibly, a great many, such offenders, do not, when punished, deserve their ordeal. If we persist in legal punishment, for society's benefit, we violate (HP), a principle of justice to which both R and TR are committed.

Let us now make a rash assumption. Only a penal system can prevent crime. No alternative can do the job. Should we then secure protection against crime by legal punishment, at the expense of (HP)?

How would our three principled philosophers view the matter?

Only U could accept the situation with equanimity. He, after all, had no commitment to (HP) in the first place.

R's dilemma, however, would be most extreme. R, we recall, feels a double obligation: to punish deservedly (A1) and not to punish undeservedly (HP). But now it seems that both sorts of punishment arrive in one package, tagged, a human penal system. Moreover R did not expect his principles to conflict. He, unlike TR, is not the man for compromise.

I imagine that R would give up and wash his hands entirely of our penal system, i.e., one not directed by an omniscient deity. Perhaps he will spend his time dreaming of a possible world where an all knowing and righteous god rains deserved suffering—just the right amount—on those who fall from virtue.

And TR? He of course is not averse to compromise. For TR, the sacrifice of (HP), to avoid a massacre, was not out of the question. But would TR endorse a penal system where injustice may be an everyday matter? Or would he, like R, turn away from a reality so resistant to his moral principles.

I say TR would face up to moral fact and strain his principles to the utmost. Perhaps he would pose the issue in the following fashion. Many offenders, punished, would not deserve to be so treated. But many who would suffer at the hands of criminals, undeterred, would not deserve to be so victimized. In that case, TR may opt for legal punishment. But he can take little pleasure in his choice.

TR aspired to that best of all plausible moral worlds, one where both justice and utility receive their due. Only in some exceptional circumstance would justice be denied. But now TR knows that in a human penal system justice may be set aside, not on some rare and grim occasion, but with dreadful regularity. In that case he could only regard the practice of legal punishment as a most unhappy compromise.

Gertrude Ezorsky

Chapter One

Concepts of Punishment

Thomas Hobbes	Of Punishments and Rewards
A. M. Quinton	On Punishment
Kurt Baier	Is Punishment Retributive?
Joel Feinberg	The Expressive Function of Punishment

Thomas Hobbes

Of Punishments and Rewards *

A *Punishment, is an Evill inflicted by publique Authority, on him that hath done, or omitted that which is Judged by the same Authority to be a Transgression of the Law; to the end that the will of men may thereby the better be disposed to obedience.*

Before I inferre any thing from this definition, there is a question to be answered, of much importance; which is, by what door the Right, or Authority of Punishing in any case, came in. For by that which has been said before, no man is supposed bound by Covenant, not to resist violence; and consequently it cannot be intended, that he gave any right to another to lay violent hands upon his person. In the making of a Common-wealth, every man giveth away the right of defending another; but not of defending himselfe. Also he obligeth himselfe, to assist him that hath the Soveraignty, in the Punishing of another; but of himselfe not. But to covenant to assist the Soveraign, in doing hurt to another, unlesse he that so covenanteth have a right to doe it himselfe, is not to give him a Right to Punish. It is manifest therefore that the Right which the Common-wealth (that is he, or they that represent it) hath to Punish, is not grounded on any concession, or gift of the Subjects. But I have also shewed formerly, that before the Institution of Common-wealth, every man had a right to every thing, and to do whatsoever he thought necessary to his own preservation; subduing, hurting, or killing any man in order thereunto. And this is the foundation of the right of Punishing, which is exercised in every Common-wealth. For the Subjects did not give the Soveraign the right; but onely in laying down theirs, strengthned him to use his own, as he should think fit, for the preservation of them

* Thomas Hobbes, *Leviathan*. (New York: E. P. Dutton & Co., 1950), pp. 266–69.

all: so that it was not given, but left to him, and to him onely; and (excepting the limits set him by naturall Law) as entire, as in the condition of meer Nature, and of warre of every one against his neighbour.

From the definition of Punishment, I inferre, First, that neither private revenges, nor injuries of private men, can properly be stiled Punishment; because they proceed not from publique Authority.

Secondly, that to be neglected, and unpreferred by the publique favour, is not a Punishment; because no new evill is thereby on any man Inflicted; he is onely left in the estate he was in before.

Thirdly, that the evill inflicted by publique Authority, without precedent publique condemnation, is not to be stiled by the name of Punishment; but of an hostile act; because the fact for which a man is Punished, ought first to be Judged by publique Authority, to be a transgression of the Law.

Fourthly, that the evill inflicted by usurped power, and Judges without Authority from the Soveraign, is not Punishment; but an act of hostility; because the acts of power usurped, have not for Author, the person condemned; and therefore are not acts of publique Authority.

Fifthly, that all evill which is inflicted without intention, or possibility of disposing the Delinquent, or (by his example) other men, to obey the Lawes, is not Punishment; but an act of hostility; because without such an end, no hurt done is contained under that name.

Sixthly, whereas to certain actions, there be annexed by nature, divers hurtfull consequences; as when a man in assaulting another, is himselfe slain, or wounded; or when he falleth into sicknesse by the doing of some unlawfull act; such hurt, though in respect of God, who is the author of Nature, it may be said to be inflicted, and therefore a Punishment divine; yet it is not contaned in the name of Punishment in respect of men, because it is not inflicted by the Authority of man.

Seventhly, If the harm inflicted be lesse than the benefit, or contentment that naturally followeth the crime committed, that harm is not within the definition; and is rather the Price, or Redemption, than the Punishment of a Crime: Because it is of the nature of Punishment, to have for end, the disposing of men to obey the Law; which end (if it be lesse than the benefit of the transgression) it attaineth not, but worketh a contrary effect.

Eighthly, If a Punishment be determined and prescribed in the Law it selfe, and after the crime committed, there be a greater Punishment inflicted, the excesse is not Punishment, but an act of hostility. For seeing the aym of Punishment is not a revenge, but terrour; and the terrour of a great Punishment unknown, is taken away by the declaration of a lesse, the unexpected addition is no part of the Punishment. But where there is no Punishment at all determined by the Law, there whatsoever is inflicted, hath the nature of Punishment. For he that goes about the violation of a Law, wherein no penalty is determined, expecteth an indeterminate, that is to say, an arbitrary Punishment.

Ninthly, Harme inflicted for a Fact done before there was a Law that forbad it, is not Punishment, but an act of Hostility: For before the Law, there is no transgression of the Law: But Punishment supposeth a fact judged, to have been a transgression of the Law; Therefore Harme inflicted before the Law made, is not Punishment, but an act of Hostility.

Tenthly, Hurt inflicted on the Representative of the Commonwealth, is not Punishment, but an act of Hostility: Because it is of the nature of Punishment, to be inflicted by publique Authority, which is the Authority only of the Representative it self.

Lastly, Harme inflicted upon one that is a declared enemy, fals not under the name of Punishment: Because seeing they were either never subject to the Law, and therefore cannot transgresse it; or having been subject to it, and professing to be no longer so, by consequence deny they can transgresse it, all the Harmes that can be done them, must be taken as acts of Hostility. But in declared Hostility, all infliction of evill is lawfull. From whence it followeth, that if a subject shall by fact, or word, wittingly, and deliberatly deny the authority of the Representative of the Common-wealth, (whatsoever penalty hath been formerly ordained for Treason,) he may lawfully be made to suffer whatsoever the Representative will: For in denying subjection, he denyes such Punishment as by the Law hath been ordained; and therefore suffers as an enemy of the Common-wealth; that is, according to the will of the Representative. For the Punishments set down in the Law, are to Subjects, not to Enemies; such as are they, that having been by their own act Subjects, deliberately revolting, deny the soveraign Power.

A. M. Quinton

On Punishment *

1. Introductory

There is a prevailing antinomy about the philosophical justification of punishment. The two great theories—retributive and ultilitarian—seem, and at least are understood by their defenders, to stand in open and flagrant contradiction. Both sides have arguments at their disposal to demonstrate the atrocious consequences of the rival theory. Retributivists, who seem to hold that there are circumstances in which the infliction of suffering is a good thing in itself, are charged by their opponents with vindictive barbarousness. Utilitarians, who seem to hold that punishment is always and only justified by the good consequences it produces, are accused of vicious opportunism. Where the former insists on suffering for suffering's sake, the latter permits the punishment of the innocent. Yet, if the hope of justifying punishment is not to be abandoned altogether, one of these apparently unsavory alternatives must be embraced. For they exhaust the possibilities. Either punishment must be self-justifying, as the retributivists claim, or it must depend for its justification on something other than itself, the general formula of "utilitarianism" in the wide sense appropriate here.

In this paper I shall argue that the antinomy can be resolved, since retributivism, properly understood, is not a moral but a logical doctrine, and that it does not provide a moral justification of the infliction of punishment but an elucidation of the use of the word. Utilitarianism, on the other hand, embraces a number of possible moral attitudes toward punishment, none of which necessarily involves the objectionable consequences commonly adduced by retributivists, provided that

* A. M. Quinton, "On Punishment," *Analysis*, 14 (1954), pp. 512-17. Reprinted by permission of the author and the publisher.

the word "punishment" is understood in the way that the essential retributivist thesis lays down. The antinomy arises from a confusion of modalities, of logical and moral necessity and possibility, of "must" and "can" with "ought" and "may." In brief, the two theories answer different questions: retributivism the question "when (logically) *can* we punish?", utilitarianism the question "when (morally) *may* we or *ought* we to punish?" I shall also describe circumstances in which there is an answer to the question "when (logically) *must* we punish?" Finally, I shall attempt to account for this difference in terms of a distinction between the establishment of rules whose infringement involves punishment from the application of these rules to particular cases.

ii. The Retributive Theory

The essential contention of retributivism is that punishment is only justified by guilt. There is a certain compellingness about the repudiation of utilitarianism that this involves. We feel that whatever other considerations may be taken into account, the primary and indispensable matter is to establish the guilt of the person to be punished. I shall try to show that the peculiar outrageousness of the rejection of this principle is a consequence, not of the brutality that such rejection might seem to permit, but of the fact that it involves a kind of lying. At any rate the first principle of retributivism is that it is necessary that a man be guilty if he is to be punished.

But this doctrine is normally held in conjunction with some or all of three others which are logically, if not altogether psychologically, independent of it. These are that the function of punishment is the negation or annulment of evil or wrongdoing, that punishment must fit the crime (the *lex talionis*) and that offenders have a right to punishment, as moral agents they ought to be treated as ends not means.

The doctrine of "annulment," however carefully wrapped up in obscure phraseology, is clearly utilitarian in principle. For it holds that the function of punishment is to bring about a state of affairs in which it is as if the wrongful act had never happened. This is to justify

punishment by its effects, by the desirable future consequences which it brings about. It certainly goes beyond the demand that only the guilty be punished. For, unlike this demand, it seeks to prescribe exactly what the punishment should be. Holding that whenever wrong has been done it must be annulled, it makes guilt—the state of one who has done wrong—the sufficient as well as the necessary condition of punishment. While the original thesis is essentially negative, ruling out the punishment of the innocent, the annulment doctrine is positive, insisting on the punishment and determining the degree of punishment of the guilty. But the doctrine is only applicable to a restricted class of cases, the order of nature is inhospitable to attempts to put the clock back. Theft and fraud can be compensated, but not murder, wounding, alienation of affection, or the destruction of property or reputation.

Realizing that things cannot always be made what they were, retributivists have extended the notion of annulment to cover the infliction on the offender of an injury equal to that which he has caused. This is sometimes argued for by reference to Moore's theory of organic wholes, the view that sometimes two blacks make a white. That this, the *lex talionis*, revered by Kant, does not follow from the original thesis is proved by the fact that we can always refrain from punishing the innocent but that we cannot always find a punishment to fit the crime. Some indeed would argue that we can never fit punishment to wrongdoing, for how are either, especially wrongdoing, to be measured? (Though, as Ross has pointed out, we can make ordinal judgments of more or less about both punishment and wrongdoing.)

Both of these views depend on a mysterious extension of the original thesis to mean that punishment and wrongdoing must necessarily be somehow equal and opposite. But this is to go even further than to regard guilt and punishment as necessitating one another. For this maintains that only the guilty are to be punished and that the guilty are always to be punished. The equal and opposite view maintains further that they are to be punished to just the extent that they have done wrong.

Finally retributivism has been associated with the view that if we are to treat offenders as moral agents, as ends and not as means, we must recognize their right to punishment. It is an odd sort of right whose holders would strenuously resist its recognition. Strictly interpreted, this view would entail that the sole relevant consideration in determining whether and how a man should be punished is his own moral regeneration. This is utilitarian and it is also immoral, since it neglects the rights of an offender's victims to compensation and of society in general to protection. A less extreme interpretation would be that we should never treat offenders merely as means in inflicting punishment but should take into account their right to treatment as moral agents. This is reasonable enough; most people would prefer a penal system which did not ignore the reformation of offenders. But it is not the most obvious correlate of the possible view that if a man is guilty he ought to be punished. We should more naturally allot the correlative right to have him punished to his victims or society in general and not to him himself.

III. The Retributivist Thesis

So far I have attempted to extricate the essentials of retributivism by excluding some traditional but logically irrelevant associates. A more direct approach consists in seeing what is the essential principle which retributivists hold utilitarians to deny. Their crucial charge is that utilitarians permit the punishment of the innocent. So their fundamental thesis must be that only the guilty are to be punished, that guilt is a necessary condition of punishment. This hardly lies open to the utilitarian countercharge of pointless and vindictive barbarity, which could only find a foothold in the doctrine of annulment and in the *lex talionis*. (For that matter, it is by no means obvious that the charge can be sustained even against them, except in so far as the problems of estimating the measure of guilt lead to the adoption of a purely formal and external criterion which would not distinguish between the doing of deliberate and accidental injuries.)

Essentially, then, retributivism is the view that only the guilty are to be punished. Excluding the punishment of the innocent, it permits the other three possibilities: the punishment of the guilty, the nonpunishment of the guilty, and the nonpunishment of the innocent. To add that guilt is also the sufficient condition of punishment, and thus to exclude the nonpunishment of the guilty, is another matter altogether. It is not entailed by the retributivist attack on utilitarianism and has none of the immediate compulsiveness of the doctrine that guilt is the necessary condition of punishment.

There is a very good reason for this difference in force. For the necessity of not punishing the innocent is not moral but logical. It is not, as some retributivists think, that we *may* not punish the innocent and *ought* only to punish the guilty, but that we *cannot* punish the innocent and *must* only punish the guilty. Of course, the suffering or harm in which punishment consists can be and is inflicted on innocent people, but this is not punishment, it is judicial error or terrorism or, in Bradley's characteristically repellent phrase, "social surgery." The infliction of suffering on a person is only properly described as punishment if that person is guilty. The retributivist thesis, therefore, is not a moral doctrine, but an account of the meaning of the word "punishment." Typhoid carriers and criminal lunatics are treated physically in much the same way as ordinary criminals; they are shut up in institutions. The essential difference is that no blame is implied by their imprisonment, for there is no guilt to which the blame can attach. "Punishment" resembles the word "murder"; it is infliction of suffering on the guilty and not simply infliction of suffering, just as murder is wrongful killing and not simply killing. Typhoid carriers are no more (usually) criminals than surgeons are (usually) murderers. This accounts for the flavor of moral outrage attending the notion of punishment of the innocent. In a sense a contradiction in terms, it applies to the common enough practice of inflicting the suffering involved in punishment on innocent people and of sentencing them to punishment with a lying imputation of their responsibility and guilt. Punishment *cannot* be inflicted on the innocent; the suffering associated with punishment may not be inflicted on them, firstly, as brutal and secondly, if it is represented as punishment, as involving a lie.

This can be shown by the fact that punishment is always *for* something. If a man says to another "I am going to punish you" and is asked "what for?" he cannot reply "nothing at all" or "something you have not done." At best, he is using "punish" here as a more or less elegant synonym for "cause to suffer." Either that or he does not understand the meaning of "punish." "I am going to punish you for something you have not done" is as absurd a statement as "I blame you for this event for which you were not responsible." "Punishment implies guilt" is the same sort of assertion as "ought implies can." It is not *pointless* to punish or blame the innocent, as some have argued, for it is often very useful. Rather the very conditions of punishment and blame do not obtain in these circumstances.

iv. An Objection

But how can it be useful to do what is impossible? The innocent can be punished and scapegoats are not logical impossibilities. We do say "they punished him for something he did not do." For A to be said to have punished B it is surely enough that A thought or said he was punishing B and ensured that suffering was inflicted on B. However innocent B may be of the offense adduced by A, there is no question that, in these circumstances, he has been punished by A. So guilt cannot be more than a *moral* precondition of punishment.

The answer to this objection is that "punish" is a member of that now familiar class of verbs whose first-person-present use is significantly different from the rest. The absurdity of "I am punishing you for something you have not done" is analogous to that of "I promise to do something which is not in my power." Unless you are guilty I am no more in a position to punish you than I am in a position to promise what is not in my power. So it is improper to say "I am going to punish you" unless you are guilty, just as it is improper to say "I promise to do this" unless it is in my power to do it. But it is only *morally* improper if I do not *think* that you are guilty or that I can do the promised act. Yet, just as it is perfectly proper to say of another "he promised to do this," whether he thought he could do it or not, provided that he *said* "I promise to do this," so it is perfectly proper to say "they punished him," whether they thought him guilty or not, provided that they *said* "we are going to punish you" and inflicted suffering on him. By the first-person-present use of these verbs we prescribe punishment and make promises; these activities involve the satisfaction of conditions over and above what is required for *reports* or *descriptions* of what their prescribers or makers represent as punishments and promises.

Understandably "reward" and "forgive" closely resemble "punish." Guilt is a precondition of forgiveness, desert—its contrary—of reward. One cannot properly say "I am going to reward you" or "I forgive you" to a man who has done nothing. Reward and forgiveness are always for something. But, again, one can say "they rewarded (or forgave) him for something he had not done." There is an interesting difference here between "forgive" and "punish" or "reward." In this last kind of assertion "forgive" seems more peculiar, more inviting to inverted commas, than the other two. The three undertakings denoted by these verbs can be divided into the utterance of a more or less ritual formula and the consequences authorized by this utterance. With punishment and reward the consequences are more noticeable than the formula, so they come to be sufficient occasion for the use of the word even if the formula is inapplicable and so improperly used. But, since the consequences of forgiveness are negative, the absence of punishment, no such shift occurs. To reward involves giving a reward, to punish inflicting a punishment, but to forgive involves no palpable consequence, e.g., handing over a written certificate of pardon.

Within these limitations, then, guilt is a *logically* necessary condition of punishment and, with some exceptions, it might be held, a morally necessary condition of the infliction of suffering. Is it in either way a sufficient condition? As will be shown in the last section there are circumstances, though they do not obtain in our legal system, nor generally in extralegal penal systems (e.g., parental), in which guilt is a logically sufficient condition of at least a sentence of punishment. The parallel moral doctrine would be that if anyone is guilty of wrongdoing he ought morally to be punished. This rather futile rigorism is not embodied in our legal system with its relaxations of penalties for first offenders. Since it entails that offenders should never be forgiven it is hardly likely to commend itself in the extralegal sphere.

v. The Utilitarian Theory

Utilitarianism holds that punishment must always be justified by the value of its consequences. I shall refer to this as "utility" for convenience without any implication that utility must consist in pleasure.

The view that punishment is justified by the value of its consequences is compatible with any ethical theory which allows meaning to be attached to moral judgments. It holds merely that the infliction of suffering is of no value or of negative value and that it must therefore be justified by further considerations. These will be such things as prevention of and deterrence from wrongoing, compensation of victims, reformation of offenders, and satisfaction of vindictive impulses. It is indifferent for our purposes whether these are valued as intuitively good, as productive of general happiness, as conducive to the survival of the human race or are just normatively laid down as valuable or derived from such a norm.

Clearly there is no *logical* relation between punishment and its actual or expected utility. Punishment *can* be inflicted when it is neither expected, nor turns out, to be of value and, on the other hand, it can be foregone when it is either expected, or would turn out, to be of value.

But that utility is the morally necessary or sufficient condition, or both, of punishment are perfectly reputable moral attitudes. The first would hold that no one should be punished unless the punishment would have valuable consequences; the second that if valuable consequences would result punishment ought to be inflicted (without excluding the moral permissibility of utility-less punishment). Most people would no doubt accept the first, apart from the rigorists who regard guilt as a morally sufficient condition of punishment. Few would maintain the second except in conjunction with the first. The first says when you may not but not when you ought to punish, the second when you ought to but not when you may not.

Neither permits or encourages the punishment of the innocent, for this is only logically possible if the word "punishment" is used in an unnatural way, for example as meaning any kind of deliberate infliction of suffering. But in that case they cease to be moral doctrine about punishment as we understand the word and become moral doctrines (respectively, platitudinous and inhuman) about something else.

So the retributivist case against the utilitarians falls to the ground as soon as what is true and essential in retributivism is extracted from the rest. This may be unwelcome to retributivists since it leaves the moral field in the possession of the utilitarians. But there is a compensation in the fact that what is essential in retributivism can at least be definitely established.

vi. Rules and Cases

So far what has been established is that guilt and the value or utility of consequences are relevant to punishment in different ways. A further understanding of this difference can be gained by making use of a distinction made by Sir David Ross in the appendix on punishment in *The Right and the Good*. This will also help to elucidate the notion of guilt which has hitherto been applied uncritically.

The distinction is between laying down a rule which attaches punishment to actions of a certain kind and the application of that rule to particular cases. It might be maintained that the utilitarian theory was an answer to the question "What kinds of action should be punished?" and the retributive theory an answer to the question "On what particular occasions should we punish?" On this view both punishment and guilt are defined by reference to these rules. Punishment is the infliction of suffering attached by these rules to certain kinds of action, guilt the condition of a person to whom such a rule applies. This accounts for the logically necessary relation holding between guilt and punishment. Only the guilty can be punished because unless a person is guilty, unless a rule applies to him, no infliction of suffering on him is properly called punishment, since punishment is infliction of suffering as laid down by such a rule. Considerations of utility, then, are alone relevant to the determination of what in general, what *kinds* of action, to punish. The outcome of this is a set of rules. Given these rules, the question of whom in particular to punish has a definite and necessary answer. Not only will guilt be the logically necessary but also the logically sufficient condition of punishment or, more exactly, of a sentence of punishment. For declaration of guilt will be a declaration that a rule applies and, if the rule applies, what the rule enjoins—a sentence of punishment—applies also.

The distinction between setting up and applying penal rules helps to explain the different parts played by utility and guilt in the justification of punishment, in particular the fact that where utility is a moral, guilt is a logical, justification. Guilt is irrelevant to the setting up of rules, for until they have been set up the notion of guilt is undefined and without application. Utility is irrelevant to the application of rules, for once the rules have been set up, punishment is determined by guilt; once they are seen to apply, the rule makes a sentence of punishment necessarily follow.

But this account is not an accurate description of the very complex penal systems actually employed by states, institutions, and parents. It is, rather, a schema, a possible limiting case. For it ignores an almost universal feature of penal systems (and of games, for that matter, where penalties attend infractions of the rules)—discretion. For few offenses against the law is one and only one fixed and definite punishment laid down. Normally only an upper limit is set. If guilt, the applicability of the rule, is established no fixed punishment is entailed but rather, for example, one not exceeding a fine of forty shillings or fourteen days' imprisonment. This is even more evident in the administration of such institutions as clubs or libraries and yet more again in the matter of parental discipline. The establishment of guilt does not close the matter; at best it entails some punishment or other. Precisely how much is appropriate must be determined by reference to considerations of utility. The variety of things is too great for any manageably concise penal code to dispense altogether with discretionary judgment in particular cases.

But this fact only shows that guilt is not a logically *sufficient* condition of punishment; it does not affect the thesis that punishment entails guilt. A man cannot be guilty unless his action falls under a penal rule and he can only be properly said to be punished if the rule in question prescribes or permits some punishment or other. So all applications of the notion of guilt necessarily contain or include all applications of the notion of punishment.

Kurt Baier

Is Punishment
Retributive?*

It would seem that punishment must of its nature be retributive, and also that it cannot be. It must be, for the infliction of hardship on someone is not punishment, unless it is as retribution *for* something he has done. It cannot be, for it makes sense to say that someone was punished for something he did not do. This seemingly simple, but actually quite intricate problem, was recently discussed by Professor A. G. N. Flew in an article entitled 'The Justification of Punishment'[1] and by Mr. A. M. Quinton in a paper entitled 'On Punishment'.[2] Both appear to me to misrepresent the nature of punishment. I shall begin by stating briefly what I hold to be the correct solution, and then point out where exactly they went wrong.

1. To say that someone has punished someone else is to say that someone entitled to administer the penalty for a certain offense has administered this penalty to the person who has been found guilty of this offence by someone with the authority to do so. The question whether or not someone has punished someone else could not even arise unless he belonged to a group which had the practice of punishing people. We could not say of a group that it had the practice of punishing people unless all the following conditions were satisfied. There must be someone, such as a father or legislator, whose job it is to prescribe or prohibit the doing of certain things or types of thing by certain people, in the form of commands or regulations, someone whose task it is to decree how a person disobeying these commands or regulations shall be treated, someone, such as a father or policeman, entrusted with the task of detecting cases of disobedience,

* Kurt Baier, "Is Punishment Retributive?" *Analysis*, 16 (1955), pp. 25–32. Reprinted by permission of the author and the publisher.
1. *Philosophy*, October, 1954.   2. *Analysis*, June, 1954.

someone, such as a father or judge, charged with meting out the penalty for such disobedience, and someone, such as a father or executioner, charged with administering it. Of course, all these different tasks may be entrusted to one and the same person, as in the case of punishment by a father or teacher.

It should be noticed that 'punishing' is the name of only a part-activity belonging to a complex procedure involving several stages. Giving orders or laying down laws, affixing penalties to them, as-certaining whether anyone has disobeyed the commands or laws, sentencing persons found guilty, are not themselves punishing or part of the activity of punishing. Yet these activities must be performed and must precede the infliction of hardship if we are to speak of punishment at all. Of course, these activities may take only rudimentary forms. A father does not legislate, but give orders; he does not necessarily affix penalties to breaches of these orders before the breaches occur, but determines the penalty after a breach or disobedience has occurred; he often does not take much trouble in finding out whether his child really is guilty, nor does he formally "find him guilty" or pronounce sentence. All this is merely tacitly implied, but it is quite definitely implied. It would be just as odd for a father to send his son to bed without supper for being late, if he had found the son not guilty of this—either because the son was not told to be home by a certain time or because he was home by the time mentioned—as it would be for a judge to pronounce sentence on the accused when he has just been acquitted by the jury.

It follows from the nature of this whole "game", consisting of rule-making, penalisation, finding guilty of a breach of a rule, pronouncing sentence, and finally administering punishment, that the last act cannot be performed unless things have gone according to the rules until then. It is one of the constitutive rules of this whole "game" that the activity called punishing, or administering punishment, cannot be performed if, at a previous stage of the "game", the person in question has been found 'not guilty'. The "game" has to proceed differently after the verdict 'not guilty', from the way it must proceed after the verdict 'guilty'. It is only if the verdict is 'guilty' that there is any question of a sentence and its being carried out. And if, after the jury has found the accused 'not guilty', the judge continues as if the jury had found him guilty, then his 'I sentence you to three years' hard labour' is not the pronouncement of the sentence, but mere words. If, for some reason, the administration acts on these words, then what they do to the accused is not the infliction of punishment, but something for which (since it never happens) we do not even have a word.

A method of inflicting hardship on someone cannot be called 'punishment' unless at least the following condition is satisfied. It must be the case that when someone is found "not guilty" it is not permissible to go on to pronounce sentence on him and carry it out. For 'punishment' is the name of a method, or system, of inflicting hardship, *the aim of which* is to hurt all and only those who are guilty of an offence. For this reason, a system of punishment requires a more or less elaborate apparatus for detecting those who are guilty and for allotting to them the hardship prescribed by the system. To say that it is of the very nature of punishment to be retributive, is to say that a system of inflicting hardship on someone could not be properly called 'punishment,' unless it is the aim of this system to hurt all and only those guilty of an offence. Hence inflicting hardship on a person who has been found 'not guilty' (logically) cannot be punishing. This is a conceptual point about punishment.

The correct answer to our problem is that punishment is indeed of its very nature retributive, since the very aim of inflicting hardship *as punishment* would be destroyed, if it were inflicted on someone who had been found 'not guilty'. But at the same time, someone may be punished, i.e. have hardship inflicted on him *as punishment*, although he was guilty of no offence, since he may have been *found* guilty without *being* guilty. For all judges and jurymen are fallible and some are corrupt.

2. Flew holds a different view. He says [3] that punishment is of its very nature retributive, but thinks that this applies only to the system of punishment as a whole, not to individual instances of punishing, because "The term 'punishment' is sufficiently vague to permit us to speak *in single cases and provided these do not become too numerous* (if they do become too numerous, then *ispo facto* the use, the meaning, of 'punishment' has changed) of punishing a man who has broken no law (or even done no wrong).' [4]

3. *Loc. cit.*, p. 298.   4. *Ibid.*, p. 299/300.

My first point is that Flew has got the analysis wrong. Punishment, whether a system or a single case, is of its nature retributive. Flew says it "would be pedantic to insist *in single cases* that people (logically) cannot be punished for what they have not done",[5] but that "a *system* of inflicting unpleasantness on scapegoats . . . could scarcely be called a system of punishment at all". These contrasts are misleading. It is not pedantic, but plain wrong, to insist in single cases that people (logically) cannot be punished for what they have not done. But this is not a statistical matter at all. True, a system of inflicting unpleasantness on scapegoats *as such* is not a system of punishment, but then a single case of inflicting unpleasantness on a scapegoat *as such* is not a case of punishment either. In Ruritania, everyone who has been punished during the last year or the last ten years may have been innocent, for in Ruritania the judges and jurymen and the police and prison authorities are very inefficient and very corrupt. A system of punishing people does not turn into a system of inflicting unpleasantness on scapegoats, simply in virtue of the fact that in this system innocent people happen frequently to get punished.

It is surely not true that, if under a certain system of punishment it happens that very many innocent people get punished, the meaning and use of 'punishment' has *ipso facto* changed. Let us envisage such a deterioration in our own legal system. It is not logically necessary that we should come to know about it. Even now many people claim to have been unjustly condemned. Every now and then we hear of a ghastly judicial error, and there may be many more than we hear of. Think of the many cases in which people accuse the police of having used third degree methods for getting "confessions". For all I know, a very large percentage of people who are found guilty and are later punished, are really innocent. At least, this is conceivable. Yet, if it were true, the meaning and use of 'punishment' could not change *eo ipso*.

Or suppose we knew about it. What would we say? Simply that judges, police, and so on, were inefficient and/or corrupt, and that very many people got punished wrongly, i.e. unjustly, or by mistake.

Flew may have confused the unsound point he is making with an-

5. *Ibid.*, p. 293.

other point which is sound. Suppose a group had what is properly called a system of punishment. It may then happen once in a while that a judge goes on to "pronounce sentence" even after the jury has found the accused 'not guilty'. Or, to take a more probable case, that a teacher goes on to hit a pupil even after he has realised, perhaps even admitted, that the pupil is innocent. Now, it is true that we would still say that the group had a system of punishment even if such cases occurred, provided they were exceptional. We would not, however, say that they had a system of punishment, if these were not exceptions, but if the group had a system of doing just this sort of thing.

This is true, but again it is not a matter of statistics, not a matter of happening frequently or infrequently. It is a matter of being an exception rather than the rule, in the sense that it is understood to be a breach of the rule, rather than merely out of the ordinary. Not merely that judges usually, but not always, discharge the accused when he has been found 'not guilty', but that it is their job or duty to do so. If, after the jury has found the accused 'not guilty', the judge says 'I sentence you to three years' hard labour', this is not just an unusual case of punishing the man who is innocent, but not a case of punishment at all. And here it would not only not be pedantic, let alone wrong, but perfectly right to say that this case was not a case of punishment.

Flew, I suspect, may have been taken in by the word 'system'. He is, of course, right in saying that a system of inflicting unpleasantness on scapegoats, or a system of 'punishing' people who had broken no laws cannot be called a system of punishment. This obvious truth, together with the obvious truth that men who have not broken any laws can be and sometimes are correctly said to have been punished, leads him to the view that the solution to the puzzle how one can say the one, but not the other, must be found in the difference between systems and single cases, which he takes to be the difference between the great majority of cases, and single cases.[6]

But it is more complicated than that. The expression "a system of 'punishing' people who had broken no laws" means "system whose

6. *Loc. cit.*, pp. 302/3.

declared and recognised nature it is to 'punish' those who had broken no laws". Hence the importance of 'exception'. If it is still the declared and recognised nature of the group's infliction of hardship on people that it is to be directed to all and only those who are found guilty of an offence, then the cases of inefficient and corrupt judges, and judges guilty of flagrant breaches of the law, are clearly exceptions. And while these single cases are exceptions, the whole system can still be called a system *of* punishment, otherwise it is a system of something else.

3. Mr. Quinton, on the other hand, does not think the solution of our problem lies in the distinction between systems and single cases of punishment, but he thinks it lies in the recognition "that 'punish' is a member of that now familiar class of verbs whose first-person-present use is significantly different from the rest".[7] As soon as we recognise that while 'I am punishing you for something you have not done' is as absurd as 'I promise to do something which is not in my power', we see that 'he punished him for something he had not done' is no more absurd than is 'he promised to do something that was not in his power'.

My first point is that it is simply not true that 'I am punishing you for something you have not done' is as absurd as 'I promise you to do something which is not in my power'. It need not be absurd at all. The executioner may whisper it to the man who has been sentenced to death. 'I am punishing you for something you have not done' would be analogous to 'I promise you to do this which is not in my power' only if to say 'I am punishing you . . .' were to punish you, just as 'I promise you . . .' is to promise you. In other words, the verb 'to promise' is a performatory word, 'to punish' is not. And if it were used performatorily in 'I hereby punish you . . .' (not, by the way, as Quinton has it, "I am punishing you . . ."), then it would mean the same as 'I hereby sentence you . . .' and saying it would still not be punishing anyone, but merely sentencing him. Thus, Quinton's account is not true of punishing but at best of sentencing.

A similar mistake was made some time ago by Professor H. L. A. Hart in his important paper "The Ascription of Responsibility and

7. *Loc. cit.*, p. 138.

Rights".[8] For the view he there expresses [9] is that judicial decisions are ascriptions of responsibility or rights and that these are "performatory utterances", "nondescriptive statements", statements not capable of being true or false. But while this is so of some judicial decisions such as pronouncing sentence, it is not true of others such as verdicts. When the jury says 'Guilty', the accused is "guilty in law" and may have no further recourse against such a judicial decision, but that does not mean that he really is guilty. The verdict 'guilty' could be a performatory utterance only if uttering these words were making the accused guilty, as uttering the words 'I promise' is making a promise. It might be said that the jury uses the word in a technical legal sense, different from the ordinary. When the jury says 'Jury-Guilty', the accused is not indeed made guilty, but he is made jury-guilty. But this won't do, for what does jury-guilty come to? It simply means 'to be held guilty', 'to be regarded or treated as guilty'. But this is not what the jury is asked to decide or what it says. The jury is asked to give its opinion on whether the accused *is* guilty, not on whether he is to be *treated as* guilty, for different considerations might enter into the second question. For the purpose of the legal consequences, the jury's opinion about his guilt is authoritative. Thus, it is not true that the jury says 'Jury-Guilty', and thereby makes the accused jury-guilty. What is true is that the jury says 'guilty' and thereby makes the accused jury-guilty that is to be held guilty. Hence the performatory model is out of place here, for when I say 'I promise', I am making a promise, not an 'uttered promise'.

It might be thought that Quinton had seen this point, for he says [10] "There is an interesting difference here between 'forgive' and 'punish' or 'reward' . . . The three undertakings denoted by these verbs can be divided into the utterance of a more or less ritual formula and the consequences authorized by this utterance. With punishment and reward the consequences are more noticeable than the formula, so they come to be sufficient occasion for the use of the word *even if the formula is inapplicable and so improperly used.* But, since the consequences of forgiveness are negative, the absence of punishment, no such shift occurs". At first sight, this distinction

8. *Proc. Arist. Soc.* 1948–9. Reprinted in Flew, *Logic and Language*, Vol. I.
9. *Logic and Language.* pp. 155, 157, 159, 161.   10. *Ibid.*, p. 139.

between the ritual formula and the consequences authorized by it might be taken to be the same distinction as the one I have drawn between sentencing and punishing. But on closer inspection, this turns out not to be so.

For while to say 'I forgive you' is indeed to use a formula, the use of this formula or ritual is not performatory in the way in which the use of 'I promise' or 'I hereby sentence you to . . .' is. For if I say the latter in the appropriate circumstances then I have promised or pronounced sentence. But when I say 'I forgive you' I may merely say so. It is moreover wrong to think that 'I forgive you' authorizes the non-imposition of punishment. The assaulted girl, with her last words, may forgive her assailant, but this does not authorize "the absence of punishment". Nor is the infliction of punishment authorized by the formula 'I don't forgive you'. The former indicates the injured party's intention not to seek revenge, to resume friendly relations, and so on, the latter the opposite. On the other hand, the infliction of punishment is authorized by the formula 'guilty' or equivalent formulae, the noninfliction by the formula 'not guilty' and perhaps the Home Secretary's pardon. Thus, the difference Quinton has in mind is not the difference I have drawn between pronouncing sentence and punishing.

Lastly, it should be emphasised that it is not true to say that punishing is the utterance of a ritual formula involving certain palpable consequences whereas forgiving is merely the utterance of a ritual formula involving no palpable consequences, and that, therefore, 'punishing' sometimes refers merely to the palpable consequences even when the ritual formula is inappropriate, whereas this never happens in the case of forgiving. On the contrary, punishing and forgiving alike are certain kinds of doings, but they are doings which presuppose the correct completion of a certain more or less formal procedure culminating in the finding someone guilty of an offence. If and only if this procedure has been followed correctly to its very conclusion, can there be any question of someone's being or not being punished or forgiven or pardoned. One of the important differences between forgiving and punishing is that they presuppose different sorts of formalities. Forgiving is involved only where a man has been found guilty of an injury. Punishment is involved only where he has been found guilty of an offence. Many systems of crime and punishment make injuries offences, but not all offences are necessarily injuries. Vindictiveness and forgiveness, revenge and turning the other cheek are individual, punishment and reward are social ways of dealing with objectionable behaviour.

Although the infliction of hardship on an individual cannot be called punishment unless it is preceded by his having been found 'guilty' of an offence, the procedure leading up to this finding need only be formally and not materially correct. That is to say, as long as he was found 'guilty' in the proper way, even though he is not in fact guilty, the infliction of hardship which then follows will be punishment, provided no further slip occurs.

Joel Feinberg

The Expressive Function
of Punishment *

It might well appear to a moral philosopher absorbed in the classical literature of his discipline, or to a moralist sensitive to injustice and suffering, that recent philosophical discussions of the problem of punishment have somehow missed the point of his interest. Recent influential articles [1] have quite sensibly distinguished between questions of definition and justification, between justifying general rules and particular decisions, between moral and legal guilt. So much is all to the good. When these articles go on to define 'punishment', however, it seems to many that they leave out of their ken altogether the very element that makes punishment theoretically puzzling and morally disquieting. Punishment is defined, in effect, as the infliction of hard treatment by an authority on a person for his prior failing in some respect (usually an infraction of a rule or command).[2] There may be a very general sense of the word 'punishment' which is well

* Joel Feinberg, "The Expressive Function of Punishment," *The Monist*, 49:3, (La Salle, Illinois, 1965), pp. 397–408. Reprinted by permission of the author and the publisher.

1. See especially the following: A. Flew, "The Justification of Punishment," *Philosophy*, 29 (1954), 291–307; S. I. Benn, "An Approach to the Problems of Punishment," *Philosophy*, 33 (1958), 325–341; and H. L. A. Hart, "'Prolegomenon to the Principles of Punishment," *Proceedings of the Aristotelian Society*, 60 (1959–60), 1–26.

2. Hart and Benn both borrow Flew's definition. In Hart's paraphrase, punishment "(i) . . . must involve pain or other consequences normally considered unpleasant. (ii) It must be for an offense against legal rules. (iii) It must be of an actual or supposed offender for his offense. (iv) It must be intentionally administered by human beings other than the offender. (v) It must be imposed and administered by an authority constituted by a legal system against which the offense is committed." (*op. cit.*, p. 4.)

expressed by this definition; but even if that is so, we can distinguish a narrower, more emphatic sense that slips through its meshes. Imprisonment at hard labor for committing a felony is a clear case of punishment in the emphatic sense; but I think we would be less willing to apply that term to parking tickets, offside penalties, sackings, flunkings, and disqualifications. Examples of the latter sort I propose to call *penalties* (merely), so that I may inquire further what distinguishes punishment, in the strict and narrow sense that interests the moralist, from other kinds of penalties.[3]

One method of answering this question is to focus one's attention on the class of nonpunitive penalties in an effort to discover some clearly identifiable characteristic common to them all, and absent from all punishments, on which the distinction between the two might be grounded. The hypotheses yielded by this approach, however, are not likely to survive close scrutiny. One might conclude, for example, that mere penalties are less severe than punishments, but although this is generally true, it is not necessarily and universally so. Again we might be tempted to interpret penalties as mere 'price-tags' attached to certain types of behavior that are generally undesirable, so that only those with especially strong motivation will be

---

3. The distinction between punishments and penalties was first called to my attention by Dr. Anita Fritz of the University of Connecticut. Similar distinctions in different terminologies have been made by many. Pollock and Maitland speak of 'true afflictive punishments' as opposed to outlawry, private vengeance, fine, and emendation. (*History of English Law*, 2d ed., II, pp. 451 ff.) The phrase 'afflictive punishment' was invented by Bentham (*Rationale of Punishment*, London, 1830): "These [corporal] punishments are almost always attended with a portion of ignominy, and this does not always increase with the organic pain, but principally depends upon the condition [social class] of the offender." (p. 83). James Stephen says of legal punishment that it "should always connote . . . moral infamy." (*History of the Criminal Law*, II, p. 171.) Lasswell and Donnelly distinguish 'condemnation sanctions' and 'other deprivations'. ("The Continuing Debate over Responsibility: An Introduction to Isolating the Condemnation Sanction," *Yale Law Journal*, 68, 1959.) The traditional common law distinction is between 'infamous' and 'noninfamous' crimes and punishments. Conviction of an 'infamous crime' rendered a person liable to such postpunitive civil disabilities as incompetence to be a witness.

willing to pay the price.[4] So, for example, deliberate efforts on the part of some western states to keep roads from urban centers to wilderness areas few in number and poor in quality are essentially no different from various parking fines and football penalties. In each case a certain kind of conduct is discouraged without being absolutely prohibited: Anyone who desires strongly enough to get to the wilderness (or park overtime, or interfere with a pass) may do so provided he is willing to pay the penalty (price). On this view penalties are, in effect, licensing fees, different from other purchased permits in that the price is often paid afterward rather than in advance. Since a similar interpretation of punishments seems implausible, it might be alleged that this is the basis of the distinction between penalties and punishments. However, while a great number of penalties can, no doubt, plausibly be treated as retroactive license fees, this is hardly true of all of them. It is certainly not true, for example, of most demotions, firings, and flunkings, that they are 'prices' paid for some already consumed benefit; and even parking fines are sanctions for rules "meant to be taken seriously as . . . standard [s] of behavior," [5] and thus are more than mere public parking fees.

Rather than look for a characteristic common and peculiar to the penalties on which to ground the distinction between penalties and punishments, we would be better advised, I think, to cast our attention to the examples of punishments. Both penalties and punishments are authoritative deprivations for failures; but apart from these common features, penalties have a miscellaneous character, whereas punishments have an important additional characteristic in common. That characteristic, or specific difference, I shall argue, is a certain expressive function. Punishment is a conventional device for the expression of attitudes of resentment and indignation, and of judg-

4. That even punishments proper are to be interpreted as taxes on certain kinds of conduct is a view often associated with O. W. Holmes, Jr. For an excellent discussion of Holmes's fluctuations of this question see Mark De Wolfe Howe, *Justice Holmes, The Proving Years* (Cambridge, Mass., 1963), pp. 74–80. See also Lon Fuller, *The Morality of Law* (New Haven, 1964), Chap. II, part 7, and H. L. A. Hart, *The Concept of Law* (Oxford, 1961), p. 39, for illuminating comparisons and contrasts of punishment and taxation.
5. H. L. A. Hart, *loc. cit.*

ments of disapproval and reprobation, either on the part of the punishing authority himself or of those "in whose name" the punishment is inflicted. Punishment, in short, has a *symbolic significance* largely missing from other kinds of penalties.

The reprobative symbolism of punishment and its character as 'hard treatment', while never separate in reality, must be carefully distinguished for purposes of analysis. Reprobation is itself painful, whether or not it is accompanied by further 'hard treatment'; and hard treatment, such as fine or imprisonment, because of its conventional symbolism, can itself be reprobatory; but still we can conceive of ritualistic condemnation unaccompanied by any *further* hard treatment, and of inflictions and deprivations which, because of different symbolic conventions, have no reprobative force. It will be my thesis in this essay that (1) both the hard treatment aspect of punishment and its reprobative function must be part of the *definition* of legal punishment; and (2) each of these aspects raises its own kind of question about the *justification* of legal punishment as a general practice. I shall argue that some of the jobs punishment does, and some of the conceptual problems it raises, cannot be intelligibly described unless (1) is true; and that the incoherence of a familiar form of the retributive theory results from failure to appreciate the force of (2).

1. Punishment As Condemnation

That the expression of the community's condemnation is an essential ingredient in legal punishment is widely acknowledged by legal writers. Henry M. Hart, for example, gives eloquent emphasis to the point:

What distinguishes a criminal from a civil sanction and all that distinguishes it, it is ventured, is the judgment of community condemnation which accompanies . . . its imposition. As Professor Gardner wrote not long ago, in a distinct but cognate connection:

'The essence of punishment for moral delinquency lies in the criminal conviction itself. One may lose more money on the stock market than in a court-room; a prisoner of war camp may well provide

a harsher environment than a state prison; death on the field of battle has the same physical characteristics as death by sentence of law. It is the expression of the community's hatred, fear, or contempt for the convict which alone characterizes physical hardship as punishment.'

If this is what a 'criminal' penalty is, then we can say readily enough what a 'crime' is. . . . It is conduct which, if duly shown to have taken place, will incur a formal and solemn pronouncement of the moral condemnation of the community. . . . Indeed the condemnation plus the added [unpleasant physical] consequences may well be considered, compendiously, as constituting the punishment.[6]

Professor Hart's compendious definition needs qualification in one respect. The moral condemnation and the 'unpleasant consequences' that he rightly identifies as essential elements of punishment are not as distinct and separate as he suggests. It is not always the case that the convicted prisoner is first solemnly condemned and then subjected to unpleasant physical treatment. It would be more accurate in many cases to say that the unpleasant treatment itself expresses the condemnation, and that this expressive aspect of his incarceration is precisely the element by reason of which it is properly characterized as punishment and not mere penalty. The administrator who regretfully suspends the license of a conscientious but accident-prone driver can inflict a deprivation without any scolding, express or implied; but the reckless motorist who is sent to prison for six months is thereby inevitably subject to shame and ignominy—the very walls of his cell condemn him and his record becomes a stigma.

To say that the very physical treatment itself expresses condemnation is to say simply that certain forms of hard treatment have become the conventional symbols of public reprobation. This is neither more nor less paradoxical than to say that certain words have become conventional vehicles in our language for the expression of certain attitudes, or that champagne is the alcoholic beverage traditionally used in celebration of great events, or that black is the color of mourning. Moreover, particular kinds of punishment are often used to express quite specific attitudes (loosely speaking, this is part of

6. Henry M. Hart, "The Aims of the Criminal Law," *Law and Contemporary Problems*, 23 (1958), II, A, 4.

their 'meaning'); note the differences, for example, between beheading a nobleman and hanging a yeoman, burning a heretic and hanging a traitor, hanging an enemy soldier and executing him by firing squad.

It is much easier to show that punishment has a symbolic significance than to say exactly what it is that punishment expresses. At its best, in civilized and democratic countries, punishment surely expresses the community's strong *disapproval* of what the criminal did. Indeed it can be said that punishment expresses the *judgment* (as distinct from any emotion) of the community that what the criminal did was wrong. I think it is fair to say of our community, however, that punishment generally expresses more than judgments of disapproval; it is also a symbolic way of getting back at the criminal, of expressing a kind of vindictive resentment. To any reader who has in fact spent time in a prison, I venture to say, even Professor Gardner's strong terms—'hatred, fear, or contempt for the convict'—will not seem too strong an account of what imprisonment is universally taken to express. Not only does the criminal feel the naked hostility of his guards and the outside world—that would be fierce enough— but that hostility is self-righteous as well. His punishment bears the aspect of legitimized vengefulness; hence there is much truth in J. F. Stephen's celebrated remark that "The criminal law stands to the passion of revenge in much the same relation as marriage to the sexual appetite." [7]

If we reserve the less dramatic term 'resentment' for the various vengeful attitudes, and the term 'reprobation' for the stern judgment of disapproval, then perhaps we can characterize *condemnation* (or denunciation) as a kind of fusing of resentment and reprobation. That these two elements are generally to be found in legal punishment was well understood by the authors of the Report of the Royal Commission on Capital Punishment:

Discussion of the principle of retribution is apt to be confused because the word is not always used in the same sense. Sometimes it is intended to mean vengeance, sometimes reprobation. In the first sense the idea is that of satisfaction by the State of a wronged individual's desire to be avenged; in the second it is that of the State's

7. *General View of the Criminal Law of England*, First ed. (London, 1863), p. 99.

marking its disapproval *of the breaking of its laws by a punishment proportionate to the gravity of the offense* [Feinberg's emphasis].[8]

II. Some Derivative Symbolic Functions of Punishment

The relation of the expressive function of punishment to its various central purposes is not always easy to trace. Symbolic public condemnation added to deprivation may help or hinder deterrence, reform, and rehabilitation—the evidence is not clear. On the other hand, there are other functions of punishment, often lost sight of in the preoccupation with deterrence and reform, that presuppose the expressive function and would be impossible without it.

1. *Authoritative Disavowal.* Consider the standard international practice of demanding that a nation whose agent has unlawfully violated the complaining nation's rights should punish the offending agent. For example, suppose that an airplane of nation *A* fires on an airplane of nation *B* while the latter is flying over international waters. Very likely high authorities in nation *B* will send a note of protest to their counterparts in nation *A* demanding, among other things, that the transgressive pilot be punished. Punishing the pilot is an emphatic, dramatic, and well understood way of *condemning* and thereby *disavowing* his act. It tells the world that the pilot had no right to do what he did, that he was on his own in doing it, that his government does not condone that sort of thing. It testifies thereby to government *A*'s recognition of the violated rights of government *B* in the affected area, and therefore to the wrongfulness of the pilot's act. Failure to punish the pilot tells the world that government *A* does not consider him to have been personally at fault. That in turn is to claim responsibility for the act, which in effect labels that act as an 'instrument of deliberate national policy', and therefore an act of war. In that case either formal hostilities or humiliating loss of face by one side or the other almost certainly follows. None of this makes any sense without the well understood reprobative symbolism of punishment. In quite parallel ways punish-

8. (London, 1953), pp. 17–18.

ment enables employers to disavow the acts of their employees (though not civil liability for those acts), and fathers the destructive acts of their sons.

2. *Symbolic Non-Acquiescence: 'Speaking in the Name of the People.'* The symbolic function of punishment also explains why even those sophisticated persons who abjure resentment of criminals and look with small favor generally on the penal law are likely to demand that certain kinds of conduct be punished when or if the law lets them go by. In the state of Texas, so-called 'paramour killings' are regarded by the law as not merely mitigated, but completely justifiable.[9] Many humanitarians, I believe, will feel quite spontaneously that a great injustice is done when such killings are left unpunished. The sense of violated justice, moreover, might be distinct and unaccompanied by any frustrated *schaden-freude* toward the killer, lust for blood or vengeance, or metaphysical concern lest the universe stay 'out of joint'. The demand for punishment in cases of this sort may instead represent the feeling that paramour killings deserve to be *condemned*, that the law in condoning, even approving of them, speaks for all citizens in expressing a wholly inappropriate attitude toward them. For, in effect, the law expresses the judgment of the 'people of Texas', in whose name it speaks, that the vindictive satisfaction in the mind of a cuckolded husband is a thing of greater value than the very life of his wife's lover. The demand that paramour killings be punished may simply be the demand that this lopsided value judgment be withdrawn and that the state *go on record* against paramour killings, and the law *testify to the recognition* that such killings are wrongful. Punishment no doubt would also help deter killers. This too is a desideratum and a closely related one, but it is not to be identified with reprobation; for deterrence might be

9. The Texas Penal Code (Art. 1220) states: "Homicide is justifiable when committed by the husband upon one taken in the act of adultery with the wife, provided the killing takes place before the parties to the act have separated. Such circumstances cannot justify a homicide when it appears that there has been on the part of the husband, any connivance in or assent to the adulterous connection." New Mexico and Utah have similar statutes. For some striking descriptions of perfectly legal paramour killings in Texas, see John Bainbridge, *The Super-Americans* (Garden City, 1961), pp. 238 ff.

achieved by a dozen other techniques, from simple penalties and forfeitures to exhortation and propaganda; but effective public denunciation and, through it, symbolic non-acquiescence in the crime, seem virtually to require punishment.

This symbolic function of punishment was given great emphasis by Kant, who, characteristically, proceeded to exaggerate its importance. Even if a desert island community were to disband, Kant argued, its members should first execute the last murderer left in its jails, "for otherwise they might all be regarded as participators in the [unpunished] murder. . . ." [10] This Kantian idea that in failing to punish wicked acts society endorses them and thus becomes *particeps criminis* does seem to reflect, however dimly, something embedded in common sense. A similar notion underlies whatever is intelligible in the widespread notion that all citizens share the responsibility for political atrocities. Insofar as there is a coherent argument behind the extravagant distributions of guilt made by existentialists and other literary figures, it can be reconstructed in some such way as this: To whatever extent a political act is done 'in one's name', to that extent one is responsible for it. A citizen can avoid responsibility in advance by explicitly disowning the government as his spokesman, or after the fact through open protest, resistance, and so on. Otherwise, by 'acquiescing' in what is done in one's name, one incurs the responsibility for it. The root notion here is a kind of 'power of attorney' a government has for its citizens.

3. *Vindication of the Law.* Sometimes the state goes on record through its statutes, in a way that might well please a conscientious citizen in whose name it speaks, but then through official evasion and unreliable enforcement, gives rise to doubts that the law really means what it says. It is murder in Mississippi, as elsewhere, for a white man intentionally to kill a Negro; but if grand juries refuse to issue indictments or if trial juries refuse to convict, and this is well understood by most citizens, then it is in a purely formal and empty sense indeed that killings of Negroes by whites are illegal in Mississippi. Yet the law stays on the books, to give ever-less-convincing lip service to a noble moral judgment. A statute honored mainly in the breach

10. *The Philosophy of Law,* trans. W. Hastie (Edinburgh, 1887), p. 198.

begins to lose its character as law, unless, as we say, it is *vindicated* (emphatically reaffirmed); and clearly the way to do this (indeed the only way) is to punish those who violate it.

Similarly, *punitive damages*, so-called, are sometimes awarded the plaintiff in a civil action, as a supplement to compensation for his injuries. What more dramatic way of vindicating his violated right can be imagined than to have a court thus forcibly condemn its violation through the symbolic machinery of punishment?

4. *Absolution of Others.* When something scandalous has occurred and it is clear that the wrongdoer must be one of a small number of suspects, then the state, by punishing one of these parties, thereby relieves the others of suspicion, and informally absolves them of blame. Moreover, quite often the absolution of an accuser hangs as much in the balance at a criminal trial as the inculpation of the accused. A good example of this can be found in James Gould Cozzens's novel, *By Love Possessed.* A young girl, after an evening of illicit sexual activity with her boy friend, is found out by her bullying mother, who then insists that she clear her name by bringing criminal charges against the boy. He used physical force, the girl charges; she freely consented, he replies. If the jury finds him guilty of rape, it will by the same token absolve her from (moral) guilt and her reputation as well as his rides on the outcome. Could not the state do this job without punishment? Perhaps, but when it speaks by punishing, its message is loud and sure of getting across. . . .

Chapter Two

The Justification of Punishment

1. Teleological Theories

Plato	Punishment as Cure
J. E. McTaggart	Hegel's Theory of Punishment
Jeremy Bentham	Utility and Punishment
H. Rashdall	Punishment and the Individual
T. L. S. Sprigge	A Utilitarian Reply to Dr. McCloskey
John Austin	Rule Utilitarianism (I)
John Rawls	Rule Utilitarianism (II)
Richard Brandt	Rule Utilitarianism (III)

2. Retributivism

Immanuel Kant	Justice and Punishment
G. W. F. Hegel	Punishment as a Right
F. H. Bradley	The Vulgar Notion of Responsibility

Plato

Punishment
as Cure *

SOCRATES: . . . of two who suffer evil either in body or in soul, which is the more wretched, the man who submits to treatment and gets rid of the evil, or he who is not treated but still retains it?

POLUS: Evidently the man who is not treated.

SOCRATES: And was not punishment admitted to be a release from the greatest of evils, namely wickedness?

POLUS: It was.

SOCRATES: Yes, because a just penalty disciplines us and makes us more just and cures us of evil.

POLUS: I agree.

SOCRATES: Then the happiest of men is he who has no evil in his soul, since this was shown to be the greatest of evils?

POLUS: That is plain.

SOCRATES: And second in order surely is he who is delivered from it.

POLUS: Apparently.

SOCRATES: And we found this was the man who is admonished and rebuked and punished.

POLUS: Yes.

SOCRATES: Then his life is most unhappy who is afflicted with evil and does not get rid of it.

POLUS: Evidently.

SOCRATES: And is not this just the man who does the greatest wrong and indulges in the greatest injustice and yet contrives to escape admonition, correction, or punishment—the very condition you de-

* Plato, Gorgias, in The Collected Dialogues of Plato, ed. with an intro. E. Hamilton and H. Cairns. (Princeton: Princeton University Press, 1961), pp. 262–63.

scribe as achieved by Archelaus and other tyrants, orators, and potentates?

POLUS: It seems so.

SOCRATES: For what these have contrived, my good friend, is pretty much as if a man afflicted with the most grievous ailments should contrive not to pay to the doctors the penalty of his sins against his body by submitting to treatment, because he is afraid, like a child, of the pain of cautery or surgery. Do you agree?

POLUS: I do.

SOCRATES: He is evidently ignorant of the meaning of health and physical fitness. For apparently, as our recent admissions prove, those who escape punishment also act much in the same way, Polus. They see its painfulness but are blind to its benefit and know not how much more miserable than a union with an unhealthy body is a union with a soul that is not healthy but corrupt and impious and evil, and so they leave nothing undone to avoid being punished and liberated from the greatest of ills, providing themselves with money and friends and the highest attainable powers of persuasive rhetoric. But if we have been right in our admissions, Polus, do you see the results of our argument, or shall we sum them up together?

POLUS: Yes, if you wish.

SOCRATES: Is not our conclusion then that injustice and the doing of wrong is the greatest of evils?

POLUS: Evidently.

SOCRATES: And it was shown that punishment rids us of this evil?

POLUS: Apparently.

SOCRATES: And when punishment is evaded, the evil abides?

POLUS: Yes.

SOCRATES: Then wrongdoing itself holds the second place among evils, but first and greatest of all evils is to do wrong and escape punishment.

POLUS: So it seems.

SOCRATES: Now did we not differ, my friend, about this very point, when you maintained that Archelaus was happy because he remained unpunished despite the enormity of his crimes, whereas I was of the contrary opinion—that Archelaus or any other man who escapes punishment for his misdeeds must be miserable far beyond all other men, and that invariably the doer of wrong is more wretched than his victim, and he who escapes punishment than he who is punished? Was not that what I was saying?

POLUS: Yes.

SOCRATES: And has it not been proved that it is true?

POLUS: Clearly.

J. E. McTaggart

Hegel's Theory
of Punishment *

. . . Hegel does not deny that punishment may deter, prevent, or improve, and he does not deny that this will be an additional advantage. But he says that none of these are the chief object of punishment, and none of them express its real nature. It would seem, therefore, that he must intend to advocate vindictive punishment. And this is confirmed by the fact that he expressly says the object of punishment is not to do "this or that" good.

Nevertheless, I believe that Hegel had not the slightest intention of advocating what we have called vindictive punishment. For he says, beyond the possibility of a doubt, that in punishment the criminal is to be treated as a moral being,—that is, one who is potentially moral, however immoral he may be in fact, and one in whom this potential morality must be called into actual existence. He complains that in the deterrent theory we treat a man like a dog to whom his master shows a whip, and not as a free being. He says that the criminal has a right to be punished, which indicates that the punishment is in a sense for his sake. And, still more emphatically, "in punishment the offender is honored as a rational being, since the punishment is looked on as his right." [1]

Now this is incompatible with the view that Hegel is here approving of vindictive punishment. For he says that a man is only to be punished because he is a moral being, and that it would be an injury to him not to punish him. The vindictive theory knows nothing of all this. It inflicts pain on a man, not for his ultimate good, but because, as it says, he has deserved to suffer pain. And, on Hegel's

* J. E. McTaggart, "Hegel's Theory of Punishment," *International Journal of Ethics*, 6 (1896), pp. 482–99.
1. "Philosophy of Law." Sections 99 and 100.

theory, punishment depends on the recognition of the criminal's rational and moral nature, so that, in his phrase, it is an honor as well as a disgrace. Nothing of the sort exists for vindictive punishment. It does not care whether the sinner can or will do good in the future. It punishes him because he has done wrong in the past. If we look at the doctrine of hell,—which is a pure case of vindictive punishment, —we see that it is possible to conceive punishment of this sort when the element of a potential moral character has entirely disappeared, for I conceive that the supporters of this doctrine would deny the possibility of repentance, since they deny the possibility of pardon.

What, then, is Hegel's theory? It is, I think, briefly this. In sin, man rejects and defies the moral law. Punishment is pain inflicted on him because he has done this, and in order that he may, by the fact of his punishment, be forced into recognizing as valid the law which he rejected in sinning, and so repent of his sin—really repent, and not merely be frightened out of doing it again.

Thus the object of punishment is that the criminal should repent of his crime, and by so doing realize the moral character, which has been temporarily obscured by his wrong action, but which is, as Hegel asserts, really his truest and deepest nature. At first sight this looks very much like the reformatory theory of punishment, which Hegel has rejected. But there is a great deal of difference between them. The reformatory theory says that we ought to reform our criminals while we are punishing them. Hegel says that punishment itself tends to reform them. The reformatory theory wishes to pain criminals as little as possible, and improve them as much as possible. Hegel's theory says that it is the pain which will improve them, and therefore, although it looks on pain in itself as an evil, is by no means particularly anxious to spare it, since it holds that through the pain the criminals will be raised, and that we have therefore no right to deny it to them.

When Hegel says, therefore, as we saw above, that the object of punishment is not to effect "this or that good," we must not, I think, take him to mean that we do not look for a good result from punishment. We must rather interpret him to mean that it is not in consequence of some *accidental* good result that punishment is to be defended, but that, for the criminal, punishment is inherently good. This use of "this or that" to express an accidental or contingent good seems in accordance with Hegel's usual style. And we must also remember that Hegel, who hated many things, hated nothing more bitterly than sentimental humanitarianism, and that he was in consequence more inclined to emphasize his divergence from a reformatory theory of punishment, than his agreement with it.

We have thus reached a theory quite different from any of the four which we started this paper by considering. It is not impossible that we may find out that the world has been acting on the Hegelian view for many ages, but as an explicit theory it has found little support. We all recognize that a man can be frightened into or out of a course of action by punishment. We all recognize that a man can sometimes be reformed by influences applied while he is being punished. But can he ever be reformed simply by punishment? Reform and repentance involve that he should either see that something was wrong which before he thought was right, or else that the intensity of his moral feelings should be so strengthened that he is enabled to resist a temptation, to which before he yielded. And why should punishment help him to do either of these things?

There is a certain class of people in the present day who look on all punishment as essentially degrading. They do not, in their saner moods, deny that there may be people for whom it is necessary. But they think that, if any one requires punishment, he proves himself to be uninfluenced by moral motives, and only to be governed by fear, which they declare to be degrading. (It is curious, by the way, that this school is rather fond of the idea that people should be governed by rewards rather than punishments. It does not seem easy to understand why it is less degrading to be bribed into virtue than to be frightened away from vice.) They look on all punishment as implying deep degradation in some one,—if it is justified, the sufferer must be little better than a brute; if it is not justified, the brutality is in the person who inflicts it.

This argument appears to travel in a circle. Punishment, they say, is degrading, therefore it can work no moral improvement. But this begs the question. For if punishment could work a moral improvement, it would not degrade but elevate. The humanitarian argument alternately proves that punishment can only intimidate because it is brutalizing, and that it is brutalizing because it can only intimidate. The real reason, apparently, of the foregone conviction which tries to justify itself by this confusion, is an unreasoning horror of the infliction of pain which has seized on many very excellent and disinterested people. That pain is an evil cannot be denied. It may, perhaps, be reasonably asserted that it is the ultimate evil. But to assert that it is always wrong to inflict it is equivalent to a declaration that there is no moral difference between a dentist and a wife-beater. No one can deny that the infliction of pain may in the long run increase happiness—as in the extraction of an aching tooth. If pain, in spite of its being evil *per se*, can thus be desirable as a means, the general objection to pain as a moral agent would seem to disappear also.

Of course, there is nothing in simple pain, as such, which can lead to repentance. If I get into a particular train, and break my leg in a collision, that cannot make me repent my action in going by the train, though it will very possibly make me regret it. For the pain in this case was not a punishment. It came, indeed, because I got into the train, but not because I had done wrong in getting in to the train.

Hegel's theory is that punishment, that is, pain inflicted because the sufferer had previously done wrong, may lead to repentance for the crime which caused the punishment. We have now to consider whether this is true. Our thesis is not that it always produces repentance—which, of course, is not the case—but that there is something in its nature as punishment which tends to produce repentance. And this, as we have seen, is not a common theory of punishment. "Men do not," says George Eliot in "Felix Holt," (Chap. 41,) —"men do not become penitent and learn to abhor themselves by having their backs cut open with the lash; rather, they learn to abhor the lash." That the principle expressed here is one which often operates, cannot be denied. Can we so far limit its application that Hegel's theory shall also be valid?

We have so far defined punishment as pain inflicted because the sufferer has done wrong. But, looking at it more closely, we should have to alter this definition, which is too narrow, and does not include cases of unjust or mistaken punishment. To bring these in we must say that it is pain inflicted because the person who inflicts it thinks that the person who suffers it has done wrong. Repentance, again, is the realization by the criminal, with sufficient vividness to govern future action, that he has done wrong. Now is there anything in the nature of punishment to cause the conviction in the mind of the judge to be reproduced in the mind of the culprit? If so, punishment will tend to produce repentance.

I submit that this is the case under certain conditions. When the culprit recognizes the punishing authority as one which embodies the moral law, and which has a right to enforce it, then punishment may lead to repentance, but not otherwise.

Let us examine this a little more closely. A person who suffers punishment may conceive the authority which inflicts it as distinctly immoral in its tendencies. In this case, of course, he will not be moved to repent of his action. The punishment will appear to him unjust, the incurring of the punishment will present itself in the light of a duty, and he will consider himself not as a criminal, but as a martyr. On the other hand, if the punishment causes him to change his line of action, this, his convictions being as we have supposed, will not be repentance, but cowardice.

Or again, he may not regard it as distinctly immoral—as punishing him for what it is his duty to do, but he may regard it as non-moral—as punishing him for what he had a right, though not a duty, to do. In this case, too, punishment will not lead to repentance. He will not regard himself as a martyr, but he will be justified in regarding himself as a very badly treated individual. If the punishment does cause him to abstain from such action in future, it will not be the result of repentance, but of prudence. He will not have come to think it wrong, but he may think it not worth the pain it will bring on him.

If, however, he regards the authority which punishes him as one which expresses, and which has a right to express, the moral law, his attitude will be very different. He will no longer regard his punishment either as a martyrdom or as an injury. On the contrary, he will feel that it is the proper consequence of his fault. And to feel this, and to be able to accept it as such, is surely repentance.

But it may be objected that this will lead to a dilemma. The punishment cannot have this moral effect on us unless it comes from an authority which we recognize as expressing the moral law, and therefore valid for us. But if we recognize this, how did we ever come to commit the sin, which consists in a defiance of the moral law? Does not the existence of the sin itself prove that we are not in that submissive position to the moral law, and to the power which is enforcing it, which alone can make the punishment a purification?

I do not think this is the case. It is, in the first place, quite possible for a recognition of the moral law to exist which is not sufficiently strong to prevent our violating it at the suggestion of our passions or our impulses, but which is yet strong enough, when the punishment follows, to make us recognize the justice of the sentence. After all, most cases of wrong-doing, which can be treated as criminal, are cases of this description, in which a man defies a moral law which he knows to be binding, because the temptations to violate it are at that moment too strong for his desire to do what he knows to be right. In these cases the moral law is, indeed, recognized,—for the offender knows he is doing wrong,—but not recognized with sufficient strength; for, if it was, he would abstain from doing wrong. And, therefore, the moral consciousness is strong enough to accept the punishment as justly incurred, though it was not strong enough to prevent the offender from incurring it. In this case, the significance of the punishment is that it tends to produce that vividness in the recognition of the moral law, which the occurrence of the offence shows to have been previously wanting. The pain and coercion involved in punishment present the law with much greater impressiveness than can, for the mass of people, be gained from a mere admission that the law is binding. On the other hand, the fact that the pain coincides with that intellectual recognition, on the part of the offender, that the law is binding, prevents the punishment having a merely intimidating effect, and makes it a possible stage in a moral advance.

Besides these cases of conscious violation of a moral law, there are others where men sincerely believe in a certain principle, and yet systematically fail to see that it applies in certain cases, not because they really think these cases are exceptions, but because indolence or prejudice has prevented them from ever applying their general principle to those particular instances. Thus there have been nations who conscientiously believed murder to be sinful, and yet fought duels with a good conscience. If pressed, they would have admitted duels to be attempts to murder. But no one ever did press them, and they never pressed themselves. As soon as a set of reformers arose, who did press the question, duels were found to be indefensible, and disappeared. So for many years the United States solemnly affirmed the right of all men to liberty, while slavery was legally recognized. Yet they would not have denied that slaves were men.

When such cases occur with a single individual, punishment might here, also, lead to repentance. For it was only possible to accept the general law, and reject the particular application, by ignoring the unanswerable question, Why do not you in this case practise what you preach? Now, you can ignore a question, but you cannot ignore a punishment, if it is severe enough. You cannot put it on one side; you must either assert that it is unjust, or admit that it is just. And in the class of cases we have now been considering, we have seen that when the question is once asked, it must condemn the previous line of action. Here, therefore, punishment may lead to repentance.

A third case is that in which the authority is recognized, but in which it is not known beforehand that it disapproved of the act for which the punishment is awarded. Here, therefore, there is no difficulty in seeing that recognition of the authority is compatible with transgression of the law, because the law is not known till after it has been transgressed. It may, perhaps, be doubted whether it is strictly correct to say in this case that punishment may lead to repentance, since there is no wilful fault to repent, as the law was, by the hypothesis, not known, at the time it was broken. The question is, however, merely verbal. There is no doubt that in such cases the punishment, coming from an authority accepted as moral, may lead a man to see that he has done wrong, though not intentionally, may lead him to regret it and to avoid it in future. Thus, at any rate, a moral advance comes from the punishment, and it is of no great importance whether we grant or deny it the name of repentance.

It may be objected, however, that punishment in the two last cases we have mentioned would be totally unjust. We ought to punish, it may be said, only those acts which were known by their perpetrators at the time when they did them to be wrong. And therefore we have no right to punish a man for any offence, which he did not know to be an offence, whether because he did not know of the existence of the law, or because he did not apply it to the particular case.

I do not think, however, that on examination we can limit the proper application of punishment to cases of conscious wrong-doing, plausible as such a restriction may appear at first sight. We must remember, in the first place, that not to know a moral law may be a sign of greater moral degradation than would be implied in its conscious violation. If a man really believed that he was morally justified in treating the lower animals without any consideration, he would not be consciously doing wrong by torturing them. But we should, I think, regard him as in a lower moral state than a man who was conscious of his duty to animals, though he occasionally disregarded it in moments of passion. Yet the latter in these moments would be consciously doing wrong. A man who could see nothing wrong in cowardice would be surely more degraded than a man who recognized the duty of courage, though he sometimes failed to carry it out. Thus, I submit, even if punishment were limited to cases of desert, there would be no reason to limit it to cases of conscious wrong-doing, since the absence of the consciousness of wrong-doing may itself be a mark of moral defect.

But we may, I think, go further. There seems no reason why we should inquire about any punishment, whether the criminal deserved it or not. For such a question really brings us, if we press it far enough, back to the old theory of vindictive punishment, which few of us, I suppose, would be prepared to advocate. On any other theory a man is to be punished, not to avenge the past evil, but to secure some future good. Of course, a punishment is only to be inflicted for a fault, for the effect of all punishment is to discourage the repetition of the action punished, and that would not be desirable unless the action was wrong. But to inquire into how far the criminal is to be blamed for his action seems irrelevant. If he has done wrong, and if the punishment will cure him, he has, as Hegel expresses it, a right to his punishment. If a dentist is asked to take out an aching tooth, he does not refuse to do so, on the ground that the patient did not deliberately cause the toothache, and that therefore it would be unjust to subject him to the pain of the extraction. And to refuse a man the chance of a moral advance—when the punishment appears to afford one—seems equally unreasonable.

Indeed, any attempt to measure punishment by desert gets us into hopeless difficulties. If we suppose that every man is equally responsible for every action which is not done under physical compulsion, we ignore the effect of inherited character, of difference of education, of difference of temptation, and, in fact, most of the important circumstances. Punishments measured out on such a system may, perhaps, be defended on the ground of utility, but certainly not on the ground of desert. On the other hand, if we endeavored to allow for different circumstances in fixing punishments, we should have no punishments at all. That a man commits an offence in given circumstances is due to his character, and, even if we allowed a certain amount of indeterminate free-will, we could never know that a change in the circumstances would not have saved him from the crime, so that we could never say that it was his own fault.

The only alternative seems to be to admit that we punish, not to avenge evil, but to restore or produce good, whether for society or the criminal. And on this principle we very often explicitly act. For example, we do not punish high treason because we condemn the traitors, who are often moved by sincere, though perhaps mistaken, patriotism. We punish it because we believe that they would, in fact, though with the best intentions, do harm to the state. Nor do parents, I suppose, punish young children for disobedience, on the ground that it is their own fault that they were not born with the habit of obedience developed. They do it, I should imagine, because punishment is the most effective way of teaching them obedience, and because it is desirable, for their own sakes, that they should learn it.

We must now return to the cases in which punishment can possibly produce repentance, from which we have been diverted by the question as to whether the punishment inflicted in the second and third cases could be considered just. There is a fourth and last case. In this the authority which inflicts the punishment was, before its infliction, recognized, indeed, theoretically and vaguely, as embodying the moral law, and therefore as being a valid authority. But the recognition was so languid and vague that it was not sufficient to prevent disobedience to the authority's commands. This, it will be seen, is rather analogous to the second case. There the law was held so vaguely that the logical applications of it were never made. Here the authority is recognized, but not actively enough to influence conduct. It is scarcely so much that the criminal recognizes it, as that he is not prepared to deny it.

Here the effect of punishment may again be repentance. For punishment renders it impossible any longer to ignore the authority, and it is, by the hypothesis, only by ignoring it that it can be disobeyed. The punishment clearly proves that the authority is in possession of the power. If it is pressed far enough, there are only two alternatives

—to definitely rebel, and declare the punishment to be unjust, or to definitely submit and to acknowledge it to be righteous. The first is here impossible, for the criminal, by the hypothesis, is not prepared definitely to reject the authority. There remains therefore only the second.

Perhaps the best example of this state of things may be found in the attitude of the lower boys of a public school towards the authority of the masters. Their conviction that this is a lawful and valid authority does not influence them to so great an extent as to produce spontaneous and invariable obedience. But it is, I think, sufficient to prevent them from considering the enforcement of obedience by punishment unjust, except in the cases where their own code of morality comes explicitly in conflict with the official code—cases which are not very frequent. In fact, almost all English school systems would break down completely, if they trusted to their punishments being severe enough to produce obedience by fear. That they do not break down would seem important evidence that punishment can produce other effects than intimidation, unless, indeed, any ingenious person should suggest that they could get on without punishment altogether.

We have now seen that when punishment is able to fulfil the office which Hegel declares to be its highest function,—that of producing repentance,—it does so by emphasizing some moral tie which the offender was all along prepared to admit, although it was too faint or incomplete to prevent the fault. Thus it essentially works on him as, at any rate potentially, a moral agent, and thus, as Hegel expresses it, does him honor. It is no contradiction of this, though it may appear so at first sight, to say that a punishment has such an effect only by the element of disgrace which all deserved punishment contains. Here it differs from deterrent punishment. A punishment deters from the repetition of the offence, not because it is a punishment, but because it is painful. An unpleasant consequence which followed the act, not as the result of moral condemnation, but as a merely natural effect, would have the same deterrent result. A man is equally frightened by pain, whether he recognizes it as just or not. And so a punishment may deter from crime quite as effectually when it is not recognized as just, and consequently produces no feeling of disgrace. But a punishment cannot lead to repentance unless it is recognized as the fitting consequence of a moral fault, and it is this recognition which makes a punishment appear disgraceful.

It seems to be a fashionable theory at present that it is both cruel and degrading to attempt to emphasize the element of disgrace in punishment, especially in the education of children. We are recommended to trust principally to rewards, and, if we should be unhappily forced to inflict pain, we must represent it rather as an inconvenience which it would be well to avoid for the future, than as a punishment for an offence which deserved it. And for this reason all punishments, which proclaim themselves to be such, are to be avoided.

I must confess that it is the modern theory which seems to me the degrading one. To attempt to influence by the pleasures of rewards and by the pain element in punishment, implies that the person to be influenced is governed by pleasure and pain. On the other hand, to trust to the fact that his punishment will appear to him a disgrace implies that he is to some degree influenced by a desire to do right; for, if not, he would feel no disgrace in a punishment for doing wrong. And on the whole it would seem that the latter view of a child's nature is the more hopeful and the less degrading of the two.

There seems to be in this argument a confusion between degradation and disgrace. A man is degraded by anything which lowers his moral nature. A punishment which did this would of course stand condemned. But he is disgraced by being made conscious of a moral defect. And to become conscious of a defect is not to incur a new one. It is rather the most hopeful chance of escaping from the old one. It can scarcely be seriously maintained that, if a fault has been committed, the offender is further degraded by being ashamed of it.

This confusion seems to be at the root of the discussion as to whether the corporal punishment of children is degrading. There is no doubt that it expresses, more unmistakably and emphatically than any substitute that has been proposed for it, the fact that it is a punishment. It follows that, unless the offender is entirely regardless of the opinions of the authority above him, that it is more calculated than other punishments to cause a feeling of disgrace. But, supposing it to be inflicted on the right occasions, this is surely the end of punishment. That it produces any degradation is entirely a separate assertion, which demands a separate proof—a demand which it would be difficult to gratify.

But although a punishment must, to fulfil its highest end, be disgraceful, it does not follow that we can safely trust to the disgrace involved in the offence itself as a punishment,—a course which is sometimes recommended. The aim of punishment is rather to produce repentance, and, as a means to it, disgrace. If we contented ourselves with using as a punishment whatever feeling of disgrace arose independently in the culprit's mind, the result would be that we should only affect those who were already conscious of their fault, and so required punishment least, while those who were impenitent, and so required it most, would escape altogether. We require, therefore, a punishment which will produce disgrace where it is not, not merely utilize it where it is. Otherwise we should not only distribute our punishments precisely in the wrong fashion, but we should also offer a premium on callousness and impenitence. As a matter of prudence, it is as well to make sure that the offender, even if he refuses to allow his punishment to be profitable to him, shall, at any rate, find it painful.

And in this connection we must also remember that the feeling of disgrace which ensues on punishment need be nothing more introspective or morbid than a simple recognition that the punishment was deserved. On the other hand, an attempt to influence any one—especially children—by causing them to reflect on the disgrace involved in the fault itself, must lead to a habitual self-contemplation, the results of which are not unlikely to be both unwholesome to the penitent and offensive to his friends.

I have thus endeavored to show that there are certain conditions under which punishment can perform the work which Hegel assigns to it. The question then arises, When are these conditions realized? We find the question of punishment prominent in jurisprudence and in education. It is found also in theology, in so far as the course of the world is so ordered as to punish sin. Now it seems to me that Hegel's view of punishment cannot properly be applied in jurisprudence, and that his chief mistake regarding it lay in supposing that it could.

In the first place, the paramount object of punishment from the point of view of the state ought, I conceive, to be the prevention of crime and not the reformation of the criminal. The interests of the innocent are to be preferred to those of the guilty—for there are more of them, and they have on the whole a better claim to be considered. And the deterrent effect of punishment is far more certain than its purifying effect. (I use the word purifying to describe the effect of which Hegel treats. It is, I fear, rather stilted, but the word reformatory, which would be more suitable, has by common consent been appropriated to a different theory.) We cannot, indeed, eradicate crime, but experience has shown that by severe and judicious punishment we can diminish it to an enormous extent. On the other hand, punishment can only purify by appealing to the moral nature of the criminal. This may be always latent, but is sometimes far too latent for us to succeed in arousing it. Moreover, the deterrent effect of a punishment acts not only on the criminal who suffers it, but on all who realize that they will suffer it if they commit a similar offence. The purifying influence can act only on those who suffer the punishment. For these reasons it would appear that if the state allows its attention to be distracted from the humble task of frightening criminals from crime, by the higher ambition of converting them to virtue, it is likely to fail in both, and so in its fundamental object of diminishing crime.

And in addition there seems grave reason to doubt whether, in a modern state, the crimes dealt with and the attitude of the criminal to the state are such that punishment can be expected to lead to repentance. The crimes which a state has to deal with may be divided into two classes. The first and smaller class is that in which the state, for its own welfare, endeavors to suppress by punishment conduct which is actuated by conscientious convictions of duty. Examples may be found in high treason and breaches of the law relating to vaccination. Now in these cases the criminal has deliberately adopted a different view of his duty to that entertained by the state. He is not likely, therefore, to be induced to repent of his act by a punishment which can teach him nothing except that he and the state disagree in their views of his duty—which he knew before. His punishment may appear to him to be unjust persecution, or may be accepted as the inevitable result of difference of opinion, but can never be admitted by him as justly deserved by his action, and cannot therefore change the way in which he regards that action.

In the second, and much larger, class of criminal offences, the same result happens, though from very different reasons. The average criminal, convicted of theft or violence, is, no doubt, like all of us, in his essential nature, a distinctly moral being. And, even in action, the vast majority of such criminals are far from being totally depraved. But, by the time a man has become subject to the criminal law for any offence, he has generally become so far callous, with regard to that particular crime, that his punishment will not bring about his repentance. The average burglar may clearly learn from his sentence that the state objects to burglary. He might even, if pressed, admit that the state was from an objective point of view more likely to be right than he was. But, although he may have a sincere abhorrence of murder, he is probably in a condition when the disapproval of the state of his offences with regard to property will rouse no moral remorse in him. In such a case repentance is not possible. Punishment can, under the circumstances I have mentioned above, convince us that we have done wrong. But it cannot inspire us with the desire to do right. The existence of this is assumed when we punish with a view to the purification of an offender, and it is for this reason that the punishment, as Hegel says, honors him. Where the desire to do right is, at any rate as regards one field of action, hopelessly dormant, punishment must fall back on its lower office of intimidation. And this would happen with a large proportion of those offences which are dealt with by the criminal law.

Many offences, no doubt,—especially those committed in a moment of passion, or by persons till then innocent,—are not of this sort, but do coexist with a general desire to do right, which has been overpowered by a particular temptation. Yet I doubt if, at the present day, repentance in such cases would be often the result of punishment by the state. If the criminal's independent moral will was sufficiently strong, he would, when the particular temptation was removed, repent without the aid of punishment. If it was not sufficiently strong, I doubt if the punishment would much aid it. The function of punishment, as we have seen, in this respect, was to enforce on the offender the disapproval with which his action was considered by an authority, whom he regarded as expressing the moral law. But why should the modern citizen regard the state as expressing the moral law? He does not regard it as something above and superior to himself, as the ancient citizen regarded his city, as the child regards his parents, or the religious man his God. The development of individual conscience and responsibility has been too great for such an attitude. The state is now for him an aggregate of men like himself. He regards obedience to it, within certain limits, as a duty. But this is because matters which concern the whole community are matters on which the whole community is entitled to speak. It does not rest on any belief that the state can become for the individual the interpreter of the moral law, so that his moral duty lies in conforming his views to its precepts. Not only does he not feel bound, but he does not feel entitled, to surrender in this way his moral independence. He must determine for himself what he is himself to hold as right and wrong. The result of this is that if he sees for himself that his action was wrong, he will repent without waiting for the state to tell him so, and, if he does not see it for himself, the opinion of the state will not convince him. I do not assert that there are no cases in which a man finds himself in the same childlike relation to the state as was possible in classical times, but they are too few to be of material importance. And except in such cases we cannot expect the punishment of jurisprudence to have a purifying effect.

Hegel's mistake, in applying his conception of punishment to criminal law, resulted from his high opinion of the state as against the individual citizen. The most significant feature of all his writings on the metaphysics of society is the low place that he gives to the conscience and opinions of the individual. He was irritated—not without cause, though with far less cause than we have to-day—at the follies of the writers who see nothing in morality but conscientious convictions, or "the good will." It would almost seem, according to some exponents of these views, that it is entirely unimportant, from a moral point of view, what you do, if only you can manage to persuade yourself that you are doing right. But he did not lay enough emphasis on the fact that, though the approval of conscience does not carry you very far, by itself, towards a satisfactory system of morality, yet that *without* the approval of the individual conscience no modern system of morality can be satisfactory. As between adult human beings, it has become in modern times impossible for one man to yield up his conscience into the hands of any other man or body of men. A child, while it is young enough to be treated entirely as a child, can and ought to find its morality in the commands of others. And those who believe in a divine revelation, will naturally endeavor to place themselves in an attitude of entire submission to what appears to them to be the divine will, whether manifested through books or through some specially flavored organization of men. But a man is not a child, and the state is not God, and the surrender of our consciences to the control of others has become impossible. A man may indeed accept the direction of a teacher whom he has chosen,—even accept it implicitly. But then this is by virtue of his own act of choice. We cannot now accept any purely outward authority as having, of its own right, the power of deciding for us on matters of right and wrong.

Jeremy Bentham

Utility and Punishment *

Chapter XIII

GENERAL VIEW OF CASES UNMEET FOR PUNISHMENT.

I. *The end of law is, to augment happiness.* The general object which all laws have, or ought to have, in common, is to augment the total happiness of the community; and therefore, in the first place, to exclude, as far as may be, every thing that tends to subtract from that happiness: in other words, to exclude mischief.

II. *But punishment is an evil.* But all punishment is mischief: all punishment in itself is evil. Upon the principle of utility, if it ought at all to be admitted, it ought only to be admitted in as far as it promises to exclude some greater evil.

III. *Therefore ought not to be admitted;* It is plain, therefore, that in the following cases punishment ought not to be inflicted.

1. *Where groundless.* Where it is *groundless*: where there is no mischief for it to prevent; the act not being mischievous upon the whole.

2. *Inefficacious.* Where it must be *inefficacious*: where it cannot act so as to prevent the mischief.

3. *Unprofitable.* Where it is *unprofitable*, or too expensive: where the mischief it would produce would be greater than what it prevented.

4. *Or needless.* Where it is *needless*: where the mischief may be prevented, or cease of itself, without it: that is, at a cheaper rate. . . .

* Jeremy Bentham, *An Introduction to the Principles of Morals and Legislation* (New York: Hafner, 1948), ch. 13, sec. 1, ch. 14, sec. 1–26.

Chapter xiv

OF THE PROPORTION BETWEEN PUNISHMENTS AND OFFENCES.

i. *Recapitulation.* We have seen that the general object of all laws is to prevent mischief; that is to say, when it is worth while; but that, where there are no other means of doing this than punishment, there are four cases in which it is *not* worth while.

ii: *Four objects of punishment.* When it *is* worth while, there are four subordinate designs or objects, which, in the course of his endeavours to compass, as far as may be, that one general object, a legislator, whose views are governed by the principle of utility, comes naturally to propose to himself.

iii. 1. *1st Object—to prevent all offences.* His first, most extensive, and most eligible object, is to prevent, in as far as it is possible, and worth while, all sorts of offences whatsoever; in other words, so to manage, that no offence whatsoever may be committed.

iv. 2. *2d Object—to prevent the worst.* But if a man must needs commit an offence of some kind or other, the next object is to induce him to commit an offence *less* mischievous, *rather* than one *more* mischievous: in other words, to choose always the *least* mischievous, of two offences that will either of them suit his purpose.

v. 3. *3d Object—to keep down the mischief.* When a man has resolved upon a particular offence, the next object is to dispose him to do *no more* mischief than is *necessary* to his purpose: in other words, to do as little mischief as is consistent with the benefit he has in view.

vi. 4. *4th Object—to act at the least expense.* The last object is, whatever the mischief be, which it is proposed to prevent, to prevent it at as cheap a rate as possible.

vii. *Rules of proportion between punishments and offences.* Subservient to these four objects, or purposes, must be the rules or canons by which the proportion of punishments to offences is to be governed.

viii. *Rule 1. Outweigh the profit of the offence.* The first object, it has been seen, is to prevent, in as far as it is worth while, all sorts of offences; therefore,

The value of the punishment must not be less in any case than what is sufficient to outweigh that of the profit of the offence.

If it be, the offence (unless some other considerations, independent of the punishment, should intervene and operate efficaciously in the character of tutelary motives) will be sure to be committed notwithstanding: the whole lot of punishment will be thrown away: it will be altogether *inefficacious*.

ix. *The propriety of taking the strength of the temptation for a ground of abatement, no objection to this rule.* The above rule has been often objected to, on account of its seeming harshness: but this can only have happened for want of its being properly understood. The strength of the temptation, ceteris paribus, is as the profit of the offence: the quantum of the punishment must rise with the profit of the offence: ceteris paribus, it must therefore rise with the strength of the temptation. This there is no disputing. True it is, that the stronger the temptation, the less conclusive is the indication which the act of delinquency affords of the depravity of the offender's disposition. So far then as the absence of any aggravation, arising from extraordinary depravity of disposition, may operate, or at the utmost, so far as the presence of a ground of extenuation, resulting from the innocence or beneficence of the offender's disposition, can operate, the strength of the temptation may operate in abatement of the demand for punishment. But it can never operate so far as to indicate the propriety of making the punishment ineffectual, which it is sure to be when brought below the level of the apparent profit of the offence.

The partial benevolence which should prevail for the reduction of it below this level, would counteract as well those purposes which such a motive would actually have in view, as those more extensive purposes which benevolence ought to have in view: it would be cruelty not only to the public, but to the very persons in whose behalf it pleads: in its effects, I mean, however opposite in its intention. Cruelty to the public, that is cruelty to the innocent, by suffering them, for want of an adequate protection, to lie exposed to the mischief of the offence: cruelty even to the offender himself, by punishing him to no purpose, and without the chance of compassing that beneficial end, by which alone the introduction of the evil of punishment is to be justified.

x. Rule 2. *Venture more against a great offence than a small one.* But whether a given offence shall be prevented in a given degree by a given quantity of punishment, is never any thing better than a chance; for the purchasing of which, whatever punishment is employed, is so much expended in advance. However, for the sake of giving it the better chance of outweighing the profit of the offence,

The greater the mischief of the offence, the greater is the expense, which it may be worth while to be at, in the way of punishment.

xi. Rule 3. *Cause the least of two offences to be preferred.* The next object is, to induce a man to choose always the least mischievous of two offences; therefore

Where two offences come in competition, the punishment for the greater offence must be sufficient to induce a man to prefer the less.

xii. Rule 4. *Punish for each particle of the mischief.* When a man has resolved upon a particular offence, the next object is, to induce him to do no more mischief than what is necessary for his purpose: therefore

The punishment should be adjusted in such manner to each particular offence, that for every part of the mischief there may be a motive to restrain the offender from giving birth to it.

xiii. Rule 5. *Punish in no degree without special reason.* The last object is, whatever mischief is guarded against, to guard against it at as cheap a rate as possible: therefore

The punishment ought in no case to be more than what is necessary to bring it into conformity with the rules here given.

xiv. Rule 6. *Attend to circumstances influencing sensibility.* It is further to be observed, that owing to the different manners and degrees in which persons under different circumstances are affected by the same exciting cause, a punishment which is the same in name will not always either really produce, or even so much as appear to others to produce, in two different persons the same degree of pain: therefore

That the quantity actually inflicted on each individual offender may correspond to the quantity intended for similar offenders in general, the several circumstances influencing sensibility ought always to be taken into account.

xv. *Comparative view of the above rules.* Of the above rules of proportion, the four first, we may perceive, serve to mark out the limits on the side of diminution; the limits *below* which a punishment ought not to be *diminished:* the fifth, the limits on the side of increase; the limits *above* which it ought not to be *increased.* The five first are calculated to serve as guides to the legislator: the sixth is calculated, in some measure, indeed, for the same purpose; but principally for guiding the judge in his endeavours to conform, on both sides, to the intentions of the legislator.

xvi. *Into the account of the value of a punishment must be taken its deficiency in point of certainty and proximity.* Let us look back a little. The first rule, in order to render it more conveniently applicable to practice, may need perhaps to be a little more particularly unfolded. It is to be observed, then, that for the sake of accuracy, it was necessary, instead of the word *quantity* to make use of the less perspicuous term *value.* For the word *quantity* will not properly include the circumstances either of certainty or proximity: circumstances which, in estimating the value of a lot of pain or pleasure, must always be taken into the account. Now, on the one hand, a lot of punishment is a lot of pain; on the other hand, the profit of an offence is a lot of pleasure, or what is equivalent to it. But the profit of the offence *is* commonly more *certain* than the punishment, or, what comes to the same thing, *appears* so at least to the offender. It is at any rate commonly more *immediate.* It follows, therefore, that, in order to maintain its superiority over the profit of the offence, the punishment must have its value made up in some other way, in proportion to that whereby it falls short in the two points of *certainty* and *proximity.* Now there is no other way in which it can receive any addition to its *value,* but by receiving an addition in point of *magnitude.* Wherever then the value of the punishment falls short, either in point of *certainty,* or of *proximity,* of that of the profit of the offence, it must receive a proportionable addition in point of *magnitude.*

xvii. *Also, into the account of the mischief, and profit of the offence, the mischief and profit of other offences of the same habit.* Yet farther. To make sure of giving the value of the punishment the superiority over that of the offence, it may be necessary, in some cases, to take into the account the profit not only of the *individual* offence to which the punishment is to be annexed, but also of such *other* offences of the *same sort* as the offender is likely to have already committed without detection. This random mode of calculation, severe as it is, it will be impossible to avoid having recourse to, in certain cases: in such, to wit, in which the profit is pecuniary, the chance of detection very small, and the obnoxious act of such a nature as indicates a habit: for example, in the case of frauds against the coin. If it be *not* recurred to, the practice of committing the offence will be sure to be, upon the balance of the account, a gainful practice. That being the case, the legislator will be absolutely sure of *not* being able to suppress it, and the whole punishment that is bestowed upon it will be thrown away. In a word (to keep to the same expressions we set out with) that whole quantity of punishment will be *inefficacious*.

xvIII. Rule 7. *Want of certainty must be made up in magnitude.* These things being considered, the three following rules may be laid down by way of supplement and explanation to Rule 1.

To enable the value of the punishment to outweigh that of the profit of the offence, it must be increased, in point of magnitude, in proportion as it falls short in point of certainty.

xIx. Rule 8. *(So also want of proximity.) Punishment must be further increased in point of magnitude, in proportion as it falls short in point of proximity.*

xx. Rule 9. *(For acts indicative of a habit punish as for the habit.) Where the act is conclusively indicative of a habit, such an increase must be given to the punishment as may enable it to outweigh the profit not only of the individual offence, but of such other like offences as are likely to have been committed with impunity by the same offender.*

xxI. *The remaining rules are of less importance.* There may be a few other circumstances or considerations which may influence, in some small degree, the demand for punishment: but as the propriety of these is either not so demonstrable, or not so constant, or the application of them not so determinate, as that of the foregoing, it may be doubted whether they be worth putting on a level with the others.

xxII. Rule 10. *(For the sake of quality, increase in quantity.) When a punishment, which in point of quality is particularly well calculated to answer its intention, cannot exist in less than a certain quantity, it may sometimes be of use, for the sake of employing it, to stretch a little beyond that quantity which, on other accounts, would be strictly necessary.*

xxIII. Rule 11. *(Particularly for a moral lesson.) In particular, this may sometimes be the case, where the punishment proposed is of such a nature as to be particularly well calculated to answer the purpose of a moral lesson.*

xxIV. Rule 12. *Attend to circumstances which may render punish-*

ment *unprofitable*. The tendency of the above considerations is to dictate an augmentation in the punishment: the following rule operates in the way of diminution. There are certain cases (it has been seen) in which, by the influence of accidental circumstances, punishment may be rendered unprofitable in the whole: in the same cases it may chance to be rendered unprofitable as to a part only. Accordingly,

In adjusting the quantum of punishment, the circumstances, by which all punishment may be rendered unprofitable, ought to be attended to.

xxv. Rule 13. *For simplicity's sake, small disproportions may be neglected.* It is to be observed, that the more various and minute any set of provisions are, the greater the chance is that any given article in them will not be borne in mind: without which, no benefit can ensue from it. Distinctions, which are more complex than what the conceptions of those whose conduct it is designed to influence can take in, will even be worse than useless. The whole system will present a confused appearance: and thus the effect, not only of the proportions established by the articles in question, but of whatever is connected with them, will be destroyed. To draw a precise line of direction in such case seems impossible. However, by way of memento, it may be of some use to subjoin the following rule.

Among provisions designed to perfect the proportion between punishments and offences, if any occur, which, by their own particular good effects, would not make up for the harm they would do by adding to the intricacy of the Code, they should be omitted.

xxvi. *Auxiliary force of the physical, moral, and religious sanction, not here allowed for—why.* It may be remembered, that the political sanction, being that to which the sort of punishment belongs, which in this chapter is all along in view, is but one of four sanctions, which may all of them contribute their share towards producing the same effects. It may be expected, therefore, that in adjusting the quantity of political punishment, allowance should be made for the assistance it may meet with from those other controlling powers. True it is, that from each of these several sources a very powerful assistance may sometimes be derived. But the case is, that (setting aside the moral sanction, in the case where the force of it is expressly adopted into and modified by the political) the force of those other powers is never determinate enough to be depended upon. It can never be reduced, like political punishment, into exact lots, nor meted out in number, quantity, and value. The legislator is therefore obliged to provide the full complement of punishment, as if he were sure of not receiving any assistance whatever from any of those quarters. If he does, so much the better: but lest he should not, it is necessary he should, at all events, make that provision which depends upon himself.

H. Rashdall

Punishment and the Individual *

It is sometimes supposed that the utilitarian view of punishment is inconsistent with a proper respect for human personality: it involves, we are told, the treatment of humanity as a means and not as an end. If by the 'utilitarian' theory is meant a view resting upon a hedonistic theory of Ethics, I have nothing to say in its favour; if by 'utilitarian' is meant simply a view which treats punishment as a means to some good, spiritual or otherwise, of some conscious being, I should entirely deny the justice of the criticism. In the first place I should contend that in a sense it is quite right and inevitable that we should treat humanity as a means. When a servant is called upon to black the boots of his master, or a soldier to face death or disease in the service of his country, society is certainly treating humanity as a means: the men do these things not for their own sakes, but for the sake of other people. Kant himself never uttered anything so foolish as the maxim which indiscreet admirers are constantly putting into his mouth, that we should never treat humanity as a means: what he did say was that we should never treat humanity *only* as a means, but always *also* as an end. When a man is punished in the interest of society, he is indeed treated as a means, but his right to be treated as an end is not thereby violated, if his good is treated as of equal importance with the end of other human beings. Social life would not be possible without the constant subordination of the claims of individuals to the like claims of a greater number of individuals; and there may be occasions when in punishing a criminal we have to think more of the good of society generally than of the individual who is punished. No doubt it is a duty to think also of the good of the individual so far as that can

* H. Rashdall, *Theory of Good and Evil,* 2d ed. (Oxford: Clarendon Press, 1924), 1, pp. 303–04.

be done consistently with justice to other individuals: it is obviously the duty of the State to endeavour to make its punishments as far as possible reformatory as well as deterrent and educational to others. And how the reformatory view of punishment can be accused of disrespect for human personality, because forsooth it uses a man's animal organism or his lower psychical nature as a means to the good of his higher self, I cannot profess to understand. The retributive view of punishment justifies the infliction of evil upon a living soul, even though it will do neither him nor any one else any good whatever. If it is to do anybody any good, punishment is not inflicted for the sake of retribution. It is the retributive theory which shows a disrespect for human personality by proposing to sacrifice human life and human Well-being to a lifeless fetish styled the Moral Law, which apparently, though unconscious, has a sense of dignity and demands the immolation of victims to avenge its injured *amour propre*. . . .

T. L. S. Sprigge

A Utilitarian Reply
to Dr. McCloskey *

. . . McCloskey's main argument against a utilitarian theory of punishment lies in examples which he presents of moral judgments which
he supposes would follow from utilitarian theory, and which clash
with our common moral consciousness, even presumably when this
has been altered to meet the demands of critical reflection. Such
examples may be of two types. They may be moral judgments regarding situations of a kind which actually occur or they may regard
situations of a kind which do not occur. Or, to put it another way,
these moral judgments may be deducible from the utility principle
and certain contingent truths (or from fictions akin to such truths)
or they may be deducible from the utility principle in conjunction
with contingent factual premises which include falsehoods. Although
McCloskey recognizes this distinction, he evidently does not think
it of much importance. For he says: 'Against the utilitarian who seeks
to argue that utilitarianism does not involve unjust punishment, there
is a very simple argument, namely, that whether or not unjust punishments are in fact useful, it is logically possible that they will at some
time become useful, in which case utilitarians are committed to them.'

Actually, I have a certain hesitation regarding the sense of this
passage. Is there an especial significance in the future tense? Presumably if it is logically possible that they will become useful, it is logically
possible that they are useful now. After all it is logically possible that
Britain and the United States are now at war. Use of the future tense
suggests that perhaps by its being logically possible that they will
become useful, McCloskey really means the quite different thing that

---

* T. L. S. Sprigge, "A Utilitarian Reply to Dr. McCloskey," *Inquiry* 8 (Univer-
sitetsforlaget, Olso, 1965), 272–84. Reprinted by permission of the author and
the publisher. Dr. McCloskey's paper is reprinted in this volume, p. 165.

for all we know they may become useful one day. It is an important question which is meant. For it is very easy indeed to establish the logical possibility that something like punishment of the innocent will be (is, or was) useful. One can for instance imagine the most basic facts of human nature altered for this purpose. But it is a more empirical task to establish that *for all we know* they will become useful one day. Since the 'we' presumably does not refer just to one perhaps ignorant person, one must show that there are not (say) well confirmed principles of psychology which give us firm reasons for saying that things will not develop that way.

Situations instanced in which utilitarian judgments are alleged to be offensive to our common moral consciousness (understand henceforth: even when purified by critical attention) may be of three kinds. First, they may be actual or relevantly akin to actual situations. Second, they may be situations not establishable as actual or akin to such, but not establishable either as such as will never have occurred. Thirdly, they may be logically possible situations, but ones which there is good reason to suppose will never have occurred. Of course, this rough classification is capable of refinement.

McCloskey presumably would think a situation on which a utilitarian judgment shocks our moral consciousness counts equally against utilitarianism to whichever type it belongs. For this he could argue as follows. The principle of utility is a theory about what would be right and wrong under any conceivable (i.e., logically possible) circumstances. Our common moral consciousness also provides us with principles about what would be right or wrong under any conceivable circumstances. If therefore they clash in their judgment on a conceivable situation, however out of the question such a situation is, they do indeed clash, and one must be discarded.

I accept this description of the principle of utility, but not of our common moral consciousness. I do not think the latter is thus thought of by most people we might consider typical vehicles of it. Plain men will probably admit that if the empirical nature of the world had been very different then different moral sentiments would often have been appropriate. For instance, Christians who urge more or less strongly the principle of turning the other cheek, are wont to support it with references to the contrary effects of love and hate. However basic such facts about love and hate are, they are in the last resort contingent. Similarly with the kind of support most people would give for our sentiments in favour of just rather than unjust punishment. Utilitarianism then is not eccentric in basing the rightness of some very fundamental moral sentiments on ultimately contingent facts.

Now if one considers some fantastic situations of the third type one does of course consider them as a person with certain moral sentiments, the strength of which in society as it is, is an important utilitarian good. These sentiments are offended. A utilitarian will see no point in trying to imagine oneself looking with approval on the imaginary situation, since this is likely to weaken the feelings while not serving as a preparation for any actual situation. If in fact punishing the innocent (say) always is and always will be harmful, it is likewise harmful to dwell on fanciful situations in which it would be beneficial, thus weakening one's aversion to such courses. Thus the utilitarian shares (quite consistently so) in the unease produced by these examples. Although he may admit that in such a situation punishment of the innocent would be right, he still regards favourably the distaste which is aroused at the idea of its being called right.

Certainly, if one imagines the world as other than it is, one may find oneself imagining a world in which utilitarianism implies moral judgments which shock our moral sentiments. But if these moral sentiments are quite appropriate to the only world there is, the real world, the utilitarian is glad that moral judgements in opposition to them seen repugnant. He sees no need for moral acrobatics relevant only to situations which in fact are quite out of the question.

We must be very careful therefore in using the fact that strong and, we feel, right-minded antipathies are aroused at the thought of certain utilitarian type judgments on type three examples, as an argument against utilitarianism. For the utilitarian himself will commend this distaste as something to be kept alive in himself and others, and is perhaps claiming for the offended moral sentiments as much as, on reflection, most people would be prepared to do.

There is another reason for caution in discussing type three situations. Suppose one describes a case where punishment of an innocent man would yield a balance of good, and insures that this is so simply by stipulating certain striking benefits which will derive from it, and explicitly eliminating all the harms one can think of. If one finds oneself still half-inclined to call such punishment wrong, it may well be because one does not really succeed in envisaging the situation just as described, but surrounds it with those circumstances of real life which would in fact create a greater probability of unhappiness in its consequences than happiness.

We may conclude that it would be more convincing if examples of conflict between the common moral consciousness and utilitarianism were looked for in type one situations rather than in type three, while situations of type two (clearly) have a degree of relevance here lying between the other two.

McCloskey's Examples

Let us now consider McCloskey's individual examples. I shall not dwell much on his first example, as he himself lays more weight on his second, which is a modified version of it. But I should like to comment on one oddity in his discussion of the first.

The sheriff is supposed to have framed an innocent negro to prevent a series of lynchings which he knows will occur if no one is 'punished' for the offence. It is urged that this is obviously the right course from a utilitarian point of view.

One line of objection to this conclusion appeals to the likelihood that the facts will become known. I may urge parenthetically that in the real world such a likelihood is likely (surely) to be pretty strong. The utilitarian may then insist on a variety of evils which would result from its becoming known, such as a loss of confidence in the impartiality and fairness of the legal system, of a belief that lawful behaviour pays, etc. Now McCloskey says that 'even if everyone came to know, surely, if utilitarianism is thought to be the true moral theory, the general body of citizens ought to be happier believing that their sheriff is promoting what is right rather than promoting non-utilitarian standards of justice'. This strikes me as absurd. Let us consider first the white citizenry. It is quite obvious that they are not utilitarians, or that even if by chance some are in theory, their feelings are not in fact governed by utilitarian theory. For if they were utilitarians they would not be charging around the country lynching people. For who could seriously believe that this was the best way of creating the greatest happiness of the greatest number? If they were utilitarians (in practice) the sheriff would not be in the situation he is in. As it is, he has to think about them as they are. How they *would* react to the fact that the sheriff framed the negro is a different matter, but for a utilitarian to expect their satisfaction because he has done the right thing from a utilitarian point of view would be absurd. You might as well suggest that a utilitarian penologist should urge that all prisons should be without bars, on the grounds that once it is explained to the offenders how useful it is for society that they should be punished they will see the wrongness of escaping. Let us now consider the negroes. There is not the same evidence within the very hypothesis that their actions and feelings are opposed to utilitarian precepts. But one may take it that whatever their ethical views, they are filled with bitterness at white behaviour. They are hardly going to be overjoyed at learning that a negro up for trial is likely to be framed in order to sate the fury of brutish whites. Will not their incentives to law-abidingness be decreased when they learn that someone else's crime may just as well get them punished as one of their own? Is racial harmony really going to be advanced by such an event?

But I shall now turn to the second supposedly more forceful example. Here a utilitarian visitor from outside the area bears incriminating false witness against a negro so that his being 'punished' for a rape will put an end to a series of riots and lynchings. One main point of thus changing the example presumably is to eliminate such harms as might be supposed to ensue from a local figure, especially a legal authority, practising the deception.

Before commenting on this example in further detail I should like to ask the reader (or McCloskey himself) to stand back for a moment and consider the prima facie implausibility of what McCloskey tries to show. Forget for a moment all question of the rightness or wrongness of utilitarian theory, forget morality, and imagine simply that you are a reasonable being with one overriding aim, to create as much happiness as possible at the cost of as little unhappiness as possible. Does it really seem on the cards that in a situation where race riots are going on as a result of a rape, you will find no more effective way of forwarding your aim in this area than to bear false witness against some unfortunate negro, thus ensuring that at least one human being is thoroughly miserable? Does not a vague unanalysed sense of how the world really works inform one that this is not a type of action which increases human happiness? People who lack this common-sense grasp of how the world runs are dangerous whatever moral backing they may claim for their actions.

Let us now turn to details. Our utilitarian is said to know 'that a quick arrest will stop the riots and lynchings'. How does he know this? How does he know that they aren't going to die down soon anyway? Even if he has good reason to think that they will go on unless such an arrest is made, does he know how intense they will be, how many people are actually going to get lynched? One thing he does know is that if he bears false witness (successfully) an innocent man is going to get punished. We are not told what the punishment will be, but it is likely either to be death or a long term of imprisonment, which will mean the ruin of the man's life. Suppose he does not bear the false witness, that the riots go on as he expected, but that no deaths or permanent injuries take place. Isn't it likely that the suffering in this case is less than that of a man sentenced to execution (together with the sufferings of his family) or languishing for long years in prison?

Utilitarian judgment that the false witness would be right must be based on its foreseeable consequences. Now an event can be foreseen as a probable (or certain) consequence of a given action on two roughly distinguishable grounds. It may be a well confirmed generalization that actions of that broad type in that broad type of situation very often (or always) have such a consequence. But an action may (also) be characterized by features too unusual to figure in such generalizations. If these are to provide a basis for prediction it must be because of some hunch about the situation which will be no more rational than an indefinite number of other hunches. Reliance on such hunches is something which often leads people wildly wrong. (This is well confirmed, I suggest.) This suggests that a product (such as happiness) will be increased in the long run more by those who base their expectations on well confirmed generalizations than on hunches, and that therefore the utilitarian should stick to the former, especially where the amounts of happiness or unhappiness are large. The situation is quite different from that of scientific research. Here the hunches are needed for major advances, and can be put to the test and abandoned if necessary, with no harm done. And indeed in ethical decisions which do not have consequences of too great import, action on such hunches may be useful as a mode of experiment.

Now I suggest that the prediction of misery for the innocent man if he is successfully framed rests on well confirmed generalizations, but that the prediction that this will stop lynchings, etc., which would otherwise have occurred, will be based on a hunch about the character of the riots. In that case the sensible utilitarian will attach a predominating weight to the former prediction, and refrain from framing the man.

McCloskey may, however, insist that the utilitarian has the very firmest grounds for his beliefs about the duration and degree of the rioting if no punishment takes place, and concerning the preventability of all this by the means in question. I'm inclined to suggest then that a man with such a rich knowledge of the nature of these riots should devote himself fully to a documented study of them with a view to putting his knowledge before such organizations as can arrange by propaganda and other means to alleviate their causes. If he has something to hide concerning his own illicit means of checking them, he will not be at ease in drawing up a report on the situation and will therefore not do his work properly, work which will stop more riot-caused suffering in the end than this isolated act.

If these last remarks seen somewhat fanciful I should urge that the situation in which a man *knows* that the riots will go on unless he tells this lie is also fanciful, and is an example of type two perilously close to type three. In an actual situation this would probably only be a hunch, of little weight besides the well supported belief that a successful frameup will produce massive suffering for the innocent man and his family. There is also good reason for believing that facing a man and telling lies which will ruin his life will blunt one's sensibilities in a way which may well lead one to use such methods again with still less justification. I should suspect, moreover, that a utilitarian who persuaded himself that such an act was useful would be finding an outlet for harmful impulses which it would behove him not to indulge; for instance an urge to exert power in a secret God-like manner, and without scruple. It is dangerously easy for someone who wants to do something for motives of which he is ashamed to persuade himself that the general good would be served by it. This gives another reason for suspicion of 'hunches'.

None of this has appealed to any such principle as that the suffering of an innocent man is a worse thing in itself than that of a guilty one. What of this principle? The utilitarian cannot consistently say that one is worse in itself if the degree of suffering is the same. But if there is reason to believe that more suffering is involved in a given punishment for an innocent man than for a guilty man this is something of which the utilitarian should take account.

There does seem some reason to believe this. An innocent man is liable to suffer more shock at being thus punished. He will suffer from an indignant fury as the guilty man will not. Whatever the utilitarian thinks of the appropriateness of such indignation (a matter too complicated for comment here) he must take it into account as a fact. But apart from the indignation, the punishment will come on him as much more of a surprise, and thus be something he is less able to cope with psychologically (accept) or even practically. The distress caused to his relatives will also probably be greater, since it is likely to come as more of a shock to them also. His wife may be ill prepared in every way for life alone, and she will also be more likely to be dismayed if she now believes her husband guilty. Moreover punishment of the innocent (especially in a case like that described) is very likely to arouse emotions leading to antisocial action on the part of someone previously law-abiding.

Of course McCloskey can deal with each specific point by imagining a situation in which it would not arise. Let the innocent man be without family and a natural pessimist always prepared for the worst. But what sort of investigation prior to his false witness is our wily utilitarian to make into these matters? It is hard to believe that a man of such tenacity will not find less costly ways of advancing racial harmony.

It seems to me, then, highly unlikely that in a situation at all like the one described by McCloskey a man guided by a cool assessment of probabilities rather than by wild surmises will see such bearing of false witness as the most felicific act. This applies even if we ignore the effects on the utilitarian's own character, still more if we take these into account.

Still, I should not say it was absolutely *out of the question* that situations may arise where a sensible utilitarian would think it right to implicate an innocent man. As I have explained at length, he could still think the resultant punishment *unjust*, although his production of it was right or justified. In such a situation the good to be achieved by the punishment would presumably be predictable as near certain on well confirmed principles, and be great enough to outweigh harms of the sort we have described, and such other evils (especially evils of injustice) as might arise. It would also have to be unobtainable at less cost. I suspect that with such goods to be gained our utilitarian's action would be such as many plain men (not just official utilitarians) would condone or approve.

What plain men would feel, however, is an uneasiness at the situation, and a deep regret about it. Now sometimes one gets a picture of the utilitarian who can feel no regret at any overriding of conventional moral principles provided his sums come out all right. This is a travesty of the utilitarian outlook.

There is indeed a certain problematicness about regret on any ethical theory. Everyone must admit that on occasion the action which on balance one ought to do, has characteristics or consequences which considered in themselves suggest the wrongness of the act. A general fighting for a good cause may well regard the dead and injured on the field of battle with a terrible regret that he should have brought this about, and yet think he acted rightly—although he always knew there would be a sacrifice like this. Moreover his regret may in a sense be a moral regret, different in character from the regret one feels at the sacrifice of one's own interests for the sake of duty. An unimaginative moral philosopher might say that such regret was inapposite, if he had really done the right thing. Most of us do not feel this way and utilitarianism offers at least two justifications for our attitude. First, a man who was not sad at producing suffering would lack the basic sentiment which inspires the utility principle, namely a revulsion at the suffering and a delight in the happiness of any sentient being. Second, sentiments such as the love of justice, respect for human life and so on, are sentiments which utilitarian considerations bid us cherish in ourselves and others. When the promptings of these sentiments have to be set aside in the interests of a greater good, the man who feels no regret can have them little developed, and the man who checks all regret will blunt them. Regret in such situations is therefore a desirable state of mind according to utilitarianism.

Feeling regret must not be confused with a judgement that it would be a good thing to feel regret. There is no such confusion here. Whether I feel regret is a psychological fact not normally in my control. All I have argued is that the utilitarian who feels regret need not think that his theory demands an attempt to set it aside as a weakness. Rather he should be troubled by his character if he does not feel it.

So even if on some rare occasion a greater good demands some such injustice as the punishment of an innocent man, the utilitarian will certainly accept this as an appropirate matter for regret.

Further Examples

Among further examples which McCloskey gives of unjust but useful laws are scapegoat punishment and collective punishment. He does not make it very clear, however, what his own moral attitude to such punishments is, or what he takes to be that of the common moral consciousness. Certainly he thinks they are unjust even when useful— and that is something with which the utilitarian can agree—but does he think that they are sometimes justified nonetheless? He seems at least to leave it open that they may be, and in one case, collective punishment in schools, he goes further. Now to say that they are unjust but all the same morally right or justified is a position which the utilitarian who really believed they produced more good than evil would probably adopt.

Consider the type of scapegoat punishment he mentions. It is within the bounds of possibility that a commander whose chances of victory demanded some sort of cooperation from the local people, and who had good reason to believe that without this victory the common good of humanity would suffer, finding this method of securing the population's cooperation the only workable one, would rightly consider that it was justified. I say that it is within the bounds of possibility, but it is also perhaps more probable that such a method is not even the most efficient for his end, or at least not more efficient than other means less damaging to the goods of justice. But if the circumstances really were as described most people who condone war at all would probably think the act was right.

In saying that such an undesirable means to a desirable end might possibly on rare occasions be justified, one is not giving one's general approval to such methods of gaining one's ends. There is, however, always the danger that when once one has allowed the justifiability of such means on one occasion, one will be ready to use them again on other occasions where although immediately convenient the same justifying conditions do not hold. The fact that an act may be a bad example to oneself and others (even if supposing this fact left out of account it would be justified) may often finally tip the balance against the rightness of doing it. As an example, I should like to take the bombing of centers of civilian population in wartime. For many such raids the British may well have had acceptable justification. This was certainly the belief of quite decent people in Britain. The victory of the allies really was an overwhelming good for humanity and this may have been an unavoidable means to it. But once moral scruples against such bombings were set aside in the interests of a greater good the capacity for moral reflection on the matter seems to have become blunted, and we have the bombing of Dresden which it is widely agreed served no essential purpose. In the same kind of way injustices in the treatment of an occupied country are likely to escalate, and this consideration should probably tip the balance in any cases (if there are such) where it might otherwise have been justified from a utilitarian point of view.

Just about the same can be said regarding collective punishments as scapegoat punishments.

In both cases one doubts whether these acts really ever are justified from a utilitarian point of view. Anyone concerned to gain the co-operation of an occupied territory without making it a slave population will presumably be concerned to gain its good will, to which end these methods are hardly conducive. The purposes for which the occupation is undertaken are obviously relevant here. On the whole, the more immoral the purposes the more such methods will seem required.

Although I am not attempting in this reply any account of what constitutes the goods (and evils) of justice (and injustice), I should perhaps mention a good of this type which would be prevented by scapegoat and collective punishment. One of the great goods furthered by various legal and quasilegal institutions when properly conducted is the increased chance they give to everyone to control their own futures (so far as these depend on human agency) within limits imposed by the common good. This can perhaps be called one of the goods of justice, when it is the result of such institutions. (A similar good arising from a different cause might not be so called.) But the good of justice with which I am concerned is rather the *maintenance* of institutions serving this purpose. This can be called a major good of justice. Among such institutions we may include various habits of people wielding authority even where they are not directed to act thus by some positive law. It should not be very controversial to urge that the maintenance of institutions which (or of those aspects of them which) increase a person's opportunities to plan his future is a great utilitarian good.

An institution which serves the purposes in question will ensure that such evils as may arise for a man through human agency and frustrate his plans, when they are also such that their attempted elimination (by—or in the case of punishment from—the institutions in question) would be predominantly harmful, are at least so far as possible predictable by him, and preferably dependent for their occurrence on circumstances within his control. Thus although customs which ensured that a man could never lose his job would doubtless be harmful on the whole, habits of employment according to which a man knows under what circumstances he will lose his job, especially if these circumstances are within his control, serve the purpose we have described and action which weakens such habits is so far unjust. Now we may accept that punishment (like the sack) is necessary evil, but granted that, we should try to preserve institutions according to which a man can predict and control the circumstances in which he will suffer it. Acts which weaken such institutions will be so far unjust, and be so even on those rare occasions where they may effect a predominating good and so be right.

It is not difficult to see that the infliction of scapegoat or collective punishment will be unjust from this point of view. There are various rules adherence to which is generally regarded as a criterion of just punishment. A main one is the rule that a man should only be punished for an action if he knew before doing it that he was likely to be punished for it, and could have refrained from the act if he had chosen. Various departures from this rule are in fact countenanced without people feeling that there is an injustice. For instance it is accepted that a man may be punished if in some sense he should have known that punishment might be inflicted for something he has done, even if in fact he did not know this. That is a rather minor departure. But there are also cases such as some punishments of war criminals where the rule is departed from more strikingly, and yet not everyone regards such punishment as unjust. I think we may say, however, that a departure from this rule always gives some reason for talk of injustice.

Adherence to this rule is an institution such as I have been describing. So long as a person is only punished in conformity to it the evil he suffers is such as he could have anticipated and avoided. If we weaken this institution we are acting against the major good of justice I have mentioned, and forwarding the opposing evil.

Now infliction of a scapegoat or collective punishment represents a breaking of the rule in question. A collective punishment can hardly be a secret affair, and it is not very clear that a scapegoat punishment can be. (For we do not call such frameups as were discussed in the last section scapegoat punishments.) In acting against the rule we create a general sense that this institution (adherence to the rule) is breaking down, and this acts in various ways to bring about that result. Even if in some examples the result is supposed avoided, it is unrealistic to imagine it possible thus to act without weakening one's own tendency to abide by the rule. One's adherence to the rule represents a personal habit and sentiment, which when once broken for what seem good reasons is much more likely than before to be broken for bad reasons. It seems then that collective and scapegoat punishment will always weaken the institution in question, and will be so far *unjust*, using this word according to the utilitarian account I have adumbrated.

It is of course theoretically possible that a punishment of this sort will bring about more good than evil, even when the weakening of the institution and the intrinsic evil of the punishment itself are both taken into account, and I would not care to insist that it was not sometimes a practical possibility. But there are two different possibilities here which must be distinguished. One is that the goods which outweigh these evils are other goods of justice. The other is that these goods are of a different type. In the former case we may wish to describe the punishment as on the whole just, in spite of seeming unjust when one aspect of the situation only is considered. Such might be the case with the punishment of war criminals. In the latter case, however, we will allow that the punishment was unjust, but urge that nonetheless it was justified by the special good it did. It seems likely that whatever other goods can be described as goods of justice besides that major one which we have considered, they will never be forwarded by scapegoat and collective punishment. So that the utilitarian can accept that such punishments are always unjust.

The possibility remains that these unjust punishments may on occasion be right and proper, because useful in some other way. This possibility seems, however, to be allowed by McCloskey. It is not at all clear in my judgment that occasions of this kind actually occur. At any rate the utilitarian has every reason for urging the serious damage done to the goods of justice on any likely occasion of scapegoat or collective punishment, and for insisting therefore on the extreme gravity of any decision to use them.

John Austin

Rule Utilitarianism *

The tendency of a human action (as its tendency is this understood)
is the whole of its tendency: the sum of its probable consequences,
in so far as they are important or material: the sum of its remote and
collateral, as well as of its direct consequences, in so far as any of its
consequences may influence the general happiness.

Trying to collect its tendency (as its tendency is thus understood),
we must not consider the action as if it were single and insulated,
but must look at the class of actions to which it belongs. The probable
specific consequences of doing that single act, of forbearing from that
single act, or of omitting that single act, are not the objects of the
inquiry. The question to be solved is this:—If acts of the class were
generally done, or generally forborne or omitted, what would be the
probable effect on the general happiness or good?

Considered by itself, a mischievous act may seem to be useful or
harmless. Considered by itself, a useful act may seem to be pernicious.

For example, If a poor man steal a handful from the heap of his
rich neighbour, the act, considered by itself, is harmless or positively
good. One man's poverty is assuaged with the superfluous wealth of
another.

But suppose that thefts were general (or that the useful right of
property were open to frequent invasions), and mark the result.

Without security for property, there were no inducement to save.
Without habitual saving on the part of proprietors, there were no
accumulation of capital. Without accumulation of capital, there were
no fund for the payment of wages, no division of labour, no elaborate
and costly machines: there were none of those helps to labour which
augment its productive power, and, therefore, multiply the enjoyments

* John Austin, *The Province of Jurisprudence Determined and The Uses of the
Study of Jurisprudence*, intro. H. L. A. Hart (New York: The Noonday Press,
1954), pp. 38–40.

of every individual in the community. Frequent invasions of property would bring the rich to poverty; and, what were a greater evil, would aggravate the poverty of the poor.

If a single and insulated theft seem to be harmless or good, the fallacious appearance merely arises from this: that the vast majority of those who are tempted to steal abstain from invasions of property; and the detriment to security, which is the end produced by a single theft, is overbalanced and concealed by the mass of wealth, the accumulation of which is produced by general security.

Again: If I evade the payment of a tax imposed by a good government, the *specific* effects of the mischievous forbearance are indisputably useful. For the money which I unduly withhold is convenient to myself; and, compared with the bulk of the public revenue, is a quantity too small to be missed. But the regular payment of taxes is necessary to the existence of the government. And I, and the rest of the community, enjoy the security which it gives, because the payment of taxes is rarely evaded.

In the cases now supposed, the act or omission is good, considered as single or insulated; but, considered with the rest of its class, is evil. In other cases, an act or omission is evil, considered as single or insulated; but, considered with the rest of its class, is good.

For example, A punishment, as a solitary fact, is an evil: the pain inflicted on the criminal being added to the mischief of the crime. But, considered as part of a system, a punishment is useful or beneficent. By a dozen or score of punishments, thousands of crimes are prevented. With the sufferings of the guilty few, the security of the many is purchased. By the lopping of a peccant member, the body is saved from decay.

It, therefore, is true generally (for the proposition admits of exceptions), that, to determine the true tendency of an act, forbearance, or omission, we must resolve the following question:—What would be the probable effect on the general happiness or good, if *similar* acts, forbearances, or omissions were general or frequent?

Such is the *test* to which we must usually resort, if we would try the true *tendency* of an act, forbearance, or omission: Meaning, by the true *tendency* of an act, forbearance, or omission, the sum of its probable effects on the general happiness or good, or its agreement or disagreement with the principle of general utility.

John Rawls

Rule Utilitarianism
(continued) *

In this paper I want to show the importance of the distinction between justifying a practice [1] and justifying a particular action falling
under it, and I want to explain the logical basis of this distinction and
how it is possible to miss its significance. While the distinction has
frequently been made,[2] and is now becoming commonplace, there

---

* John Rawls, "Two Concepts of Rules," *The Philosophical Review*, 44 (1955),
intro., sec. 1. pp. 3–13. Reprinted by permission of the author and *The Philosophical Review*.

1. I use the word "practice" throughout as a sort of technical term meaning any
form of activity specified by a system of rules which defines offices, roles, moves,
penalties, defenses, and so on, and which gives the activity its structure. As examples one may think of games and rituals, trials and parliaments.

2. The distinction is central to Hume's discussion of justice in *A Treatise of
Human Nature*, bk. III, pt. 11, esp. secs. 2–4. It is clearly stated by John Austin
in the second lecture of *Lectures on Jurisprudence* (4th ed.; London, 1873), I,
116ff. (1st ed., 1832). Also it may be argued that J. S. Mill took it for granted in
Utilitarianism; on this point cf. J. O. Urmson, "The Interpretation of the Moral
Philosophy of J. S. Mill," *Philosophical Quarterly*, Vol. III (1953) [reprinted in
this volume, pp. 13–24]. In addition to the arguments given by Urmson there are
several clear statements of the distinction in *A System of Logic* (8th ed.; London,
1872), bk. VI, ch. xii pars. 2, 3, 7. The distinction is fundamental to J. D.
Mabbott's important paper, "Punishment," *Mind*, n.s., vol. XLVIII (April,
1939). More recently the distinction has been stated with particular emphasis by
S. E. Toulmin in *The Place of Reason in Ethics* (Cambridge, 1950), see esp.
ch. xi, where it plays a major part in his account of moral reasoning. Toulmin
doesn't explain the basis of the distinction, nor how one might overlook its
importance, as I try to in this paper, and in my review of his book (*Philosophical
Review*, Vol. LX [October, 1951]), as some of my criticisms show, I failed to
understand the force of it. See also H. D. Aiken, "The Levels of Moral Discourse,"

---

remains the task of explaining the tendency either to overlook it altogether, or to fail to appreciate its importance.

To show the importance of the distinction I am going to defend utilitarianism against those objections which have traditionally been made against it in connection with punishment and the obligation to keep promises. I hope to show that if one uses the distinction in question then one can state utilitarianism in a way which makes it a much better explication of our considered moral judgments than these traditional objections would seem to admit.[3] Thus the importance of the distinction is shown by the way it strengthens the utilitarian view regardless of whether that view is completely defensible or not.

To explain how the significance of the distinction may be overlooked, I am going to discuss two conceptions of rules. One of these conceptions conceals the importance of distinguishing between the justification of a rule or practice and the justification of a particular action falling under it. The other conception makes it clear why this distinction must be made and what is its logical basis.

I

The subject of punishment, in the sense of attaching legal penalties to the violation of legal rules, has always been a troubling moral question.[4] The trouble about it has not been that people disagree as to whether or not punishment is justifiable. Most people have held that, freed from certain abuses, it is an acceptable institution. Only a few have rejected punishment entirely, which is rather surprising

---

Ethics, vol. LXII (1952), A. M. Quinton, "Punishment," *Analysis,* vol. XIV (June, 1954), and P. H. Nowell-Smith, *Ethics* (London, 1954), pp. 236–239, 271–273.

3. On the concept of explication see the author's paper *Philosophical Review,* Vol. LX (April, 1951).

4. While this paper was being revised, Quinton's appeared; footnote 2 supra. There are several respects in which my remarks are similar to his. Yet as I consider some further questions and rely on somewhat different arguments, I have retained the discussion of punishment and promises together as two test cases for utilitarianism.

when one considers all that can be said against it. The difficulty is with the justification of punishment: various arguments for it have been given by moral philosophers, but so far none of them has won any sort of general acceptance; no justification is without those who detest it. I hope to show that the use of the aforementioned distinction enables one to state the utilitarian view in a way which allows for the sound points of its critics.

For our purposes we may say that there are two justifications of punishment. What we may call the retributive view is that punishment is justified on the grounds that wrongdoing merits punishment. It is morally fitting that a person who does wrong should suffer in proportion to his wrongdoing. That a criminal should be punished follows from his guilt, and the severity of the appropriate punishment depends on the depravity of his act. The state of affairs where a wrongdoer suffers punishment is morally better than the state of affairs where he does not; and it is better irrespective of any of the consequences of punishing him.

What we may call the utilitarian view holds that on the principle that bygones are bygones and that only future consequences are material to present decisions, punishment is justifiable only by reference to the probable consequences of maintaining it as one of the devices of the social order. Wrongs committed in the past are, as such, not relevant considerations for deciding what to do. If punishment can be shown to promote effectively the interest of society it is justifiable, otherwise it is not.

I have stated these two competing views very roughly to make one feel the conflict between them: one feels the force of *both* arguments and one wonders how they can be reconciled. From my introductory remarks it is obvious that the resolution which I am going to propose is that in this case one must distinguish between justifying a practice as a system of rules to be applied and enforced, and justifying a particular action which falls under these rules; utilitarian arguments are appropriate with regard to questions about practices, while retributive arguments fit the application of particular rules to particular cases.

We might try to get clear about this distinction by imagining how a father might answer the question of his son. Suppose the son asks, "Why was *J* put in jail yesterday?" The father answers, "Because he robbed the bank at *B*. He was duly tried and found guilty. That's why he was put in jail yesterday." But suppose the son had asked a different question, namely, "Why do people put other people in jail?" Then the father might answer, "To protect good people from bad people" or "To stop people from doing things that would make it uneasy for all of us; for otherwise we wouldn't be able to go to bed at night and sleep in peace." There are two very different questions here. One question emphasizes the proper name: it asks why J was punished rather than someone else, or it asks what he was punished for. The other question asks why we have the institution of punishment: why do people punish one another rather than, say, always forgiving one another?

Thus the father says in effect that a particular man is punished, rather than some other man, because he is guilty, and he is guilty because he broke the law (past tense). In his case the law looks back, the judge looks back, the jury looks back, and a penalty is visited upon him for something he did. That a man is to be punished, and what his punishment is to be, is settled by its being shown that he broke the law and that the law assigns that penalty for the violation of it.

On the other hand we have the institution of punishment itself, and recommend and accept various changes in it, because it is thought by the (ideal) legislator and by those to whom the law applies that, as a part of a system of law impartially applied from case to case arising under it, it will have the consequence, in the long run, of furthering the interests of society.

One can say, then, that the judge and the legislator stand in different positions and look in different directions: one to the past, the other to the future. The justification of what the judge does, qua judge, sounds like the retributive view; the justification of what the (ideal) legislator does, qua legislator, sounds like the utilitarian view. Thus both views have a point (this is as it should be since intelligent and sensitive persons have been on both sides of the argument); and one's initial confusion disappears once one sees that these views apply to persons holding different offices with different duties, and situated differently with respect to the system of rules that make up the criminal law.[5]

5. Note the fact that different sorts of arguments are suited to different offices. One way of taking the differences between ethical theories is to regard them as accounts of the reasons expected in different offices.

One might say, however, that the utilitarian view is more fundamental since it applies to a more fundamental office, for the judge
carries out the legislator's will so far as he can determine it. Once the
legislator decides to have laws and to assign penalties for their violation (as things are there must be both the law and the penalty) an
institution is set up which involves a retributive conception of particular cases. It is part of the concept of the criminal law as a system of
rules that the application and enforcement of these rules in particular
cases should be justifiable by arguments of a retributive character. The
decision whether or not to use law rather than some other mechanism
of social control, and the decision as to what laws to have and what
penalties to assign, may be settled by utilitarian arguments, but if one
decides to have laws then one has decided on something whose working in particular cases is retributive in form.[6]

The answer, then, to the confusion engendered by the two views
of punishment is quite simple: one distinguishes two offices, that of the
judge and that of the legislator, and one distinguishes their different
stations with respect to the system of rules which make up the law;
and then one notes that the different sorts of considerations which
would usually be offered as reasons for what is done under the cover
of these offices can be paired off with the competing justifications of
punishment. One reconciles the two views by the time-honored
device of making them apply to different situations.

But can it really be this simple? Well, this answer allows for the
apparent intent of each side. Does a person who advocates the retributive view necessarily advocate, as an *institution*, legal machinery
whose essential purpose is to set up and preserve a correspondence
between moral turpitude and suffering? Surely not.[7] What retributionists have rightly insisted upon is that no man can be punished
unless he is guilty, that is, unless he has broken the law. Their fundamental criticism of the utilitarian account is that, as they interpret it,
it sanctions an innocent person's being punished (if one may call it
that) for the benefit of society.

On the other hand, utilitarians agree that punishment is to be

6. In this connection see Mabbott, *op. cit.*, pp. 163–164.
7. On this point see Sir David Ross, *The Right and the Good* (Oxford, 1930),
pp. 57–60.

inflicted only for the violation of law. They regard this much as understood from the concept of punishment itself.[8] The point of the utilitarian account concerns the institution as a system of rules: utilitarianism seeks to limit its use by declaring it justifiable only if it can be shown to foster effectively the good of society. Historically it is a protest against the indiscriminate and ineffective use of the criminal law.[9] It seeks to dissuade us from assigning to penal institutions the improper, if not sacrilegious, task of matching suffering with moral turpitude. Like others, utilitarians want penal institutions designed so that, as far as humanly possible, only those who break the law run afoul of it. They hold that no official should have discretionary power to inflict penalties whenever he thinks it for the benefit of society; for on utilitarian grounds an institution granting such power could not be justified.[10]

The suggested way of reconciling the retributive and the utilitarian

8. See Hobbes's definition of punishment in *Leviathan*, ch. xxviii; and Bentham's definition in *The Principle of Morals and Legislation*, ch. xii, par. 36, ch. xv, par. 28, and in *The Rationale of Punishment*, (London, 1830), bk. I, ch. i. They could agree with Bradley that: "Punishment is punishment only when it is deserved. We pay the penalty, because we owe it, and for no other reason; and if punishment is inflicted for any other reason whatever than because it is [8] merited by wrong, it is a gross immorality, a crying injustice, an abominable crime, and not what it pretends to be." *Ethical Studies* (2nd ed.; Oxford, 1927), 26–27. Certainly by definition it isn't what it pretends to be. The innocent can only be punished by mistake; deliberate "punishment" of the innocent necessarily involves fraud.

9. Cf. Leon Radzinowicz, A *History of English Criminal Law: The Movement for Reform 1750–1833* (London, 1948), esp. ch. xi on Bentham.

10. Bentham discusses how corresponding to a punitory provision of a criminal law there is another provision which stands to it as an antagonist and which needs a name as much as the punitory. He calls it, as one might expect, the *anaetiosostic*, and of it he says: 'The punishment of guilt is the object of the former one: the preservation of innocence that of the latter." In the same connection he asserts that it is never thought fit to give the judge the option of deciding whether a thief (that is, a person whom he believes to be a thief, for the judge's belief is what the question must always turn upon) should hang or not, and so the law writes the provision: "The judge shall not cause a thief to be hanged unless he have been duly convicted and sentenced in course of law" (*The Limits of Jurisprudence Defined*, ed. C. W. Everett [New York, 1945], pp. 238–239).

justifications of punishment seems to account for what both sides have wanted to say. There are, however, two further questions which arise, and I shall devote the remainder of this section to them.

First, will not a difference of opinion as to the proper criterion of just law make the proposed reconciliation unacceptable to retributionists? Will they not question whether, if the utilitarian principle is used as the criterion, it follows that those who have broken the law are guilty in a way which satisfies their demand that those punished deserve to be punished? To answer this difficulty, suppose that the rules of the criminal law are justified on utilitarian grounds (it is only for laws that meet his criterion that the utilitarian can be held responsible). Then it follows that the actions which the criminal law specifies as offenses are such that, if they were tolerated, terror and alarm would spread in society. Consequently, retributionists can only deny that those who are punished deserve to be punished if they deny that such actions are wrong. This they will not want to do.

The second question is whether utilitarianism doesn't justify too much. One pictures it as an engine of justification which, if consistently adopted, could be used to justify cruel and arbitrary institutions. Retributionists may be supposed to concede that utilitarians *intend* to reform the law and to make it more humane; that utilitarians do not *wish* to justify any such thing as punishment of the innocent; and that utilitarians may appeal to the fact that punishment presupposes guilt in the sense that by punishment one understands an institution attaching penalties to the infraction of legal rules, and therefore that it is logically absurd to suppose that utilitarians in justifying *punishment* might also have justified punishment (if we may call it that) of the innocent. The real question, however, is whether the utilitarian, in justifying punishment, hasn't used arguments which commit him to accepting the infliction of suffering on innocent persons if it is for the good of society (whether or not one calls this punishment). More generally, isn't the utilitarian committed in principle to accepting many practices which he, as a morally sensitive person, wouldn't want to accept? Retributionists are inclined to hold that there is no way to stop the utilitarian principle from justifying too much except by adding to it a principle which distributes certain rights to individuals. Then the amended criterion is not the greatest benefit of society *simpliciter*, but the greatest benefit of society subject to the constraint that no one's rights may be violated. Now while I think that the classical utilitarians proposed a criterion of this more complicated sort, I do not want to argue that point here.[11] What I want to show is that there is *another* way of preventing the utilitarian principle from justifying too much, or at least of making it much less likely to do so: namely, by stating utilitarianism in a way which accounts for the distinction between the justification of an institution and the justification of a particular action falling under it.

I begin by defining the institution of punishment as follows: a person is said to suffer punishment whenever he is legally deprived of some of the normal rights of a citizen on the ground that he has violated a rule of law, the violation having been established by trial according to the due process of law, provided that the deprivation is carried out by the recognized legal authorities of the state, that the rule of law clearly specifies both the offense and the attached penalty, that the courts construe statutes strictly, and that the statute was on the books prior to the time of the offense.[12] This definition specifies what I shall understand by punishment. The question is whether utilitarian arguments may be found to justify institutions widely different from this and such as one would find cruel and arbitrary.

This question is best answered, I think, by taking up a particular accusation. Consider the following from Carritt:

. . . *the utilitarian must hold that we are justified in inflicting pain always and only to prevent worse pain or bring about greater happiness. This, then, is all we need to consider in so-called punishment, which must be purely preventive. But if some kind of very cruel crime becomes common, and none of the criminals can be caught, it might be highly expedient, as an example, to hang an innocent man, if a charge against him could be so framed that he were universally thought guilty; indeed this would only fail to be an ideal instance of utilitarian 'punishment' because the victim himself would not have been so likely as a real felon to commit such a crime in the future; in*

11. By the classical utilitarians I understand Hobbes, Hume, Bentham, J. S. Mill, and Sidgwick.

12. All these features of punishment are mentioned by Hobbes; cf. *Leviathan*, ch. xxviii.

all other respects it would be perfectly deterrent and therefore felicific.[13]

Carritt is trying to show that there are occasions when a utilitarian argument would justify taking an action which would be generally condemned; and thus that utilitarianism justifies too much. But the failure of Carritt's argument lies in the fact that he makes no distinction between the justification of the general system of rules which constitutes penal institutions and the justification of particular applications of these rules to particular cases by the various officials whose job it is to administer them. This becomes perfectly clear when one asks who the "we" are of whom Carritt speaks. Who is this who has a sort of absolute authority on particular occasions to decide that an innocent man shall be "punished" if everyone can be convinced that he is guilty? Is this person the legislator, or the judge, or the body of private citizens, or what? It is utterly crucial to know who is to decide such matters, and by what authority, for all of this must be written into the rules of the institution. Until one knows these things one doesn't know what the institution is whose justification is being challenged; and as the utilitarian principle applies to the institution one doesn't know whether it is justifiable on utilitarian grounds or not.

Once this is understood it is clear what the countermove to Carritt's argument is. One must describe more carefully what the *institution* is which his example suggests, and then ask oneself whether or not it is likely that having this institution would be for the benefit of society in the long run. One must not content oneself with the vague thought that, when it's a question of *this* case, it would be a good thing if *somebody* did something even if an innocent person were to suffer.

Try to imagine, then, an institution (which we may call "telishment") which is such that the officials set up by it have authority to arrange a trial for the condemnation of an innocent man whenever they are of the opinion that doing so would be in the best interests of society. The discretion of officials is limited, however, by the rule that they may not condemn an innocent man to undergo such an ordeal unless there is, at the time, a wave of offenses similar to that

13. *Ethical and Political Thinking* (Oxford, 1947), p. 65.

with which they charge him and telish him for. We may imagine that the officials having the discretionary authority are the judges of the higher courts in consultation with the chief of police, the minister of justice, and a committee of the legislature.

Once one realizes that one is involved in setting up an *institution*, one sees that the hazards are very great. For example, what check is there on the officials? How is one to tell whether or not their actions are authorized? How is one to limit the risks involved in allowing such systematic deception? How is one to avoid giving anything short of complete discretion to the authorities to telish anyone they like? In addition to these considerations, it is obvious that people will come to have a very different attitude towards their penal system when telishment is adjoined to it. They will be uncertain as to whether a convicted man has been punished or telished. They will wonder whether or not they should feel sorry for him. They will wonder whether the same fate won't at any time fall on them. If one pictures how such an institution would actually work, and the enormous risks involved in it, it seems clear that it would serve no useful purpose. A utilitarian justification for this institution is most unlikely.

It happens in general that as one drops off the defining features of punishment one ends up with an institution whose utilitarian justification is highly doubtful. One reason for this is that punishment works like a kind of price system: by altering the prices one has to pay for the performance of actions it supplies a motive for avoiding some actions and doing others. The defining features are essential if punishment is to work in this way; so that an institution which lacks these features, e.g., an institution which is set up to "punish" the innocent, is likely to have about as much point as a price system (if one may call it that) where the prices of things change at random from day to day and one learns the price of something after one has agreed to buy it.[14]

14. The analogy with the price system suggests an answer to the question how utilitarian considerations insure that punishment is proportional to the offense. It is interesting to note that Sir David Ross, after making the distinction between justifying a penal law and justifying a particular application of it, and after stating that utilitarian considerations have a large place in determining the former, still holds back from accepting the utilitarian justification of punishment on the grounds that justice requires that punishment be proportional to the offense, and

If one is careful to apply the utilitarian principle to the institution which is to authorize particular actions, then there is *less* danger of its justifying too much. Carritt's example gains plausibility by its indefiniteness and by its concentration on the particular case. His argument will only hold if it can be shown that there are utilitarian arguments which justify an institution whose publicly ascertainable offices and powers are such as to permit officials to exercise that kind of discretion in particular cases. But the requirement of having to build the arbitrary features of the particular decision into the institutional practice makes the justification much less likely to go through.

---

that utilitarianism is unable to account for this. Cf. *The Right and the Good* (Oxford: Clarendon Press, 1930), pp. 61–62. I do not claim that utilitarianism can account for this requirement as Sir David might wish, but it happens, nevertheless, that if utilitarian considerations are followed penalties will be proportional to offenses in this sense: the order of offenses according to seriousness can be paired off with the order of penalties according to severity. Also the absolute level of penalties will be as low as possible. This follows from the assumption that people are rational (i.e., that they are able to take into account the "prices" the state puts on actions), the utilitarian rule that a penal system should provide a motive for preferring the less serious offense, and the principle that punishment as such is an evil. All this was carefully worked out by Bentham in *The Principles of Morals and Legislation*, chs. xiii–xv.

Richard Brandt

Rule Utilitarianism
(continued) *

The essence of the rule-utilitarian theory, we recall, is that our actions, whether legislative or otherwise, should be guided by a set of prescriptions, the conscientious following of which by all would have maximum net expectable utility. As a result, the utilitarian is not, just as such, committed to any particular view about how anti-social behavior should be treated by society—or even to the view that society should do anything at all about immoral conduct. It is only the utilitarian principle *combined* with statements about the kind of laws and practices which will maximize expectable utility that has such consequences. Therefore, utilitarians are free to differ from one another about the character of an ideal system of criminal justice; some utilitarians think that the system prevalent in Great Britain and the United States essentially corresponds to the ideal, but others think that the only system that can be justified is markedly different from the actual systems in these Western countries. We shall concentrate our discussion, however, on the traditional line of utilitarian thought which holds that roughly the actual system of criminal law, say in the United States, is morally justifiable, and we shall follow roughly the classic exposition of the reasoning given by Jeremy Bentham—but modifying this freely when we feel amendment is called for. At the end of the chapter we shall look briefly at a different view.

Traditional utilitarian thinking about criminal justice has found the rationale of the practice, in the United States, for example, in three main facts. (Those who disagree think the first two of these "facts" happen not to be the case.) (1) People who are tempted to misbehave, to trample on the rights of others, to sacrifice public welfare for personal gain, can usually be deterred from misconduct by

* Richard B. Brandt, *Ethical Theory: The Problems of Normative and Critical Ethics* (Englewood Cliffs, New Jersey: Prentice-Hall, Inc., 1959), pp. 490–95.

fear of punishment, such as death, imprisonment, or fine. (2) Imprisonment or fine will teach malefactors a lesson; their characters may be improved, and at any rate a personal experience of punishment will make them less likely to misbehave again. (3) Imprisonment will certainly have the result of physically preventing past malefactors from misbehaving, during the period of their incarceration.

In view of these suppositions, traditional utilitarian thinking has concluded that having laws forbidding certain kinds of behavior on pain of punishment, and having machinery for the fair enforcement of these laws, is justified by the fact that it maximizes expectable utility. Misconduct is not to be punished just for its own sake; malefactors must be punished for their past acts, according to law, as a way of maximizing expectable utility.

The utilitarian principle, of course, has implications for decisions about the severity of punishment to be administered. Punishment is itself an evil, and hence should be avoided where this is consistent with the public good. Punishment should have precisely such a degree of severity (not more or less) that the probable disutility of greater severity just balances the probable gain in utility (less crime because of the more serious threat). The cost, in other words, should be counted along with the value of what is bought; and we should buy protection up to the point where the cost is greater than the protection is worth. How severe will such punishment be? Jeremy Bentham had many sensible things to say about this. Punishment, he said, must be severe enough so that it is to no one's advantage to commit an offense even if he receives the punishment; a fine of $10 for bank robbery would give no security at all. Further, since many criminals will be undetected, we must make the penalty heavy enough in comparison with the prospective gain from crime, that a prospective criminal will consider the risk hardly worth it, even considering that it is not certain he will be punished at all. Again, the more serious offenses should carry the heavier penalties, not only because the greater disutility justifies the use of heavier penalties in order to prevent them, but also because criminals should be motivated to commit a less serious rather than a more serious offense. Bentham thought the prescribed penalties should allow for some variation at the discretion of the judge, so that the actual suffering caused should roughly be the same in all cases; thus, a heavier fine will be imposed on a rich man than on a poor man.

Bentham also argued that the goal of maximum utility requires that certain facts should excuse from culpability, for the reason that punishment in such cases "must be inefficacious." He listed as such (1) the fact that the relevant law was passed only after the act of the accused, (2) that the law had not been made public, (3) that the criminal was an infant, insane, or was intoxicated, (4) that the crime was done under physical compulsion, (5) that the agent was ignorant of the probable consequences of his act or was acting on the basis of an innocent misapprehension of the facts, such that the act the agent thought he was performing was a lawful one, and (6) that the motivation to commit the offense was so strong that no threat of law could prevent the crime. Bentham also thought that punishment should be remitted if the crime was a collective one and the number of the guilty so large that great suffering would be caused by its imposition, or if the offender held an important post and his services were important for the public, or if the public or foreign powers would be offended by the punishment; but we shall ignore this part of his view.

Bentham's account of the logic of legal "defenses" needs amendment. What he should have argued is that *not* punishing in certain types of cases (cases where such defenses as those just indicated can be offered) reduces the amount of suffering imposed by law and the insecurity of everybody, and that failure to impose punishment in these types of case will cause only a negligible increase in the incidence of crime.

How satisfactory is this theory of criminal justice? Does it have any implications that are far from being acceptable when compared with concrete justified convictions about what practices are morally right? [1]

Many criminologists, as we shall see at the end of this chapter, would argue that Bentham was mistaken in his facts: The deter-

1. Act-utilitarians face some special problems. For instance, if I am an act-utilitarian and serve on a jury, I shall work to get a verdict that will do the most good, irrespective of the charges of the judge, and of any oath I may have taken to give a reasonable answer to certain questions on the basis of the evidence presented—unless I think my doing so will have indirect effects on the institution of the jury, public confidence in it, and so on. This is certainly not what we think a juror should do. Of course, neither a juror nor a judge can escape his prima facie obligation to do what good he can; this obligation is present in some form in every theory. The act-utilitarian, however, makes this the whole of one's responsibility.

rence value of threat of punishment, they say, is much less than he imagined, and criminals are seldom reformed by spending time in prison. If these contentions are correct, then the ideal rules for society's treatment of malefactors are very different from what Bentham thought, and from what actual practice is today in the United States. To say all this, however, is not to show that the utilitarian *principle* is incorrect, for in view of these facts presumably the attitudes of a "qualified" person would not be favorable to criminal justice as practiced today. Utilitarian theory might still be correct, but its implications would be different from what Bentham thought—and they might coincide with justified ethical judgments. We shall return to this.

The whole utilitarian approach, however, has been criticized on the ground that it ought not in consistency to approve of *any* excuses from criminal liability.[2] Or at least, it should do so only after careful empirical inquiries. It is not obvious, it is argued, that we increase net expectable utility by permitting such defenses. At the least, the utilitarian is committed to defend the concept of "strict liability." Why? Because we could get a more strongly deterrent effect if everyone knew that *all behavior* of a certain sort would be punished, irrespective of mistaken supposals of fact, compulsion, and so on. The critics admit that knowledge that all behavior of a certain sort will be punished will hardly deter from crime the insane, persons acting under compulsion, persons acting under erroneous beliefs about facts, and others, but, as Professor Hart points out, it does not follow from this that general knowledge that certain acts will always be punished will not be salutary.

The utilitarian, however, has a solid defense against charges of this sort. We must bear in mind (as the critics do not) that the utilitarian principle, *taken by itself, implies nothing whatever* about whether a system of law should excuse persons on the basis of certain defenses. What the utilitarian does say is that, when we *combine* the principle of utilitarianism with *true* propositions about a certain thing

2. See H. L. A. Hart, "Legal Responsibility and Excuses," in Sidney Hook (ed.), *Determinism and Freedom* (New York: New York University Press, 1958), pp. 81–104; and David Braybrooke, "Professor Stevenson, Voltaire, and the Case of Admiral Byng," *Journal of Philosophy*, LIII (1956), 787–96.

or situation, then we shall come out with true statements about obligations. The utilitarian is certainly not committed to saying that one will derive true propositions about obligations if one starts with *false* propositions about fact or about what will maximize welfare, or with *no* such propositions at all. Therefore the criticism sometimes made (for example, by Hart), that utilitarian theory does not render it "obviously" or "necessarily" the case that the recognized excuses from criminal liability should be accepted as excusing from punishment, is beside the point. Moreover, in fact the utilitarian can properly claim that we do have excellent reason for believing that the general public would be no better motivated to avoid criminal offenses than it now is, if the insane and others were also punished along with intentional wrongdoers. Indeed, he may reasonably claim that the example of punishment of these individuals could only have a hardening effect—like public executions. Furthermore, the utilitarian can point out that abolition of the standard exculpating excuses would lead to serious insecurity. Imagine the pleasure of driving an automobile if one knew one could be executed for running down a child whom it was absolutely impossible to avoid striking! One certainly does not maximize expectable utility by eliminating the traditional excuses. In general, then, the utilitarian theory is not threatened by its implications about exculpating excuses.

It might also be objected against utilitarianism that it cannot recognize the validity of *mitigating* excuses (which presumably have the support of "qualified" attitudes). Would not consequences be better if the distinction between premeditated and impulsive acts were abolished? The utilitarian can reply that people who commit impulsive crimes, in the heat of anger, do not give thought to legal penalties; they would not be deterred by a stricter law. Moreover, such a person is unlikely to repeat his crime, so that a mild sentence saves an essentially good man for society.[3] Something can also be said in support of the practice of judges in giving a milder sentence when a person's temptation is severe: at least the *extended* rule-utilitarian

3. The utilitarian must admit that the same thing is true for many deliberate murders, and probably he should also admit that some people who commit a crime in the heat of anger would have found time to think had they known a grave penalty awaited them.

can say, in defense of the practice of punishing less severely the crime of a man who has had few opportunities in life, that a judge ought to do what he can to repair inequalities in life, and that a mild sentence to a man who has had few opportunities is one way of doing this. There are, then, utilitarian supports for recognizing the mitigating excuses.

Sometimes it is objected to utilitarianism that it must view imprisonment for crime as morally no different from quarantine. This, it is said, shows that the utilitarian theory must be mistaken, since actually there is a vast moral difference between being quarantined and being imprisoned for crime. Why is it supposed utilitarian theory must view imprisonment as a kind of quarantine? The answer is that utilitarianism looks to the future; the treatment it prescribes for individuals is treatment with an eye to maximizing net expectable utility. The leper is quarantined because otherwise he will expose others to disease. The criminal is imprisoned because otherwise he, or others who are not deterred by the threat of punishment, will expose the public to crime. Both the convicted criminal and the leper are making contributions to the public good. So, quarantine and imprisonment are essentially personal sacrifices for the public welfare, if we think of punishment as the utilitarian does. But in fact, the argument goes on, we feel there is a vast difference. The public is obligated to do what is possible to make the leper comfortable, to make his necessary sacrifice as easy for him and his family as possible. But we feel no obligation to make imprisonment as comfortable as possible.

Again the utilitarian has a reply. He can say that people cannot help contracting leprosy, but they can avoid committing crimes—and the very discomforts and harshness of prison life are deterring factors. If prison life were made attractive, there might be more criminals—not to mention the indolent who would commit a crime in order to enjoy the benefits of public support. Furthermore, the utilitarian can say, why should we feel that we "ought to make it up to" a quarantined leper? At least partly because it is useful to encourage willingness to make such sacrifices. But we do not at all wish to encourage the criminal to make his "sacrifice"; rather, we wish him not to commit his crimes. There is all the difference between the kind of treatment justified on utilitarian grounds for a person who may have to make a sacrifice for the public welfare through no fault of his own, and for a person who is required to make a sacrifice because he has selfishly and deliberately trampled on the rights of others, in clear view of the fact that if he is apprehended society must make an example of him. There are all sorts of utilitarian reasons for being kindly to persons of the former type, and stern with people of the latter type.

Another popular objection to the utilitarian theory is that the utilitarian must approve of prosecutors or judges occasionally withholding evidence known to them, for the sake of convicting an innocent man, if the public welfare really is served by so doing. Critics of the theory would not deny that there *can* be circumstances where the dangers are so severe that such action is called for; they only say that utilitarianism calls for it all too frequently. Is this criticism justified? Clearly, the utilitarian is not committed to advocating that a provision should be written into the *law* so as to permit punishment of persons for crimes they did not commit if to do so would serve the public good. Any such provision would be a shattering blow to public confidence and security. The question is only whether there should be an informal moral rule to the same effect, for the guidance of judges and prosecutors. Will the rule-utilitarian necessarily be committed to far too sweeping a moral rule on this point? We must recall that he is not in the position of the act-utilitarian, who must say that an innocent man must be punished if in *his particular case* the public welfare would be served by his punishment. The rule-utilitarian rather asserts only that an innocent man should be punished if he falls within a class of cases such that net expectable utility is maximized if *all* members of the class are punished, taking into account the possible disastrous effects on public confidence if it is generally known that judges and prosecutors are guided by such a rule. Moreover, the "extended" rule-utilitarian has a further reason for not punishing an innocent man unless he has had more than his equal share of the good things of life already; namely, that there is an obligation to promote equality of welfare, whereas severe punishment is heaping "illfare" on one individual person. When we take these considerations into account, it is *not* obvious that the rule-utilitarian (or the "extended" rule-utilitarian) is committed to action that we are justifiably convinced is immoral.[4]

4. In any case, a tenable theory of punishment must approve of punishing persons who are *morally* blameless. Suppose someone commits treason for moral reasons. We may have to say that his deed is not reprehensible at all, and might even

In recent years, some philosophers have sought to rescue the utilitarian from his supposed difficulty of being committed to advocate the punishment of innocent men, by a verbal point. Their argument is that it is *logically* guaranteed that only a guilty man be *punished.* "Punishment," it is said, like "reward" and "forgive," has a backward reference; we properly speak of "punishing *for* . . .," and if we inflict suffering on someone for the sake of utility and irrespective of guilt for some offense, it is a misuse of the word "punishment" to speak of such a person as being punished.[5] It is not clear, however, that anything is accomplished by this verbal move. If these writers are correct, then it is self-contradictory to say "innocent men may be punished for the sake of the public good," and no one can say that utilitarian theory commits one to uttering such a self-contradiction. But it may still be that utilitarian theory commits one to advocating that prosecutors suppress evidence on certain occasions, that judges aid in conducting unfair trials and pronounce sentences out of line with custom for a particular type of case in times of public danger, and, in short, that innocent men be *locked up* or *executed*—only not "*punished*"—for the sake of the public welfare. So, if there is a difficulty here at all for the utilitarian theory, the verbal maneuver of these philosophers seems not to remove it.

Everything considered, the utilitarian theory seems to be in much less dire distress, in respect of its implications for criminal justice, than has sometimes been supposed. It does not seem possible to show that in any important way its implications are clearly in conflict with our valid convictions about what is right. The worst that can be said is that utilitarian theory does not in a clear-cut way definitely require us to espouse some practices we are inclined to espouse. But to this the utilitarian may make two replies. First, that there is reason to think our ordinary convictions about punishment for crime ought to be thoroughly re-examined in important respects. We shall briefly

---

(considering the risk he took for his principles) be morally admirable. Yet we think such persons must be punished no matter what their motives; people cannot be permittted to take the law into their own hands.

5. For some discussion of the grammar of "punish," see A. M. Quinton, "On Punishment," *Analysis*, XIV (1954), 133–42; and K. Baier, "Is Punishment Retributive?" *Analysis*, XVI (1955), 25–32.

examine later some proposals currently receiving the strong support of criminologists. Second, the utilitarian may reply that if we consider our convictions about the punishments we should administer as a *parent*—and this is the point where our moral opinions are least likely to be affected by the sheer weight of tradition—we shall find that we think according to the principles of rule-utilitarianism. Parents do regard their punishment of their children as justified only in view of the future good of the child, and in order to make life in the home tolerable and in order to distribute jobs and sacrifices equally.

Immanuel Kant

Justice and Punishment *

What we call good must be, in the judgment of every reasonable man, an object of the faculty of desire, and the evil must be, in everyone's eyes, an object of aversion. Thus, in addition to sense, this judgment requires reason. So it is with truthfulness as opposed to a lie, with L. W. Beck (New York: Liberal Arts Press, 1956), part 1, bk. 1, from ch. 2. justice in contrast to violence, etc. But we can call something an ill, however, which everyone at the same time must acknowledge as good, either directly or indirectly.

Whoever submits to a surgical operation feels it without doubt as an ill, but by reason he and everyone else will describe it as good. When, however, someone who delights in annoying and vexing peace-loving folk receives at last a right good beating, it is certainly an ill, but everyone approves of it and considers it as good in itself even if nothing further results from it; nay, even he who gets the beating must acknowledge, in his reason, that justice has been done to him, because he sees the proportion between welfare and well-doing, which reason inevitably holds before him, here put into practice.

* Immanuel Kant, *Critique of Practical Reason*, trans. and ed. with an intro.

Immanuel Kant

Justice and Punishment
(continued) *

E. The Right of Punishing and of Pardoning

I. THE RIGHT OF PUNISHING

The right of administering punishment, is the right of the sovereign as the supreme power to inflict pain upon a subject on account of a crime committed by him. The head of the state cannot therefore be punished; but his supremacy may be withdrawn from him. Any transgression of the public law which makes him who commits it incapable of being a citizen, constitutes a *crime*, either simply as a private crime (*crimen*), or also as a *public* crime (*crimen publicum*). Private crimes are dealt with by a civil court; public crimes by a criminal court.—Embezzlement or peculation of money or goods entrusted in trade, fraud in purchase or sale, if done before the eyes of the party who suffers, are private crimes. On the other hand, coining false money or forging bills of exchange, theft, robbery, etc., are public crimes, because the commonwealth, and not merely some particular individual, is endangered thereby. Such crimes may be divided into those of a *base* character (*indolis abjectae*) and those of a *violent* character (*indolis violentiae*).

Judicial or juridical punishment (*poena forensis*) is to be distinguished from natural punishment (*poena naturalis*), in which crime as vice punishes itself, and does not as such come within the cognizance of the legislator. Juridical punishment can never be administered merely as a means for promoting another good, either with regard to the criminal himself or to civil society, but must in all cases be im-

* Immanuel Kant, *The Philosophy of Law*, Part II, translated by W. Hastie, (Edinburgh: T. T. Clark, 1887), pp. 194–8.

posed only because the individual on whom it is inflicted *has committed a crime*. For one man ought never to be dealt with merely as a means subservient to the purpose of another, nor be mixed up with the subjects of real right. Against such treatment his inborn personality has a right to protect him, even although he may be condemned to lose his civil personality. He must first be found guilty and *punishable*, before there can be any thought of drawing from his punishment any benefit for himself or his fellow-citizens. The penal law is a categorical imperative; and woe to him who creeps through the serpent-windings of utilitarianism to discover some advantage that may discharge him from the justice of punishment, or even from the due measure of it, according to the pharisaic maxim: 'It is better that *one* man should die than that the whole people should perish.' For if justice and righteousness perish, human life would no longer have any value in the world.—What, then, is to be said of such a proposal as to keep a criminal alive who has been condemned to death, on his being given to understand that if he agreed to certain dangerous experiments being performed upon him, he would be allowed to survive if he came happily through them? It is argued that physicians might thus obtain new information that would be of value to the commonweal. But a court of justice would repudiate with scorn any proposal of this kind if made to it by the medical faculty; for justice would cease to be justice, if it were bartered away for any consideration whatever.

But what is the mode and measure of punishment which public justice takes as its principle and standard? It is just the principle of equality, by which the pointer of the scale of justice is made to incline no more to the one side than the other. It may be rendered by saying that the undeserved evil which any one commits on another, is to be regarded as perpetrated on himself. Hence it may be said: 'If you slander another, you slander yourself; if you steal from another, you steal from yourself; if you strike another, you strike yourself; if you kill another, you kill yourself.' This is the right of retaliation (*jus talionis*); and properly understood, it is the only principle which in regulating a public court, as distinguished from mere private judgment, can definitely assign both the quality and the quantity of a just penalty. All other standards are wavering and uncertain; and on account of other considerations involved in them, they contain no principle conformable to the sentence of pure and strict justice. It may appear, however, that difference of social status would not admit the application of the principle of retaliation, which is that of 'like with like.' But although the application may not in all cases be possible according to the letter, yet as regards the effect it may always be attained in practice, by due regard being given to the disposition and sentiment of the parties in the higher social sphere. Thus a pecuniary penalty on account of a verbal injury, may have no direct proportion to the injustice of slander; for one who is wealthy may be able to indulge himself in this offence for his own gratification. Yet the attack committed on the honour of the party aggrieved may have its equivalent in the pain inflicted upon the pride of the aggressor, especially if he is condemned by the judgment of the court, not only to retract and apologize, but to submit to some meaner ordeal, as kissing the hand of the injured person. In like manner, if a man of the highest rank has violently assaulted an innocent citizen of the lower orders, he may be condemned not only to apologize but to undergo a solitary and painful imprisonment, whereby, in addition to the discomfort endured, the vanity of the offender would be painfully affected, and the very shame of his position would constitute an adequate retaliation after the principle of 'like with like.' But how then would we render the statement: 'If you *steal* from another, you steal from yourself'? In this way, that whoever steals anything makes the property of all insecure; he therefore robs himself of all security in property, according to the right of retaliation. Such a one has nothing, and can acquire nothing, but he has the will to live; and this is only possible by others supporting him. But as the state should not do this gratuitously, he must for this purpose yield his powers to the state to be used in penal labour; and thus he falls for a time, or it may be for life, into a condition of slavery.—But whoever has committed murder, must *die*. There is, in this case, no juridical substitute or surrogate, that can be given or taken for the satisfaction of justice. There is no *likeness* or proportion between life, however painful, and death; and therefore there is no equality between the crime of murder and the retaliation of it but what is judicially accomplished by the execution of the criminal. His death, however, must be kept free from all maltreatment that would make the humanity suffering in his person loathsome or abominable. Even if a civil society resolved to dissolve itself with the consent of all its members—as might be supposed in the case of a people inhabiting an island resolving to separate and scatter themselves throughout the whole world—the last murderer lying in the prison ought to be executed before the resolution was carried out. This ought to be done in order that every one may realize the desert of his deeds, and that bloodguiltiness may not remain upon the people; for otherwise they might all be regarded as participators in the murder as a public violation of justice.

The equalization of punishment with crime, is therefore only possible by the cognition of the judge extending even to the penalty of death, according to the right of retaliation . . .

G. W. F. Hegel

Punishment as
a Right *

The injury [the penalty] which falls on the criminal is not merely
implicitly just—as just, it is *eo ipso* his implicit will, an embodiment
of his freedom, his right; on the contrary, it is also a right *established*
within the criminal himself, i.e., in his objectively embodied will, in
his action. The reason for this is that his action is the action of a rational being and this implies that it is something universal and that
by doing it the criminal has laid down a law which he has explicitly
recognized in his action and under which in consequence he should
be brought as under his right.

As is well known, Beccaria denied to the state the right of inflicting capital punishment. His reason was that it could not be presumed
that the readiness of individuals to allow themselves to be executed
was included in the social contract, and that in fact the contrary
would have to be assumed. But the state is not a contract at all nor is
its fundamental essence the unconditional protection and guarantee
of the life and property of members of the public as individuals. On
the contrary, it is that higher entity which even lays claim to this very
life and property and demands its sacrifice. Further, what is involved
in the action of the criminal is not only the concept of crime, the
rational aspect present in crime as such whether the individual wills
it or not, the aspect which the state has to vindicate, but also the
abstract rationality of the individual's *volition*. Since that is so, punishment is regarded as containing the criminal's right and hence by
being punished he is honoured as a rational being. He does not receive this due of honour unless the concept and measure of his punishment are derived from his own act. Still less does he receive it if he is

* G. W. F. Hegel, *The Philosophy of Right*, trans. T. M. Knox (London:
Oxford University Press, 1969), sec. 100.

treated either as a harmful animal who has to be made harmless, or with a view to deterring and reforming him.

Moreover, apart from these considerations, the form in which the righting of wrong exists in the state, namely punishment, is not its only form, nor is the state a precondition of the principle of righting wrong. [A.]

F. H. Bradley

The Vulgar Notion
of Responsibility *

If there is any opinion to which the man of uncultivated morals is attached, it is the belief in the necessary connexion of punishment and guilt. Punishment is punishment, only where it is deserved. We pay the penalty, because we owe it, and for no other reason; and if punishment is inflicted for any other reason whatever than because it is merited by wrong, it is a gross immorality, a crying injustice, an abominable crime, and not what it pretends to be. We may have regard for whatever considerations we please—our own convenience, the good of society, the benefit of the offender; we are fools, and worse, if we fail to do so. Having once the right to punish, we may modify the punishment according to the useful and the pleasant; but these are external to the matter, they can not give us a right to punish, and nothing can do that but criminal desert. This is not a subject to waste words over: if the fact of the vulgar view is not palpable to the reader, we have no hope, and no wish, to make it so.

I am not to be punished, on the ordinary view, unless I deserve it. Why then (let us repeat) on this view do I merit punishment? It is because I have been guilty. I have done 'wrong.' I have taken into my will, made a part of myself, have realized my being in something which is the negation of 'right,' the assertion of not-right. Wrong can be imputed to me. I *am* the realization and the standing assertion of wrong. Now the plain man may not know what he means by 'wrong,' but he is sure that, whatever it is, it 'ought' not to exist, that it calls and cries for obliteration; that, if he can remove it, it is his business to do so; that, if he does not remove it, it rests also upon him, and that the destruction of guilt, whatever be the consequences, and even

* F. H. Bradley, *Ethical Studies*, 2d ed. (London: Oxford University Press, 1927), pp. 26–29.

if there be no consequences at all, is still a good in itself; and this, not because a mere negation is a good, but because the denial of wrong is the assertion of right (whatever 'right' means); and the assertion of right is an end in itself.

Punishment is the denial of wrong by the assertion of right, and the wrong exists in the self, or will, of the criminal; his self is a wrongful self, and is realized in his person and possessions; he has asserted in them his wrongful will, the incarnate denial of right; and in denying that assertion, and annihilating, whether wholly or partially, that incarnation by fine, or imprisonment, or even by death, we annihilate the wrong and manifest the right; and since this, as we saw, was an end in itself, so punishment is also an end in itself.

Yes, in despite of sophistry, and in the face of sentimentalism, with well-nigh the whole body of our self-styled enlightenment against them, our people believe to this day that *punishment is inflicted for the sake of punishment*; though they know no more than our philosophers themselves do, that there stand on the side of the unthinking people the two best-known names of modern philosophy.

But, even were we able, it is not our task here to expound to the reader, what this, or again what the other metaphysician understands by punishment. The above is no more than the theoretical expression of the popular view, viz. that punishment is justice; that justice implies the giving what is due; that suppression of its existence, in one form or other, is due to guilt, and so to the guilty person; and that, against his will, to give or take from a man what is not due, is, on the other hand, injustice.

G. E. Moore

An Organic Unity *

There remains one point which must not be omitted in a complete description of the kind of questions which Ethics has to answer. The main division of those questions is, as I have said, into two; the question what things are good in themselves, and the question to what other things these are related as effects. The first of these, which is the primary ethical question and is presupposed by the other, includes a correct comparison of the various things which have intrinsic value (if there are many such) in respect of the degree of value which they have; and such comparison involves a difficulty of principle which has greatly aided the confusion of intrinsic value with mere 'goodness as a means.' It has been pointed out that one difference between a judgment which asserts that a thing is good in itself, and a judgment which asserts that it is a means to good, consists in the fact that the first, if true of one instance of the thing in question, is necessarily true of all; whereas a thing which has good effects under some circumstances may have bad ones under others. Now it is certainly true that all judgments of intrinsic value are in this sense universal; but the principle which I have now to enunciate may easily make it appear as if they were not so but resembled the judgment of means in being merely general. There is, as will presently be maintained, a vast number of different things, each of which has intrinsic value; there are also very many which are positively bad; and there is a still larger class of things, which appear to be indifferent. But a thing belonging to any of these three classes may occur as part of a whole, which includes among its other parts other things belonging both to the same and to the other two classes; and these wholes, as such, may also have intrinsic value. The paradox, to which it is necessary to call attention, is that *the value of such a whole bears no regu-*

* G. E. Moore, *Principia Ethica* (Cambridge: Cambridge University Press, 1903), ch. 1, sec. 18, 19, ch. 6, sec. 128, 130.

lar proportion to the sum of the values of its parts. It is certain that a good thing may exist in such a relation to another good thing that the value of the whole thus formed is immensely greater than the sum of the values of the two good things. It is certain that a whole formed of a good thing and an indifferent thing may have immensely greater value than that good thing itself possesses. It is certain that two bad things or a bad thing and an indifferent thing may form a whole much worse than the sum of badness of its parts. And it seems as if indifferent things may also be the sole constituents of a whole which has great value, either positive or negative. Whether the addition of a bad thing to a good whole may increase the positive value of the whole, or the addition of a bad thing to a bad may produce a whole having positive value, may seem more doubtful; but it is, at least, possible, and this possibility must be taken into account in our ethical investigations. However we may decide particular questions, the principle is clear. *The value of a whole must not be assumed to be the same as the sum of the values of its parts.*

A single instance will suffice to illustrate the kind of relation in question. It seems to be true that to be conscious of a beautiful object is a thing of great intrinsic value; whereas the same object, if no one be conscious of it, has certainly comparatively little value, and is commonly held to have none at all. But the consciousness of a beautiful object is certainly a whole of some sort in which we can distinguish as parts the object on the one hand and the being conscious on the other. Now this latter factor occurs as part of a different whole, whenever we are conscious of anything; and it would seem that some of these wholes have at all events very little value, and may even be indifferent or positively bad. Yet we cannot always attribute the slightness of their value to any positive demerit in the object which differentiates them from the consciousness of beauty; the object itself may approach as near as possible to absolute neutrality. Since, therefore, mere consciousness does not always confer great value upon the whole of which it forms a part, even though its object may have no great demerit, we cannot attribute the great superiority of the consciousness of a beautiful thing over the beautiful thing itself to the mere addition of the value of consciousness to that of the beautiful thing. Whatever the intrinsic value of consciousness may be, it does not give to the whole of which it forms a part a value proportioned to the sum of its value and that of its object. If this be so, we have here an instance of a whole possessing a different intrinsic value from the sum of that of its parts; and whether it be so or not, what is meant by such a difference is illustrated by this case.

There are, then, wholes which possess the property that their value is different from the sum of the values of their parts; and the relations which subsist between such parts and the whole of which they form a part have not hitherto been distinctly recognized or received a separate name. Two points are especially worthy of notice. (1) It is plain that the existence of any such part is a necessary condition for the existence of that good which is constituted by the whole. And exactly the same language will also express the relation between a means and the good thing which is its effect. But yet there is a most important difference between the two cases, constituted by the fact that the part is, whereas the means is not, a part of the good thing for the existence of which its existence is a necessary condition. The necessity by which, if the good in question is to exist, the means to it must exist is merely a natural or causal necessity. If the laws of nature were different, exactly the same good might exist, although what is now a necessary condition of its existence did not exist. The existence of the means has no intrinsic value; and its utter annihilation would leave the value of that which it is now necessary to secure entirely unchanged. But in the case of a part of such a whole as we are now considering, it is otherwise. In this case the good in question cannot conceivably exist, unless the part exist also. The necessity which connects the two is quite independent of natural law. What is asserted to have intrinsic value is the existence of the whole; and the existence of the whole includes the existence of its part. Suppose the part removed, and what remains is *not* what was asserted to have intrinsic value; but if we suppose a means removed, what remains is just what *was* asserted to have intrinsic value. And yet (2) the existence of the part may *itself* have no more intrinsic value than that of the means. It is this fact which constitutes the paradox of the relation which we are discussing. It has just been said that what has intrinsic value is the existence of the whole, and that this includes the existence of the part; and from this it would seem a natural inference that the existence of the part has intrinsic value. But the inference would be as false as if we were to conclude that, because the number of two stones was two, each of the stones was also two. The part of a valuable whole retains exactly the same value when it is, as when it is not, a part of that whole. If it had value under other circumstances, its value is not any greater, when it is part of a far more valuable whole; and if it had no value by itself, it has none still, however great be that of the whole of which it now forms a part. We are not then justified in asserting that one and the same thing is under some circumstances intrinsically good, and under others not so; as we are justified in asserting of a means that it sometimes does and sometimes does not produce good results. And yet we are justified in asserting that it is far more desirable that a certain thing should exist under some circumstances than under others; namely when other things will exist in such relations to it as to form a more valuable whole. *It* will not have more intrinsic value under these circumstances than under others; *it* will not necessarily even be a means to the existence of things having more intrinsic value; but it will, like a means, be a necessary condition for the existence of that which *has* greater intrinsic value, although, unlike a means, it will itself form a part of this more valuable existent. . . .

But, finally, it must be insisted that pleasure and pain are completely analogous in this: that we cannot assume either that the presence of pleasure always makes a state of things better *on the whole*, or that the presence of pain always makes it worse. That is the truth which is most liable to be overlooked with regard to them; and it is because this is true, that the common theory, that pleasure is the only good and pain the only evil, has its grossest consequences in misjudgments of value. Not only is the pleasantness of a state *not* in proportion to its intrinsic worth; it may even add positively to its vileness. We do not think the successful hatred of a villain the less vile and odious, because he takes the keenest delight in it; nor is there the least need, in logic, why we should think so, apart from an unintelligent prejudice in favour of pleasure. In fact it seems to be the case that wherever pleasure is added to an evil state of either of our first two classes, the whole thus formed is *always* worse than if no pleasure had been there. And similarly with regard to pain. If pain be added to an evil state of either of our first two classes, the whole thus formed is *always* better, *as a whole*, than if no pain had been there; though here, if the pain be too intense, since that is a great evil, the state may not be better *on the whole*. It is in this way that the theory of vindictive punishment may be vindicated. The infliction of pain on a person whose state of mind is bad may, if the pain be not too intense, create a state of things that is better *on the whole* than if the evil state of mind had existed unpunished. Whether such a state of things can ever constitute a *positive* good, is another question. . . .

But what we have now to consider are cases or wholes, in which one or more parts have a great *negative* value—are great positive evils. And first of all, we may take the *strongest* cases, like that of retributive punishment, in which we have a whole, exclusively composed of two great positive evils—wickedness and pain. Can such a whole ever be positively good *on the whole?*

(1) I can see no reason to think that such wholes ever are positively good *on the whole*. But from the fact that they may, nevertheless, be less evils, than either of their parts taken singly, it follows that they have a characteristic which is most important for the correct decision of practical questions. It follows that, quite apart from *consequences* or any value which an evil may have as a mere means, it may, *supposing* one evil already exists, be worth while to create another, since, by the mere creation of this second, there may be constituted a whole less bad than if the original evil had been left to exist by itself. And similarly, with regard to all the wholes which I am about to consider, it must be remembered, that, even if they are not goods *on the whole*, yet, where an evil already exists, as in this world evils do exist, the existence of the other part of these wholes will constitute a thing desirable *for its own sake*—that is to say, not merely a means to future goods, but one of the *ends* which must be taken into account in estimating what that best possible state of things is, to which every right action must be a means.

Herbert Morris

Persons and Punishment *

... Let us first turn attention to the institutions in which punishment is involved. The institutions I describe will resemble those we ordinarily think of as institutions of punishment; they will have, however, additional features we associate with a system of just punishment.

Let us suppose that men are constituted roughly as they now are, with a rough equivalence in strength and abilities, a capacity to be injured by each other and to make judgments that such injury is undesirable, a limited strength of will, and a capacity to reason and to conform conduct to rules. Applying to the conduct of these men are a group of rules, ones I shall label 'primary,' which closely resemble the core rules of our criminal law, rules that prohibit violence and deception and compliance with which provides benefits for all persons. These benefits consist in noninterference by others with what each person values, such matters as continuance of life and bodily security. The rules define a sphere for each person, then, which is immune from interference by others. Making possible this mutual benefit is the assumption by individuals of a burden. The burden consists in the exercise of self-restraint by individuals over inclinations that would, if satisfied, directly interfere or create a substantial risk of interference with others in proscribed ways. If a person fails to exercise self-restraint even though he might have and gives in to such inclinations, he renounces a burden which others have voluntarily assumed and thus gains an advantage which others, who have restrained themselves, do not possess. This system, then, is one in which the rules establish a mutuality of benefit and burden and in which the benefits of noninterference are conditional upon the assumption of burdens.

Connecting punishment with the violation of these primary rules, and making public the provision for punishment, is both reasonable

* Herbert Morris, "Persons and Punishment," *The Monist*, 52:4 (La Salle, Illinois, 1968), pp. 476–79. Reprinted by permission of the publisher and the author.

and just. First, it is only reasonable that those who voluntarily comply with the rules be provided some assurance that they will not be assuming burdens which others are unprepared to assume. Their disposition to comply voluntarily will diminish as they learn that others are with impunity renouncing burdens they are assuming. Second, fairness dictates that a system in which benefits and burdens are equally distributed have a mechanism designed to prevent a maldistribution in the benefits and burdens. Thus, sanctions are attached to noncompliance with the primary rules so as to induce compliance with the primary rules among those who may be disinclined to obey. In this way the likelihood of an unfair distribution is diminished.

Third, it is just to punish those who have violated the rules and caused the unfair distribution of benefits and burdens. A person who violates the rules has something others have—the benefits of the system—but by renouncing what others have assumed, the burdens of self-restraint, he has acquired an unfair advantage. Matters are not even until this advantage is in some way erased. Another way of putting it is that he owes something to others, for he has something that does not rightfully belong to him. Justice—that is punishing such individuals—restores the equilibrium of benefits and burdens by taking from the individual what he owes, that is, exacting the debt. It is important to see that the equilibrium may be restored in another way. Forgiveness—with its legal analogue of a pardon—while not the righting of an unfair distribution by making one pay his debt is, nevertheless, a restoring of the equilibrium by forgiving the debt. Forgiveness may be viewed, at least in some types of cases, as a gift after the fact, erasing a debt, which had the gift been given before the fact, would not have created a debt. But the practice of pardoning has to proceed sensitively, for it may endanger in a way the practice of justice does not, the maintenance of an equilibrium of benefits and burdens. If all are indiscriminately pardoned less incentive is provided individuals to restrain their inclinations, thus increasing the incidence of persons taking what they do not deserve.

There are also in this system we are considering a variety of operative principles compliance with which provides some guarantee that the system of punishment does not itself promote an unfair distribution of benefits and burdens. For one thing, provision is made for a variety of defenses, each one of which can be said to have as its object diminishing the chances of forcibly depriving a person of benefits others have if that person has not derived an unfair advantage. A person has not derived an unfair advantage if he could not have restrained himself or if it is unreasonable to expect him to behave otherwise than he did. Sometimes the rules preclude punishment of classes of persons such as children. Sometimes they provide a defense if on a particular occasion a person lacked the capacity to conform his conduct to the rules. Thus, someone who in an epileptic seizure strikes another is excused. Punishment in these cases would be punishment of the innocent, punishment of those who do not voluntarily renounce a burden others have assumed. Punishment in such cases, then, would not equalize but rather cause an unfair distribution in benefits and burdens.

Along with principles providing defenses there are requirements that the rules be prospective and relatively clear so that persons have a fair opportunity to comply with the rules. There are, also, rules governing, among other matters, the burden of proof, who shall bear it and what it shall be, the prohibition on double jeopardy, and the privilege against self-incrimination. Justice requires conviction of the guilty, and requires their punishment, but in setting out to fulfill the demands of justice we may, of course, because we are not omniscient, cause injustice by convicting and punishing the innocent. The resolution arrived at in the system I am describing consists in weighing as the greater evil the punishment of the innocent. The primary function of the system of rules was to provide individuals with a sphere of interest immune from interference. Given this goal, it is determined to be a greater evil for society to interfere unjustifiably with an individual by depriving him of good than for the society to fail to punish those that have unjustifiably interfered.

Finally, because the primary rules are designed to benefit all and because the punishments prescribed for their violation are publicized and the defenses respected, there is some plausibility in the exaggerated claim that in choosing to do an act violative of the rules an individual has chosen to be punished. This way of putting matters brings to our attention the extent to which, when the system is as I have described it, the criminal "has brought the punishment upon himself" in contrast to those cases where it would be misleading to say "he has brought it upon himself," cases, for example, where one does not know the rules or is punished in the absence of fault . . .

H. J. McCloskey

A Non-Utilitarian
Approach to Punishment *

Although the view that punishment is to be justified on utilitarian grounds has obvious appeal, an examination of utilitarianism reveals that, consistently and accurately interpreted, it dictates unjust punishments which are unacceptable to the common moral consciousness. In this rule-utilitarianism is no more satisfactory than in act-utiliarianism. Although the production of the greatest good, or the greatest happiness, of the greatest number is obviously a relevant consideration when determining which punishments may properly be inflicted, the question as to which punishment is just is a distinct and more basic question and one which must be answered before we can determine which punishments are morally permissible. That a retributivist theory, which is a particular application of a general principle of justice, can account more satisfactorily for our notion of justice in punishment is a positive reason in its support.

I. Introduction

At first glance there are many obvious considerations which seem to suggest a utilitarian approach to punishment. Crime is an evil and what we want to do is not so much to cancel it out after it occurs as to prevent it. To punish crime when it occurs is, at best, an imperfect state of affairs. Further, punishment, invoking as it does evils such as floggings, imprisonment, and death, is something which does not commend itself to us without argument. An obvious way of at-

* H. J. McCloskey, "A Non-Utilitarian Approach to Punishment," *Inquiry*, 8 (1965), pp. 239–255. Reprinted by permission of the author and the publisher. A reply to Dr. McCloskey is reprinted in this volume p. 66.

tempting to justify such deliberately created evils would be in terms of their utility.

This is how crime and punishment impress on first sight. A society in which there was no crime and no punishment would be a much better society than one with crime and resulting punishments. And punishment, involving evils such as deliberately inflicted suffering and even death, and consequential evils such as the driving of some of its victims into despair and even insanity, etc., harming and even wrecking their subsequent lives, and often also the lives of their relatives and dependents, obviously needs justification. To argue that it is useful, that good results come from such punishment, is to offer a more plausible justification than many so-called retributive justifications. It is obviously more plausible to argue that punishment is justified if and because it is useful than to argue that punishment is justified because society has a right to express its indignation at the actions of the offender, or because punishment annuls and cancels out the crime, or because the criminal, being a human being, merits respect and hence has a right to his punishment. Such retributive type justifications have some point, but they are nonetheless implausible in a way that the utilitarian justification is not. Yet I shall be concerned to argue that the key to the morality of punishment is to be found in terms of a retributive theory, namely, the theory that evils should be distributed according to desert and that the vicious deserve to suffer. In so arguing, I shall be bringing together and adding to a number of arguments I have set out elsewhere.[1]

II. How Our Common Moral Consciousness Views Punishment

Is the punishment which commends itself to the moral consciousness always useful punishment? And is all punishment that is useful such that we should consider it to be morally just and permissible? Pun-

1. "An Examination of Restricted Utilitarianism," *Philosophical Review*, Vol. LXVI, 4 (Oct., 1957); 'The Complexity of the Concepts of Punishment,' *Philosophy*, Vol. XXXVII, pp. 307–325 (Oct., 1962).

ishment which we commonly consider to be just is punishment which is deserved. To be deserved, punishment must be of an offender who is guilty of an offence in the morally relevant sense of 'offence.' For instance, the punishing of a man known to be innocent of any crime shocks our moral consciousness and is seen as a grave injustice. Similarly, punishment of a person not responsible for his behaviour, e.g., a lunatic, is evidently unjust and shocking. Punishment for what is not an offence in the morally significant sense of 'offence' is equally unjust. To punish a man who has tried his hardest to secure a job during a period of acute and extensive unemployment for 'having insufficient means of support,' or to punish a person under a retroactive law is similarly unjust. So too, if the offence for which the person punished is one against a secret law which it was impossible for him to know of, the punishment is gravely unjust. Similarly, punishment of other innocent people—e.g., as scapegoats—to deter others, is unjust and morally wrong. So too is collective punishment—killing all the members of a village or family for the offences of one member. Whether such punishments successfully deter seems irrelevant to the question of their justice. Similarly, certain punishments of persons who are offenders in the morally relevant sense of 'offenders' also impress us as gravely unjust. We now consider to have been gravely unjust the very severe punishments meted out to those punished by hanging or transportation and penal servitude for petty thefts in the 18th century. Comparable punishments, e.g., hanging for shoplifting from a food market, would be condemned today as equally unjust. It is conceivable that such unjust punishments may, in extreme circumstances, become permissible, but this would only be so if a grave evil has to be perpetrated to achieve a very considerable good.

In brief, our moral consciousness suggests that punishment, to be just, must be merited by the committing of an offence. It follows from this that punishment, to be justly administered, must involve care in determining whether the offending person is really a responsible agent. And it implies that the punishment must not be excessive. It must not exceed what is appropriate to the crime. We must always be able to say of the person punished that he deserved to be punished as he was punished. It is not enough to say that good results were achieved by punishing him. It is logically possible to say that the punishment was useful but undeserved, and deserved but not useful. It is not possible to say that the punishment was just although undeserved.

These features of ordinary moral thinking about just punishment appear to be features of which any defensible theory of punishment needs to take note. Punishment of innocent people—through collective punishments, scapegoat punishment, as a result of inefficient trial procedures, corrupt police methods, mistaken tests of responsibility, etc., or by using criteria of what constitute offences which allow to be offences, offences under secret and retroactive laws—is unjust punishment, as is punishment which is disproportionate with the crime. Thus the punishment which we consider, after critical reflection, to be just punishment, is punishment which fits a retributive theory. It is to be noted that it is just punishment, not morally permissible punishment, of which this is being claimed. Sometimes it is morally permissible and obligatory to override the dictates of justice. The retributive theory is a theory about justice in punishment and tells only part of the whole story about the morality of punishment. It points to a very important consideration in determining the morality of punishment—namely, its justice—and explains what punishments are just and why they are just.

Before proceeding further, some comment should be made concerning these allusions to 'what our common moral consciousness regards as just or unjust.' Utilitarians frequently wish to dismiss such appeals to our moral consciousness as amounting to an uncritical acceptance of our emotional responses. Obviously they are not that. Our uncritical moral consciousness gives answers which we do not accept as defensible after critical reflection, and it is the judgements which we accept after critical reflection which are being appealed to here. In any case, before the utilitarian starts questioning this approach, he would do well to make sure that he himself is secure from similar criticism. It might well be argued that his appeal to the principle of utility itself rests upon an uncritical emotional acceptance of what prima facie appears to be a high-minded moral principle but which, on critical examination, seems to involve grave moral evils. Thus the problem of method, and of justifying the use of this method, is one which the utilitarian shares with the nonutilitarian. It is not possible here to argue for the soundness of this mode of argument beyond noting that whether an intuitionist or non-cognitivist meta-ethic be true, this sort of appeal is what such meta-ethical theories suggest to be appropriate.

III. What Utilitarianism Appears to Entail in Respect of Punishment

Is all useful punishment just punishment, and is all just punishment useful? Here it is necessary first to dispose of what might not unfairly be described as 'red herring.' A lot of recent utilitarian writing is to the effect that punishment of the innocent is logically impossible, and hence that utilitarianism cannot be committed to punishment of the innocent. Their point is that the concept of punishment entails that the person being punished be an actual or supposed offender, for otherwise we do not call it punishment but injury, harm-infliction, social quarantining, etc. There are two good reasons for rejecting this argument as nothing but a red herring. Not all unjust punishment is punishment of the innocent. Much is punishment which is excessive. Thus even if punishment of the innocent were not logically possible, the problem of justice in punishment would remain in the form of showing that only punishments commensurate with the offence were useful. Secondly, the verbal point leaves the issue of substance untouched. The real quarrel between the retributionist and the utilitarian is whether a system of inflictions of suffering on people without reference to the gravity of their offences or ever to whether they have committed offences, is just and morally permissible. It is immaterial whether we call such deliberate inflictions of sufferings punishment, social surgery, social quarantining, etc. In any case, as I have elsewhere tried to show, the claim is evidently false. We the observers and the innocent victims of such punishment call it punishment, unjust punishment. In so referring to it there is no straining of language.

To consider now whether all useful punishment is just punishment. When the problem of utilitarianism in punishment is put in this way, the appeal of the utilitarian approach somewhat diminishes. It appears to be useful to do lots of things which are unjust and undesirable. Whilst it is no doubt true that harsh punishment isn't necessarily the most useful punishment, and that punishment of the guilty person is usually the most useful punishment, it is nonetheless easy to call to mind cases of punishment of innocent people, of mentally deranged people, of excessive punishment, etc., inflicted because it was believed to be useful. Furthermore, the person imposing such punishment seems not always to be mistaken. Similarly, punishment which is just may be less useful than rewards. With some criminals, it may be more useful to reward them. As Ross observes:

> A utilitarian theory, whether of the hedonistic or of the 'ideal' kind, if it justifies punishment at all, is bound to justify it solely on the ground of the effects it produces. . . . In principle, then, the punishment of a guilty person is treated by utilitarians as not different in kind from the imposition of inconvenience, say by quarantine regulations, on innocent individuals for the good of the community.[2]

What is shocking about this, and what most utilitarians now seek to avoid admitting to be an implication of utilitarianism, is the implication that grave injustices in the form of punishment of the innocent, of those not responsible for their acts, or harsh punishments of those guilty of trivial offences, are dictated by their theory. We may sometimes best deter others by punishing, by framing, an innocent man who is generally believed to be guilty, or by adopting rough and ready trial procedures, as is done by army courts martial in the heat of battle in respect of deserters, etc.; or we may severely punish a person not responsible for his actions, as so often happens with military punishments for cowardice, and in civil cases involving sex crimes where the legal definition of insanity may fail to cover the relevant cases of insanity. Sometimes we may deter others by imposing ruthless sentences for crimes which are widespread, as with car stealing and shoplifting in food markets. We may make people very thoughtful about their political commitments by having retroactive laws about their political affiliations, and we may, by secret laws, such as make to be major crimes what are believed simply to be antisocial practices and not crimes at all, usefully encourage a watchful, public-spirited behaviour. If the greatest good or the greatest

2. W. D. Ross, *The Right and the Good*, Oxford University Press, Oxford 1930, p. 56.

happiness of the greatest number is the foundation of the morality and justice of punishment, there can be no guarantee that some such injustices may not be dictated by it. Indeed, one would expect that it would depend on the details of the situation and on the general features of the society, which punishments and institutions of punishment were most useful. In most practical affairs affecting human welfare, e.g., forms of government, laws, social institutions, etc., what is useful is relative to the society and situation. It would therefore be surprising if this were not also the case with punishment. We should reasonably expect to find that different punishments and systems of punishment were useful for different occasions, times, communities, peoples, and be such that some useful punishments involved grave and shocking injustices. Whether this is in fact the case is an empirical matter which is best settled by social and historical research, for there is evidence available which bears on which of the various types of punishments and institutions work best in the sense of promoting the greatest good. Although this is not a question for which the philosopher qua philosopher is well equipped to deal, I shall nonetheless later briefly look at a number of considerations which are relevant to it, but only because the utilitarian usually bases his defence of utilitarianism on his alleged knowledge of empirical matters of fact, upon his claim to know that the particular punishments and that system of punishment which we regard as most just, are most conducive to the general good. J. Bentham, and in our own day, J. J. C. Smart, are among the relatively few utilitarians who are prepared— in the case of Smart, albeit reluctantly—to accept that utilitarian punishment may be unjust by conventional standards, but morally right nonetheless.

Against the utilitarian who seeks to argue that utilitarianism does not involve unjust punishment, there is a very simple argument, namely, that whether or not unjust punishments are in fact useful, it is logically possible that they will at some time become useful, in which case utilitarians are committed to them. Utilitarianism involves the conclusion that if it is useful to punish lunatics, mentally deranged people, innocent people framed as being guilty, etc., it is obligatory to do so. It would be merely a contingent fact, if it were a fact at all, that the punishment which works is that which we consider to be morally just. In principle, the utilitarian is committed to saying that we should ask "Is the punishment deserved?" The notion of desert does not arise for him. The only relevant issue is whether the punishment produces greater good.

IV. What Utilitarianism in Fact Entails in the Light of Empirical Considerations

What is the truth about the utility of the various types of punishments? As I have already suggested, it would be astonishing if, in the sphere of punishment, only those punishments and that institution of punishment we consider to be just, worked best. To look at particular examples.

In an article cited above, I argued that a utilitarian would be committed to unjust punishment, and used the example of a sheriff framing an innocent Negro in order to stop a series of lynchings which he knew would occur if the guilty person were not immediately found, or believed to have been found.[3] I suggested that if the sheriff were a utilitarian he would frame an innocent man to save the lives of others. Against this example, it is suggested that we cannot know with certainty what the consequences of framing the Negro would be, and that there may be other important consequences besides the prevention of lynchings. Utilitarians point to the importance of people having confidence in the impartiality and fairness of the legal system, a belief that lawful behavior pays, etc. However, as the example is set up, only the sheriff, the innocent victim and the guilty man and not the general public, would know there had been a frameup. Further, even if a few others knew, this would not mean that everyone knew; and even if everyone came to know, surely, if utilitarianism is thought to be the true moral theory, the general body of citizens ought to be happier believing that their sheriff is promoting what is right rather than promoting nonutilitarian standards of justice. Since complex factors are involved, this example is not as decisive as is desirable. It can readily be modified so as to avoid

3. "An Examination of Restricted Utilitarianism," *op. cit.*, pp. 468–469 [reprinted above, pp. 120–121].

many of these complications and hence become more decisive. Suppose a utilitarian were visiting an area in which there was racial strife, and that, during his visit, a Negro rapes a white woman, and that race riots occur as a result of the crime, white mobs, with the connivance of the police, bashing and killing Negroes, etc. Suppose too that our utilitarian is in the area of the crime when it is committed such that his testimony would bring about the conviction of a particular Negro. If he knows that a quick arrest will stop the riots and lynchings, surely, as a utilitarian, he must conclude that he has a duty to bear false witness in order to bring about the punishment of an innocent person. In such a situation, he has, on utilitarian theory, an evident duty to bring about the punishment of an innocent man. What unpredictable consequences, etc., are present here other than of a kind that are present in every moral situation? Clearly, the utilitarian will not be corrupted by bearing false witness, for he will be doing what he believes to be his duty. It is relevant that it is rare for any of us to be in a situation in which we can usefully and tellingly bear false witness against others.

We may similarly give possible examples of useful punishments of other unjust kinds. Scapegoat punishment need not be and typically is not of a framed person. It may be useful. An occupying power which is experiencing trouble with the local population may find it useful to punish, by killing, some of the best loved citizen leaders, each time an act of rebellion occurs; but such punishments do not commend themselves to us as just and right. Similarly, collective punishment is often useful—consider its use in schools. There we consider it unjust but morally permissible because of its great utility. Collective punishments of the kind employed by the Nazis in Czechoslovakia—destroying a village and punishing its inhabitants for the acts of a few—are notorious as war crimes. Yet they appear to have been useful in the sense of achieving Nazi objectives. It may be objected that the Nazi sense of values was mistaken, that such punishment would not contribute towards realizing higher values and goods. But it is partly an accident of history that it was the Nazis who, in recent times, resorted to this method. If we had had to occupy a Nazi territory with inadequate troops, this might have been the only effective way of maintaining order. As with human affairs generally, it would depend on many factors, including the strength of our troops, the degree of hostility of the occupied people, their temper and likely reaction to this sort of collective punishment, etc. Punishment of relatives could also be useful. It would be an interesting social experiment in those modern democracies which are plagued by juvenile delinquency, for parents as well as the teenage delinquents to be punished. Such punishment would be unjust but it might well be useful. It would need a number of social experiments to see whether it is or is not useful. It is not a matter we can settle by intuitive insight. If it did prove useful, it is probable people would come to think of such punishment of parents as punishment for the offence of being a parent of a delinquent! This would obscure the awareness of the injustice of such punishment, but it would nonetheless be unjust punishment.

Similarly with punishment for offences under secret and retroactive laws. Such laws, it is true, would be useful only if used sparingly and for very good reasons but it is not hard to imagine cases where the use of a retroactive law might be useful in the long as well as in the short run. That a plausible case could have been made out for introducing retroactive laws in postwar Germany on utilitarian grounds as well as on the other sorts of grounds indicated by legal theorists, suggests that such cases do occur. They may be the most useful means, they may, in the German case, even have been morally permissible means and the means of achieving greater total justice; but they are nonethless means which in themselves are unjust. Retroactive laws are really a kind of secret law. Their injustice consists in this; and secret laws, like them, seem useful if used sparingly and with discretion. The Nazis certainly believed them to be very useful but again it will no doubt be said that this was because their system of values was mistaken. However, unless the system of values includes respect for considerations of justice, such secret laws are possibly useful instruments for promoting good.

In our own community we define 'offence' in such a way, with various laws, that we condone unjust punishment because of its utility. The vagrancy law is a very useful law but what it declares to be an offence is hardly an offence in the morally relevant sense. And it is not difficult to imagine countries in which it would be useful to have a law making it an offence to arouse the suspicions of the government. Suppose there were a democratic revolution in Spain, or in

Russia, which led to the perilous existence of a democratic government. Such a government might find that the only way in which it could safely continue in existence was by having such a law and similar laws involving unjust punishments. It would then have to consider which was morally more important—to avoid the unjust punishments which such a law involves, or to secure and make permanent a democratic form of government which achieved greater over-all injustice. That is, it would face conflicting claims of justice.

In an ignorant community it might well be useful to punish as responsible moral agents 'criminals' who in fact were not responsible for their actions but who were generally believed to be responsible agents. The experts suggest that many sex offenders and others who commit the more shocking crimes, are of this type, but even in reasonably enlightened communities the general body of citizens do not always accept the judgments of the experts. Thus, in communities in which enlightened opinion generally prevails (and these are few) punishment of mentally deranged 'criminals' would have little if any deterrent value, whereas in most communities some mentally deranged people may usefully be punished, and in ignorant, backward communities very useful results may come from punishing those not responsible for their actions. Similarly, very undesirable results may come from not punishing individuals generally believed to be fully responsible moral agents. Yet, clearly, the morality of punishing such people does not depend on the degree of the enlightenment of the community. Utilitarian theory suggests that it does, that such punishment is right and just in ignorant, prejudiced communities, unjust in enlightened communities. The utility of such punishment varies in this way, but not its justice. The tests of responsible action are very difficult to determine, although this need not worry the utilitarian who should use the test of utility in this area as elsewhere. However, to make my point, we need not consider borderline cases. The more atrocious and abominable the crime, the more pointless its brutality is, the more likely it is that the criminal was not responsible and the more likely that the general public will believe him to be fully responsible and deserving of the severest punishment.

Utilitarians often admit that particular punishments may be useful but unjust and argue that utilitarianism becomes more plausible and indeed, acceptable, if it is advanced as a theory about the test of rules and institutions. These utilitarians argue that we should not test particular punishments by reference to their consequences; rather, we should test the whole institution of punishment in this way, by reference to the consequences of the whole institution.

This seems an incredible concession; yet rule-utilitarianism enjoys widespread support and is perhaps the dominant version of utilitarianism. It is argued that particular utilitarian punishments may be unjust but that useful systems of punishment are those which are just systems in the judgment of our reflective moral consciousness. This modification of utilitarianism involves a strange concession. After all, if the test of right and wrong rules and institutions lies in their utility, it is surely fantastic to suggest that this test should be confined to rules and institutions, unless it is useful so to confine its application. Clearly, when we judge the utility of particular actions, we should take note of the effects on the institution or rule, but surely, it is individual acts and their consequences which utimately matter for the utilitarian. There are therefore good reasons for believing that the half-hearted utilitarianism of rule-utilitarianism involves an indefensible compromise between act-utilitarianism and Ross's theory of a plurality of irreducible prima facie duties.

To consider now the implications of rule-utilitarianism. As with act-utilitarianism, it would be surprising if what was useful was also at all times just, and that what was the most useful institution of punishment was the same under all conditions and for all times. For example, what we in Australia regard as useful and just, fair trial procedures—and these are an important part of justice in punishment—for example, rules about the burden of proof, strict limitation of newspaper comment before and during the trial, selection of the jury, provision of legal aid for the needy, etc., differ from those found useful in dictatorships. Also, obviously a country emerging from the instability of a great revolution cannot afford to take risks with criminals and counter-revolutionaries which a stable, secure, well established community can afford to take. In Australia we can take the risk of allowing a few traitors to escape deserved punishment as a result of our careful procedures directed at ensuring that the innocent be not punished in error. During a war we may take fewer risks but at the expense of injustices. In an unstable community, immediately after a revolution, a more cavalier approach to justice is usually found to be the most useful approach. And there are differences within any one community. What is useful for civil courts is not necessarily what is most useful for military courts, and the most useful 'institution' for the whole community may be a mixture of different systems of justice and punishment. Thus not only particular punishments but also whole institutions of punishment may be useful but of a kind we consider to be gravely unjust. It is these difficulties of utilitarianism—of act- and rule-utilitarianism—and the facts which give rise to these difficulties which give to the retributive theory, that the vicious deserve to suffer, its initial plausibility.

V. Positive Considerations for a Retributive Theory of Punishment

There are many positive considerations in support of the retributive theory of punishment, if it is constructed as the theory that the vicious deserve to suffer. Firstly, it is a particular application of a general principle of justice, namely, that equals should be treated equally and unequals unequally. This is a principle which has won very general acceptance as a self-evident principle of justice. It is the principle from which the more celebrated, yet opposed accounts of justice, are derived. It is a principle which has wide application and which underlies our judgments of justice in the various areas. We think of it as applying—other things being equal—to fair prices, wages, and treatment generally. It is in terms of such a principle that we think that political discrimination against women and peoples of special races is unjust, and that against children, just. Justice in these areas involves treating equals equally, unequals unequally— where the equals are equal in the relevant respect, and the unequals unequal in the relevant respect. Hence it is that we think it just to deny women some jobs because of their weaker physique, but unjust to exclude a woman from a post such as librarian or violinist if she is more proficient as such than other candidates for the post. So too with justice and punishment. The criminal is one who has made himself unequal in the relevant sense. Hence he merits unequal treatment. In this case, unequal treatment amounts to deliberate infliction of evils—suffering or death.

We need now to consider whether our retributive theory implies that there is a duty to punish with full, deserved punishment. Look at the other areas of justice, for example, wage justice. If it is just, say, to pay a labourer £20 a week, there is no breach of justice if the employer shows benevolence and pays £25, whereas there is a grave breach if he pays only £15. Similarly with retributive justice, but in a reverse way. We do not act unjustly if, moved by benevolence, we impose less than is demanded by justice, but there is a grave injustice if the deserved punishment is exceeded. If the deserved punishment is inflicted, all we need to do to justify it is to point out that the crime committed deserved and merited such punishment. Suppose that the just punishment for murder is imprisonment for 15 years. Suppose also that the judge knows that the murderer he is about to sentence will never be tempted to commit another murder, that he is deeply and genuinely remorseful, and that others will not be encouraged to commit murders if he is treated leniently. If the judge imposed a mild penalty we should probably applaud his humanity, but if he imposed the maximum penalty we should not be entitled to condemn him as unjust. What we say in cases like this is that the judge is a hard, even harsh, man, not that he is an unjust man.

Is only deserved punishment morally permissible? Obviously not. Here we might take an analogy with other parts of morality. It is wrong to lie, to break promises, or to steal. This is not to say that we are never obliged to lie, break promises, steal, etc. What it means is that we need to have another, conflicting, more stringent duty which overrides the duty to tell the truth, keep our promise, or not steal, if we are to be justified in lying, breaking our promise, or stealing. Similarly with justice in punishment. The fact that a punishment is just entitles the appropriate authority to inflict it, but that is not to say that it must be inflicted nor that more cannot properly be inflicted. Many considerations may weigh with the relevant authority and make it morally right to inflict more or less than is strictly just; and not all such considerations will be utilitarian considerations— some may be other considerations of justice. We determine what punishment ought to be inflicted by taking into account firstly what punishment is deserved, and then other considerations. Relevant here are considerations such as that the criminal's wife and children may be the real victims of the punishment, that the criminal would be unable to make restitution to the person whose property he has stolen; of benevolence, e.g., in not imposing the punishment because the criminal has already suffered greatly in blinding himself in attempting to blow a safe; of the general good, as in making an example of the criminal and inflicting more than the deserved punishment because of the grave consequences that will come about if this type of crime is not immediately checked, etc. Production of the greatest good is obviously a relevant consideration when determining which punishment may properly be inflicted, but the question as to which punishment is just is a much more basic and important consideration. When considering that question we need to determine whether the person to be punished committed an offence in the morally relevant sense of 'offence' and what punishment is commensurate with the offence.

It is important here to note and dismiss a commonly made criticism of this retributive theory, namely, that there is no objective test of the gravity of a crime except in terms of the penalty attached to the crime. If the penalty is hanging, then, it is argued, the crime is a serious one; if the penalty is a £2 fine, it is a trivial offence. This criticism is often reinforced by the contention that if all the people in any given group were to make out lists of crimes in order of their gravity, they would give significantly different lists such that what appear as grave crimes on one list are minor crimes on other lists. Obviously, if this criticism were sound, it would mean that one very important element of the retributive theory would be nullified, for punishment could not be other than commensurate with the offence. However, this criticism is unsound and rests on a number of confusions.

It is true that we speak of a crime as serious if the penalty is hanging, but this is not to say that it is therefore a grave crime in the morally significant sense of 'grave crime.' The fact that hanging was the penalty for stealing a loaf of bread made that a serious offence in one sense but not in another, for we speak of the punishment as gravely disproportionate and as treating the offence as much more serious than it really is. It is on this basis that we can and do speak of penalties as being too light or too heavy, even where similar offences have similar penalties. It is unjust that the theft of a loaf of bread should meet with the same punishment as murder. Further, the fact that we reach different conclusions about the relative gravity of different crimes constitutes no difficulty for the retributive theory. Most of us would agree that murder is a very serious crime and that shoplifting a cake of soap is a considerably lesser offence. We should perhaps differ about such questions as to whether kidnapping is more or less serious than blackmail, whether embezzlement should be treated as a lesser crime than housebreaking, whether stealing a car worth £2,000 is less serious than stealing £2,000 worth of jewelry. We do disagree, and most of us would have doubts about the right order of the gravity of crimes. This shows very little. We have the same doubts—and disagreements—in other areas of morality where we are uncertain about which duties are more stringent, and where we differ from others in our ordering of duties. Similarly, utilitarians differ among themselves about goods such that if a group of utilitarians were asked to list goods in their order of goodness we could confidently expect different lists of different goods and of goods listed in different orders. But this would not show that utilitarianism is therefore a theory to be discounted. It shows simply that whatever theory of punishment is adopted, there will be disagreements and uncertainties as to precisely what it dictates. With the utilitarian theory, the uncertainty and doubts arise concerning the assessments of the value of the goods and the determination of which goods should be promoted by punishment. With the retributive theory the difficulties arise in determining the relative gravity of offences; and there, clearly, the appropriate method of seeking to resolve our doubts is neither to look at what punishments are in fact imposed, nor at what punishments will produce the greatest good, but rather to look at the nature of the offence itself.

St. Thomas Aquinas

Whether Vengeance is Lawful *

Vengeance consists in the infliction of a penal evil on one who has sinned. Accordingly, in the matter of vengeance, we must consider the mind of the avenger. For if his intention is directed chiefly to the evil of the person on whom he takes venegance, and rests there, then his vengeance is altogether unlawful: because to take pleasure in another's evil belongs to hatred, which is contrary to the charity whereby we are bound to love all men. Nor is it an excuse that he intends the evil of one who has unjustly inflicted evil on him, as neither is a man excused for hating one that hates him: for a man may not sin against another just because the latter has already sinned against him, since this is to be overcome by evil, which was forbidden by the Apostle, who says (Rom. xii. 21): *Be not overcome by evil, but overcome evil by good.*

If, however, the avenger's intention be directed chiefly to some good, to be obtained by means of the punishment of the person who has sinned (for instance that the sinner may amend, or at least that he may be restrained and others be not disturbed, that justice may be upheld, and God honored), then vengeance may be lawful, provided other due circumstances be observed.

* St. Thomas Aquinas, *Summa Theologica* (New York: Benziger, Inc., 1947), II, part 2–2, quest. 108, first article.

K. G. Armstrong

The Right to Punish *

Before we leave the question of penalty-fixing it is worth asking why it should be so often thought that Retributive theories in this area are necessarily barbarous. The charge springs from the misconception, which I mentioned before, that there is only one such theory—the lex talionis. In fact, all that a Retributive theory of penalty-fixing needs to say to deserve the name is that there should be a proportion between the severity of the crime and the severity of the punishment. It sets an upper limit to the punishment, suggests what is due. But the 'repayment' (so to speak) need not be in kind; indeed in some cases it could not be. What would the lex talionis prescribe for a blind man who blinded someone else? Even in those cases where repayment in kind of violent crime is possible there is no reason why we should not substitute a more civilized equivalent punishment; the scale of equivalent punishments will, of course, vary from society to society. There is also no reason, having got some idea of the permissible limits of a man's punishment from Retributive considerations, why we should not be guided in our choice of the form of the penalty by Deterrent and Reformatory considerations. . . .

A vital point here is that justice gives the appropriate authority the right to punish offenders up to some limit, but one is not necessarily and invariably obliged to punish to the limit of justice. Similarly, if I lend a man money I have a right, in justice, to have it returned; but if I choose not to take it back I have not done anything unjust. I cannot claim more than is owed to me but I am free to claim less, or even to claim nothing. For a variety of reasons (amongst them the hope of reforming the criminal) the appropriate authority may choose to punish a man less than it is entitled to, but it is never just to punish a man more than he deserves.

* K. G. Armstrong, "The Retributivist Hits Back," Mind, 70 (1961), pp. 486–87. Reprinted by permission of the author and D. W. Hamlyn, the editor of Mind.

A. C. Ewing

On "Retributivism" *

It seems to me that Armstrong's defence [1] of the retributive theory can only be described as an evacuation. He reduces the theory to the negative conditions that a man should not be punished unless he is guilty and even if guilty should not be punished excessively out of proportion to the offence. These principles also seem evident to me, but I think that more can be said by way of explanation of them and it is far less clear that a utilitarian explanation is not available than he thinks. But I must first point out that his form of the retributive theory provides no positive reason for punishment at all but merely declares that there is an insuperable objection against punishment unless a certain condition (guilt) is satisfied to an extent proportionate to the punishment. It does not make it a duty in itself or even a prima facie duty to punish. It is still for him only a duty if it serves a utilitarian purpose. The theory is really only utilitarianism with one *vital* reservation supposed not to be justifiable on utilitarian grounds. Thus understood the "retributive theory" is no doubt not open to most of the criticism I and others have brought, which has force only against those who suppose it to be an end in itself that an offender should be made to suffer in proportion to his deserts. Incidentally, the retributive definition, "Punishment is the infliction of pain, by an appropriate authority, on a person because he is guilty of a crime" is ambiguous. If the "because" clause signifies the ultimate reason, then it implies that we ought to punish a man just because he has done wrong and not for the sake of consequences i.e., that the punishment of the guilty is an end in itself; if it is intended to be compatible with "because" not signifying an ultimate

* A. C. Ewing, "Armstrong on the Retributive Theory," *Mind*, 72 (1963), pp. 121-24. Reprinted by permission of the author and D. W. Hamlyn, the editor of *Mind*.
1. *Mind* Oct. 1961 vol. LXX p. 471 ff.

reason, it is compatible with utilitarianism. Armstrong holds that it gives a necessary condition but not any positive reason, I think, let alone a sufficient reason for punishment. Whether we call his theory retributive or not is a question of terminology, but it is certainly not what I and most others who have criticized the "retributive theory" have understood by it, and if so his use of the term seems liable to lead to dangerous confusions. But I agree with what he calls a "retributive definition" of punishment, provided this is not taken to imply that retribution is to be regarded as a positive ultimate reason for punishment. I further agree with him that you cannot reconcile utilitarianism with justice by merely saying that, if the man punished is innocent, it is not really punishment. If we heard an innocent man had been sentenced for the good of others, such an argument, as far as it goes, would enable us to say only—The judge has been incorrect in his terminology, he ought not to have called it a "punishment"—not that it is in any way worse than if a guilty man had been condemned with the same supposedly good consequences. I should, however, prefer not to define "punishment" as "the infliction of pain on a man . . . because he is guilty" but as "the infliction of pain because he is supposed guilty". Then we can properly speak of punishing the innocent.

But I think the utilitarian could do very much more than Armstrong admitted to explain why it is wrong to be unjust. He argues that on the deterrent theory cruel punishments would be justified as more effective deterrents and that we may deter others by punishing the innocent, and that on the reformatory theory it might be justifiable to punish people before they had committed any crime at all. But no utilitarian worth his salt would hold that we need not consider the indirect harm done by punishing the innocent or the sufferings of people who were punished excessively but should just concentrate on the deterrent and reformatory effects and ignore all other results. There are very obvious utilitarian reasons why we should avoid punishing people not guilty of definite offences defined by law or have recourse to a reign of terror. The miserable insecurity produced by such unjust punishment has been sufficiently exemplified in certain states in the last years as well as in earlier history. But, it may be said, this will only apply if such action is taken frequently; there may well be occasional cases where the punishment of the innocent is useful. But the utilitarian has still a possible reply. He may admit that there are cases where this is so but deny that any human authority could be trusted to decide which these cases are. It is all very well to say that the innocence of the man punished might be kept secret, but could the authorities ever be quite sure that they would succeed in doing this (unless at least they imposed an extreme dictatorship, which would be open to other objections)? And, if they recognised that they might punish the innocent sometimes, would not there be a great danger of their going too far in this practice? Against the tangible advantages that they saw or might think they saw have to be set a number of considerations which are very important and yet hardly susceptible of measurement—the psychological effects of being punished when one knew oneself innocent, the risk of discovery, the effects on the relatives of the person punished, the bad psychological effects on the punisher. As with most cases of adopting means generally condemned morally in order to produce good results, we should realize that besides any definitely foreseeable results there is reason to think that the unforseeable results of such action will tend to be bad rather than good and these ought to be allowed for. I think this generalization is supported by the empirical evidence. But an authority which adopted the practice of making exceptions when it thought more good could be done by this would be liable to be biased in favour of the apparent concrete advantages as against these intangibles because they are easier to be reckoned with, and in any case it would be so hard to decide when the good consequences outweighed the bad, and such a power would be so liable to abuse that it might well be argued on purely utilitarian grounds that it would be best to take it as an absolutely unbreakable rule that the innocent ought never to be punished. For, although there probably are cases where it would do more good than harm to punish an innocent man, authorities who did not make it a general law never to punish the innocent, but allowed the making of exceptions on the ground of consequences, would be likely to do more harm by punishing innocent men when the consequences were really bad, although thought good, than authorities who stuck to the general law did by not punishing innocent people in the rare cases when the consequences would have been good.

Or is this going a little too far? Miss Anscombe expressed the greatest horror at the normal philosophers who suggested that it might ever be justifiable to condemn an innocent man to death even to avoid a war, but suppose the question were not whether he was to be put to death but whether he was to be given a month's imprisonment (or fined £20)? Suppose this were all that was needed to mollify a mad dictator who would otherwise declare war? If we admitted that in such a case it might be right to punish the innocent, that would be sufficient to make us give up the absoluteness of the principle and substitute "almost always" for "always." But this would only show that everybody had in certain cases to agree with the utilitarian.

As for excessive punishment inflicted on deterrent grounds, the pain caused may easily outweigh the evils of the crimes prevented and, in general, over-severe punishments have other detrimental effects besides the sheer suffering. They make people feel sympathy with the suffering offender rather than with the law, they make juries reluctant to convict, and they tend to the brutalization of society. Society may pay too great a price for the diminution of crimes.

The utilitarian may further urge that the reformatory function of punishment, at any rate, is essentially and not only incidentally connected with its justice. For how can punishment as such reform? Only by making a man realize more vividly the wrongness of what he has been doing. A punishment functions as a way of telling a man more emphatically than by mere words that he has done very wrong, and this has no reformatory point if the man has not done wrong. Offenders can, of course, be reformed by other means, e.g., psychological treatment while they are in prison, but, as McTaggart said, we must distinguish between reforming a man while he is being punished and reforming him by punishment. Certain psychological treatments may be unpleasant, but that does not make them punishments, and some may be undesirable because they violate the rights of individuals, but that does not make them unjust punishments. Deterrence is connected more loosely with justice and may occur without it (generally with disastrous effects), but even the deterrent force of punishment commonly depends a good deal on its being considered a disgrace because it implies that the man punished has acted very wrongly.

But I am not satisfied that the objection to unjust punishment lies simply in its effects. Suppose it could be strictly proved that, everything taken into account, the consequences of punishing a particular innocent man would be better than the consequences of acquitting him, I should not necessary think it right to punish him. This is not necessarily incompatible with utilitarianism ("ideal"), though it is with hedonism, because the utilitarian may include among things bad in themselves certain actions and attitudes of mind or will. The action and the attitude of mind inseparable from it might be intrinsically evil, although its effects in a particular instance were on the whole rather good than bad. Why should this be? It is not merely or mainly because it is a case of doing undeserved harm to a man. We must of course avoid harming people as far as possible, but there are many instances where laws harm the interests of some people for the sake of others. It is not unjust or terribly deplorable that the well-to-do have to pay extra taxes for the benefit of the poor, though, unless we say it is wrong to have plenty of money at all, this harm is not deserved by previous wrong-doing. It is not unjust to accept a man's offer to volunteer for a hopelessly dangerous but necessary job in war, though he has not thereby deserved death or the extreme risk of death. Thus what makes punishment of the innocent so wrong seems to be not mainly the fact that it is undeserved, but the pretence of guilt. This brings one back to Quinton's (and my) suggestion that the evil consists in a lying imputation of guilt, and this is certainly a very important, but I should not be prepared to say the only, factor. There is also the breach of faith involved in the violation of the tacit understanding that people will not be punished if they obey the laws. To inflict the worse kinds of harm on an innocent man against his will for the sake of others may be said grossly to violate a principle which perhaps must be taken as ultimate, i.e. the principle which Kant expressed by saying that a man ought never to be treated as a mere means, but it is not clear why this should not be the case even if the man is guilty. I do not know whether there are any other factors involved. Ross (who might have been mentioned, since Armstrong adopts a very similar view to his) also invokes the principle that it is good in itself that a man's happiness or unhappiness should be in proportion to his moral goodness or badness, but for the reasons I have given above I think we can maintain that the punishment of the innocent is intrinsically evil without accepting this (properly retributive) principle, of the truth of which I am very doubtful indeed. But I shall not discuss this matter, for I do not think Armstrong either accepts it as a reason for punishment.

D. Daiches Raphael

Justice *

... I agree with the utilitarian theory of punishment to the extent of thinking that where there is an obligation to punish, the obligation arises from utility. The strength of the so-called retributive (or, as I prefer to call it, the desert) theory of punishment lies, not in the justification of a positive obligation to punish the guilty, but in the protection of innocence. The utilitarian theory, taken alone, requires us to say, with Samuel Butler's Erewhonians, that sickness is a crime which deserves the punishment of medicine. It also requires us to say, when 'it is expedient that one man should die for the people,' that he deserves this as a punishment. It is here that common sense protests against the 'injustice' of utilitarianism, and it is here that the 'retributive' theory of punishment has greatest force. Punishment is permissible only if it is deserved. But this does not of itself give rise to an obligation to punish. An obligation to inflict punishment, where punishment is permitted by desert, arises from the social utility of its infliction. The desert permits this socially useful action to be taken although it means pain to the particular person concerned. Where there is no guilt, the infliction of pain on a particular person may still be socially useful, but the claim of social utility is opposed by the claim of the individual to be treated as an 'end-in-himself' and not merely as a means to the ends of society. Where, however, a person is guilty of having wilfully done wrong, he has thereby forfeited part of his claim to be treated as an end-in-himself; in acting as a nonmoral being he leaves it open to his fellows to use him as such.[1] Such forfeit of his claim not to be pained does not of itself give rise

* D. Daiches Raphael, Moral Judgement (London: George Allen & Unwin Ltd., 1955), pp. 70–73, reprinted by permission of the author and Shaw Maclean, London.

1. Cf. W. G. Maclagan, "Punishment and Retribution," Philosophy, July, 1939, section v.

to an obligation to pain him, for his ill-desert consists in the removal, not the creation, of a claim with its corresponding obligation. The guilt does not constitute, or give rise to, a claim on the part of the guilty person to be punished i.e., an obligation on the part of others to punish him. It removes, to the degree to which he has infringed another's rights, his normal claim not to be pained; i.e., it removes, to that degree, the obligations of others not to pain him. Where there is a positive obligation to punish him, this is the obligation to the public at large to safeguard their secuirty, and the corresponding claim is the claim of the public to have their security safeguarded.

This obligation to, or claim of, the public at large, exists of course at all times, and if the fulfilment of it involves pain for an innocent individual it still has its force. But the claim of the public in such circumstances conflicts with the claim of the individual not to be pained, to be treated as an end, and sometimes the one claim, sometimes the other, is thought to be paramount in the circumstances. If it should be thought necessary to override the claim of the individual for the sake of the claim of society, our decision is coloured by compunction, which we express by saying that the claim of justice has to give way to that of utility. Where the individual has been guilty of deliberate wrongdoing, however, his claim not to be pained is thought to be removed; there is held to be no conflict of claims now, no moral *obstat* [2] raised by justice to the fulfilment of the claim of utility. This thought is expressed by saying that the individual 'deserves' his pain, and the pain is called 'punishment', which is simply a way of saying that in this situation the infliction of pain, for the sake of social utility, involves no trespass on the claims of justice, no conflict between utility and justice. What is called 'punishment' is not a different sort of *fact* from any other pain inflicted for utilitarian purposes; it receives a different *name* to express the thought that the pain is inflicted in circumstances where it commits no offence against justice. Justice is 'satisfied' by the 'punishment,' for justice has not, in the circumstances of guilt, a countervailing claim that would have been breached by pursuing the path of utility.

2. There is always the weaker *obstat* of unfittingness in the infliction of pain. My point is that the *obstat* of a moral claim is not only greater in degree but also different in kind, and the difference of kind is marked by the use of different language.

In giving this interpretation of the saying that 'justice is satisfied by punishment,' I do not imply that the statement has always had the meaning which I am now attributing to it (or rather, recommending for it). Clearly it used to have a more positive meaning. No doubt it originally referred to the satisfaction of the desire for vengeance. My point is that our present moral thinking recoils, as opponents of the retributive theory rightly insist, from justifying punishment by mere retaliation, but at the same time it does give an important place to justice in the idea of punishment. This role of justice, I am suggesting, is the protection of innocence, the raising of a moral *obstat* to the infliction of pain on an innocent individual. Where we think that, despite the moral *obstat* of justice, the pain must be inflicted for the sake of utility, we recognize the claim of justice at least to the extent of using different language. It may be *expedient*, but not just, that one man should die for the people. 'Expediency' then has the a-moral or anti-moral connotation which it bears when 'expediency' is contrasted with 'principle.' But where the victim of expediency is guilty, he has forfeited the claim of justice; now we may speak of his pain as 'punishment', as 'deserved.' Expediency here does not conflict with 'principle', i.e., with justice, but conforms to 'principle.' Not that the punishment is now *required* by justice. The 'principle' that requires the 'punishment' is the principle of safeguarding public security, i.e., expediency itself. Justice does not demand the punishment; justice stands aside, for it is satisfied that its claims raise no obstruction. It does demand *reparation*, where possible, for the person wronged, and thereby lays an obligation on the wrongdoer toward the person he has wronged. But it lays no obligation on others to *punish* the wrongdoer. It permits the punishment by withdrawing its protection against the claims of expediency. The obligation to punish comes from expediency.

Of course, expediency does not become 'principle' only when justice stands aside. The claim of social utility is always a valid claim. It is the claim of the members of society in general not to be harmed. In denying earlier that there is a moral obligation to produce good as such, I was not denying the partial truth of hedonistic utilitarianism. There is an obligation to relieve and to prevent pain in others. When I say that the utility of punishment gives rise to an obligation, the obligation is to the members of society who will thereby be protected from harm. . . .

W. D. Ross

Punishment *

In connection with the discussion of rights it is proper to consider a question which has always interested and usually puzzled moralists, and which forms a crucial example for the testing of moral theories—the question of punishment. A utilitarian theory, whether of the hedonistic or of the 'ideal' kind, if it justifies punishment at all, is bound to justify it solely on the ground of the effects it produces. The suffering of pain by the person who is punished is thought to be in itself a bad thing, and the bringing of this bad thing into the world is held to need justification, and to receive it only from the fact that the effects are likely to be so much better than those that would follow from his nonpunishment as to outweigh the evil of his pain. The effects usually pointed to are those of deterrence and of reformation. In principle, then, the punishment of a guilty person is treated by utilitarians as not different in kind from the imposition of inconvenience, say by quarantine regulations, on innocent individuals for the good of the community. Or again, if a state found to be prevalent some injury to itself or to its members that had not been legislated against, and proceeded to punish the offenders, its action would in principle be justified by utilitarians in the same way as it punishment of offenders against the law is justified by them, viz., by the good of the community. No doubt the state would have greater difficulty in justifying its action, for such action would produce bad consequences which the punishment of law-breakers does not. But the difference would be only in degree. Nay more, a government which found some offence against the law prevalent, and in its inability to find the offenders punished innocent people on the strength of manufactured evidence, would still be able to justify its action on the same general principle as before.

*W. D. Ross, *The Right and the Good* (Oxford: Clarendon Press, 1965), pp. 56–64. Reprinted by permission of the publisher.

Plain men, and even perhaps most people who have reflected on moral questions, are likely to revolt against a theory which involves such consequences, and to exclaim that there is all the difference in the world between such action and the punishment of offenders against the law. They feel the injustice of such action by the state, and are ready to say, in the words imputed to them by Mr. Bradley: 'Punishment is punishment, only when it is deserved. We pay the penalty because we owe it, and for no other reason; and if punishment is inflicted for any other reason whatever than because it is merited by wrong, it is a gross immorality, a crying injustice, an abominable crime, and not what it pretends to be. We may have regard for whatever considerations we please—our own convenience, the good of society, the benefit of the offender; we are fools, and worse, if we fail to do so. Having once the right to punish, we may modify the punishment according to the useful and the pleasant; but these are external to the matter, they cannot give us a right to punish, and nothing can do that but criminal desert.' [1]

There is one form of utilitarian view which differs in an important respect from that above ascribed to utilitarians. Professor Moore admits the possibility, which follows from his doctrine of organic unities, that punishment may not need to be justified merely by its after-effects. He points out [2] that it may well be the case that though crime is one bad thing and pain another, the union of the two in the same person may be a less evil than crime unpunished, and might even be a positive good. And to this extent, while remaining perfectly consistent with his own type of utilitarianism, he joins hands with intuitionists most of whom, at any rate, would probably hold that the combination of crime and punishment is a lesser evil than unpunished crime.

Most intuitionists would perhaps take the view that there is a fundamental and underivative duty to reward the virtuous and to punish the vicious. I am inclined to diverge from this view. Two things seem to me to be clear: that we have a prima facie duty to do this, and that a state of affairs in which the good are happy and the bad unhappy is better than one in which the good are unhappy and the bad happy. Now if the first of these is an underivative fact,

1. *Ethical Studies*, ed. 2, 26–7.   2. *Principia Ethica*, 214.

the two facts are logically unconnected. For it can be an underivative fact only if the intuitionist view is true, and if that view is true the superiority of the one state of affairs over the other cannot follow from the duty of producing it, since on the intuitionist view there are duties other than the duty of producing good. But an intuitionist may with propriety perform the reverse derivation; he may derive the prima facie duty of reward and punishment from the superiority of the state of affairs produced, since he may—and, as I think, must—admit that if a state of affairs is better than its alternatives there is a prima facie duty to produce it if we can. The duty of reward and punishment seems to me to be in this way derivative. It can be subsumed under the duty of producing as much good as we can; though it must be remembered that the good to be produced in this case is very different from the other goods we recognize (say virtue, knowledge, and pleasure), consisting as it does in a certain relative arrangement of virtue, vice, pleasure, and pain.

But if we hold that there is this duty, it must be admitted that it is one which it is very difficult for us to see our way to performing, since we know so little about the degrees of virtue and vice, and of happiness and unhappiness, as they occur in our fellow men. And in particular there are two grave objections to holding that the principle of punishing the vicious, for the sake of doing so, is that on which the state should proceed in its bestowal of punishments.

(1) What we perceive to be good is a condition of things in which the total pleasure enjoyed by each person in his life as a whole is proportional to his virtue similarly taken as a whole. Now it is by no means clear that we should help to bring about this end by punishing particular offences in proportion to their moral badness. Any attempt to bring about such a state of affairs should take account of the whole character of the persons involved, as manifested in their life taken as a whole, and of the happiness enjoyed by them throughout their life taken as a whole, and it should similarly take account of the virtue taken as a whole, and of the happiness taken as a whole, of each of the other members of the community, and should seek to bring about the required adjustments. In the absence of such a view of the whole facts, the criminals that a retributive theory of state punishment would call on us to punish for the sake of doing so may well be persons who are more sinned against than sinning, and may be, quite

apart from our intervention, already enjoying less happiness than a perfectly fair distribution would allow them. The offences which the state legislates against are only a small part of the wrong acts which are being done every day, and a system which punishes not all wrong acts, but only those which have been forbidden by law, and does not attempt to reward all good acts—such an occasional and almost haphazard system of intervention does not hold out any good hope of promoting the perfect proportionment of happiness to virtue. Nor would it be in the least practicable for the state to attempt the thorough review of the merit and the happiness of all its members, which alone would afford a good hope of securing this end.

(2) Even if it were practicable, it is by no means clear that it is the business of the state to aim at this end. Such a view belongs, I think, to an outworn view of the state, one which identifies the state with the whole organization of the community. In contrast to this, we have come to look upon the state as the organization of the community for a particular purpose, that of the protection of the most important rights of individuals, those without which a reasonably secure and comfortable life is impossible; and to leave the promotion of other good ends to the efforts of individuals and of other organizations, such as churches, trade unions, learned and artistic societies, clubs. Now it cannot, I think, be maintained that the apportionment of happiness to merit is one of the essential conditions to the living of a reasonably secure and comfortable life. Life has gone on for centuries being lived with reasonable security and comfort though states have never achieved or even attempted with any degree of resolution to effect this apportionment. And in fact for the state to make such an attempt would seriously interfere with its discharge of its proper work. Its proper work is that of protecting rights. Now rights are (as we have seen) rights to be treated in certain ways and not to be treated in certain ways from certain motives; what the state has to take account of, therefore, is not morally bad actions, but wrong acts, and it has to take account of them in such a way as to diminish the chance of their repetition. And this attempt would only be interfered with if the state were at the same time trying to effect a proportionment of happiness to moral worth in its members. The latter task, involving as it would a complete review of the merit and happiness of all its members, would involve leaving the punishment for each offence un-

determined by law, and to be determined in the light of all the circumstances of each case; and punishment so completely undetermined in advance would be quite ineffective as a protector of rights.

But to hold that the state has no duty of retributive punishment is not necessarily to adopt a utilitarian view of punishment. It seems possible to give an account of the matter which retains elements in punishment other than that of expediency, without asserting that the state has any duty properly defined as the duty of punishing moral guilt. The essential duty of the state is to protect the most fundamental rights of individuals. Now, rights of any human being are correlative to duties incumbent on the owner of rights, or, to put it otherwise, to rights owned by those against whom he has rights; and the main element in any one's right to life or liberty or property is extinguished by his failure to respect the corresponding right in others.[3] There is thus a distinction in kind which we all in fact recognize, but which utilitarianism cannot admit, between the punishment of a person who has invaded the rights of others and the infliction of pain or restraint on one who has not. The state ought, in its effort to maintain the rights of innocent persons, to take what steps are necessary to prevent violations of these rights; and the offender, by violating the life or liberty or property of another, has lost his own right to have his life, liberty, or property respected, so that the state has no prima facie duty to spare him, as it has a prima facie duty to spare the innocent. It is morally at liberty to injure him as he has injured others, or to inflict any lesser injury on him, or to spare him, exactly as consideration both of the good of the community and of his own good requires. If, on the other hand, a man has respected the rights of others, there is a strong and distinctive objection to the state's inflicting any penalty on him with a view to the good of the community or even to his own good. The interests of the society may sometimes be so deeply involved as to make it right to punish an innocent man 'that the whole nation perish not.' But then the prima facie duty of consulting the general interest has proved more obligatory than the perfectly distinct prima facie duty of respecting the rights of those who have respected the rights of others.

This is, I believe, how most thoughtful people feel about the

3. Cf. pp. 54–5.

affixing of penalties to the invasion of the rights of others. They may have lost any sense they or their ancestors had that the state should inflict retributive punishment for the sake of doing so, but they feel that there is nevertheless a difference of kind between the community's right to punish people for offences against others, and any right it may have to inconvenience or injure innocent people in the public interest. This arises simply from the fact that the state has a prima facie duty not to do the latter and no such duty not to do the former.

We can, I think, help ourselves towards an understanding of the problem by distinguishing two stages which are not usually kept apart in discussions of it. The infliction of punishment by the state does not, or should not, come like a bolt from the blue. It is preceded by the making of a law in which a penalty is affixed to a crime; or by the custom of the community and the decisions of judges a common law gradually grows up in which a penalty is so affixed. We must, I think, distinguish this stage, that of the affixing of the penalty, from that of its infliction, and we may ask on what principles the state or its officials should act at each stage.

At the earlier stage a large place must be left for considerations of expediency. We do not claim that laws should be made against all moral offences, or even against all offences by men against their neighbours. Legislators should consider such questions as whether a given law would be enforced if it were made, and whether a certain type of offence is important enough to make it worth while to set the elaborate machinery of the law at work against it, or is better left to be punished by the injured person or by public opinion. But even at this stage there is one respect in which the notion of justice, as something quite distinct from expediency, plays a part in our thoughts about the matter. We feel sure that if a law is framed against a certain type of offence the punishment should be proportional to the offence. However strong the temptation to commit a certain type of offence may be, and however severe the punishment would therefore have to be in order to be a successful deterrent, we feel certain that it is unjust that very severe penalties should be affixed to very slight offenses. It is difficult, no doubt, to define the nature of the relation which the punishment should bear to the crime. We do not see any *direct* moral relation to exist between wrongdoing and suffering so that we may say directly, such and such an offence deserves so much suffering, neither more nor less. But we do think that the injury to be inflicted on the offender should be not much greater than that which he has inflicted on another. Ideally, from this point of view, it should be no greater. For he has lost his prima facie rights to life, liberty, or property, only in so far as these rested on an explict or implicit undertaking to respect the corresponding rights in others, and in so far as he has failed to respect those rights. But laws must be stated in general terms, to cover a variety of cases, and they cannot in advance affix punishments which shall never be greater than the injury inflicted by the wrongdoer. We are therefore content with an approximation to what is precisely just. At the same time we recognize that this, while it is a prima facie duty, is not the only prima facie duty of the legislator; and that, as in the selection of offences to be legislated against, so in the fixing of the penalty, he must consider expediency, and may make the penalty more or less severe as it dictates. His action should, in fact, be guided by regard to the prima facie duty of injuring wrongdoers only to the extent that they have injured others, and also to the prima facie duty of promoting the general interest. And I think that we quite clearly recognize these as distinct and specifically different elements in the moral situation. To say this is not to adopt a compromise between the intuitionist and the utilitarian view; for it can fairly be claimed that one of the duties we apprehend intuitively is that of promoting the general interest so far as we can.

When the law has been promulgated and an offence against it committed, a new set of considerations emerges. The administrator of the law has not to consider what is the just punishment for the offence, nor what is the expedient punishment, except when the law has allowed a scale of penalties within which he can choose. When that is the case, he has still to have regard to the same considerations as arose at the earlier stage. But that, when the penalty fixed by law is determinate, this and no other should be inflicted, and that, when a scale of penalties is allowed, no penalty above or below the scale should be inflicted, depends on a prima facie duty that did not come in at the earlier stage, viz. that of fidelity to promise. Directly, the law is not a promise: it is a threat to the guilty, and a threat is not a promise. The one is an undertaking to do or give to the promisee something mutually understood to be advantageous to him; the other, an announcement of intention to do to him something mutually understood to be disadvantageous to him. Punishment is sometimes justified on the ground that to fail to punish is to break faith with the offender. It is said that he has a right to be punished, and that not to punish him is not to treat him with due respect as a moral agent responsible for his actions, but as if he could not have helped doing them. This is, however, not a point of view likely to be adopted by a criminal who escapes punishment, and seems to be a somewhat artificial way of looking at the matter, and to ignore the difference between a threat and a promise.

But while the law is not a promise to the criminal, it is a promise to the injured person and his friends, and to society. It promises to the former, in certain cases, compensation, and always the satisfaction of knowing that the offender has not gone scot-free, and it promises to the latter this satisfaction and the degree of protection against further offences which punishment gives. At the same time the whole system of law is a promise to the members of the community that if they do not commit any of the prohibited acts they will not be punished.

Thus to our sense that prima facie the state has a right to punish the guilty, over and above the right which it has, in the last resort, of inflicting injury on any of its members when the public interest sufficiently demands it, there is added the sense that promises should prima facie be kept; and it is the combination of these considerations that accounts for the moral satisfaction that is felt by the community when the guilty are punished, and the moral indignation that is felt when the guilty are not punished, and still more when the innocent are. There may be cases in which the prima facie duty of punishing the guilty, and even that of not punishing the innocent, may have to give way to that of promoting the public interest. But these are not cases of a wider expediency overriding a narrower, but of one prima facie duty being more obligatory than two others different in kind from it and from one another.

H. L. A. Hart

Principles of
Punishment *

1. Introductory

The main object of this paper is to provide a framework for the discussion of the mounting perplexities which now surround the institution of criminal punishment, and to show that any morally tolerable account of this institution must exhibit it as a compromise between distinct and partly conflicting principles.

General interest in the topic of punishment has never been greater than it is at present and I doubt if the public discussion of it has ever been more confused. The interest and the confusion are both in part due to relatively modern scepticism about two elements which have figured as essential parts of the traditionally opposed 'theories' of punishment. On the one hand, the old Benthamite confidence in fear of the penalties threatened by the law as a powerful deterrent, has waned with the growing realization that the part played by calculation of any sort in anti-social behaviour has been exaggerated. On the other hand a cloud of doubt has settled over the keystone of 'retributive' theory. Its advocates can no longer speak with the old confidence that statements of the form 'This man who has broken the law could have kept it' had a univocal or agreed meaning; or where scepticism does not attach to the *meaning* of this form of statement, it has shaken the confidence that we are generally able to distinguish the

* H. L. A. Hart, "Prolegomenon to the Principles of Punishment," in *Punishment and Responsibility* (Oxford: Clarendon Press, 1968), pp. 1–13. The original version of this essay was the 1959 Inaugural Address to the Aristotelian Society, pub. in *Proc. Arist. Soc.*, 60 (1959–60). Reprinted by permission of the author and the publisher.

cases where a statement of this form is true from those where it is not.[1]

Yet quite apart from the uncertainty engendered by these fundamental doubts, which seem to call in question the accounts given of the efficacy, and the morality of punishment by all the old competing theories, the public utterances of those who conceive themselves to be expounding, as plain men for other plain men, orthodox or common-sense principles (untouched by modern psychological doubts) are uneasy. Their words often sound as if the authors had not fully grasped their meaning or did not intend the words to be taken quite literally. A glance at the parliamentary debates or the *Report of the Royal Commission on Capital Punishment* [2] shows that many are now troubled by the suspicion that the view that there is just one supreme value or objective (e.g. Deterrence, Retribution or Reform) in terms of which *all* questions about the justification of punishment are to be answered, is somehow wrong; yet, from what is said on such occasions no clear account of what the different values or objectives are, or how they fit together in the justification of punishment, can be extracted.[3]

No one expects judges or statesmen occupied in the business of sending people to the gallows or prison, or in making (or unmaking) laws which enable this to be done, to have much time for philosophical discussion of the principles which make it morally tolerable to do these things. A judicial bench is not and should not be a professorial chair. Yet what is said in public debates about punishment by those specially concerned with it as judges or legislators is important. Few are likely to be more circumspect, and if what they say seems, as

1. See Barbara Wootton *Social Science and Social Pathology* (1959) for a comprehensive modern statement of these doubts.

2. (1953) Cmd. 8932.

3. In the Lords' debate in July 1956 the Lord Chancellor agreed with Lord Denning that 'the ultimate justification of any punishment is not that it is a deterrent but that it is the emphatic denunciation by the community of a crime' yet also said that 'the real crux' of the question at issue is whether capital punishment is a uniquely effective deterrent. See 198 *H. L. Deb* (5th July) 576, 577, 596 (1956). In his article, 'An Approach to the Problems of Punishment,' *Philosophy* (1958), Mr. S. I. Benn rightly observes of Lord Denning's view that denunciation does not imply the deliberate imposition of suffering which is the feature needing justification (p. 328, n. 1).

it often does, unclear, one-sided and easily refutable by pointing to some aspect of things which they have overlooked, it is likely that in our inherited ways of talking or thinking about punishment there is some persistent drive towards an over-simplification of multiple issues which require separate consideration. To counter this drive what is most needed is *not* the simple admission that instead of a single value or aim (Deterrence, Retribution, Reform or any other) a plurality of different values and aims should be given as a conjunctive answer to some *single* question concerning the justification of punishment. What is needed is the realization that different principles (each of which may in a sense be called a 'justification') are relevant at different points in any morally acceptable account of punishment. What we should look for are answers to a number of different questions such as: What justifies the general practice of punishment? To whom may punishment be applied? How severely may we punish? In dealing with these and other questions concerning punishment we should bear in mind that in this, as in most other social institutions, the pursuit of one aim may be qualified by or provide an opportunity, not to be missed, for the pursuit of others. Till we have developed this sense of the complexity of punishment (and this prolegomenon aims only to do this) we shall be in no fit state to assess the extent to which the whole institution has been eroded by, or needs to be adapted to, new beliefs about the human mind.

2. Justifying Aims and Principles of Distribution

There is, I think, an analogy worth considering between the concept of punishment and that of property. In both cases we have to do with a social institution of which the centrally important form is a structure of *legal* rules, even if it would be dogmatic to deny the names of punishment or property to the similar though more rudimentary rule-regulated practices within groups such as a family, or a school, or in customary societies whose customs may lack some of the standard or salient features of law (e.g. legislation, organized sanctions, courts). In both cases we are confronted by a complex institution presenting different inter-related features calling for separate explanation; or, if the morality of the institution is challenged, for separate justification. In both cases failure to distinguish separate questions or attempting to answer them all by reference to a single principle ends in confusion. Thus in the case of property we should distinguish between the question of the *definition* of property, the question why and in what circumstance it is a *good* institution to maintain, and the questions in what ways individuals may become *entitled* to acquire property and *how much* they should be allowed to acquire. These we may call questions of *Definition*, *General Justifying Aim*, and *Distribution* with the last subdivided into questions of *Title* and *Amount*. It is salutary to take some classical exposition of the idea of property, say Locke's chapter 'Of Property' in the *Second Treatise*,[4] and to observe how much darkness is spread by the use of a single notion (in this case 'the labour of [a man's] body and the work of his hands') to answer all these different questions which press upon us when we reflect on the institution of property. In the case of punishment the beginning of wisdom (though by no means its end) is to distinguish similar questions and confront them separately.

(a) Definition

Here I shall simply draw upon the recent admirable work scattered through English philosophical [5] journals and add to it only an admonition of my own against the abuse of definition in the philosopical discussion of punishment. So with Mr. Benn and Professor Flew I shall define the standard or central case of 'punishment' in terms of five elements:

(i) It must involve pain or other consequences normally considered unpleasant.
(ii) It must be for an offence against legal rules.
(iii) It must be of an actual or supposed offender for his offence.
(iv) It must be intentionally administered by human beings other than the offender.

4. Chapter V.
5. K. Baier, "Is Punishment Retributive?," *Analysis* (1955), p. 25. A. Flew, "The Justification of Punishment," *Philosophy* (1954), p. 291. S. I. Benn, *op. cit.*, pp. 325–6.

(v) It must be imposed and administered by an authority constituted by a legal system against which the offence is committed.

In calling this the standard or central case of punishment I shall relegate to the position of sub-standard or secondary cases the following among many other possibilities:

(a) Punishments for breaches of legal rules imposed or administered otherwise than by officials (decentralised sanctions).

(b) Punishments for breaches of nonlegal rules or orders (punishments in a family or school).

(c) Vicarious or collective punishment of some member of a social group for actions done by others without the former's authorization, encouragement, control or permission.

(d) Punishment of persons (otherwise than under [c]) who neither are in fact nor supposed to be offenders.

The chief importance of listing these substandard cases is to prevent the use of what I shall call the 'definitional stop' in discussions of punishment. This is an abuse of definition especially tempting when use is made of conditions (ii) and (iii) of the standard case in arguing against the utilitarian claim that the practice of punishment is justified by the beneficial consequences resulting from the observance of the laws which it secures. Here the stock 'retributive' argument [6] is: If *this* is the justification of punishment, why not apply it, when it pays to do so, to those innocent of any crime, chosen at random, or to the wife and children of the offender? And here the wrong reply is: *That*, by definition, would not be 'punishment' and it is the justification of punishment which is in issue.[7] Not only will this definitional stop fail to satisfy the advocate of 'Retribution', it would prevent us from investigating the very thing which modern skepticism most calls in question: namely the rational and moral status of our preference for a system of punishment under which

6. A. C. Ewing, *The Morality of Punishment*, D. J. B. Hawkins, *Punishment and Moral Responsibility* (The King's Good Servant, p. 92), J. D. Mabbott, "Punishment," *Mind* (1939), p. 152.

7. Mr. Benn seemed to succumb at times to the temptation to give 'the short answer to the critics of utilitarian theories of punishment—that they are theories of *punishment* not of any sort of technique involving suffering' (*op. cit.*, p. 332). He has since told me that he does not now rely on the definitional stop.

measures painful to individuals are to be taken against them only when they have committed an offence. Why do we prefer this to other forms of social hygiene which we might employ to prevent anti-social behaviour and which we do employ in special circumstances sometimes with reluctance? No account of punishment can afford to dismiss this question with a definition.

(b) The nature of an offence

Before we reach any question of justification we must identify a preliminary question to which the answer is so simple that the question may not appear worth asking; yet it is clear that some curious 'theories' of punishment gain their only plausibility from ignoring it, and others from confusing it with other questions. The question is: Why are certain kinds of action forbidden by law and so made crimes or offences? The answer is: To announce to society that these actions are not to be done and to secure that fewer of them are done. These are the common immediate aims of making any conduct a criminal offence and until we have laws made with these primary aims we shall lack the notion of a 'crime' and so of a 'criminal'. Without recourse to the simple idea that the criminal law sets up, in its rules, standards of behaviour to encourage certain types of conduct and discourage others we cannot distinguish a punishment in the form of a fine from a tax on a course of conduct.[8] This indeed is one grave objection to those theories of law which in the interests of simplicity or uniformity obscure the distinction between primary laws setting standards for behaviour and secondary laws specifying what officials must or may do when they are broken. Such theories insist that all legal rules are 'really' directions to officials to exact 'sanctions' under certain conditions, e.g. if people kill.[9] Yet only if we keep alive the distinction

8. This generally clear distinction may be blurred. Taxes may be imposed to discourage the activities taxed though the law does not announce this as it does when it makes them criminal. Conversely fines payable for some criminal offenses because of a depreciation of currency become so small that they are cheerfully paid and offences are frequent. They are then felt to be mere taxes because the sense is lost that the rule is meant to be taken seriously as a standard of behavior. 9. cf. Kelsen. *General Theory of Law and State* (1945), pp. 30–33, 33–34, 143–4. Law is the primary norm, which stipulates the sanction. . . .' (ibid. 61).

(which such theories thus obscure) between the primary objective of the law in encouraging or discouraging certain kinds of behaviour, and its merely ancillary sanction or remedial steps, can we give sense to the notion of a crime or offence.

It is important however to stress the fact that in thus identifying the immediate aims of the criminal law we have not reached the stage of justification. There are indeed many forms of undesirable behaviour which it would be foolish (because ineffective or too costly) to attempt to inhibit by use of the law and some of these may be better left to educators, trades unions, churches, marriage guidance councils or other nonlegal agencies. Conversely there are some forms of conduct which we believe cannot be effectively inhibited without use of the law. But it is only too plain that in fact the law may make activities criminal which it is morally important to promote and the suppression of these may be quite unjustifiable. Yet confusion between the simple immediate aim of any criminal legislation and the justification of punishment seems to be the most charitable explanation of the claim that punishment is *justified* as an 'emphatic denunciation by the community of a crime'. Lord Denning's dictum that this is the ultimate justification of punishment [10] can be saved from Mr. Benn's criticism, noted above, only if it is treated as a blurred statement of the truth that the aim not of punishment, but of criminal legislation is indeed to denounce certain types of conduct as something not to be practised. Conversely the immediate aim of criminal legislation cannot be any of the things which are usually mentioned as justifying punishment: for until it is settled what conduct is to be legally denounced and discouraged we have not settled from what we are to *deter* people, or who are to be considered *criminals* from whom we are to exact *retribution*, or on whom we are to wreak *vengeance*, or whom we are to *reform*.

Even those who look upon human law as a mere instrument for enforcing 'morality as such' (itself conceived as the law of God or Nature) and who at the stage of justifying punishment wish to appeal not to socially beneficial consequences but simply to the intrinsic value of inflicting suffering on wrongdoers who have disturbed by

10. In evidence to the Royal Commission on Capital Punishment, Cmd. 8932. para. 53 (1953). *Supra*, p. 2, n. 3.

their offence the moral order, would not deny that the aim of criminal legislation is to set up types of behaviour (in this case conformity with a pre-existing moral law) as legal standards of behaviour and to secure conformity with them. No doubt in all communities certain moral offences, e.g., killing, will always be selected for suppression as crimes and it is conceivable that this may be done not to protect human beings from being killed but to save the potential murderer from sin; but it would be paradoxical to look upon the law as designed not to discourage murder at all (even conceived as sin rather than harm) but simply to extract the penalty from the murderer.

(c) General Justifying Aim

I shall not here criticize the intelligibility or consistency or adequacy of those theories that are united in denying that the practice of a system of punishment is justified by its beneficial consequences and claim instead that the main justification of the practice lies in the fact that when breach of the law involves moral guilt the application to the offender of the pain of punishment is itself a thing of value. A great variety of claims of this character, designating 'Retribution' or 'Expiation' or 'Reprobation' as the justifying aim, fall in spite of differences under this rough general description. Though in fact I agree with Mr. Benn [11] in thinking that these all either avoid the question of justification altogether or are in spite of their protestations disguised forms of Utilitarianism, I shall assume that Retribution, defined simply as the application of the pains of punishment to an offender who is morally guilty, may figure among the conceivable justifying aims of a system of punishment. Here I shall merely insist that it is one thing to use the word Retribution *at this point* in an account of the principle of punishment in order to designate the General Justifying Aim of the system, and quite another to use it to secure that to the question 'To whom may punishment be applied?' (the question of Distribution), the answer given is 'Only to an offender for an offense.' Failure to distinguish Retribution as a General Justifying Aim from retribution as the simple insistence that only

11. *Op. cit.*, pp. 326–35.

those who have broken the law—and voluntarily broken it—may be punished, may be traced in many writers: even perhaps in Mr. J. D. Mabbott's [12] otherwise most illuminating essay. We shall distinguish the latter from Retribution in General Aim as 'retribution in Distribution.' Much confusing shadow-fighting between utilitarians and their opponents may be avoided if it is recognized that it is perfectly consistent to assert *both* that the General Justifying Aim of the practice of punishment is its beneficial consequences *and* that the pursuit of this General Aim should be qualified or restricted out of deference to principles of Distribution which require that punishment should be only of an offender for an offence. Conversely it does not in the least follow from the admission of the latter principle of retribution in Distribution that the General Justifying Aim of punishment is Retribution though of course Retribution in General Aim entails retribution in Distribution.

We shall consider later the principles of justice lying at the root of retribution in Distribution. Meanwhile it is worth observing that both the old-fashioned Retributionist (in General Aim) and the most modern skeptic often make the same (and, I think, wholly mistaken) assumption that sense can only be made of the restrictive principle that punishment be applied only to an offender for an offense if the General Justifying Aim of the practice of punishment is Retribution. The skeptic consequently imputes to all systems of punishment (when they are restricted by the principle of retribution in Distribution) all the irrationality he finds in the idea of Retribution as a General Justifying Aim; conversely the advocates of the latter think the admission of retribution in Distribution is a refutation of the utilitarian claim that the social consequences of punishment are its Justifying Aim.

The most general lesson to be learned from this extends beyond the topic of punishment. It is, that in relation to any social institution, after stating what general aim or value its maintenance fosters we should enquire whether there are any and if so what principles limiting the unqualified pursuit of that aim or value. Just because the pursuit of any single social aim always has its restrictive qualifier, our

12. *Op. cit. supra*, n. 6. It is not always quite clear what he considers a 'retributive' theory to be.

main social institutions always possess a plurality of features which can only be understood as a compromise between partly discrepant principles. This is true even of relatively minor legal institutions like that of a contract. In general this is designed to enable individuals to give effect to their wishes to create structures of legal rights and duties, and so to change, in certain ways, their legal position. Yet at the same time there is need to protect those who, in good faith, understand a verbal offer made to them to mean what it would ordinarily mean, accept it, and then act on the footing that a valid contract has been concluded. As against them, it would be unfair to allow the other party to say that the words he used in his verbal offer or the interpretation put on them did not express his real wishes or intention. Hence principles of 'estoppel' or doctrines of the 'objective sense' of a contract are introduced to prevent this and to qualify the principle that the law enforces contracts in order to give effect to the joint wishes of the contracting parties.

(d) Distribution

This as in the case of property has two aspects (i) Liability (Who may be punished?) and (ii) Amount. In this section I shall chiefly be concerned with the first of these.[13]

From the foregoing discussions two things emerge. First, though we may be clear as to what value the practice of punishment is to promote, we have still to answer as a question of Distribution 'Who may be punished?' Secondly, if in answer to this question we say 'only an offender for an offence' this admission of retribution in Distribution is not a principle from which anything follows as to the severity or amount of punishment; in particular it neither licenses nor requires, as Retribution in General Aim does, more severe punishments than deterrence or other utilitarian criteria would require.

The root question to be considered is, however, why we attach the moral importance which we do to retribution in Distribution. Here I shall consider the efforts made to show that restriction of punishment to offenders is a simple consequence of whatever principles (Retributive or Utilitarian) constitute the Justifying Aim of punishment.

13. Amount is considered below in Section III (in connection with Mitigation) and Section V.

The standard example used by philosophers to bring out the importance of retribution in Distribution is that of a wholly innocent person who has not even unintentionally done anything which the law punishes if done intentionally. It is supposed that in order to avert some social catastrophe officials of the system fabricate evidence on which he is charged, tried, convicted and sent to prison or death. Or it is supposed that without resort to any fraud more persons may be deterred from crime if wives and children of offenders were punished vicariously for their crimes. In some forms this kind of thing may be ruled out by a consistent sufficiently comprehensive utilitarianism.[14] Certainly expedients involving fraud or faked charges might be very difficult to justify on utilitarian grounds. We can of course imagine that a Negro might be sent to prison or executed on a false charge of rape in order to avoid widespread lynching of many others; but a *system* which openly empowered authorities to do this kind of thing, even if it succeeded in averting specific evils like lynching, would awaken such apprehension and insecurity that any gain from the exercise of these powers would by any utilitarian calculation be offset by the misery caused by their existence. But official resort to this kind of fraud on a particular occasion in breach of the rules and the subsequent indemnification of the officials responsible might save many lives and so be thought to yield a clear surplus of value. Certainly vicarious punishment of an offender's family might do so and legal systems have occasionally though exceptionally resorted to this. An example of it is the Roman *Lex Quisquis* providing for the punishment of the children of those guilty of *majestas*.[15] In extreme cases many might still think it right to resort to these expedients but we should do so with the sense of sacrificing an important principle. We should be conscious of choosing the lesser of two evils, and this would be inexplicable if the principle sacrificed to utility were itself only a requirement of utility.

Similarly the moral importance of the restriction of punishment to the offender cannot be explained as merely a consequence of the principle that the General Justifying Aim is Retribution for immorality involved in breaking the law. Retribution in the Distribution of

14. See J. Rawls, "Two Concepts of Rules," *Philosophical Review* (1955), pp. 4–13.

punishment has a value quite independent of Retribution as Justifying Aim. This is shown by the fact that we attach importance to the restrictive principle that only offenders may be punished, even where breach of this law might not be thought immoral. Indeed even where the laws themselves are hideously immoral as in Nazi Germany, e.g., forbidding activities (helping the sick or destitute of some racial group) which might be thought morally obligatory, the absence of the principle restricting punishment to the offender would be a further *special* iniquity; whereas admission of this principle would represent some residual respect for justice shown in the administration of morally bad laws.

J. D. Mabbott

Punishment *

I propose in this paper to defend a retributive theory of punishment
and to reject absolutely all utilitarian considerations from its justification. I feel sure that this enterprise must arouse deep suspicion
and hostility both among philosophers (who must have felt that the
retributive view is the only moral theory except perhaps psychological
hedonism which has been definitely destroyed by criticism) and
among practical men (who have welcomed its steady decline in our
penal practice).

The question I am asking is this. Under what circumstances is the
punishment of some particular person justified and why? The theories of reform and deterrence which are usually considered to be the
only alternatives to retribution involve well-known difficulties. These
are considered fully and fairly in Dr. Ewing's book, *The Morality of
Punishment*, and I need not spend long over them. The central difficulty is that both would on occasion justify the punishment of an
innocent man, the deterrent theory if he were believed to have been
guilty by those likely to commit the crime in future, and the reformatory theory if he were a bad man though not a criminal. To this may
be added the point against the deterrent theory that it is the threat
of punishment and not punishment itself which deters, and that
when deterrence seems to depend on actual punishment, to imple-
ment the threat, it really depends on publication and may be achieved
if men believe that punishment has occurred even if in fact it has not.
As Bentham saw, for a Utilitarian apparent justice is everything, real
justice is irrelevant.

Dr. Ewing and other moralists would be inclined to compromise
with retribution in the face of the above difficulties. They would

* J. D. Mabbott, "Punishment," *Mind*, 48 (1939), pp. 150–67. Reprinted by
permission of the author and D. W. Hamlyn, the editor of *Mind*.

admit that one fact and one fact only can justify the punishment of this man, and that is a *past* fact, that he has committed a crime. To this extent reform and deterrence theories, which look only to the consequences, are wrong. But they would add that retribution can determine only *that* a man should be punished. It cannot determine how or how much, and here reform and deterrence may come in. Even Bradley, the fiercest retributionist of modern times, says "Having once the right to punish we may modify the punishment according to the useful and the pleasant, but these are external to the matter; they cannot give us a right to punish and nothing can do that but criminal desert." Dr. Ewing would maintain that the whole estimate of the amount and nature of a punishment may be effected by considerations of reform and deterrence. It seems to me that this is a surrender which the upholders of retribution dare not make. As I said above, it is publicity and not punishment which deters, and the publicity though often spoken of as "part of a man's punishment" is no more part of it than his arrest or his detention prior to trial, though both these may be also unpleasant and bring him into disrepute. A judge sentences a man to three years' imprisonment not to three years *plus* three columns in the press. Similarly with reform. The visit of the prison chaplain is not part of a man's punishment nor is the visit of Miss Fields or Mickey Mouse.

The truth is that while punishing a man and punishing him justly, it is possible to deter others, and also to attempt to reform him, and if these additional goods are achieved the total state of affairs is better than it would be with the just punishment alone. But reform and deterrence are not modifications of the punishment, still less reasons for it. A parallel may be found in the case of tact and truth. If you have to tell a friend an unpleasant truth you may do all you can to put him at his ease and spare his feelings as much as possible, while still making sure that he understands your meaning. In such a case no one would say that your offer of a cigarette beforehand or your apology afterwards are modifications of the truth still less reasons for telling it. You do not tell the truth in order to spare his feelings, but having to tell the truth you also spare his feelings. So Bradley was right when he said that reform and deterrence were "external to the matter," but therefore wrong when he said that they may "modify the punishment." Reporters are admitted to our trials so that punishments may become public and help to deter others. But the punishment would be no less just were reporters excluded and deterrence not achieved. Prison authorities may make it possible that a convict may become physically or morally better. They cannot ensure either result; and the punishment would still be just if the criminal took no advantage of their arrangements and their efforts failed. Some moralists see this and exclude these "extra" arrangements for deterrence and reform. They say that it must be the punishment *itself* which reforms and deters. But it is just my point that the punishment *itself* seldom reforms the criminal and never deters others. It is only "extra" arrangements which have any chance of achieving either result. As this is the central point of my paper, at the cost of labored repetition I would ask the upholders of reform and deterrence two questions. Suppose it could be shown that a particular criminal had not been improved by a punishment and also that no other would-be criminal had been deterred by it, would that prove that the punishment was unjust? Suppose it were discovered that a particular criminal had lived a much better life after his release and that many would-be criminals believing him to have been guilty were influenced by his fate, but yet that the "criminal" was punished for something he had never done, would these excellent results prove the punishment just?

It will be observed that I have throughout treated punishment as a purely legal matter. A "criminal" means a man who has broken a law, not a bad man; an "innocent" man is a man who has not broken the law in connection with which he is being punished, though he may be a bad man and have broken other laws. Here I dissent from most upholders of the retributive theory—from Hegel, from Bradley, and from Dr. Ross. They maintain that the essential connection is one between punishment and moral or social wrong-doing.

My fundamental difficulty with their theory is the question of *status*. It takes two to make a punishment, and for a moral or social wrong I can find no punisher. We may be tempted to say when we hear of some brutal action "that ought to be punished"; but I cannot see how there can be duties which are nobody's duties. If I see a man ill-treating a horse in a country where cruelty to animals is not a legal offence, and I say to him "I shall now punish you," he will reply, rightly, "What has it to do with you? Who made you a judge and a ruler over me?" I may have a duty to try to stop him and one way of stopping him may be to hit him, but another way may be to buy the horse. Neither the blow nor the price is a punishment. For a moral offence, God alone has the *status* necessary to punish the offender; and the theologians are becoming more and more doubtful whether even God has a duty to punish wrong-doing.

Dr. Ross would hold that not all wrong-doing is punishable, but only invasion of the rights of others; and in such a case it might be thought that the injured party had a right to punish. His right, however, is rather a right to reparation, and should not be confused with punishment proper.

This connection, on which I insist, between punishment and crime, not between punishment and moral or social wrong, alone accounts for some of our beliefs about punishment, and also meets many objections to the retributive theory as stated in its ordinary form. The first point on which it helps us is with regard to retrospective legislation. Our objection to this practice is unaccountable on reform and deterrent theories. For a man who commits a wrong before the date on which a law against it is passed, is as much in need of reform as a man who commits it afterwards; nor is deterrence likely to suffer because of additional punishments for the same offence. But the orthodox retributive theory is equally at a loss here, for if punishment is given for moral wrongdoing or for invasion of the rights of others, that immorality or invasion existed as certainly before the passing of the law as after it.

My theory also explains, where it seems to me all others do not, the case of punishment imposed by an authority who believes the law in question is a bad law. I was myself for some time disciplinary officer of a college whose rules included a rule compelling attendance at chapel. Many of those who broke this rule broke it on principle. I punished them. I certainly did not want to reform them; I respected their characters and their views. I certainly did not want to drive others into chapel through fear of penalties. Nor did I think there had been a wrong done which merited retribution. I wished I could have believed that I would have done the same myself. My position was clear. They had broken a rule; they knew it and I knew it. Nothing more was necessary to make punishment proper.

I know that the usual answer to this is that the judge enforces a bad law because otherwise law in general would suffer and good laws would be broken. The effect of punishing good men for breaking bad laws is that fewer bad men break good laws.

[*Excursus on Indirect Utilitarianism.* The above argument is a particular instance of a general utilitarian solution of all similar problems. When I am in funds and consider whether I should pay my debts or give the same amount to charity, I must choose the former because repayment not only benefits my creditor (for the benefit to him might be less than the good done through charity) but also upholds the general credit system. I tell the truth when a lie might do more good to the parties directly concerned, because I thus increase general trust and confidence. I keep a promise when it might do more immediate good to break it, because indirectly I bring it about that promises will be more readily made in future and this will outweigh the immediate loss involved. Dr. Ross has pointed out that the effect on the credit system of my refusal to pay a debt is greatly exaggerated. But I have a more serious objection of principle. It is that in all these cases the indirect effects do not result from my wrong action—my lie or defalcation or bad faith—but from the publication of these actions. If in any instance the breaking of the rule were to remain unknown then I could consider only the direct or immediate consequences. Thus in my "compulsory chapel" case I could have considered which of my culprits were lawabiding men generally and unlikely to break any other college rule. Then I could have sent for each of these separately and said "I shall let you off if you will tell no one I have done so." By these means the general keeping of rules would not have suffered. Would this course have been correct? It must be remembered that the proceedings need not deceive everybody. So long as they deceive would-be lawbreakers the good is achieved.

As this point is of crucial importance and as it has an interest beyond the immediate issue, and gives a clue to what I regard as the true general nature of law and punishment, I may be excused for expanding and illustrating it by an example or two from other fields. Dr. Ross says that two men dying on a desert island would have duties to keep promises to each other even though their breaking them would not affect the future general confidence in promises at all. Here is certainly the same point. But as I find that desert-island morality always rouses suspicion among ordinary men I should like to quote two instances from my own experience which also illustrate the problem.

(i) A man alone with his father at his death promises him a private and quiet funeral. He finds later that both directly and indirectly the keeping of this promise will cause pain and misunderstanding. He can see no particular positive good that the quiet funeral will achieve. No one yet knows that he has made the promise nor need anyone ever know. Should he therefore act as though it had never been made?

(ii) A college has a fund given to it for the encouragement of a subject which is now expiring. Other expanding subjects are in great need of endowment. Should the authorities divert the money? Those who oppose the diversion have previously stood on the past, the promise. But one day one of them discovers the "real reason" for this slavery to a dead doner. He says "We must consider not only the value of this money for these purposes, since on all direct consequences it should be diverted at once. We must remember the effect of this diversion on the general system of benefactions. We know that benefactors like to endow special objects, and this act of ours would discourage such benefactors in future and leave learning worse off." Here again is the indirect utilitarian reason for choosing the alternative which direct utilitarianism would reject. But the immediate answer to this from the most ingenious member of the opposition was crushing and final. He said, "Divert the money but keep it dark." This is obviously correct. It is not the act of diversion which would diminish the stream of benefactions but the news of it reaching the ears of benefactors. Provided that no possible benefactor got to hear of it no indirect loss would result. But the justification of our action would depend entirely on the success of the measures for "keeping it dark." I remember how I felt and how others felt that whatever answer was right this result was certainly wrong. But it follows that indirect utilitarianism is wrong in all such cases. For its argument can always be met by "Keep it dark."]

The view, then, that a judge upholds a bad law in order that law in general should not suffer is indefensible. He upholds it simply because he has no right to dispense from punishment.

The connection of punishment with law-breaking and not with wrongdoing also escapes moral objections to the retributive theory as held by Kant and Hegel or by Bradley and Ross. It is asked how we can measure moral wrong or balance it with pain, and how pain can wipe out moral wrong. Retributivists have been pushed into holding that pain *ipso facto* represses the worse self and frees the better, when this is contrary to the vast majority of observed cases. But if punishment is not intended to measure or balance or negate moral wrong then all this is beside the mark. There is the further difficulty of reconciling punishment with repentance and with forgiveness. Repentance is the reaction morally appropriate to moral wrong and punishment added to remorse is an unnecessary evil. But if punishment is associated with lawbreaking and not with moral evil the punisher is not entitled to consider whether the criminal is penitent any more than he may consider whether the law is good. So, too, with forgiveness. Forgiveness is not appropriate to law-breaking. (It is noteworthy that when, in divorce cases, the law has to recognize forgiveness it calls it "condonation," which is symptomatic of the difference of attitude.) Nor is forgiveness appropriate to moral evil. It is appropriate to personal injury. No one has any right to forgive me except the person I have injured. No judge or jury can do so. But the person I have injured has no right to punish me. Therefore there is no clash between punishment and forgiveness since these two duties do not fall on the same person nor in connection with the same characteristic of my act. (It is the weakness of vendetta that it tends to confuse this line, though even there it is only by personifying the family that the injured party and the avenger are identified. Similarly we must guard against the plausible fallacy of personifying society and regarding the criminal as "injuring society," for then once more the old dilemma about forgiveness would be insoluble.) A clergyman friend of mine catching a burglar red-handed was puzzled about his duty. In the end he ensured the man's punishment by information and evidence, and at the same time showed his own forgiveness by visiting the man in prison and employing him when he came out. I believe any "good Christian" would accept this as representing his duty. But obviously if the punishment is thought of as imposed *by* the victim or *for* the injury or immorality then the contradiction with forgiveness is hopeless.

So far as the question of the actual punishment of any individual is concerned this paper could stop here. No punishment is morally retributive or reformative or deterrent. Any criminal punished for any one of these reasons is certainly unjustly punished. The only justification for punishing any man is that he has broken a law.

In a book which has already left its mark on prison administration I have found a criminal himself confirming these views. *Walls Have Mouths*, by W. F. R. Macartney, is prefaced, and provided with appendices to each chapter, by Compton Mackenzie. It is interesting to notice how the novelist maintains that the proper object of penal servitude should be reformation,[1] whereas the prisoner himself accepts the view I have set out above. Macartney says "To punish a man is to treat him as an equal. To be punished *for an offence against rules* is a sane man's right." [2] It is striking also that he never uses "injustice" to describe the brutality or provocation which he experienced. He makes it clear that there were only two types of prisoner who were *unjustly* imprisoned, those who were insane and not responsible for the acts for which they were punished [3] and those who were innocent and had broken no law.[4] It is irrelevant, as he rightly observes, that some of these innocent men were, like Steinie Morrison, dangerous and violent characters, who on utilitarian grounds might well have been restrained. That made their punishment no whit less unjust.[5] To these general types may be added two specific instances of injustice. First, the sentences on the Dartmoor mutineers. "The Penal Servitude Act . . . lays down specific punishments for mutiny and incitement to mutiny, which include flogging.. . . . Yet on the occasion of the only big mutiny in an English prison, men are not dealt with by the Act specially passed to meet mutiny in prison, but are taken out of gaol and tried under an Act expressly passed to curb and curtail the Chartists—a revolutionary movement." [6] Here again the injustice does not lie in the actual effect the sentences are likely to have on the prisoners (though Macartney has some searching suggestions about that also) but in condemning men for breaking a law they did not break and not for breaking the law they did break. The second specific instance is that of Coulton, who served his twenty years and then was brought back to prison to do another eight years and to die. This is due to the "unjust order that no lifer shall be released unless he has either relations or a job to whom he can go: and it is actually sug-

1. p. 97.   2. p. 165. My italics.   3. pp. 165–166.   4. p. 298.
5. p. 301.   6. p. 255.

gested that this is really for the lifer's own good. Just fancy, you admit that the man in doing years upon years in prison had expiated his crime: but, instead of releasing him, you keep him a further time —perhaps another three years—because you say he has nowhere to go. Better a ditch and hedge than prison! True, there are abnormal cases who want to stay in prison, but Lawrence wanted to be a private soldier, and men go into monasteries. Because occasionally a man wants to stay in prison, must every lifer who has lost his family during his sentence (I was doing only ten years and I lost all my family) be kept indefinitely in gaol after he has paid his debt?" [7] Why is it unjust? Because he has paid his debt. When that is over it is for the man himself to decide what is for his own good. Once again the reform and utilitarian arguments are summarily swept aside. Injustice lies not in bad treatment or treatment which is not in the man's own interest, but in restriction which, according to the law, he has not merited.

It is true that Macartney writes, in one place, a paragraph of general reflection on punishment in which he confuses, as does Compton Mackenzie, retribution with revenge and in which he seems to hold that the retributive theory has some peculiar connection with private property. "Indeed it is difficult to see how, in society as it is today constituted, a humane prison system could function. All property is sacred, although the proceeds of property may well be reprehensible, therefore any offence against property is sacrilege and must be punished. Till a system eventuates which is based not on exploitation of man by man and class by class, prisons must be dreadful places, but at least there might be an effort to ameliorate the more savage side of the retaliation, and this could be done very easily." [8] The alternative system of which no doubt he is thinking is the Russian system described in his quotations from *A Physician's Tour in Soviet Russia*, by Sir James Purves-Stewart, the system of "correctional colonies" providing curative "treatment" for the different types of criminal.[9] There are two confusions here, to one of which we shall return later. First, Macartney confuses the retributive system with the punishment of one particular type of crime, offences against property, when he must have known that the majority of offenders against

7. p. 400.   8. pp. 166, 167.   9. p. 229.

property do not find themselves in Dartmoor or even in Wandsworth. After all his own offence was not one against property—it was traffic with a foreign Power—and it was one for which in the classless society of Russia the punishment is death. It is surely clear that a retributive system may be adopted for any class of crime. Secondly, Macartney confuses injustice within a penal system with the wrongfulness of a penal system. When he pleads for "humane prisons" as if the essence of the prison should be humanity, or when Compton Mackenzie says the object of penal servitude should be reform, both of them are giving up punishment altogether, not altering it. A Russian "correctional colony," if its real object is curative treatment, is no more a "prison" than is an isolation hospital or a lunatic asylum. To this distinction between abolishing injustice in punishment and abolishing punishment altogether we must now turn.

It will be objected that my original question "Why ought X to be punished?" is an illegitimate isolation of the issue. I have treated the whole set of circumstances as determined. X is a citizen of a state. About his citizenship, whether willing or unwilling, I have asked no questions. About the government, whether it is good or bad, I do not enquire. X has broken a law. Concerning the law, whether it is well-devised or not, I have not asked. Yet all these questions are surely relevant before it can be decided whether a particular punishment is just. It is the essence of my position that none of these questions is relevant. Punishment is a corollary of lawbreaking by a member of the society whose law is broken. This is a static and an abstract view but I see no escape from it. Considerations of utility come in on two quite different issues. Should there be laws, and what laws should there be? As a legislator I may ask what general types of action would benefit the community, and, among these, which can be "standardized" without loss, or should be standardized to achieve their full value. This, however, is not the primary question since particular laws may be altered or repealed. The choice which is the essential *prius* of punishment is the choice that there should be laws. The choice is not Hobson's. Other methods may be considered. A government might attempt to standardize certain modes of action by means of advice. It might proclaim its view and say "Citizens are requested" to follow this or that procedure. Or again it might decide to deal with each case as it arose in the manner most effective for the common welfare. Anarchists have wavered between these two alternatives and a third—that of doing nothing to enforce a standard of behavior but merely giving arbitrational decisions between conflicting parties, decisions binding only by consent.

I think it can be seen without detailed examination of particular laws that the method of law-making has its own advantages. Its orders are explicit and general. It makes behaviour reliable and predictable. Its threat of punishment may be so effective as to make punishment unnecessary. It promises to the good citizen a certain security in his life. When I have talked to business men about some inequity in the law of liability they have usually said "Better a bad law than no law, for then we know where we are."

Someone may say I am drawing an impossible line. I deny that punishment is utilitarian; yet now I say that punishment is a corollary of law and we decide whether to have laws and which laws to have on utilitarian grounds. And surely it is only this corollary which distinguishes law from good advice or exhortation. This is a misunderstanding. Punishment is a corollary not of law but of lawbreaking. Legislators do not choose to punish. They hope no punishment will be needed. Their laws would succeed even if no punishment occurred. The criminal makes the essential choice: he "brings it on himself." Other men obey the law because they see its order is reasonable, because of inertia, because of fear. In this whole area, and it may be the major part of the state, law achieves its ends without punishment. Clearly, then, punishment is not a corollary of law.

We may return for a moment to the question of amount and nature of punishment. It may be thought that this also is automatic. The law will include its own penalties and the judge will have no option. This, however, is again an initial choice of principle. If the laws do include their own penalties then the judge has no option. But the legislature might adopt a system which left complete or partial freedom to the judge, as we do except in the case of murder. Once again, what are the merits (regardless of particular laws, still more of particular cases) of fixed penalties and variable penalties? At first sight it would seem that all the advantages are with the variable penalties; for men who have broken the same law differ widely in degree of wickedness and responsibility. When, however, we remember that punishment is not an attempt to balance moral guilt this advantage is diminished. But there are still degrees of responsibility; I do not mean degrees of freedom of will but, for instance, degrees of complicity in a crime. The danger of allowing complete freedom to the judicature in fixing penalties is not merely that it lays too heavy a tax on human nature but that it would lead to the judge expressing in his penalty the degree of his own moral aversion to the crime. Or he might tend on deterrent grounds to punish more heavily a crime which was spreading and for which temptation and opportunity were frequent. Or again on deterrent grounds he might "make examples" by punishing ten times as heavily those criminals who are detected in cases in which time nine out of ten evade detection. Yet we should revolt from all such punishments if they involved punishing theft more heavily than blackmail or negligence more heavily than premeditated assault. The death penalty for sheep-stealing might have been defended on such deterrent grounds. But we should dislike equating sheep-stealing with murder. Fixed penalties enable us to draw these distinctions between crimes. It is not that we can say how much imprisonment is right for a sheep-stealer. But we can grade crimes in a rough scale and penalties in a rough scale, and keep our heaviest penalties for what are socially the most serious wrongs regardless of whether these penalties will reform the criminal or whether they are exactly what deterrence would require. The compromise of laying down maximum penalties and allowing judges freedom below these limits allows for the arguments on both sides.

To return to the main issue, the position I am defending is that it is essential to a legal system that the infliction of a particular punishment should *not* be determined by the good *that particular punishment* will do either to the criminal or to "society." In exactly the same way it is essential to a credit system that the repayment of a particular debt should not be determined by the good that particular payment will do. One may consider the merits of a legal system or of a credit system, but the acceptance of either involves the surrender of utilitarian considerations in particular cases as they arise. This is in effect admitted by Ewing in one place where he says "It is the penal system as a whole which deters and not the punishment of any individual offender." [10]

10. *The Morality of Punishment*, p. 66.

To show that the choice between a legal system and its alternatives is one we do and must make, I may quote an early work of Lenin in which he was defending the Marxist tenet that the state is bound to "wither away" with the establishment of a classless society. He considers the possible objection that some wrongs by man against man are not economic and therefore that the abolition of classes would not ipso facto eliminate crime. But he sticks to the thesis that these surviving crimes should not be dealt with by law and judicature. "We are not Utopians and do not in the least deny the possibility and inevitability of excesses by *individual persons*, and equally the need to suppress such excesses. But for this no special machine, no special instrument of repression is needed. This will be done by the armed nation itself as simply and as readily as any crowd of civilized people even in modern society parts a pair of combatants or does not allow a woman to be outraged." [11] This alternative to law and punishment has obvious demerits. Any injury not committed in the presence of the crowd, any wrong which required skill to detect or pertinacity to bring home would go untouched. The lynching mob, which is Lenin's instrument of justice, is liable to error and easily deflected from its purpose or driven to extremes. It must be a mob, for there is to be no "machine." I do not say that no alternative machine to ours could be devised but it does seem certain that the absence of all "machines" would be intolerable. An alternative machine might be based on the view that "society" is responsible for all criminality, and a curative and protective system developed. This is the system of Butler's "Erewhon" and something like it seems to be growing up in Russia except for cases of "sedition."

We choose, then, or we acquiesce in and adopt the choice of others of, a legal system as one of our instruments for the establishment of the conditions of a good life. This choice is logically prior to and independent of the actual punishment of any particular persons or the passing of any particular laws. The legislators choose particular laws within the framework of this predetermined system. Once again a small society may illustrate the reality of these choices and the distinction between them. A Headmaster launching a new school must explicitly make both decisions. First, shall he have any

11. *The State and Revolution* (Eng. Trans.), p. 93. Original italics.

rules at all? Second, what rules shall he have? The first decision is a genuine one and one of great importance. Would it not be better to have an "honour" system, by which public opinion in each house or form dealt with any offence? (This is the Lenin method.) Or would complete freedom be better? Or should he issue appeals and advice? Or should he personally deal with each malefactor individually, as the case arises, in the way most likely to improve his conduct? I can well imagine an idealistic Headmaster attempting to run a school with one of these methods or with a combination of several of them and therefore without punishment. I can even imagine that with a small school of, say, twenty pupils all open to direct personal psychological pressure from authority and from each other, these methods involving no "rules" would work. The pupils would of course grow up without two very useful habits, the habit of having some regular habits and the habit of obeying rules. But I suspect that most Headmasters, especially those of large schools, would either decide at once, or quickly be driven, to realize that some rules were necessary. This decision would be "utilitarian" in the sense that it would be determined by consideration of consequences. The question "what rules?" would then arise and again the issue is utilitarian. What action must be regularized for the school to work efficiently? The hours of arrival and departure, for instance, in a day school. But the one choice which is now no longer open to the Headmaster is whether he shall punish those who break the rules. For if he were to try to avoid this he would in fact simply be returning to the discarded method of appeals and good advice. Yet the Headmaster does not decide to punish. The pupils make the decision there. He decides actually to have rules and to threaten, but only hypothetically, to punish. The one essential condition which makes actual punishment just is a condition he *cannot* fulfil—namely that a rule should be broken.

I shall add a final word of consolation to the practical reformer. Nothing that I have said is meant to counter any movement for "penal reform" but only to insist that none of these reforms have anything to do with punishment. The only type of reformer who can claim to be reforming the system of punishment is a follower of Lenin or of Samuel Butler who is genuinely attacking the *system* and who believes there should be no laws and no punishments. But our great

British reformers have been concerned not with punishment but with its accessories. When a man is sentenced to imprisonment he is not sentenced also to partial starvation, to physical brutality, to pneumonia from damp cells and so on. And any movement which makes his food sufficient to sustain health, which counters the permanent tendency to brutality on the part of his warders, which gives him a dry or even a light and well-aired cell, is pure gain and does not touch the theory of punishment. Reformatory influences and prisoners' aid arrangements are also entirely unaffected by what I have said. I believe myself that it would be best if all such arrangements were made optional for the prisoner, so as to leave him in these cases a freedom of choice which would make it clear that they are not part of his punishment. If it is said that every such reform lessens a man's punishment, I think that is simply muddled thinking which, if it were clear, would be mere brutality. For instance, a prisoners' aid society is said to lighten his punishment, because otherwise he would suffer not merely imprisonment but also unemployment on release. But he was sentenced to imprisonment, not imprisonment *plus* unemployment. If I promise to help a friend and through special circumstances I find that keeping my promise will involve upsetting my day's work, I do not say that I really promised to help him and to ruin my day's work. And if another friend carries on my work for me I do not regard him as carrying out part of my promise, nor as stopping me from carrying it out myself. He merely removes an indirect and regrettable consequence of my keeping my promise. So with punishment. The Prisoners' Aid Society does not alter a man's punishment nor diminish it, but merely removes an indirect and regrettable consequence of it. And anyone who thinks that a criminal cannot make this distinction and will regard all the inconvenience that comes to him as punishment, need only talk to a prisoner or two to find how sharply they resent these wanton additions to a punishment which by itself they will accept as just. Macartney's chapter on "Food" in the book quoted above is a good illustration of this point, as are also his comments on Clayton's administration. "To keep a man in prison for many years at considerable expense and then to free him charged to the eyes with uncontrollable venom and hatred generated by the treatment he has received in gaol, does not appear to be sensible." Clayton "endeavoured to send a man out of prison in a reasonable state of mind. 'Well, I've done my time. They were not too bad to me. Prison is prison and not a bed of roses. Still they didn't rub it in. . . .' " [12] This "reasonable state of mind" is one in which a prisoner on release feels he has been punished but not *additionally* insulted or ill-treated. I feel convinced that penal reformers would meet with even more support if they were clear that they were *not* attempting to alter the system of punishment but to give its victims "fair play." We have no more right to starve a convict than to starve an animal. We have no more right to keep a convict in a Dartmoor cell "down which the water trickles night and day" [13] than we have to keep a child in such a place. If our reformers really want to alter the system of punishment, let them come out clearly with their alternative and preach, for instance, that no human being is responsible for any wrong-doing, that all the blame is on society, that curative or protective measures should be adopted, forcibly if necessary, as they are with infection or insanity. Short of this let them admit that the essence of prison is deprivation of liberty for the breaking of law, and that deprivation of food or of health or of books is unjust. And if our sentimentalists cry "coddling of prisoners," let us ask them also to come out clearly into the open and incorporate whatever starvation and disease and brutality they think necessary *into the sentences they propose*.[14] If it is said that some prisoners will prefer such reformed prisons, with adequate food and aired cells, to the outer world, we may retort that their numbers are probably not greater than those of the masochists who like to be flogged. Yet we do not hear the same "coddling" critics suggest abolition of the lash on the grounds that some criminals may like it. Even if the abolition from our prisons of all maltreatment other than that imposed by law results in a few down-and-outs breaking a window (as O. Henry's hero did) to get a night's lodging, the country will lose less than she does by her present method of sending

12. p. 152.   13. *Op. cit.*, p. 258.

14. One of the minor curiosities of jail life was that they quickly provided you with a hundred worries which left you no time or energy for worrying about your sentence, long or short. . . . Rather as if you were thrown into a fire with spikes in it, and the spikes hurt you so badly that you forget about the fire. But then your punishment would *be* the spikes not the fire. Why did they pretend it was only the fire, when they knew very well about the spikes?" (From *Lifer*, by Jim Phelan, p. 40.)

out her discharged convicts "charged with vernom and hatred" because of the additional and unconvenanted "rubbing it in" which they have received.

I hope I have established both the theoretical importance and the practical value of distinguishing between penal reform as we know and approve it—that reform which alters the accompaniments of punishment without touching its essence—and those attacks on punishment itself which are made not only by reformers who regard criminals as irresponsible and in need of treatment, but also by every judge who announces that he is punishing a man to deter others or to protect society, and by every juryman who is moved to his decision by the moral baseness of the accused rather than by his legal guilt.

Chapter Three

Strict Liability

St. Thomas Aquinas

Those Who Have Sinned Involuntarily *

... according to human judgment a man should never be condemned without fault of his own to an inflictive punishment, such as death, mutilation or flogging. But a man may be condemned, even according to human judgment, to a punishment of forfeiture, even without any fault on his part, but not without cause: and this in three ways.

First, through a person becoming, without any fault of his, disqualified for having or acquiring a certain good: thus for being infected with leprosy a man is removed from the administration of the Church: and for bigamy, or through pronouncing a death sentence a man is hindered from receiving sacred orders.

Secondly, because the particular good that he forfeits is not his own but common property: thus that an episcopal see be attached to a certain church belongs to the good of the whole city, and not only to the good of the clerics.

Thirdly, because the good of one person may depend on the good of another: thus in the crime of high treason a son loses his inheritance through the sin of his parent.

* St. Thomas Aquinas, *Summa Theologica* (New York: Benziger, Inc., 1947), II, part 2–2, quest. 108, fourth article.

Jeremy Bentham

Inefficacious Punishment *

Cases in Which Punishment Must be Inefficacious

These are,

1. Where the penal provision is *not established* until after the act is done. Such are the cases, 1. Of an ex-post-facto law; where the legislator himself appoints not a punishment till after the act is done. 2. Of a sentence beyond the law; where the judge, of his authority, appoints a punishment which the legislator had not appointed.

2. Where the penal provision, though established, is *not conveyed* to the notice of the person on whom it seems intended that it should operate. Such is the case where the law has omitted to employ any of the expedients which are necessary, to make sure that every person whatsoever, who is within the reach of the law, be apprized of all the cases whatsoever, in which (being in the station of life he is in) he can be subjected to the penalties of the law [1].

3. Where the penal provision, though it were conveyed to a man's notice, *could produce no effect* on him, with respect to the preventing him from engaging in any act of the *sort* in question. Such is the case, 1. In extreme *infancy*; where a man has not yet attained that state or disposition of mind in which the prospect of evils so distant as those which are held forth by the law, has the effect of influencing his conduct. 2. In *insanity*; where the person, if he has attained to that disposition, has since been deprived of it through the influence of some permanent though unseen cause. 3. In *intoxication*; where he has been deprived of it by the transient influence of a visible cause:

---

* Jeremy Bentham, *An Introduction to the Principles of Morals and Legislation* (New York: Hafner, 1948), pp. 172–75.

1. See B. II. Appendix, tit. iii. [Promulgation].

such as the use of wine, or opium, or other drugs, that act in this manner on the nervous system: which condition is indeed neither more nor less than a temporary insanity produced by an assignable cause [2].

4. Where the penal provision (although, being conveyed to the party's notice, it might very well prevent his engaging in acts of the sort in question, provided he knew that it related to those acts) could not have this effect, with regard to the *individual* act he is about to engage in: to wit, because he knows not that it is of the number of those to which the penal provision relates. This may happen, 1. In the case of *unintentionality*; where he intends not to engage, and thereby knows not that he is about to engage, in the act in which eventually he is about to engage.[3] 2. In the case of *unconsciousness*; where, although he may know that he is about to engage in the act itself, yet, from not knowing all the material *circumstances* attending it, he knows not of the *tendency* it has to produce that mischief, in contemplation of which it has been made penal in most instances. 3. In the case of *missupposal*; where, although he may know of the tendency the act has to produce that degree of mischief, he supposes it, though mistakenly, to be attended with some circumstance, or set

---

2. Notwithstanding what is here said, the cases of infancy and intoxication (as we shall see hereafter) cannot be looked upon in practice as affording sufficient grounds for absolute impunity. But this exception in point of practice is no objection to the propriety of the rule in point of theory. The ground of the exception is neither more nor less than the difficulty there is of ascertaining the matter of fact: viz., whether at the requisite point of time the party was actually in the state of question; that is, whether a given case comes really under the rule. Suppose the matter of fact capable of being perfectly ascertained, without danger or mistake, the impropriety of punishment would be as indubitable in these as in any other.

The reason that is commonly assigned for the establishing an exemption from punishment in favour of infants, insane persons, and persons under intoxication, is either false in fact, or confusedly expressed. The phrase is, that the will of these persons concurs not with the act; that they have no vicious will; or, that they have not the free use of their will. But suppose all this to be true? What is it to the purpose? Nothing: except in as far as it implies the reason given in the text.

3. See ch. 2. [Intentionality].

of circumstances, which, if it had been attended with, it would either not have been productive of that mischief, or have been productive of such a greater degree of good, as has determined the legislator in such a case not to make it penal.[4]

5. Where, though the penal clause might exercise a full and prevailing influence, were it to act alone, yet by the *predominant* influence of some opposite cause upon the will, it must necessarily be ineffectual; because the evil which he sets himself about to undergo, in the case of his *not* engaging in the act, is so great, that the evil denounced by the penal clause, in case of his engaging in it, cannot appear greater. This may happen, 1. In the case of *physical danger;* where the evil is such as appears likely to be brought about by the unassisted powers of *nature.* 2. In the case of a *threatened mischief;* where it is such as appears likely to be brought about through the intentional and conscious agency of *man.*

6. Where (though the penal clause may exert a full and prevailing influence over the *will* of the party) yet his *physical faculties* (owing to the predominant influence of some physical cause) are not in a condition to follow the determination of the will: insomuch that the act is absolutely *involuntary.* Such is the case of physical *compulsion* or *restraint,* by whatever means brought about; where the man's hand, for instance, is pushed against some object which his will disposes him *not* to touch; or tied down from touching some object which his will disposes him to touch.

4. See ch. 3. [Consciousness].

H. L. A. Hart

The Rationale of
Excuses *

The admission of excusing conditions is a feature of the Distribution of punishment and it is required by distinct principles of Justice which restrict the extent to which general social aims may be pursued at the cost of individuals. The moral importance attached to these in punishment distinguishes it from other measures which pursue similar aims (e.g. the protection of life, wealth or property) by methods which like punishment are also often unpleasant to the individuals to whom they are applied, e.g., the detention of persons of hostile origin or association in war time, or of the insane, or the compulsory quarantine of persons suffering from infectious disease. To these we resort to avoid damage of a catastrophic character.

Every penal system in the name of some other social value compromises over the admissions of excusing conditions and no system goes as far (particularly in cases of mental disease) as many would wish. But it is important (if we are to avoid a superficial but tempting answer to modern skepticism about the meaning or truth of the statement that a criminal could have kept the law which he has broken) to see that our moral preference for a system which does recognize such excuses cannot, any more than our reluctance to engage in the cruder business of false charges or vicarious punishment, be explained by reference to the General Aim which we take to justify the practice of punishment. Here, too, even where the laws appear to us morally iniquitous or where we are uncertain as to their moral character so that breach of law does not entail moral guilt, punishment of those

* H. L. A. Hart, "Prolegomenon to the Principles of Punishment," in *Punishment and Responsibility* (Oxford: Clarendon Press, 1968), pp. 17–24. The original version of this essay was the 1959 Inaugural Address to the Aristotelian Society, pub. in *Proc. Arist. Soc.*, 60 (1959–60). Reprinted by permission of the author and the publisher.

who break the law unintentionally would be an added wrong and refusal to do this some sign of grace.

Retributionists (in General Aim) have not paid much attention to the rationale of this aspect of punishment; they have usually (wrongly) assumed that it has no status except as a corollary of Retribution in General Aim. But Utilitarians have made strenuous, detailed efforts to show that restriction of the use of punishment to those who have voluntarily broken the law is explicable on purely utilitarian lines. Bentham's efforts are the most complete and their failure is an instructive warning to contemporaries.

Bentham's argument was a reply to Blackstone who, in expounding the main excusing conditions recognized in the criminal law of his day,[1] claimed that 'all the several pleas and excuses which protect the committer of a forbidden act from punishment which is otherwise annexed thereto may be reduced to this single consideration: the want or defect of *will*' . . . . [and to the principle] 'that to constitute a crime . . . . there must be first, a vitious will.' In his Introduction to the Principles of Morals and Legislation[2] under the heading 'Cases unmeet for punishment' Bentham sets out a list of the main excusing conditions similar to Blackstone's; he then undertakes to show that the infliction of punishment on those who have done, while in any of these conditions, what the law forbids 'must be inefficacious: it cannot act so as to prevent the mischief.' All the common talk about want or defect of will or lack of a 'vitious' will is, he says, 'nothing to the purpose,' except so far as it implies the reason (inefficacy of punishment) which he himself gives for recognising these excuses.

Bentham's argument is in fact a spectacular non sequitur. He sets out to prove that to *punish* the mad, the infant child or those who break the law unintentionally or under duress or even under 'necessity' must be inefficacious; but all that he proves (at the most) is the quite different proposition that the *threat* of punishment will be ineffective so far as the class of persons who suffer from these conditions is concerned. Plainly it is possible that though (as Bentham says) the *threat* of punishment could not have operated on them, the actual *infliction* of punishment on those persons, may secure a higher measure of conformity to law on the part of normal persons than is secured

1. *Commentaries*, Book IV, Chap. II.   2. Chap. XIII esp. para. 9, n. 1.

by the admission of excusing conditions. If this is so and if Utilitarian principles only were at stake, we should, without any sense that we were sacrificing any principle of value or were choosing the lesser of two evils, drop from the law the restriction on punishment entailed by the admission of excuses: unless, of course, we believed that the terror or insecurity or misery produced by the operation of laws so Draconic was worse than the lower measure of obedience to law secured by the law which admits excuses.

This objection to Bentham's rationale of excuses is not merely a fanciful one. Any increase in the number of conditions required to establish criminal liability increases the opportunity for deceiving courts or juries by the pretence that some condition is not satisfied. When the condition is a psychological factor the chances of such pretence succeeding are considerable. Quite apart from the provision made for mental disease, the cases where an accused person pleads that he killed in his sleep or accidentally or in some temporary abnormal state of unconsciousness show that deception is certainly feasible. From the Utilitarian point of view this may lead to two sorts of "losses." The belief that such deception is feasible may embolden persons who would not otherwise risk punishment to take their chance of deceiving a jury in this way. Secondly, a criminal who actually succeeds in this deception will be left at large, though belonging to the class which the law is concerned to incapacitate. Developments in Anglo-American law since Bentham's day have given more concrete form to this objection to his argument. There are now offences (known as offences of 'strict liability') where it is not necessary for conviction to show that the accused either intentionally did what the law forbids or could have avoided doing it by use of care: selling liquor to an intoxicated person, possessing an altered passport, selling adulterated milk[3] are examples out of a range of 'strict liability' offences where it is no defence that the accused did not offend intentionally, or through negligence, e.g., that he was under some mistake against which he had no opportunity to guard. Two things should be noted about them. First, the common justification of this form of criminal liability is that if proof of intention or lack of care

3. See Glanville Williams, *Criminal Law*, 2nd edn., Chap. VI, for a discussion of the protest against 'strict responsibility.'

were required guilty persons would escape. Secondly, 'strict liability' is generally viewed with great odium and admitted as an exception to the general rule, with the sense that an important principle has been sacrificed to secure a higher measure of conformity and conviction of offenders. Thus Bentham's argument curiously ignores both the two possibilities which have been realized. First, actual punishment of these who act unintentionally or in some other normally excusing manner may have a utilitarian value in its effects on others; and secondly, when because of this probability, strict liability is admitted and the normal excuses are excluded, this may be done with the sense that some other principle has been overridden.

On this issue modern extended forms of Utilitarianism fare no better than Bentham's whose main criterion here of 'effective' punishment was deterrence of the offender or of others by example. Sometimes the principle that punishment should be restricted to those who have voluntarily broken the law is defended not as a principle which is rational or morally important in itself but as something so engrained in popular conceptions of justice [4] in certain societies, including our own, that not to recognize it would lead to disturbances, or to the nullification of the criminal law since officials or juries might refuse to co-operate in such a system. Hence to punish in these circumstances would either be impracticable or would create more harm than could possibly be offset by any superior deterrent force gained by such a system. On this footing, a system should admit excuses much as, in order to prevent disorder or lynching, concessions might be made to popular demands for more savage punishment than could be defended on other grounds. Two objections confront this wider pragmatic form of Utilitarianism. The first is the factual observation that even if a system of strict liability for all or very serious crime would be unworkable, a system which admits it on its periphery for relatively minor offences is not only workable but an actuality which we have, though many object to it or admit it with reluctance. The second objection is simply that we do not dissociate ourselves from the principle that it is wrong to punish the hopelessly insane or those who act unintentionally, etc., by treating it as something merely em-

4. Michael and Wechsler, "A Rationale of the Law of Homicide" (1937), 37 C.L.R., 701, esp. pp. 752–7, and Rawls, *op. cit.*

bodied in popular mores to which concessions must be made sometimes. We condemn legal systems where they disregard this principle; whereas we try to educate people out of their preference for savage penalties even if we might in extreme cases of threatened disorder concede them.

It is therefore impossible to exhibit the principle by which punishment is excluded for those who act under the excusing conditions merely as a corollary of the general Aim—Retributive or Utilitarian —justifying the practice of punishment. Can anything positive be said about this principle except that it is one to which we attach moral importance as a restriction on the pursuit of any aim we have in punishing?

It is clear that like all principles of Justice it is concerned with the adjustment of claims between a multiplicity of persons. It incorporates the idea that each individual person is to be protected against the claim of the rest for the highest possible measure of security, happiness or welfare which could be got at his expense by condemning him for a breach of the rules and punishing him. For this a moral licence is required in the form of proof that the person punished broke the law by an action which was the outcome of his free choice, and the recognition of excuses is the most we can do to ensure that the terms of the licence are observed. Here perhaps, the elucidation of this restrictive principle should stop. Perhaps we (or I) ought simply to say that it is a requirement of Justice, and Justice simply consists of principles to be observed in adjusting the competing claims of human beings which (i) treat all alike as persons by attaching special significance to human voluntary action and (ii) forbid the use of one human being for the benefit of others except in return for his voluntary actions against them. I confess however to an itch to go further; though what I have to say may not add to these principles of Justice. There are, however, three points which even if they are restatements from different points of view of the principles already stated, may help us to identify what we now think of as values in the practice of punishment and what we may have to reconsider in the light of modern skepticism.

(a) We may look upon the principle that punishment must be reserved for voluntary offences from two different points of view. The first is that of the rest of society considered as *harmed* by the offence (either because one of its members has been injured or because the authority of the law essential to its existence has been challenged or both). The principle then appears as one securing that the suffering involved in punishment falls upon those who have voluntarily harmed others: this is valued, not as the Aim of punishment, but as the only fair terms on which the General Aim (protection of society, maintenance of respect for law, etc.) may be pursued.

(b) The second point of view is that of society concerned not as harmed by the crime but as *offering* individuals including the criminal the protection of the laws on terms which are fair, because they not only consist of a framework of reciprocal rights and duties, but because within this framework each individual is given a *fair* opportunity to choose between keeping the law required for society's protection or paying the penalty. From the first point of view the actual punishment of a criminal appears not merely as something useful to society (General Aim) but as justly extracted from the criminal who has voluntarily done harm; from the second it appears as a price justly extracted because the criminal had a fair opportunity beforehand to avoid liability to pay.

(c) Criminal punishment as an attempt to secure desired behaviour differs from the manipulative techniques of the Brave New World (conditioning, propaganda, etc.) or the simple incapacitation of those with antisocial tendencies, by taking a risk. It defers action till harm has been done; its primary operation consists simply in announcing certain standards of behaviour and attaching penalties for deviation, making it less eligible, and then leaving individuals to choose. This is a method of social control which maximizes individual freedom within the coercive framework of law in a number of different ways, or perhaps, different senses. First, the individual has an option between obeying or paying. The worse the laws are, the more valuable the possibility of exercising this choice becomes in enabling an individual to decide how he shall live. Secondly, this system not only enables individuals to exercise this choice but increases the power of individuals to identify beforehand periods when the law's punishments will not interfere with them and to plan their lives accordingly. This very obvious point is often overshadowed by the other merits of restricting punishment to offenses voluntarily committed, but is worth separate attention. Where punishment is not so restricted individuals will be liable to have their plans frustrated by punishments for what they do unintentionally, in ignorance, by accident or mistake. Such a system of strict liability for all offences, if logically possible,[5] would not only vastly increase the number of punishments, but would diminish the individual's power to identify beforehand particular periods during which he will be free from them. This is so because we can have very little ground for confidence that during a particular period we will not do something unintentionally, accidentally, etc.; whereas from their own knowledge of themselves many can say with justified confidence that for some period ahead they are not likely to engage intentionally in crime and can plan their lives from point to point in confidence that they will be left free during that period. Of course the confidence thus justified, though drawn from knowledge of ourselves, does not amount to certainty. My confidence that I will not during the next twelve months intentionally engage in any crime and will be free from punishment, may turn out to be misplaced; but it is both greater and better justified than my belief that I will not do unintentionally any of the things which our system punishes if done intentionally.

5. Some crimes, e.g., demanding money by menaces, cannot (logically) be committed unintentionally.

R. Wasserstrom

Strict Liability
in the Criminal Law *

The proliferation of so-called "strict liability" offenses in the criminal law has occasioned the vociferous, continued, and almost unanimous criticism of analysts and philosophers of the law.[1] The imposition of severe criminal sanctions[2] in the absence of any requisite mental element has been held by many to be incompatible with the basic requirements of our Anglo-American, and, indeed, any civilized jurisprudence.

The Model Penal Code, for example, announces that its provisions for culpability make a "frontal attack" upon the notion of strict, or absolute, liability.[3] Francis B. Sayre, in his classic article on "Public Welfare Offenses," contends that since the real menace to society is the intentional commission of undesirable acts, evil intent must remain an element of the criminal law. "To inflict substantial punishment upon one who is morally entirely innocent, who caused injury through reasonable mistake or pure accident, would so outrage the feelings of the community as to nullify its own enforcement."[4]

* Richard Wasserstrom, "Strict Liability in the Criminal Law," *Stanford Law Review*, 12 (1959–60), pp. 730–45. Reprinted by permission of the author and the *Stanford Law Review*.

1. The history of those strict liability offenses which are of legislative origin is of quite recent date. One of the first cases in which a statute was interpreted as imposing strict criminal liability was Regina v. Woodrow, 15 M. & W. 404, 153 Eng. Rep. 907 (1846). For an exhaustive account of the early history of these statutory offenses see Sayre, "Public Welfare Offenses," 33 *Colum. L. Rev.* 55, 56–66 (1933).

2. "Severe criminal sanctions" refer to imprisonment as opposed to the mere imposition of a fine.

3. Model Penal Code § 2.05, comment (Tent. Draft No. 4, 1955).

4. Sayre, *supra* nore 1, at 56.

And Jerome Hall, perhaps the most active and insistent critic of such offenses, has consistently denounced the notion of strict liability as anathema to the coherent development of a rational criminal law: "It is impossible to defend strict liability in terms of or by reference to the only criteria that are available to evaluate the influence of legal controls on human behavior. What then remains but the myth that through devious, unknown ways some good results from strict liability in 'penal' law?" [5]

Without attempting to demonstrate that strict liability offenses are inherently or instrumentally desirable, one can question the force of the arguments which have been offered against them. It is not evident, for example, that strict liability statutes cannot have a deterrent effect greater than that of ordinary criminal statutes. Nor, is it clear that all strict liability statutes can most fruitfully be discussed and evaluated as members of a single class of criminality. The notion of "fault" is sufficiently ambiguous, perhaps, so as to obscure the sense or senses in which these statutes do impose liability "without fault." And finally, the similarities between strict liability and criminal negligence are such that it seems difficult to attack the former without at the same time calling the latter into comparable question. Issues of this kind are, then, the explicit subjects for examination here.

The Concept of Strict Criminal Liability

Neither the arguments against the imposition of strict criminal liability nor the justifications for such imposition can be evaluated intelligently until the meaning of the phrase "strict criminal liability" has been clarified. One possible approach—and the one selected here as appropriate for the scope of this analysis—is that of ostensive definition. That is to say, a small, but representative, sample of the kinds of offenses which are usually characterized as strict liability offenses can be described briefly so as to make the common characteristics of this class relatively obvious upon inspection.

5. Hall, *General Principles of Criminal Law* (1947), pp. 304–5. See also Willims, *Criminal Law* (1953), §§ 70–76; Hart, "The Aims of Criminal Law," 23 *Law & Contemp. Prob.*, pp. 401, 422–25 (1958).

At the outset, it is essential that strict liability offenses not be confused with Sayre's "public welfare" offenses, i.e., those which he defines as essentially regulative in function and punishable by fine rather than imprisonment.[6] This inquiry is concerned with those offenses which cannot be distinguished from other criminal conduct by virtue of the fact that the punishment involved is consistently less than imprisonment.[7] Thus, the cases here selected as exemplary of strict criminal liability are all cases in which the prescribed sentences are surely not minimal in degree or merely regulative in function.

The landmark case in American jurisprudence is undoubtedly *United States v. Balint.*[8] The defendant was indicted under a statute which made it unlawful to sell narcotics without a written order. The defendant claimed that the indictment was insufficient because it failed to allege that he had known that the drugs sold were narcotics. The United States Supreme Court held that his conviction did not deny due process.

Another classic example is *State v. Lindberg.*[9] The statute in question provided that "every director and officer of any bank . . . who shall borrow . . . any of its funds in an excessive amount . . . shall . . . be guilty of a felony."[10] The defendant contended that he had borrowed the money in question only after he had been assured by another official of the bank that the money had come from a bank other than his own. But the court held that the reasonableness of the defendant's mistake was not a defense.

The final case, *Regina v. Prince,*[11] is famous in both English and American jurisprudence. Prince was indicted under a statute which made it a misdemeanor to "unlawfully take . . . any unmarried Girl, being under the Age of Sixteen Years, out of the Possession and against the Will of her Father or Mother . . . ."[12] One of the de-

6. Sayre, *supra* note 1, at 83.

7. If the offenses were always punishable by something less than imprisonment then it would surely be relevant to ask in what sense they were penal in anything but name. This appears in part to be Hall's criticism of Sayre's article. See Hall, *op. cit. supra* note 5, at 279.

8.   258 U.S. 250 (1922).   9.   125 Wash. 51, 215 Pac. 41 (1923).

10.   Wash. Comp. Stat. § 3259 (Remington 1922).

11.   13 Cox Crim. Cas. 138 (1875).

12.   Offenses Against the Person Act, 1861, 24 & 25 Vict., c. 100, § 55.

fenses which Prince sought to interpose rested upon the reasonableness of his belief that the girl in question was over sixteen years old. The majority of the court interpreted the statute to make the reasonableness of a belief as to the girl's age irrelevant, and found Prince guilty.

Assuming these cases to be representative,[13] strict liability offenses might be tentatively described (although not defined) as those in which the sole question put to the jury is whether the jury believes the defendant to have committed the act proscribed by the statute.[14] If it finds that he did the act, then it is obliged to bring in a verdict of guilty.[15] Whether this characterization of the above three cases is either precise or very helpful is a question which must await further discussion below. For the present, however, it is perhaps sufficient to observe that whatever it is that the concept of mens rea is thought to designate, it is this which needs not be shown to be predicable of the defendant.[16]

The Justification of Strict Liability

Before attempting to assess the arguments for and against the notion of strict criminal liability, it should be made clear that the author agrees with most of the critics in not finding many of the usual justi-

13. Exhaustive enumerations of leading strict liability cases can be found in Sayre, "Public Welfare Offenses," 33 Colum. L. Rev. 55 (1933).

14. Jackson, "Absolute Prohibition in Statutory Offenses," 6 Camb. L.J. 83, 88 (1938).

15. There is, of course, a sense in which the notion of having "committed an act" is far from unambiguous. Depending upon how "act" is defined, it may or may not be true that the sole question is whether the defendant committed the act. The fact that the defendant was sleepwalking or insane at the time might be treated as bearing upon the issue of whether the "act" was committed. There is an obvious sense in which even this determination requires some inquiry into the defendant's state of mind.

16. This would be true whether mens rea is interpreted as requiring only that the person "intend" to do the act, or as requiring that the person intend to do something which is morally wrong. The latter interpretation is advanced in Mueller, "On Common Law Mens Rea," 42 Minn. L. Rev. 1043 (1958).

fications of strict liability at all persuasive. The fact, for example, that slight penalties are usually imposed, or that mens rea would be peculiarly unsusceptible of proof in these cases, does not, either singly or in combination, justify the presence of these offenses in the criminal law. But to reject these and comparable arguments is not necessarily to prove that plausible justifications cannot be located. In fact, it is precisely when the "stronger" arguments of the opponents of strict liability are considered in detail that the case against strict liability is found to be less one-sided than the critics so unanimously suppose.

Critics of strict criminal liability usually argue that the punishment of persons in accordance with the minimum requirements of strict liability (1) is inconsistent with any or all of the commonly avowed aims of the criminal law; and (2) runs counter to the accepted standards of criminal culpability which prevail in the community. They assert that the imposition of criminal sanctions in a case in which—conceivably—the defendant acted both reasonably and with no intention to produce the proscribed events cannot be justified by an appeal to the deterrent, the rehabilitative, or the incarcerative functions of punishment.[17] And, in fact, they assert the practical effect of strict liability offenses is simply to create that anomalous situation in which persons not morally blamed by the community are nevertheless branded criminal.[18] Although the two lines of criticism are intimately related, for purposes of discussion they will be treated somewhat separately.

17. One author has suggested that the question of whether a crime has been committed ought to be determined solely by deciding whether the defendant committed the specific act proscribed by the statute. The actor's mental state would be relevant to the separate question of the actor's punishment. Levitt, "Extent and Function of the Doctrine of Mens Rea," 17 *Ill. L. Rev.* 578 (1923). This bifurcation is unobjectionable in so far as it recognizes that one of the factors to be considered in the sentencing of an individual is his mental state at the time of the crime. The author seems to imply that in the absence of a finding of the requisite mental element it would be proper for the court not to punish the defendant at all. This, too, is perhaps in itself unobjectionable. The question remains then whether it makes any sense to speak of this defendant as having committed a crime.

18. Hall, *General Principles of Criminal Law* pp. 302–3 (1947); Williams, *Criminal Law* § 76, at 269 (1953); Sayre, "Public Welfare Offenses," 33 *Colum. L. Rev.* 55, 56 (1933).

The notion that strict liability statutes can be defended as efficacious deterrents has been consistently rejected. It has been proposed, for example, that strict liability offenses cannot be a deterrent simply because they do not proscribe the kind of activity which is obviously incompatible with the moral standards of the community. Thus Gerhard Mueller argues that the substance of common-law *mens rea* is the "awareness of evil, *the sense of doing something which one ought not....*" [19] Since all common-law crimes involved the commission of some act which was known by all the members of the community to be morally wrong, there was, he suggests, no problem in finding the presence of *mens rea* in cases of common-law criminal acts. Such, he insists, is not true of strict liability offenses. They do not punish those activities which a person would know to be wrong independently of the existence of a particular statute. Thus strict liability statutes are to be condemned because they necessarily imply that a person might be punished even though he could not have appealed to that one certain indicia of criminality—the moral laws of the community—to decide whether he was doing something which would violate the law.

If I understand Mr. Mueller's argument correctly, then it clearly proves too much to be of any special significance as a criticism of strict liability offenses. The argument rests upon the obviously sound premise that a person cannot be deterred if he does not know or have reason to believe that his intended action will violate the law. And if this theory about common-law *mens rea* is correct, it only demonstrates that everyone either knew or should have known that certain kinds of activity would be legally punishable. These two points, however, at best imply that ignorance of the law ought—on deterrent grounds—to be always admitted as a complete defense to any criminal prosecution founded upon a statute which does not incorporate an express moral rule or practice into the criminal law.[20]

19. Mueller, *op. cit. supra* note 16, at 1060.
20. Mueller cites the recent case of Lambert v. California, 355 U.S. 225 (1957) as implicitly attacking all strict liability statutes on this ground. Such a reading of the case seems plainly incorrect. At *most*, the reasoning of the Court can be construed as suggesting that strict liability statutes of which the defendant neither had nor ought to have had notice might violate due process. More plausibly, the Court struck down the conviction in *Lambert* because the statute there reached a very general kind of activity which the defendant could not reasonably have supposed to be regulated by statute at all: namely, the mere fact that the defendant

Concomitantly, if a person knew of the existence and import of a statute of this kind, it seems wholly irrelevant to distinguish strict liability statutes from those requiring some greater "mental element." It is just as possible to know that one might be violating a strict liability statute as it is to know that one might be violating some other kind of criminal statute. Thus, unless special reasons exist for believing that strict liability offenses are not effective deterrents, Mr. Mueller's argument leaves them undifferentiated from many other statutory crimes which do not incorporate the moral law of the community.[21]

Just such special reasons for rejecting the deterrent quality of strict liability offenses are offered by Jerome Hall, among others. He rejects the argument that a strict liability statute is a more efficacious deterrent than an ordinary criminal statute for at least two reasons: (a) it is not plausible to suppose that the "strictness" of the liability renders it more of a deterrent than the liability of ordinary criminal statutes; and (b) persons are not, as a matter of fact, deterred by those penalties usually imposed for the violation of a strict liability offense.[22]

The first of these objections is, it is submitted, inconclusive. For there seem to be at least two respects in which strict liability statutes might have a greater deterrent effect than "usual" criminal statutes. In the first place, it should be noted that Hall's first proposition is just as apt to be false as to be true. That is to say, it might be the case that a person engaged in a certain kind of activity would be more careful precisely because he knew that this kind of activity was governed by a strict liability statute. It is at least plausible to suppose that the knowledge that certain criminal sanctions will be imposed if

---

came into a city and failed to register with the sheriff as an ex-convict. Surely, it is reading too much into the opinion to find a disposition on the part of the Court to group all strict liability statutes in this class.

21. It is assumed throughout the remainder of this Article that knowledge of the relevant strict liability statutes is possessed or is readily capable of being possessed by those subject to the statutes.

22. "There is, first, the opinion of highly qualified experts that the present rules are regarded by unscrupulous persons merely 'as a license fee for doing an illegitimate business.' " Hall, *op. cit. supra* note 18, at 301.

certain consequences ensue might induce a person to engage in that activity with much greater caution than would be the case if some lesser standard prevailed.

In the second place (and this calls Hall's second premise into question as well), it seems reasonable to believe that the presence of strict liability offenses might have the added effect of keeping a relatively large class of persons from engaging in certain kinds of activity.[23] A person who did not regard himself as capable of conducting an enterprise in such a way so as not to produce the deleterious consequences proscribed by the statute might well refuse to engage in that activity at all. Of course, if the penalties for violation of the statute are minimal—if payment of fines is treated merely as a license to continue in operation—then unscrupulous persons will not be deterred by the imposition of this sanction. But this does not imply that unscrupulous persons would be quite so willing to engage in these activities if the penalties for violation were appreciably more severe. In effect, Hall's second argument, if it proves anything, shows only that stronger penalties are needed if strict liability statutes are to be effective.

If the above analysis of the possible deterrent effect of strict liability offenses is plausible, then one of the results of their continued existence and enforcement might very well be that few if any persons would be willing to engage in certain kinds of conduct. The presence of statutes such as that in the Lindberg case might have the effect of inducing persons not to engage in banking as an occupation since the risks, one might suppose, are just too great to be compensated by the possible rewards. More plausibly, such a statute might merely have the effect of discouraging bankers from borrowing money—or possibly only from borrowing money from banks. But these effects, too, might conceivably make banking a less attractive occupation, although they would probably not cause the disappearance of banking as an institution in society. However, if we assume the strongest of all re-

23. Glanville Williams concedes both of these points. Williams, op. cit. supra note 18, § 73, at 258. But he argues in part that this kind of deterrent places an "undesirable restraint on proper activities." Ibid. Yet, to a considerable extent, this only succeeds in raising the precise point at issue; namely, whether the restraint which is imposed upon activity is undesirable. The legislature might believe that for certain kinds of activity, at least, the restraint was less undesirable than the production of those consequences proscribed by the statute.

sults—that a statute of this kind would lead to the disappearance of the institution involved—what conclusions are to be drawn?

The case of socially undesirable activity is easy. If the operation of the felony murder rule has the effect of inducing persons to refuse to commit felonies, there are surely few if any persons who would object to this consequence.[24] Where socially beneficial activities, such as banking and drug distribution,[25] are concerned, the case is more troublesome. If it is further assumed that at least some of the strict liability statutes in these areas have been rigidly enforced, it is also to be noted that these institutions have not disappeared from the society. One possible conclusion to be drawn is that these strict liability offenses have been deemed to impose a not unreasonable risk. The fact that banking is still considered an extremely attractive endeavor (despite the possibility of a prison sentence for borrowing money from one's own bank) might be interpreted as evidence that people believe they can be successful bankers without violating this or a comparable strict liability statute. They believe, in other words, that they can operate with sufficient care so as not to violate the statute. Admittedly, the evidence in support of this thesis is not particularly persuasive. Perhaps most people who have gone into banking never even knew of the existence of the statute. Perhaps there is no such statute in most jurisdictions. Perhaps they knew of the statute but believed it would never attach to their conduct. And perhaps they took the statute into account incorrectly and should have been deterred by the statute. In part, the difficulty stems from the fact that there is so little empirical evidence available. It is suggested only that the above interpretation of the extant evidence is just as plausible as are the contrary inferences so often drawn.

24. Nor do there appear to be any very serious undesirable societal consequences in discouraging persons from having intercourse with females who may be around the age of sixteen. See Regina v. Prince, 13 Cox Crim. Cas. 138 (1875).

25. See the more recent federal case, United States v. Dotterweich, 320 U.S. 277 (1943), where the defendant, president of a drug company, was indicted and convicted under the Federal Food, Drug, and Cosmetic Act, 52 Stat. 1040 (1938), 21 U.S.C. §§ 301–92 (1958) for shipping misbranded and adulterated drugs in interstate commerce. There was no showing that Dotterweich personally was either negligently or intentionally engaged in the proscribed conduct. It was sufficient that he was the president of the company.

The fact that strict liability statutes might cause the disappearance of socially desirable undertakings raises, in a specific context, one important feature of the kind of justification which might be offered for these statutes. If it is conceded that strict liability statutes have an additional deterrent effect, then a fairly plausible utilitarian argument can be made for their perpetuation.

To the extent to which the function of the criminal law is conceived to be that of regulating various kinds of conduct, it becomes relevant to ask whether this particular way of regulating conduct leads to more desirable results than possible alternative procedures. The problem is not peculiar to strict liability statutes but is endemic to the legal system as a whole. Consider, for instance, one such justification of the present jury system. In order to prevent the conviction of persons who did not in fact commit the crimes of which they are accused, is is required that a unanimous jury of twelve persons find, among other things, that they believe the accused did the act in question. Perhaps if the concern were solely with guaranteeing that no innocent man be convicted, a twenty- or thirty-man jury in which unanimous consent was required for conviction would do a better job. But such is not the sole concern of the criminal law; there is also the need to prevent too many guilty persons from going free. Here, a twelve-man jury is doubtless more effective than a thirty-man jury. Requiring unanimous vote for acquittal would be a still more efficacious means of insuring that every guilty man be convicted. The decision to have a twelve-man jury which must be unanimous for conviction can be justified, in other words, as an attempt to devise an adjudicatory procedure (perhaps it is unsuccessful) which will yield a greater quantity of desirable results than would any of the alternatives.

Precisely the same kind of analysis can be made of strict liability offenses. One of the ways to prevent the occurrence of certain kinds of consequences is to enact strict liability offenses, since, ex hypothesi, these will be an added deterrent. One of the deleterious consequences of strict liability offenses is the possibility that certain socially desirable institutions will be weakened or will disappear. The problem is twofold: first, one must decide whether the additional deterrent effect of the strict liability statutes will markedly reduce the occurrence of those events which the statute seeks quite properly to prevent. And second, one must decide whether this additional reduction in undesirable occurrences is more beneficial to society than the possible deleterious effects upon otherwise desirable activities such as banking or drug distribution. For even if it be conceded that strict liability offenses may have the additionally undesirable effect of holding as criminal some persons who would not on other grounds be so regarded, strict liability could be supported on the theory that the need to prevent certain kinds of occurrences is sufficiently great so as to override the undesirable effect of punishing those who might in some other sense be "innocent."

I do not urge that either or both of these arguments for strict liability offenses are either irrefutable or even particularly convincing. But I do submit that this is a perfectly plausible kind of argument which cannot be met simply by insisting either that strict liability is an inherently unintelligible concept or that the legislative judgment of the desirability of strict criminal liability is necessarily irrational.[26] It is one thing to attack particular legislative evaluations on the grounds that they have misconstrued either the beneficial effects of strict liability or its attendant deleterious consequences, but it is quite another thing to attack the possible rationality of any such comparative determination.[27]

26. In this connection, it has been suggested that there is little evidence that legislatures consciously intend criminal statutes to be strict liability statutes. The most exhaustive examination of this issue is in a recent study conducted by the *Wisconsin Law Review*. 1956 *Wis. L. Rev.* 625. And while it seems clear that there is little affirmative evidence on this score, what evidence is available seems to indicate that at times the legislature has consciously intended the statute to be a strict criminal liability statute. *Cf. id.* at 644. Additionally, Glanville Williams argues that Parliament seems to have intended to retain strict liability in the statute interpreted by the court in the *Prince* case. See Williams, *op. cit. supra* note 18, § 73, at 259-60.

27. *Cf.* Note, 74 *L.Q. Rev.* 321, 343 (1958). "It must always be remembered that primary purpose of the criminal law is to prevent the commission of certain acts which it regards as being against the public interest and not to punish or to reform a wrongdoer. It may, therefore, be necessary to provide for strict liability when this is the only practical way to guard against the commission of the harmful act."

While I do not feel committed to the view that the primary function of the criminal law is that of the prevention of certain acts, the writer of the Note seems

As was observed earlier, the second of the two major kinds of criticism directed against strict criminal liability is that punishment of persons in accordance with the minimal requirements of strict liability—the punishment of persons in the absence of *mens rea*—is irreconcilable with those fundamental, long extant standards of criminal culpability which prevail in the community. As usually propounded the thesis is a complex one; it is also considerably more ambiguous than many of its proponents appear to have noted. One possible, although less interesting, implication concerns the notion of criminal culpability. The claim is made that the imposition of strict liability is inconsistent with the concept of criminal culpability—criminal culpability being defined to mean "requiring *mens rea*." But unless the argument is to be vacuous it must be demonstrated that independent reasons exist for selecting just this definition which precludes strict liability offenses from the class of actions to which the criminal sanctions are to attach.

A more troublesome and related question is whether the proposition is presented as a *descriptive* or *prescriptive assertion*. It is not clear whether the imposition of strict liability is thought to be incompatible with the accepted values of society or whether the prevalence of strict liability is inconsistent with what ought to be accepted values.

As an empirical assertion the protest against strict liability on the grounds that it contravenes public sentiment is, again, at best an open hypothesis. Those who seek to substantiate its correctness turn to the fact that minimal penalties are often imposed. They construe this as indicative of the felt revulsion against the concept of strict criminal liability. That judges and juries often refuse to impose those sanctions which would be imposed in the comparable cases involving the presence of *mens rea* is taken as additional evidence of community antipathy.

The evidence is, however, no less (and probably no more) persuasive on the other side. The fact that most strict liability offenses are creatures of statute has already been alluded to. While few per-

---

correct in suggesting that if an essentially utilitarian view of the criminal law is adopted, then the justification of many strict liability offenses becomes increasingly plausible.

sons would seriously wish to maintain that the legislature is either omniscient or a wholly adequate reflection of general or popular sentiment, the fact that so many legislatures have felt such apparently little compunction over enacting such statutes is surely indicative of the presence of a comparable community conviction. Strict liability offenses, as the critics so persistently note, are not mere sports, mere sporadic legislative oversights or anomalies. They are, again as the critics note, increasing in both number and scope. It may very well be the case that strict liability offenses ought to be condemned by the community; it is much more doubtful that they are presently held in such contumely.

"Mental" Requirements, Strict Liability, and Negligence

The arguments against strict liability offenses which remain to be examined go to what is conceived to be the very heart of a strict liability offense; namely, the imposition of criminal sanctions in the absence of any *fault* on the part of the actor.

Since that liability [strict liability] is meaningful only in its complete exclusion of fault, it is patently inconsistent to assert, e.g., that a businessman is honest, exercises care and skill; and also, if a misbranded or adulterated package of food somehow, unknown to anyone, is shipped from his establishment, that he should be punished or coercively educated to increase his efficiency.[28]

The actor has, ex *hypothesi*, lacked precisely those mental attributes upon which fault is properly predicated—indeed, proof of his state of mind is irrelevant. Thus, the argument concludes, the vicious character of convictions founded upon strict liability is revealed. Intelligent understanding and evaluation of this objection must await, however, the clarification of several critically ambiguous notions. In particular, the ways in which a strict liability offense may fail to take the defendant's state of mind into account are far from clearly delineated.

28. Hall, *op. cit. supra* note 18, at 304.

More seriously, still, there seem to be a variety of alternative meanings of "fault" which should be explored and discriminated.

That certain offers of proof concerning the defendant's state of mind might not be irrelevant even in the case of a putative violation is apparent. Quite apart from the ambiguous meaning of the word "act," [29] there are several other questions about the defendant's mental state which might be permitted in a strict liability prosecution. For example, suppose the defendant in the *Lindberg* case were to offer to prove that he had never intended to become a director or officer of the bank and that he reasonably believed that he was merely becoming an employee. Is it clear that this offer would be rejected as irrelevant? Or, suppose the offer of proof was that the defendant had never intended to borrow any money and reasonably believed that he was receiving a bonus. Would this statement be excluded? Thus, it can be argued that if strict liability statutes are to be characterized as "strict" because of their failure to permit inquiry as to the defendant's state of mind, this description is too broad. More appropriately, each criminal statute must be examined to determine in what respects it is "strict."

The ambiguity in the notion of "fault" can be illustrated by a hypothetical situation. Consider a statute which reads: "If a bank director borrows money in excess of [a certain amount] from the bank of which he is a director, then the directors of any other bank shall be punishable by not more than ten years in the state prison." Suppose that there is no connection between the various banks in the jurisdiction, that a director of bank A had borrowed money in excess of the statutory amount from his own bank, and that a director of bank B, a wholly unrelated bank, was accused and convicted. This, it is submitted, would be a case of "stricter" liability. The example is surely chimerical; the point is not. It serves to illustrate the way in which ordinary strict liability statutes do require "fault."

If the notion of fault requires that there be some sort of causal relationship between the accused and the act in question, it is arguable that the *Lindberg* case takes account of such a relationship. The defendant in the *Lindberg* case by virtue of his position *qua* officer of the bank had considerable control over the affairs of that bank. And

29. See note 15 *supra*.

he had even greater control over his own borrowing activities. If the element of control is sufficient to permit some kind of causal inference as to events occurring within that control, then a finding of fault in this sense does not seem arbitrary in the same manner in which a finding of fault in the hypothetical clearly would be.

Admittedly, there is a second, more restricted sense of "fault" which was clearly not present in the *Lindberg* case. This would require that the actor intended to have the particular act—borrowing money *from his own bank*—occur. And yet, there was a conscious intent to engage in just that activity—banking—which the defendant knew or should have known to be subject to criminal sanctions if certain consequences ensued. And there was a still clearer intent to do the more specific act—borrow money—which the defendant knew or should have known to be subject to criminal sanctions under certain specified circumstances. Strict liability offenses can be interpreted as legislative judgments that persons who intentionally engage in certain activities and occupy some peculiar or distinctive position of control are to be held accountable for the occurrence of certain consequences.

It is entirely possible that such a characterization of fault might still be regarded as unsatisfactory.[30] The mere fact that there was control over the general activity may be insufficient to justify a finding of fault in every case in which certain results ensue. The kind of fault which must be present before criminal sanctions ought to be imposed, so the argument might continue, is one which is predicated upon some affirmative state of mind with respect to the particular act or consequence.

There may be good reasons why this more restrictive concept of fault ought to be insisted upon in the criminal law. Indeed, I think such reasons exist and are persuasive. Furthermore, "deontological" arguments, which rest upon analysis of what ought to be entailed by concepts of justice, criminal guilt, and culpability might support the more restrictive definition. Arguments of this nature will not be challenged here, for to a considerable extent this article is written in the hope that others will feel the need to articulate these contentions

---

30. Hall, *op. cit. supra note* 18, at 304, clearly regards such a definition as unsatisfactory.

more precisely. However, there remains one final thesis which must be questioned. That is, that a person who accepts this more restrictive notion of fault can consistently believe that negligent acts ought to be punished by the criminal law.[31]

If the objection to the concept of strict liability is that the defendant's state of mind is irrelevant, then a comparable objection seems to lie against offenses founded upon criminal negligence. For the jury in a criminal negligence prosecution asks only whether the activity of the defendant violated some standard of care which a reasonable member of the community would not have violated.[32] To the extent that strict liability statutes can be interpreted as legislative judgments that conduct which produces or permits certain consequences is unreasonable, strict criminal liability is similar to a jury determination that conduct in a particular case was unreasonable.

There are, of course, important differences between the two kinds of offenses. Precisely because strict liability statutes require an antecedent judgment of per se unreasonableness, they necessarily require a more general classification of the kind of activity which is to be regulated. They tend, and perhaps inherently so, to neglect many features which ought to be taken into account before such a judgment is forthcoming. Criminal negligence, on the other hand, demands an essentially *a posteriori* judgment as to the conduct in the particular

---

31. The "Model Penal Code," §§ 2.02, 2.05 (Tent. Draft No. 4, 1955), appears to take this approach.

32. I find highly unpersuasive, attempts to treat negligence as in fact requiring *mens rea*. It has been argued that "in the case of negligence . . . the law operates with an objective standard which, based upon experience, closely approximates that under which the defendant must have operated in fact. In my opinion, therefore, we are here confronted with the use of a schematic and crude way of establishing the *mens rea*, but one which nevertheless evidences the law's concern for the mental attitude of the defendant." Mueller, *supra* note 16, at 1063–64.

If Mueller is suggesting merely that when certain kinds of consequences occur in certain kinds of situations it is reasonable to infer that the defendant in fact had a certain state of mind, then I find nothing objectionable about this claim. But, of course, *mutatis mutandis*, the same can be said for many strict liability offenses. If, on the other hand, he is suggesting that negligence in fact requires the jury to make a determination as to the presence or absence of the defendant's *mens rea*, then I do not understand in what sense this is accurate.

case. As such, it surely provides more opportunity for the jury to consider just those factors which are most significant in determining whether the standard of care was observed.

In spite of these important distinctions, in so far as strict liability statutes are condemned because they fail to require a mental element, negligence as a category of criminality ought to be likewise criticized. There may be independent reasons for urging the retention or rejection of the category of criminal negligence—just as there may be such reasons for accepting or disallowing strict liability offenses. But the way in which the two kinds of criminal liability are similar must be kept in mind whenever they are evaluated.

Conclusion

It is readily conceded that many strict liability statutes do not perform any very meaningful or desirable social function. It is admitted, too, that legislatures may have been both negligent and unwise in their selection of strict criminal liability as the means by which to achieve certain ends. But until the issues raised in the preceding discussion have been considered more carefully and precisely, it will not be immediately evident that all strict liability statutes are inherently vicious and irrational legislative or judicial blunders.

Lady B. Wootton

The Function of
the Courts *

Before I embark on discussion of the function of the criminal courts perhaps a word may be said about the atmosphere in which this function is performed. It is, in the higher courts at least, an atmosphere of archaic majesty and ritual. Moreover the members of the Bar, whether on or off the Bench, constitute a sodality that is, surely, unique among English professions; nor is there anything in their training which might widen their social horizons or enlarge their social observations. In consequence, there is perhaps no place in English life where the divisions of our society are more obtrusive: nowhere where one is more conscious of the division into "them" and "us." Of the effect of this each must judge for himself. Many of those who gave evidence before the Streatfeild Committee [1] expressed the view (though the Committee itself maintained a skeptical attitude) that the formality of the superior courts, along with the period of waiting before trial and the risk of incurring a substantial sentence, had a salutary effect upon offenders. There may indeed be cases where this is so. But my own opinion is that an opposite effect is more often likely: that the formal and unfamiliar language, the wigs and robes, the remoteness of the judge from the lives and temptations of many defendants detract from, rather than add to, the effectiveness of British justice.

Be that as it may, of the twin functions of the courts in identifying and dealing with (here I deliberately choose what I hope is a wholly neutral word) offenders, the first raises fewer controversies than the

* Barbara Wootton, Crime and the Criminal Law (London: Stevens and Son Ltd., 1963), pp. 48–57. Reprinted by permission of the author and the publisher.
1. Interdepartmental Committee on the Business of the Criminal Courts, Report (H.M.S.O.) 1961, Cmnd. 1289, para. 93.

second. But even here certain of the customary procedures seem incongruous in a scientific age.

For instance, the legal process of examination, cross-examination and re-examination can hardly be rated highly as an instrument for ascertaining the facts of past history. At least no scientist would expect to extract the truth from opposite distortions, although it is perhaps not unknown for scientific controversies to resolve themselves—I nearly said degenerate—to this level. The accusatorial method is, however, so deeply rooted in our history that it would be idle to embark on any comparison of its merits with those of its inquisitorial rival. I will therefore only call attention in passing to the present Lord Chancellor's observation (though in a totally different context) that "where the task of a body is to ascertain what has happened, there is not, as far as I can see, any escape from an inquisitorial procedure" [2]—with its implication that in the courts the ascertainment of the facts cannot be the primary concern. That the place of historical truth in the legal process is indeed only secondary is no doubt acceptable legal doctrine—otherwise it would scarcely be possible for a distinguished lawyer to express his admiration of the success of another distinguished lawyer in obtaining an "almost impossible" verdict, as Lord Hailsham once did to the late Lord Birkett.[3] Nevertheless it is hard to see how the discovery of the truth and the protection of the innocent from unjust conviction can be regarded as alternative objectives: the more accurately the relevant facts are established the less the probability that a wrongful conviction will result. When, however, the facts are in doubt the price that must be paid for safeguarding the innocent is the risk that the guilty will go free; and the greater the doubt the higher this price will be.

Even within its own terms of reference, however, the process of trial might, perhaps, benefit from a little modernization. No one can fail to be struck by the contrast between the high degree of sophistication attained by forensic science in the detection of crime, and the pre-scientific character of the criminal process itself—between the skill and zeal with which modern scientific methods are seized upon in order to bring an offender to justice, and the neglect of such

2. House of Lords Debates, May 8, 1963, col. 712.
3. House of Lords Debates, February 8, 1962, col. 342.

methods in what happens when he gets there. Consider for a moment some of the familiar aspects of a criminal trial. In order to arrive at a verdict it is necessary to disentangle the truth about past events from conflicting, incomplete, distorted and often deliberately falsified accounts. At the best of times and in the best of hands this is bound to be an extremely difficult matter. Many psychological experiments have demonstrated the unreliability of the ordinary person's recollection of previous happenings, even in circumstances in which every effort is made to achieve accuracy and in which there can be no motive for falsification. Yet in our criminal courts in the vast majority of cases, including those of the utmost gravity, this task devolves upon completely inexperienced juries or upon untrained magistrates; and in the case of juries, upon whom the heaviest responsibility rests, the sacred secrecy of the jury room precludes any investigation into the methods by which, or the efficiency with which, they discharge their task. Nor do these amateurs even enjoy the help of modern technical devices. Without benefit of tape recorder or transcription, juries are not even furnished with elementary facilities for taking notes. The facts upon which their verdict should be based are recorded only in their memory of the witnesses' memory of the original events: or in their memory of the judge's summing-up of the witnesses' memory of the original events. Indeed in the use of modern recording instruments our courts are almost unbelievably antiquated. To this day in London magistrates' courts evidence is written down by the clerk in longhand—a procedure which I have never found paralleled, although I have visited similar courts in the United States, Canada, Australia, India, Japan and Ghana, as well as in Europe.

Some of these inadequacies are inevitable. Trials cannot be held on the spot, and memories are bound to fade. Trivial events which later prove to be of vital significance are bound to be overlooked at the time or imperfectly recollected. But even so, something could I think be done to improve the criminal process as a method of historical investigation. Juries might be supplied with transcriptions of the evidence—or better still with tape recordings, since it is not only what a witness says, but how he says it, which is important; or, at the very least, a recording should be available in the jury room of the judge's summing-up, for this alone in an important case can be long enough to impose a serious tax on memory: in the A6 trial it lasted for ten hours. Admittedly such changes would add to the cost of trials; but hardly in proportion to the risk of convictions or acquittals not justified by the facts.

Memories, too, might be greener if the interval between the commission of an offence and the trial of the person charged were kept to a minimum. So far as the period between committal and trial is concerned, the Criminal Justice Administration Act of 1962, following on the recommendations of the Streatfield Committee, should now make it possible for the interval between committal and trial never to exceed eight weeks, and normally to approximate to the four-week period which is already usual at the Old Bailey and such other courts as are in more or less continuous session. These improvements, however, relate only to the lapse of time between committal proceedings and subsequent trial, and do nothing to mitigate the long delays which sometimes occur before a prosecution is initiated. Even if such delays are sometimes unavoidable in serious charges, where evidence can often only be collected with difficulty and over a considerable period of time, this does not explain the long interval that often elapses—in London at any rate—particularly in motoring cases, between the commission of an offence and the resulting proceedings in the magistrates' court. At the best of times evidence in traffic cases is apt to be singularly elusive; but the supposition that speeds and distances and traffic conditions in a single incident on the road can be accurately recollected six, seven or eight months later can only be described as farcical.

Better recording and quicker trials would certainly do something to improve the efficiency of fact-finding in the criminal courts. Is it impertinent for a layman to suggest that changes in the conventions of advocacy might do more? In spite of the extreme conservatism of the legal profession, these conventions need not be regarded as wholly immutable. Indeed they are subtly changing all the time. The extravagant and often irrelevant oratory of an earlier age, for instance, has today given way to a more sober style, and the highly emotional approach of a generation or two ago sounds very oddly in contemporary ears. So it is not unreasonable to hope for further changes. In particular one could wish to see less readiness to pose unanswerable questions. Justice is not promoted by asking a witness, as I have heard a witness asked, why he did not see the trafficator on a vehicle which he has already said he did not see at all; nor by pressing a cyclist who was thrown into the air by collision with a motorcycle to state exactly on what part of his machine the impact occurred. Too often, also, inferences from shaky premises become clothed with an air of spurious certainty, as when elaborate and convincing explanations are based on the behaviour of a hypothetical person whose presence nobody can confidently remember, but equally no one can categorically deny. By the time that counsel has finished, this hypothetical figure has become so real that the court can almost picture what he was wearing; and, most sinister of all, the witness who first cast doubt upon his existence is now wholly convinced of his reality. Truth would be better served if professional etiquette could be extended to require that the distinction between the hypothetical and the agreed (between "he could have been there" and "he was there") must not be blurred. Witnesses, too, ought surely to be more explicitly encouraged to admit the limitations of their own memory or observation; and to appreciate that, understandable as is their reluctance continually to repeat "I do not know" or "I do not remember," there is nothing discreditable in doing so. Particularly is this true in the many cases in which the minutiae of time or space are important. Judges, magistrates and lawyers might indeed do well to study more closely the known facts of the psychology of perception, and to take to heart Professor Vernon's warning that "experiments indicate that it is not possible to perceive and attend to two events separately and independently if these coincide too nearly in time or space. Either one will cancel out the other or they will be combined in some way if this is at all possible.[4]

In other words, even within an accusatorial procedure, more weight might be given on both sides to the ascertainment of fact. After all, in England at any rate, a criminal trial is not a free-for-all. The prosecutor at least operates within many conventional restraints: he does not, as in some other countries, clamour for the imposition of a particular penalty; and he is often scrupulously fair in exposing the weaknesses in his own case. Is it so certain that the interests of justice or even the interests of defendants are served by the gross distortions of fact and indeed the unmitigated nonsense which is often advanced by

4. M. D. Vernon, *The Psychology of Perception* (Penguin Books, 1962), p. 171.

defending counsel? For my part I could wish—and I suspect that many experienced magistrates would say the same—that the whole question of the conventions of defense advocacy, and even more of the efficiency of present criminal procedure as a means of arriving at the truth, might be examined by the Bar. The moment for such suggestions seems moreover to be opportune, for the profession appears to be in a remarkably receptive mood. Within two days of each other, first the Attorney-General is reported to have reminded the Bar Council that "the public could have no confidence in any profession unless it were alert frequently to review its practices and to see that they correspond to the requirements of the modern age," [5] and, second, the Lord Chancellor is said to have suggested at the judges' Mansion House dinner that the wind of change must be felt in the corridors of the courts "if we, in the law, are to keep abreast of the times." [6]

Proposals for the modernisation of the methods by which the criminal courts arrive at their verdicts do not, however, raise any question as to the object of the whole exercise. Much more fundamental are the issues which arise after conviction, when many a judge or magistrate must from time to time have asked himself just what it is that he is trying to achieve. Is he trying to punish the wicked, or to prevent the recurrence of forbidden acts? The former is certainly the traditional answer and is still deeply entrenched both in the legal profession and in the minds of much of the public at large; and it has lately been reasserted in uncompromising terms by a former Lord Chief Justice. At a meeting of magistrates earlier this year Lord Goddard is reported to have said that the duty of the criminal law was to punish—and that reformation of the prisoner was not the courts' business.[7] Those who take this view doubtless comfort themselves with the belief that the two objectives are nearly identical: that the punishment of the wicked is also the best way to prevent the occurrence of prohibited acts. Yet the continual failure of a mainly punitive system to diminish the volume of crime strongly suggests that such comfort is illusory; and it will indeed be a principal theme of these lectures that the choice between the punitive and the preven-

5. *The Times,* July 16, 1963.   6. *The Times,* July 18, 1963.
7. *The Observer,* May 5, 1963.

tive [8] concept of the criminal process is a real one; and that, according as that choice is made, radical differences must follow in the courts' approach to their task. I shall, moreover, argue that in recent years a perceptible shift has occurred away from the first and towards the second of these two conceptions of the function of the criminal law; and that this movement is greatly to be welcomed and might with advantage be both more openly acknowledged and also accelerated.

First, however, let us examine the implications of the traditional view. Presumably the wickedness which renders a criminal liable to punishment must be inherent either in the actions which he has committed or in the state of mind in which he has committed them. Can we then in the modern world identify a class of inherently wicked actions? Lord Devlin, who has returned more than once to this theme, holds that we still can, by drawing a sharp distinction between what he calls the criminal and the quasi-criminal law. The distinguishing mark of the latter, in his view, is that a breach of it does not mean that the offender has done anything morally wrong. "Real" crimes, on the other hand, he describes as "sins with legal definitions"; and he adds that "It is a pity that this distinction, which I believe the ordinary man readily recognises, is not acknowledged in the administration of justice." "The sense of obligation which leads the citizen to obey a law that is good in itself is," he says, "different in quality from that which leads to obedience to a regulation designed to secure a good end." Nor does his Lordship see any reason "why the quasi-criminal should be treated with any more ignominy than a man who has incurred a penalty for failing to return a library book in time." [9] And in a personal communication he has further defined the "real" criminal law as any part of the criminal law, new or old, which the good citizen does not break without a sense of guilt.

Nevertheless this attempt to revive the lawyer's distinction between *mala in se* and *mala prohibita*—things which are bad in themselves and things which are merely prohibited—cannot, I think, succeed. In

8. I use this word throughout to describe a system the primary purpose of which is to prevent the occurrence of offences, whether committeed by persons already convicted or by other people. The relative importance of these two ("special" and "general") aspects of prevention is discussed in Chap. 4 below. See pp. 97–102.
9. Sir Patrick (now Lord) Devlin, *Law and Morals* (University of Birmingham 1961), pp. 3, 7, 8, 9.

the first place the statement that a real crime is one about which the good citizen would feel guilty is surely circular. For how is the good citizen to be defined in this context unless as one who feels guilty about committing the crimes that Lord Devlin classifies as "real"? And in the second place the badness even of those actions which would most generally be regarded as *mala in se is* inherent, not in the physical acts themselves, but in the circumstances in which they are performed. Indeed it is hard to think of any examples of actions which could, in a strictly physical sense, be said to be bad in themselves. The physical act of stealing merely involves moving a piece of matter from one place to another: what gives it its immoral character is the framework of property rights in which it occurs. Only the violation of these rights transforms an inherently harmless movement into the iniquitous act of stealing. Nor can bodily assaults be unequivocally classified as *mala in se*; for actions which in other circumstances would amount to grievous bodily harm may be not only legal, but highly beneficial, when performed by competent surgeons; and there are those who see no wrong in killing in the form of judicial hanging or in war.

One is indeed tempted to suspect that actions classified as *mala in se* are really only *mala antiqua*—actions, that is to say, which have been recognised as criminal for a very long time; and that the tendency to dismiss sundry modern offences as "merely quasi-crimes" is simply a mark of not having caught up with the realities of the contemporary world. The criminal calendar is always the expression of a particular social and moral climate, and from one generation to another it is modified by two sets of influences. On the one hand ideas about what is thought to be right or wrong are themselves subject to change; and on the other hand new technical developments constantly create new opportunities for antisocial actions which the criminal code must be extended to include. To a thorough-going Marxist these two types of change would not, presumably, be regarded as mutually independent: to the Marxist it is technical innovations which cause moral judgments to be revised. But for present purposes it does not greatly matter whether the one is, or is not, the cause of the other. In either case the technical and the moral are distinguishable. The fact that there is nothing in the Ten Commandments about the iniquity of driving a motor vehicle under the influence of drink cannot be read as evidence that the ancient Israelites regarded this offence more leniently than the contemporary British. On the other hand the divergent attitudes of our own criminal law and that of most European countries to homosexual practices has no obvious relation to technical development, and is clearly the expression of differing moral judgments, or at the least to different conceptions of the proper relation between morality and the criminal law.

One has only to glance, too, at the maximum penalties which the law attaches to various offences to realise how profoundly attitudes change in course of time. Life imprisonment, for example, is not only the obligatory sentence for noncapital murder and the maximum permissible for manslaughter. It may also be imposed for blasphemy or for the destruction of registers of births or baptisms. Again, the crime of abducting an heiress carries a potential sentence of fourteen years, while that for the abduction of a child under fourteen years is only half as long. For administering a drug to a female with a view to carnal knowledge a maximum of two years is provided, but for damage to cattle you are liable to fourteen years' imprisonment. For using unlawful oaths the maximum is seven years, but for keeping a child in a brothel it is a mere six months. Such sentences strike us today as quite fantastic; but they cannot have seemed fantastic to those who devised them.

For the origins of the supposed dichotomy between real crimes and quasicrimes we must undoubtedly look to theology, as Lord Devlin's use of the term "sins with legal definitions" itself implies. The links between law and religion are both strong and ancient. Indeed, as Lord Radcliffe has lately reminded us, it has taken centuries for "English judges to realize that the tenets and injunctions of the Christian religion were not part of the common law of England" [10]; and even today such realisation does not seem to be complete. As recently as 1961, in the "Ladies Directory" case, the defendant Shaw, you may remember, was convicted of conspiring to corrupt public morals, as well as of offences against the Sexual Offences Act of 1956 and the Obscene Publications Act of 1959, on account of his publication of a directory in which the ladies of the town advertised their services, sometimes, it would seem, in considerable detail. In reject-

10. Lord Radcliffe, *The Law and Its Compass* (Faber, 1961), p. 12.

ing Shaw's appeal to the House of Lords on the charge of conspiracy, Lord Simonds delivered himself of the opinion that without doubt "there remains in the courts a residual power to . . . conserve not only the safety but also the moral welfare of the state"; and Lord Hodson, concurring, added that "even if Christianity be not part of the law of England, yet the common law has its roots in Christianity." [11]

In the secular climate of the present age, however, the appeal to religious doctrine is unconvincing, and unlikely to be generally acceptable. Instead we must recognise a range of actions, the badness of which is inherent not in themselves, but in the circumstances in which they are performed, and which stretches in a continuous scale from wilful murder at one end to failure to observe a no parking rule or to return on time a library book (which someone else may be urgently wanting) at the other. (Incidentally a certain poignancy is given to Lord Devlin's choice of this last example by a subsequent newspaper report that a book borrower in Frankfurt who omitted, in spite of repeated requests, to return a book which he had borrowed two years previously was brought before a local magistrate actually—though apparently by mistake—in handcuffs.[12]) But however great the range from the heinous to the trivial, the important point is that the gradation is continuous; and in the complexities of modern society a vast range of actions, in themselves apparently morally neutral, must be regarded as in varying degrees anti-social, and therefore in their contemporary settings as no less objectionable than actions whose criminal status is of greater antiquity. The good citizen will doubtless experience different degrees of guilt according as he may have stabbed his wife, engaged in homosexual intercourse, omitted to return his library book or failed to prevent one of his employees from watering the milk sold by his firm. Technically these are all crimes; whether or not they are also sins is a purely theological matter with which the law has no concern. If the function of the criminal law is to punish the wicked, then everything which the law forbids must in the circumstances in which it is forbidden be regarded as in its appropriate measure wicked.

Although this is, I think, the inevitable conclusion of any argument

11. *Shaw v. Director of Public Prosecutions* [1961] 2 W.L.R. 897.
12. *The Times*, November 11, 1961.

which finds wickedness inherent in particular classes of action, it seems to be unpalatable to Lord Devlin and others who conceive the function of the criminal law in punitive terms. It opens the door too wide. Still the door can be closed again by resort to the alternative theory that the wickedness of an action is inherent not in the action itself, but in the state of mind of the person who performs it. To punish people merely for what they have done, it is argued, would be unjust, for the forbidden act might have been an accident for which the person who did it cannot be held to blame. Hence the requirement, to which traditionally the law attaches so much importance, that a crime is not, so to speak, a crime in the absence of *mens rea*.

Today, however, over a wide front even this requirement has in fact been abandoned. Today many, indeed almost certainly the majority, of the cases dealt with by the criminal courts are cases of strict liability in which proof of a guilty mind is no longer necessary for conviction. A new dichotomy is thus created, and one which in this instance exists not merely in the minds of the judges but is actually enshrined in the law itself—that is to say, the dichotomy between those offences in which the guilty mind is, and those in which it is not, an essential ingredient. In large measure, no doubt, this classification coincides with Lord Devlin's division into real and quasicrimes; but whether or no this coincidence is exact must be a question of personal judgment. To drive a car when your driving ability is impaired through drink or drugs is an offence of strict liability: it is no defence to say that you had no idea that the drink would affect you as it did, or to produce evidence that you were such a seasoned drinker that any such result was, objectively, not to be expected.

Nothing has dealt so devastating a blow at the punitive conception of the criminal process as the proliferation of offences of strict liability; and the alarm has forthwith been raised. Thus Dr. J. Ll. J. Edwards has expressed the fear that there is a real danger that the "widespread practice of imposing criminal liability independent of any moral fault" will result in the criminal law being regarded with contempt. "The process of basing criminal liability upon a theory of absolute prohibition," he writes, "may well have the opposite effect to that intended and lead to a weakening of respect for the law." [13] Nor, in

13. J. Ll. J. Edwards, *Mens Rea in Statutory Offences* (Macmillan, 1955), p. 247.

his view, is it an adequate answer to say that absolute liability can be tolerated because of the comparative unimportance of the offences to which it is applied and because, as a rule, only a monetary penalty is involved; for, in the first place, there are a number of important exceptions to this rule (drunken driving for example); and, secondly, as Dr. Edwards himself points out, in certain cases the penalty imposed by the court may be the least part of the punishment. A merchant's conviction for a minor trading offence may have a disastrous effect upon his business.

Such dislike of strict liability is not by any means confined to academic lawyers. In the courts, too, various devices have been used to smuggle mens rea back into offences from which, on the face of it, it would appear to be excluded. To the lawyer's ingenious mind the invention of such devices naturally presents no difficulty. Criminal liability, for instance, can attach only to voluntary acts. If a driver is struck unconscious with an epileptic seizure, it can be argued that he is not responsible for any consequences because his driving thereafter is involuntary: indeed he has been said not to be driving at all. If on the other hand he falls asleep, this defence will not serve since sleep is a condition that comes on gradually, and a driver has an opportunity and a duty to stop before it overpowers him. Alternatively, recourse can be had to the circular argument that anyone who commits a forbidden act must have intended to commit it and must, therefore, have formed a guilty intention. As Lord Devlin puts it, the word "knowingly" or "wilfully" can be read into acts in which it is not present; although as his Lordship points out this subterfuge is open to the criticism that it fails to distinguish between the physical act itself and the circumstances in which this becomes a crime.[14] All that the accused may have intended was to perform an action (such as firing a gun or driving a car) which is not in itself criminal. Again, in yet other cases such as those in which it is forbidden to permit or to allow something to be done the concept of negligence can do duty as a watered down version of mens rea: for how can anyone be blamed for permitting something about which he could not have known?

All these devices, it cannot be too strongly emphasised, are necessitated by the need to preserve the essentially punitive function of the

14. Lord Devlin, *Samples of Law Making* (O.U.P., 1962), pp. 71–80.

criminal law. For it is not, as Dr. Edwards fears, the criminal law which will be brought into contempt by the multiplication of offences of strict liability, so much as this particular conception of the law's function. If that function is conceived less in terms of punishment than as a mechanism of prevention these fears become irrelevant. Such a conception, however, apparently sticks in the throat of even the most progressive lawyers. Even Professor Hart, in his Hobhouse lecture on *Punishment and the Elimination of Responsibility*,[15] seems to be incurably obsessed with the notion of punishment, which haunts his text as well as figuring in his title. Although rejecting many traditional theories, such as that punishment should be "retributive" or "denunciatory," he nevertheless seems wholly unable to envisage a system in which sentence is not automatically equated with "punishment." Thus he writes of "values quite distinct from those of retributive punishment which the system of responsibility does maintain, and which remain of great importance even if our aims in *punishing* are the forward-looking aims of social protection"; and again "even if we *punish* men not as wicked but as nuisances . . ." while he makes many references to the principle that liability to punishment must depend on a voluntary act. Perhaps it requires the naïveté of an amateur to suggest that the forward-looking aims of social protection might, on occasion, have absolutely no connection with punishment.

If, however, the primary function of the courts is conceived as the prevention of forbidden acts, there is little cause to be disturbed by the multiplication of offences of strict liability. If the law says that certain things are not to be done, it is illogical to confine this prohibition to occasions on which they are done from malice aforethought; for at least the material consequences of an action, and the reasons for prohibiting it, are the same whether it is the result of sinister malicious plotting, of negligence or of sheer accident. A man is equally dead and his relatives equally bereaved whether he was stabbed or run over by a drunken motorist or by an incompetent one; and the inconvenience caused by the loss of your bicycle is unaffected by the question whether or no the youth who removed it had the intention of putting it back, if in fact he had not done so at the time

15. H. L. A. Hart, *Punishment and the Elimination of Responsibility* (Athlone Press, 1962), pp. 27, 28. Italics mine.

of his arrest. It is true, of course, as Professor Hart has argued,[16] that the material consequences of an action by no means exhaust its effects. "If one person hits another, the person struck does not think of the other as *just* a cause of pain to him. . . . If the blow was light but deliberate, it has a significance for the person struck quite different from an accidental much heavier blow." To ignore this difference, he argues, is to outrage "distinctions which not only underlie morality, but pervade the whole of our social life." That these distinctions are widely appreciated and keenly felt no one would deny. Often perhaps they derive their force from a purely punitive or retributive attitude; but alternatively they may be held to be relevant to an assessment of the social damage that results from a criminal act. Just as a heavy blow does more damage than a light one, so also perhaps does a blow which involves psychological injury do more damage than one in which the hurt is purely physical.

The conclusion to which this argument leads is, I think, not that the presence or absence of the guilty mind is unimportant, but that *mens rea* has, so to speak—and this is the crux of the matter—*got into the wrong place*. Traditionally, the requirement of the guilty mind is written into the actual definition of a crime. No guilty intention, no crime, is the rule. Obviously this makes sense if the law's concern is with wickedness: where there is no guilty intention, there can be no wickedness. But it is equally obvious, on the other hand, that an action does not become innocuous merely because whoever performed it meant no harm. If the object of the criminal law is to prevent the occurrence of socially damaging actions, it would be absurd to turn a blind eye to those which were due to carelessness, negligence or even accident. The question of motivation is *in the first instance* irrelevant.

But only in the first instance. At a later stage, that is to say, after what is now known as a conviction, the presence or absence of guilty intention is all-important for its effect on the appropriate measures to be taken to prevent a recurrence of the forbidden act. The prevention of accidential deaths presents different problems from those involved in the prevention of wilful murders. The results of the actions of the careless, the mistaken, the wicked and the merely unfortunate may be indistinguishable from one another, but each case calls for a

16. *Op. cit.*, pp. 29, 30.

different treatment. Tradition, however, is very strong, and the notion that these differences are relevant only after the fact has been established that the accused committed the forbidden act seems still to be deeply abhorrent to the legal mind. Thus Lord Devlin, discussing the possibility that judges might have taken the line that all "unintentional" criminals might be dealt with simply by the imposition of a nominal penalty, regards this as the "negation of law." "It would," [17] he says, "confuse the function of mercy which the judge is dispensing when imposing the penalty with the function of justice. It would have been to deny to the citizen due process of law because it would have been to say to him, in effect: 'Although we cannot think that Parliament intended you to be punished in this case because you have really done nothing wrong, come to us, ask for mercy, and we shall grant mercy.' . . . In all criminal matters the citizen is entitled to the protection of the law . . . and the mitigation of penalty should not be adopted as the prime method of dealing with accidental offenders."

Within its implied terms of reference the logic is unexceptionable. If the purpose of the law is to dispense punishment tempered with mercy, then to use mercy as a consolation for unjust punishment is certainly to give a stone for bread. But these are not the implied terms of reference of strict liability. In the case of offences of strict liability the presumption is not that those who have committed forbidden actions must be punished, but that appropriate steps must be taken to prevent the occurrence of such actions.

Here, as often in other contexts also, the principles involved are admirably illustrated by the many driving offences in which conviction does not involve proof of mens rea. If, for instance, the criterion of gravity is the amount of social damage which a crime causes, many of these offences must be judged extremely grave. In 1961 299 persons were convicted on charges of causing death by dangerous driving, that is to say more than five times as many as were convicted of murder (including those found guilty but insane) and 85 per cent more than the total of convictions for all other forms of homicide (namely murder, manslaughter and infanticide) put together. It is, moreover, a peculiarity of many driving offences that the offender seldom intends the actual damage which he causes. He may be to

17. Lord Devlin, *Samples of Law Making* (O.U.P., 1962), p. 73.

blame in that he takes a risk which he knows may result in injury to other people or to their property, but such injury is neither an inevitable nor an intended consequence of the commission of the offence: which is not true of, for example, burglary. Dangerous or careless driving ranges in a continuous series from the almost wholly accidental, through the incompetent and the negligent to the positively and grossly culpable; and it is quite exceptionally difficult in many of these cases to establish just to what point along this scale any particular instance should be assigned. In consequence the gravity of any offence tends to be estimated by its consequences rather than by the state of mind of the perpetrator—which is less usual (although attempted murder or grievous bodily harm may turn into murder, if the victim dies) in the case of other crimes. In my experience it is exceptional (though not unknown) for a driving charge to be made unless an accident actually occurs, and the nature of the charge is apt to be determined by the severity of the accident. I recall, for example, a case in which a car driver knocked down an elderly man on a pedestrian crossing, and a month later the victim died in hospital after an operation, his death being, one must suppose, in spite, rather than because, of this. Thereupon the charge, which had originally been booked by the police as careless, not even dangerous, driving was upgraded to causing death by dangerous driving.

For all these reasons it is recognised that if offences in this category are to be dealt with by the criminal courts at all, this can only be on a basis of strict liability. This particular category of offences thus illustrates all too vividly the fact that in the modern world in one way or another, as much and more damage is done by negligence, or by indifference to the welfare or safety of others, as by deliberate wickedness. In technically simpler societies this is less likely to be so, for the points of exposure to the follies of others are less numerous, and the daily chances of being run over, or burnt or infected or drowned because someone has left undone something that he ought to have done are less ominous. These new complexities were never envisaged by the founders of our legal traditions, and it is hardly to be wondered at if the law itself is not yet fully adapted to them. Yet it is by no means certain that the last chapter in the long and chequered history of the concept of guilt, which is so deeply rooted in our traditions, has yet been written. Time was when inanimate objects—the rock that fell on you, the tree that attracted the lightning that killed you —were held to share the blame for the disasters in which they were instrumental; and it was properly regarded as a great step forward when the capacity to acquire a guilty mind was deemed to be one of the distinctive capacities of human beings.[18] But now, perhaps, the time has come for the concept of legal guilt to be dissolved into a wider concept of responsibility or at least accountability, in which there is room for negligence as well as purposeful wrong doing; and for the significance of a conviction to be reinterpreted merely as evidence that a prohibited act has been committed, questions of motivation being relevant only in so far as they bear upon the probability of such acts being repeated.

I am not, of course, arguing that all crimes should immediately be transferred into the strict liability category. To do so would in some cases involve formidable problems of definition—as, for instance, in that of larceny. But I do suggest that the contemporary extension of strict liability is not the nightmare that it is often made out to be, that it does not promise the decline and fall of the criminal law, and that it is, on the contrary, a sensible and indeed inevitable measure of adaptation to the requirements of the modern world; and above all I suggest that its supposedly nightmarish quality disappears once it is accepted that the primary objective of the criminal courts is preventive rather than punitive. Certainly we need to pay heed to Mr. Nigel Walker's reminder [19] that "under our present law it is possible for a person to do great harm in circumstances which suggest that there is a risk of his repeating it, and yet to secure an acquittal." In two types of case, in both of which such harm can result, the concept of the guilty mind has become both irrelevant and obstructive. In this lecture I have been chiefly concerned with the first of these categories— that of cases of negligence. The second category—that of mental abnormality—will be the theme of that which follows.

18. There could be an argument here, into which I do not propose to enter, as to whether this capacity is not shared by some of the higher animals.
19. N. Walker, "Queen Victoria Was Right," *New Society*, June 27, 1963.

H. L. A. Hart

Changing Conceptions
of Responsibility *

I have said that the change made by the introduction of diminished responsibility was both meagre and half-hearted. Nonetheless it marked the end of an era in the criticism of the law concerning the criminal responsibility of the mentally abncrmal. From this point on criticism has largely changed its character. Instead of demanding that the court should take more seriously the task of dividing law-breakers into two classes—those fully responsible and justly punishable because they had an unimpaired capacity to conform to the law, and those who were to be excused for lack of this—critics have come to think this a mistaken approach. Instead of seeking an expansion of the doctrine of mens rea they have argued that it should be eliminated and have welcomed the proliferation of offences of strict liability as a step in the right direction and a model for the future. The bolder of them have talked of the need to 'by-pass' or 'dispense with' questions of responsibility and have condemned the old efforts to widen the scope of the M'Naghten Rules as waste of time or worse. Indeed, their attitude to such reforms is like that of the Communist who condemns private charity in a capitalist system because it tends to hide the radical errors of the system and thus preserve it. By far the best informed, most trenchant and influential advocate of these new ideas is Lady Wootton whose powerful work on the subject of criminal responsibility has done much to change and, in my opinion, to raise, the whole level of discussion.[1]

* H. L. A. Hart, "Changing Conceptions of Responsibility," in *Punishment and Responsibility* (Oxford: Clarendon Press, 1968), pp. 93–209. Reprinted by permisson of the author and the publisher.
1. See her *Social Science and Social Pathology* (1959) esp. Chapter VIII on

Hence, since 1957 a new skepticism going far beyond the old criticisms has developed. It is indeed a skepticism of the whole institution of criminal punishment so far as it contains elements which differentiate it from a system of purely forward-looking social hygiene in which our only concern, when we have an offender to deal with, is with the future and the rational aims of the prevention of further crime, the protection of society and the care and if possible the cure of the offender. For criminal punishment, as even the most progressive older critics of the M'Naghten Rules conceived of it, is *not* mere social hygiene. It differs from such a purely forward-looking system in the stress that it places on something in the past: the state of mind of the accused at the time, not of his trial, but when he broke the law.

To many modern critics this backward-looking reference to the accused's past state of mind as a condition of his liability to compulsory measures seems a useless deflection from the proper forward-looking aims of a rational system of social control. The past they urge is over and done with, and the offender's past state of mind is only important as a diagnosis of the causes of his offence and a prognosis of what can be done now to counter these causes. Nothing in the past, according to this newer outlook, can in itself justify or be required to license what we do to the offender now; that is something to be determined exclusively by reference to the consequences to society and to him. Lady Wootton argues that if the aim of the criminal law is to be the prevention of 'socially damaging actions' not retribution for past wickedness, the conventional doctrine puts *mens rea* 'into the wrong place.'[2] *Mens rea* is on her view relevant only *after* conviction as a guide to what measures should be taken to prevent a recurrence of the forbidden act. She considers it 'illogical' if the aim of the criminal law is prevention to make *mens rea* part of the definition of a crime

---

"Mental Disorder and the Problem of Moral and Criminal Responsibility"; "Diminished Responsibility: A Layman's View," 76 *L.Q.R.* (1960), p. 224; *Crime and the Criminal Law* (1963).

2. See *Crime and the Criminal Law*, p. 52. But she does not consider explicitly whether, even if the aim of the criminal law is to prevent crime, there are not moral objections to applying its sanctions even as preventives to those who lacked the capacity to conform to the Law. See *infra*, pp. 207–8.

and a necessary condition of the offender's liability to compulsory measures.[3]

This way of thinking leads to a radical revision of the penal system which in crude outline and in its most extreme form is as follows: Once it has been proved in a court that a person's outward conduct fits the legal definition of some crime, this without proof of any *mens rea*, is sufficient to bring him within the scope of compulsory measures. These may be either of a penal or therapeutic kind or both; or it may be found that no measures are necessary in a particular case and the offender may be discharged. But the choice between these alternatives is not to be made by reference to the offender's past mental state—his culpability—but by consideration of what steps, in view of his present mental state and his general situation, are likely to have the best consequences for him and for society.

I have called this the extreme form of the new approach because as I have formulated it it is generally applicable to all offenders alike. It is not a system reserved solely for those who could be classed as mentally abnormal. The whole doctrine of *mens rea* would on this extreme version of the theory be dropped from the law; so that the distinctions which at present we draw and think vital to draw before convicting an offender, between, for example, intentional and unintentional wrongdoing, would no longer be relevant at this stage. To show that you have struck or wounded another unintentionally or without negligence would not save you from conviction and liability to such treatment, penal or therapeutic, as the court might deem advisable on evidence of your mental state and character.

This is, as I say, the extreme form of the theory, and it is the form that Lady Wootton now advances.[4] But certainly a less extreme though more complex form is conceivable which would replace, not the whole doctrine of *mens rea*, but only that part of it which concerns the legal responsibility of the mentally abnormal. In this more moderate form of the theory a mentally normal person would still escape conviction if he acted unintentionally or without some other

3. *Op. cit.*, p. 51.

4. In *Crime and the Criminal Law* she makes it clear that the elimination or 'withering away' of *mens rea* as a condition of liability is to apply to all its elements not merely to its provision for mental abnormality. Hence strict liability is welcomed as the model for the future (*op. cit.*, pp. 46–57).

requisite mental element forming part of the definition of the crime charged. The innovation would be that no form of insanity or mental abnormality would bar a conviction, and this would no longer be investigated before conviction.[5] It would be something to be investigated only after conviction to determine what measures of punishment or treatment would be most efficacious in the particular case. It is important to observe that most advocates of the elimination of responsibility have been mainly concerned with the inadequacies or absurdities of the existing law in relation to mentally abnormal offenders, and some of these advocates may have intended only the more moderate form of the theory which is limited to such offenders. But I doubt if this is at all representative, for many, including Lady Wootton, have said that no satisfactory line can be drawn between the mentally normal and abnormal offenders: there simply are no clear or reliable criteria. They insist that general definitions of mental health are too vague and too conflicting; we should be freed from all such illusory classifications to treat, in the most appropriate way from the point of view of society, all persons who have actually manifested the behaviour which is the *actus reus* of a crime.[6] The fact that harm was done unintentionally should not preclude an investigation of what steps if any are desirable to prevent a repetition. This scepticism of the possibility of drawing lines between the normal and abnormal offenders commits advocates of the elimination of responsibility to the extreme form of the theory.

Such then are the essentials of the new idea. Of course the phrase 'eliminating responsibility' does sound very alarming and when Lady Wootton's work first made it a centre of discussion the columns of *The Times* newspaper showed how fluttered legal and other dovecotes were. But part at least of the alarm was unnecessary because it arose from the ambiguities of the word 'responsibility'; and it is, I think, still important to distinguish two of the very different things this difficult word may mean. To say that someone is legally responsible for something often means only that under legal rules he is liable to be made either to suffer or to pay compensation in certain eventualities. The expression 'he'll pay for it' covers both these things. In this the primary sense of the word, though a man is normally only

---

5. Save as indicated *infra* p. 205, n. 31.   6. See Wootton, *op. cit.*, p. 51.

responsible for his own actions or the harm he has done, he may be also responsible for the actions of other persons if legal rules so provide. Indeed in this sense a baby in arms or a totally insane person might be legally responsible—again, if the rules so provide; for the word simply means liable to be made to account or pay and we might call this sense of the word 'legal accountability'. But the new idea— the programme of eliminating responsibility—is not, as some have feared, meant to eliminate legal accountability: persons who break the law are not just to be left free. What is to be eliminated are enquiries as to whether a person who has done what the law forbids was responsible at the time he did it and responsible in this sense does not refer to the legal status of accountability. It means the capacity, so far as this is a matter of a man's mind or will, which normal people have to control their actions and conform to law. In this sense of responsibility a man's responsibility can be said to be 'impaired'. That is indeed the language of s. 2 of the Homicide Act 1957 which introduced into English law the idea of diminished responsibility: it speaks of a person's 'mental' responsibility and in the rubric to s. 2 even of persons 'suffering from' diminished responsibility. It is of course easy to see why this second sense of responsibility (which might be called 'personal responsibility') has grown up alongside the primary idea of legal accountability. It is no doubt because the law normally, though not always, confines legal accountability to persons who are believed to have normal capacities of control.

So perhaps the new ideas are less alarming than they seem at first. They are also less new, and those who advocate them have always been able to point to earlier developments within English law which seem to foreshadow these apparently revolutionary ideas. Lady Wootton herself makes much of the fact that the doctrine of mens rea in the case of normal offenders has been watered down by the introduction of strict liability and she deprecates the alarm this has raised. But apart from this, the Courts have often been able to deal with mentally abnormal persons accused of crime without confronting the issue of their personal responsibility at the time of their offence. There are in fact several different ways in which this question may be avoided. A man may be held on account of his mental state to be unfit to plead when brought to trial; or he may be certified insane before trial; or, except on a charge of murder, an accused person might enter a plea of guilty with the suggestion that he should be put on probation with a condition of mental treatment.[7] In fact, only a very small percentage of the mentally abnormal have been dealt with under the M'Naghten Rules, a fact which is understandable since a successful plea under those Rules means detention in Broadmoor for an indefinite period and many would rather face conviction and imprisonment and so may not raise the question of mental abnormality at all. So the old idea of treating mental abnormality as bearing on the question of the accused's responsibility and to be settled before conviction, has with few exceptions only been a reality in murder cases to which alone is the plea of diminished responsibility applicable.

But the most important departure from received ideas incorporated in the doctrine of mens rea is the Mental Health Act, 1959, which expands certain principles of older legislation. S. 60 of this Act provides that in any case, except where the crime is not punishable by imprisonment or the sentence is fixed by the law (and this latter exception virtually excludes only murder), the courts may, after conviction of the offender, if two doctors agree that the accused falls into any of four specified categories of mental disorder, order his detention for medical treatment instead of passing a penal sentence, though it requires evidence that such detention is warranted. The four categories of mental disorder are very wide and include even psychopathic disorder in spite of the general lack of clear or agreed criteria of this condition. The courts are told by the statute that in exercising their choice between penal or medical measures to have regard to the nature of the offence and the character and antecedents of the offender. These powers have come to be widely used [8] and are available even in cases where a murder charge has been reduced to manslaughter on a plea of provocation or diminished responsibility.

Advocates of the programme of eliminating responsibility welcome the powers given by the Mental Health Act to substitute compulsory treatment for punishment, but necessarily they view it as a com-

7. In 1962 the number of persons over 17 treated in these ways were respectively 36 (unfit to plead), 5 (insane before trial), and 836 (probation with mental treatment). See *Criminal Statistics* 1962.
8. In 1962 hospital orders under this section were made in respect of 1187 convicted persons (*Criminal Statistics* 1962).

promise falling short of what is required, and we shall understand their own views better if we see why they think so. It falls short in four respects. First the power given to courts to order compulsory treatment instead of punishment is discretionary, and even if the appropriate medical evidence is forthcoming the courts may still administer conventional punishment if they choose. The judges may still think in terms of responsibility, and it is plain that they occasionally do so in these cases. Thus in the majority of cases of conviction for manslaughter following on a successful plea of diminished responsibility, the courts have imposed sentences of imprisonment notwithstanding their powers under s. 60 of the Mental Health Act, and the Lord Chief Justice has said that in such cases the prisoner may on the facts be shown to have some responsibility for which he must be punished.[9] Secondly, the law itself still preserves a conception of penal methods, such as imprisonment, coloured by the idea that it is a payment for past wickedness and not just an alternative to medical treatment; for though the courts may order medical treatment or punish, they cannot combine these. This of course is a refusal to think, as the new critics demand we should think,[10] of punitive and medical measures as merely different forms of social hygiene to be used according to a prognosis of their effects on the convicted person. Thirdly, as it stands at present, the scheme presupposes that a satisfactory distinction can be drawn on the basis of its four categories of mental disorder between those who are mentally abnormal and those who are not. But the more radical reformers are not merely sceptical about the adequacy of the criteria which distinguish, for example, the psychopath from the normal offender: they would contend that there may exist propensities to certain types of socially harmful behaviour in people who are in other ways not abnormal and that a rational system should attend to these cases.

But fourthly, and this is most important, the scheme is vitiated for these critics because the courts' powers are only exercisable after the conviction of an offender and, for this conviction, proof of *mens rea* at the time of his offence is still required: the question of the accused's mental abnormality may still be raised before conviction as

9. R. v. *Morris* (1961) 45 Cr. App. Rep. 185.
10. See Wootton, *op. cit.*, pp. 79–80.

a defence if the accused so wishes. So the Mental Health Act does not 'by-pass' the whole question of responsibility: it does not eliminate the doctrine of mens rea. It expands the courts' discretion in dealing with a convicted person, enabling it to choose between penal and therapeutic measures and making this choice in practice largely independent of the offender's state of mind at the time of his offence. Its great merit is that the mentally abnormal offender who would before have submitted to a sentence of imprisonment rather than raise a plea of insanity under the M'Naghten Rules (because success would mean indeterminate detention in Broadmoor) may now be encouraged to bring forward his mental condition after conviction, in the hope of obtaining a hospital order rather than a sentence of imprisonment.

The question which now awaits our consideration is the merits of the claim that we should proceed from such a system as we now have under the Mental Health Act to one in which the criminal courts were freed altogether from the doctrine of mens rea and could proceed to the use of either penal or medical measures at discretion simply on proof that the accused had done the outward acts of a crime. Prisons and hospitals under such a scheme will alike 'be simply "places of safety" in which offenders receive the treatment which experience suggests is most likely to evoke the desired response.' [11]

The case for adopting these new ideas in their entirety has been supported by arguments of varying kinds and quality, and it is very necessary to sift the wheat from the chaff. The weakest of the arguments is perhaps the one most frequently heard, namely, that our concern with personal responsibility incorporated in the doctrine of mens rea only makes sense if we subscribe to a retributive theory of punishment according to which punishment is used and justified as an 'appropriate' or 'fitting' return for past wickedness and not merely as a preventive of anti-social conduct. This, as I have argued elsewhere,[12] is a philosophical confusion and Lady Wootton falls a victim to it because she makes too crude a dichotomy between 'punishment' and 'prevention.' She does not even mention a moral outlook on punish-

11. Wootton, op. cit., pp. 79–80.
12. 'Punishment and the Elimination of Responsibility', Chap. VII, supra.

ment which is surely very common, very simple and except perhaps for the determinist perfectly defensible. This is the view that out of considerations of fairness or justice to individuals we should restrict even punishment designed as a 'preventive' to those who had a normal capacity and a fair opportunity to obey. This is still an intelligible ideal of justice to the individuals whom we punish even if we punish them to protect society from the harm that crime does and not to pay back the harm that they have done. And it remains intelligible even if in securing this form of fairness to those whom we punish we secure a lesser measure of conformity to law than a system of total strict liability which repudiated the doctrine of mens rea.

But of course it is certainly arguable that, at present, in certain cases, in the application of the doctrine of mens rea, we recognize this principle of justice in a way which plays too high a price in terms of social security. For there are indeed cases where the application of mens rea operates in surprising and possibly dangerous ways. A man may cause very great harm, may even kill another person, and under the present law neither be punished for it nor subjected to any compulsory medical treatment or supervision. This happened, for example, in February 1961 when a United States Air Force sergeant,[13] after a drunken party, killed a girl, according to his own story, in his sleep. He was tried for murder but the jury were not persuaded by the prosecution, on whom the legal burden of proof rests, that the sergeant's story was false and he was accordingly acquitted and discharged altogether. It is worth observing that in recent years in cases of dangerous driving where the accused claims that he suffered from 'automatism' or a sudden lapse of consciousness, the courts have striven very hard to narrow the scope of this defence because of the obvious social dangers of an acquittal of such persons, unaccompanied by any order for compulsory treatment. They have produced a most complex body of law distinguishing between 'sane' and 'insane' automatism each with their special burdens of proof.[14] No doubt such dangerous cases are not very numerous and the risk of their occurrence is one which many people might prefer to run rather than introduce a new system dispensing altogether with proof of mens rea.

13. *The Times*, 18 February 1961 (Staff Sergeant Boshears).
14. See *Bratty v. Att. Gen. for Northern Ireland* (1961), 3 All E.R., 523 and Cross, 'Reflections on Bratty's Case' 78 *L.Q.R.* (1962), p. 236.

In any case something less extreme than the new system might deal with such cases; for the courts could be given powers in the case of such physically harmful offences to order, notwithstanding an acquittal, any kind of medical treatment or supervision that seemed appropriate.

But the most important arguments in favour of the more radical system in which proof of the outward act alone is enough to make the accused liable to compulsory measures of treatment or punishment, comes from those who, like Lady Wootton, have closely scrutinized the actual working of the old plea of insanity and the plea of diminished responsibility introduced in 1957 by the Homicide Act into cases of homicide. The latter treats mental abnormality as an aspect of *mens rea* and forces the Courts before the verdict to decide the question whether the accused's 'mental responsibility,' that is, his capacity to control his actions was 'substantially impaired' at the time of his offence when he killed another person. The conclusion drawn by Lady Wootton from her impressive and detailed study of all the cases (199 in number) in which this plea was raised down to mid-September of 1962, is that this question which is thus forced upon the Courts should be discarded as unanswerable. Here indeed she echoes the cry, often in earlier years thundered from the Bench, that it is impossible to distinguish between an irresistible impulse and an impulse which was merely not resisted by the accused.

But here too if we are to form a balanced view we must distinguish between dubious philosophical contentions and some very good sense. The philosophical arguments (which I will not discuss here in detail) pitch the case altogether too high: they are supposed to show that the question whether a man could have acted differently is *in principle unanswerable* and not merely that in Law Courts we do not usually have clear enough evidence to answer it. Lady Wootton says that a man's responsibility or capacity to resist temptation is something 'buried in [his] consciousness, into which no human being can enter',[15] known if at all only to him and to God: it is not something which other men may ever know; and since 'it is not possible to get inside another man's skin'[16] it is not something of which they can ever form even a reasonable estimate as a matter of probability. Yet

15. See 'Diminished Responsibility: A Layman's view' 76 L.Q.R. (1960), p. 232.
16. See *Crime and the Criminal Law*, p. 74.

strangely enough she does not take the same view of the question which arises under the M'Naghten Rules whether a man knew what he was doing or that it was illegal, although a man's knowledge is surely as much, or as little, locked in his breast as his capacity for self-control. Questions about the latter indeed may often be more difficult to answer than questions about a man's knowledge; yet in favourable circumstances if we know a man well and can trust what he says about his efforts or struggles to control himself we may have as good ground for saying 'Well he just could not do it though he tried' as we have for saying 'He didn't know that the pistol was loaded.' And we sometimes may have good general evidence that in certain conditions, e.g., infancy or a clinically definable state, such as depression after childbirth, human beings are unable or less able than the normal adult to master certain impulses. We are not forced by the facts to say of a child or mental defective, who has struggled vainly with tears, merely 'he usually cries when that happens.' We say—and why not?—'he could not stop himself crying though he tried as hard as he could.'

It must however be conceded that such clear cases are very untypical of those that face the Courts where an accused person is often fighting for his life or freedom. Lady Wootton's best arguments are certainly independent of her more debatable philosophical points about our ability to know what is locked in another's mind or breast. Her central point is that the evidence put before Courts on the question whether the accused lacked the capacity to conform to the law, or whether it was substantially impaired, at the best only shows the *propensity* of the accused to commit crimes of certain sorts. From this, she claims, it is a fallacy to infer that he could not have done otherwise than commit the crime of which he is accused. She calls this fallacious argument 'circular': we infer the accused's lack of capacity to control his actions from his propensity to commit crimes and then both explain this propensity and excuse his crimes by his lack of capacity. Lady Wootton's critics have challenged this view of the medical and other evidence on which the Courts act in these cases.[17] They would admit that it is at any rate in part *through* studying a man's crimes that we may discern his incapacity to control his

17. See N. Walker, 'M'Naghten's Ghost', *The Listener*, 29 Aug. 1963, p. 303.

actions. Nonetheless the evidence for this conclusion is not merely the bare fact that he committed these crimes repeatedly, but the manner and the circumstances and the psychological state in which he did this. Secondly in forming any conclusion about a man's ability to control his action much more than his repeated crimes are taken into account. Antisocial behaviour is not just used to explain and excuse itself, even in the case of the psychopath, the definition of whose disorder presents great problems. I think there is much in these criticisms. Nonetheless the forensic debate before judge and jury of the question whether a mentally disordered person could have controlled his action or whether his capacity to do this was or was not 'substantially impaired' seems to me very often very unreal. The evidence tendered is not only often conflicting, but seems to relate to the specific issue of the accused's power or capacity for control on a specific past occasion only very remotely. I can scarcely believe that on this, the supposed issue, anything coherent penetrates to the minds of the jury after they have heard the difficult expert evidence and heard the judge's warning that these matters are 'incapable of scientific proof.' [18] And I sympathize with the judges in their difficult task of instructing juries on this plea. In Israel there are no juries to be instructed and the judges themselves must confront these same difficulties in deciding in accordance with the principle of the Mandelbrot case whether or not the action of a mentally abnormal person who knew what he was doing occurred 'independently of the exercise of his will.'

Because of these difficulties I would prefer to the present law the scheme which I have termed the 'moderate' form of the new doctrine. Under this scheme mens rea would continue to be a necessary condition of liability to be investigated and settled before conviction except so far as it relates to mental abnormality. The innovation would be that an accused person would no longer be able to adduce any form of mental abnormality as a bar to conviction. The question of his mental abnormality would under this scheme be investigated only after conviction and would be primarily concerned with his present rather than his past mental state. His past mental state at the time of his crime would only be relevant so far as it provided ancil-

18. Per Parker C. J. in R. v. Byrne (1960) 44 Cr. App. 246 at 258.

lary evidence of the nature of his abnormality and indicated the appropriate treatment. This position could perhaps be fairly easily reached by eliminating the pleas of insanity and diminished responsibility and extending the provisions of the Mental Health Act, 1959 to all offences including murder. But I would further provide that in cases where the appropriate direct evidence of mental disorder was forthcoming the Courts should no longer be permitted to think in terms of responsibility and mete out penal sentences instead of compulsory medical treatment. Yet even his moderate reform certainly raises some difficult questions requiring careful consideration.[19]

Many I think would wish to go further than this 'moderate' scheme and would join Lady Wootton in a demand for the elimination of the whole doctrine of *mens rea* or at least in the hope that it will 'wither away'. My reasons for not joining them consist of misgivings on three principal points. The first concerns individual freedom. In a system in which proof of *mens rea* is no longer a necessary condition for conviction, the occasions for official interferences with our lives and for compulsion will be vastly increased. Take, for example, the notion of a criminal assault. If the doctrine of *mens rea* were swept away, every

19. Of these difficult questions the following seem the most important.

(1) If the post-conviction inquiry into the convicted person's mental abnormality is to focus on his present state, what should a court do with an offender (a) who suffered some mental disorder at the time of his crime but has since recovered? (b) who was 'normal' at the time of the crime but at the time of his conviction suffers from mental disorder?

(2) The Mental Health Act does not by its terms require the court to be satisfied before making a hospital order that there was any causal connexion between the accused's disorder and his offense, but only provides that the court in the exercise of its discretion shall have regard to the nature of the offence. Would this still be satisfactory if the Courts were bound to make a hospital order if the medical evidence of abnormality is forthcoming?

(3) The various elements of *mens rea* (knowledge, intention, and the minimum control of muscular movements required for an act) may be absent either in a person otherwise normal or may be absent because of some mental disorder (compare the distinctions now drawn between 'sane' and 'insane' automatism). (See *supra*, p. 202). Presumably it would be desirable that in the latter case there should not be an acquittal; but to identify such cases where there were grounds for suspecting mental abnormality, some investigation of mental abnormality would be necessary before the verdict.

blow, even if it was apparent to a policeman that it was purely accidental or merely careless and therefore not, according to the present law, a criminal assault, would be a matter for investigation under the new scheme, since the possibilities of a curable or treatable condition would have to be investigated and the condition if serious treated by medical or penal methods. No doubt under the new dispensation, as at present, prosecuting authorities would use their common sense; but very considerable discretionary powers would have to be entrusted to them to sift from the mass the cases worth investigation as possible candidates for thereapeutic or penal treatment. No one could view this kind of expansion of police powers with equanimity, for with it will come great uncertainty for the individual: official interferences with his life will be more frequent but he will be less able to predict their incidence if any accidental or careless blow may be an occasion for them.

My second misgiving concerns the idea to which Lady Wootton attaches great importance: that what we now call punishment (imprisonment and the like) and compulsory medical treatment should be regarded just as alternative forms of social hygiene to be used according to the best estimate of their future effects, and no judgment of responsibility should be required before we apply to a convicted person those measures, such as imprisonment, which we now think of as penal. Lady Wootton thinks this will present no difficulty as long as we take a firm hold of the idea that the purpose and justification of the criminal law is to prevent crime and not to pay back criminals for their wickedness. But I do not think objections to detaching the use of penal methods from judgments of responsibility can be disposed of so easily. Though Lady Wootton looks forward to the day when the 'formal distinction' between hospitals and prisons will have disappeared, she does not suggest that we should give up the use of measures such as imprisonment. She contemplates that 'those for whom medicine has nothing to offer' [20] may be sentenced to 'places of safety' to receive 'the treatment which experience suggests is most likely to evoke the desired responses', and though it will only be for the purposes of convenience that their 'places of safety' will be separate from those for whom medicine has something to offer, she

20. *Op. cit.*, p. 79–80 ('places of safety' are in quotation marks in her text).

certainly accepts the idea that imprisonment may be used for its deterrent effect on the person sentenced to it.

This vision of the future evokes from me two different responses: one is a moral objection and the other a sociological or criminological doubt. The moral objection is this: If we imprison a man who has broken the law in order to deter him and by his example others, we are using him for the benefit of society, and for many people, including myself, this is a step which requires to be justified by (*inter alia*) the demonstration that the person so treated could have helped doing what he did. The individual according to this outlook, which is surely neither esoteric nor confused, has a right not to be used in this way unless he could have avoided doing what he did. Lady Wootton would perhaps dismiss this outlook as a disguised form of a retributive conception of punishment. But it is in fact independent of it as I have attempted to show: for though we must seek a moral license for punishing a man in his voluntary conduct in breaking the law, the punishment we are then licensed to use may still be directed solely to preventing future crimes on his part or on others' and not to 'retribution'.

To this moral objection it may be replied that it depends wholly on the assumption that imprisonment for deterrent purposes will, under the new scheme, continue to be regarded by people generally as radically distinct from medical treatment and still requiring justification in terms of responsibility. It may be said that this assumption should not be made; for the operation of the system itself will in time cause this distinction to fade, and conviction by a court, followed by a sentence of imprisonment, will in time be assimilated to such experiences as a compulsory medical inspection followed by detention in an isolation hospital. But here my sociological or criminological doubts begin. Surely there are two features which, at present, are among those distinguishing punishment from medical treatment and will have to be stripped away before this assimilation can take place, and the moral objection silenced. One of these is that, unlike medical treatment, we use deterrent punishment to deter not only the individual punished but others by the example of his punishment and the severity of the sentence may be adjusted accordingly. Lady Wootton is very skeptical of the whole notion that we can deter in this way potential offenders and therefore she may be prepared to forego this aspect of punishment altogether. But can we on the present available evidence safely adopt this course for all crime? The second feature distinguishing punishment from treatment is that unlike a medical inspection followed by detention in hospital, conviction by a court followed by a sentence of imprisonment is a public act expressing the odium, if not the hostility, of society for those who break the law. As long as these features attach to conviction and a sentence of imprisonment, the moral objection to their use on those who could not have helped doing what they did will remain. On the other hand, if they cease to attach, will not the law have lost an important element in its authority and deterrent force—as important perhaps for some convicted persons as the deterrent force of the actual measures which it administers.

My third misgiving is this. According to Lady Wootton's argument it is a mistake, indeed 'illogical,' to introduce a reference to mens rea into the definition of an offence. But it seems that a code of criminal law which omitted any reference in the definition of its offences to mental elements could not possibly be satisfactory. For there are some socially harmful activities which are now and should always be treated as criminal offences which can only be identified by reference to intention or some other mental element. Consider the idea of an attempt to commit a crime. It is obviously desirable that persons who attempt to kill or injure or steal, even if they fail, should be brought before courts for punishment or treatment; yet what distinguishes an attempt which fails from an innocent activity is just the fact that it is a step taken with the intention of bringing about some harmful consequence.

I do not consider my misgivings on these three points as necessarily insuperable objections to the programme of eliminating responsibility. For the first of them rests on a judgment of the value of individual liberty as compared with an increase in social security from harmful activities, and with this comparative judgment others may disagree. The second misgiving in part involves a belief about the dependence of the efficacy of the criminal law on the publicity and odium at present attached to conviction and sentence and on deterrence by example; psychological and sociological researches may one day show that this belief is false. The third objection may perhaps be surmounted by some ingenuity or compromise, since there are many important offences to which it does not apply. Nonetheless I am certain that the questions I have raised here should worry advocates of the elimination of responsibility more than they do; and until they have been satisfactorily answered I do not think we should move the whole way into this part of the Brave New World.

Chapter Four

The Death Penalty

The Deterrent Value of
Capital Punishment *

The Function of Capital Punishment

50. We cannot hope to find reasoned answers to these questions unless we first consider what purpose capital punishment is intended to serve and how far, as now applied in this country, it achieves that purpose. This is a difficult and controversial subject, long and hotly debated; and it evoked strongly conflicting views from our witnesses. It is generally agreed that the scope of this drastic and irrevocable punishment should be no wider than is necessary for the protection of society, but there is no such agreement about how wide a scope the protection of society demands.

51. It is commonly said that punishment has three principal purposes—retribution, deterrence and reformation. The relative importance of these three principles has been differently assessed at different periods and by different authorities; and philosophers and penologists have emphasized one or another of them, sometimes even to the exclusion of the others. For the purposes of our inquiry, however, we may accept this traditional classification, and consider the importance of each of the three principles in relation to capital punishment in Great Britain at the present time.

52. Discussion of the principle of *retribution* is apt to be confused because the word is not always used in the same sense. Sometimes it is intended to mean vengeance, sometimes reprobation. In the first sense the idea is that of satisfaction by the State of a wronged individual's desire to be avenged; in the second it is that of the State's

* *Royal Commission on Capital Punishment* 1949–53 *Report* (London: H.M.S.O., 1953), 17–24. Reprinted by permission of the Controller of Her Britannic Majesty's Stationery Office.

marking its disapproval of the breaking of its laws by a punishment proportionate to the gravity of the offence. Modern penological thought discounts retribution in the sense of vengeance. Lord Templewood [1] went so far as to say that recently "the reforming element has come to predominate and that the other two are carried incidentally to the reforming element." Sir John Anderson [2] attached greater importance to deterrence, but agreed in excluding retribution:

"I think there would be general agreement that the justification for the capital sentence, as for other salient features of our penal system, must be sought in the protection of society and that alone. . . . There is no longer in our regard of the criminal law any recognition of such primitive conceptions as atonement or retribution. We have, over the years, fortunately succeeded to a very large extent, if not entirely, in relegating the purely punitive aspect of our criminal law to the background."

53. Lord Templewood and Sir John Anderson had in mind retribution in the sense of vengeance or atonement. But in another sense retribution must always be an essential element in any form of punishment; punishment presupposes an offence and the measure of the punishment must not be greater than the offence deserves. Moreover, we think it must be recognized that there is a strong and widespread demand for retribution in the sense of reprobation—not always unmixed in the popular mind with that of atonement and expiation. As Lord Justice Denning put it [3]:

"The punishment inflicted for grave crimes should adequately reflect the revulsion felt by the great majority of citizens for them. It is a mistake to consider the objects of punishment as being deterrent or reformative or preventive and nothing else. . . . The ultimate justification of any punishment is not that it is a deterrent, but that it is the emphatic denunciation by the community of a crime: and from this point of view, there are some murders which, in the present state of public opinion, demand the most emphatic denunciation of all, namely the death penalty."

1. Q. 8533.
2. House of Commons, Official Report, 14th April, 1948, cols. 998–999.
3. p. 207 (1, 3).

The Archbishop of Canterbury, while expressing no opinion about the ethics of capital punishment, agreed with Lord Justice Denning's view about the ultimate justification of any punishment.[4] By reserving the death penalty for murder the criminal law stigmatises the gravest crime by the gravest punishment; and it may be argued that, by so doing, the law helps to foster in the community a special abhorrence of murder as "the crime of crimes," so that the element of retribution merges into that of deterrence. Whatever weight may be given to this argument, the law cannot ignore the public demand for retribution which heinous crimes undoubtedly provoke; it would be generally agreed that, though reform of the criminal law ought sometimes to give a lead to public opinion, it is dangerous to move too far in advance of it.

54. The *reformation* of the individual offender is usually regarded as an important function of punishment. But it can have no application where the death penalty is exacted, if "reformation" is taken to mean not merely repentance,[5] but reestablishment in normal life as a good citizen.[6] Not that murderers in general are incapable of reformation; the evidence plainly shows the contrary. Indeed, as we shall see later,[7] the experience of countries without capital punishment indicates that the prospects of reformation are at least as favourable with murderers as with those who have committed other kinds of serious crimes.

55. Discussion of the value of capital punishment has been largely devoted to the aspect of *deterrence*. This is an issue on which it is extraordinarily difficult to find conclusive arguments either way. Both

4. Fisher, Q. 4087–8.

5. It has sometimes been suggested that the death penalty has a unique value as a stimulus to repentance. The Royal Commission on Capital Punishment of 1864–66 were informed that in the opinion of the Governor, Chaplain and Chief Clerk of Millbank Prison "criminals deserving death generally are not likely to reform with ordinary opportunities, but they do repent before hanging." (Minutes of Evidence, p. 639).

6. It might be argued, as Professor Sellin pointed out that the death sentence, subsequently commuted, has a stronger reformative effect in some cases than an original sentence of life imprisonment would have had; but we received no evidence which might support this hypothesis.

7. Paragraphs 651–2 and Appendix 15.

sides are commonly argued by wide generalisations confidently expressed with little positive evidence to support them. We heard much evidence about it from numerous witnesses, and were furnished with much relevant information, largely statistical. The greater part of this information will be found in our Minutes of Evidence, including the evidence obtained from other countries; but, as much of it is not readily available elsewhere, we have thought it useful to give a full summary of it in an appendix to this Report.[8]

56. Supporters of capital punishment commonly maintain that it has a uniquely deterrent force, which no other form of punishment has or could have. The arguments adduced both in support of this proposition and against it fall into two categories. The first consists of what we may call the common-sense argument from human nature, applicable particularly to certain kinds of murders and certain kinds of murderers. This a priori argument was supported by evidence given by representatives of all ranks of the police and of the prison service. The second comprises various arguments based on examination of statistics.

57. The arguments in the first category are not only the simplest and most obvious, but are perhaps the strongest that can be put forward in favor of the uniquely deterrent power of capital punishment. The case was very clearly stated by Sir James Fitzjames Stephen nearly a hundred years ago [9]:

"No other punishment deters men so effectually from committing crimes as the punishment of death. This is one of those propositions which it is difficult to prove, simply because they are in themselves more obvious than any proof can make them. It is possible to display ingenuity in arguing against it, but that is all. The whole experience of mankind is in the other direction. The threat of instant death is the one to which resort has always been made when there was an absolute necessity for producing some result. . . . No one goes to certain inevitable death except by compulsion. Put the matter the other way. Was there ever yet a criminal who, when sentenced to death and brought out to die, would refuse the offer of a commutation of his sentence for the severest secondary punishment? Surely not. Why

8. Appendix 6 (pp. 328 ff).
9. "Capital Punishments" in Fraser's Magazine, Vol. LXIX, June, 1864, p. 753.

is this? It can only be because 'All that a man has will he give for his life.' In any secondary punishment, however terrible, there is hope; but death is death; its terrors cannot be described more forcibly."

58. It is true, as has often been pointed out in reply to this argument, that capital punishment as applied in Great Britain falls very far short of a threat of instant and certain death to every murderer. This is clearly shown by the figures in Tables 1 and 2 of Appendix 3. During the 50 years 1900–1949, 7,454 murders were known to the police in England and Wales. In 1,674 cases the suspect committed suicide. During the same period 4,173 persons were arrested on a charge of murder and 3,129 were committed for trial at assizes.[10] Of those committed for trial 658 were acquitted or not tried, 428 were found insane on arraignment and 798 were found guilty but insane. Of those convicted of murder 35 were sentenced to penal servitude for life or detention during H.M. pleasure and 1,210 were sentenced to death. Of those sentenced to death 23 had their conviction quashed on appeal, 47 were certified insane and 506 were reprieved. There remain 632 (621 men and 11 women) who were executed for murder. There was therefore only one execution for every 12 murders known to the police. In Scotland the proportion was even lower. In that country during the same period 612 murders were known to the police, 59 persons were convicted of murder and sentenced to death and 23 (22 men and 1 woman) were executed. There was therefore less than one execution to every 25 murders known to the police. But these odds against being hanged for murder are probably realised only vaguely, if at all, by would-be murderers. Those who, like Stephen, are convinced that the fear of death cannot fail to have a more potent effect on most men and women than the fear of any other punishment are not likely to be shaken in that conviction by these figures.

59. Capital punishment has obviously failed as a deterrent when a murder is committed. We can number its failures. But we cannot number its successes. No one can ever know how many people have refrained from murder because of the fear of being hanged. For that

10. Owing to the basis on which the Criminal Statistics are compiled, this figure does not include persons charged with murder and convicted of manslaughter or some other lesser offense; but for the present purpose this defect is immaterial.

we have to rely on indirect and inconclusive evidence. We have been told that the first thing a murderer says when he is arrested is often "Shall I be hanged?" or "I did it and I am ready to swing for it," or something of that kind. What is the inference to be drawn from this? Clearly not that the death penalty is an effective deterrent, for he has not been deterred; nor that he consciously considered the risk of the death penalty and accepted it; still less that the death penalty was not so effective a deterrent as some other punishment might have been. The true inference seems to us to be that there is a strong association between murder and the death penalty in the popular imagination. We think it is reasonable to suppose that the deterrent force of capital punishment operates not only by affecting the conscious thoughts of individuals tempted to commit murder, but also by building up in the community, over a long period of time, a deep feeling of peculiar abhorrence for the crime of murder. "The fact that men are hung for murder is one great reason why murder is considered so dreadful a crime." This widely diffused effect on the moral consciousness of society is impossible to assess, but it must be at least as important as any direct part which the death penalty may play as a deterrent in the calculations of potential murderers. It is likely to be specially potent in this country, where the punishment for lesser offences is much more lenient than in many other countries, and the death penalty stands out in the sharper contrast.

60. We have already remarked that the deterrent effect of capital punishment may naturally be expected to operate more strongly to prevent some kinds of murders than others, and to deter some kinds of individuals more than others. To form any idea of the extent to which, and the way in which, this expectation coincides with experience, it would be necessary to have some classification of murders according to motives or causes. Attempts at such a classification have been made, notably by the Home Office in 1905 and by the Home Office and Scottish Home Department in 1949. But these are inevitably very general and tentative and for several reasons can hardly fail to be misleading if they are taken as more than a rough guide. Such a classification can only be framed in somewhat crude categories. If it is in terms of motives, it is unsatisfactory, because many murders are prompted by a combination of motives, or by hidden motives, or have no obvious motive. If, like the tables prepared for us by the

Home Office and Scottish Home Department, they classify murders in terms of the relationship between the murderer and his victim, they can give only an approximate indication of the motive that inspired the crime. Although the murder of a wife, for example, will in many cases be committed for reasons which may broadly be described as of a sexual character, it may be inspired by the widest range of motives—jealousy, boredom, pity, exasperation, revenge, a wish to be free to marry another woman or a desire to dispose of the wife's fortune. Such analyses can do no more than lend some support to conclusions that can be reached by commonsense, namely that capital punishment is likely to act as a deterrent more of premeditated murders than of impulsive ones, and on normal persons more than on the mentally abnormal. Even these generalisations are subject to many exceptions. Premeditated murders are committed in spite of the existence of the death penalty—in them the offender will often calculate on escaping detection—and it can hardly be doubted that impulsive murders are prevented by it. Mentally normal persons do commit murder, and, though the deterrent effect of capital punishment will certainly be negligible on the severely deranged, the question how far persons suffering from lesser forms of mental abnormality, and especially that difficult and amorphous category known as psychopaths, are capable of being deterred by the fear of punishment is far from clear. Our evidence was that some are and some are not. It was even suggested that in some very rare cases the existence of capital punishment may act as an incitement to murder on the mentally abnormal.[11]

61. Of more importance was the evidence of the representatives of the police and prison service. From them we received virtually unanimous evidence in both England and Scotland, to the effect that they were convinced of the uniquely deterrent value of capital punishment in its effect on professional criminals. On these the fear of the death penalty may not only have the direct effect of deterring them from using lethal violence to accomplish their purpose, or to avoid detection by silencing the victim of their crime, or to resist arrest. It may also have the indirect effect of deterring them from carrying a

11. Howard League, p. 279 (4), Calvert, Q. 3561–2; Henderson, p. 462 ** (17); Institute of Pyscho-Analysis, p. 546 (6(ii)(e)); Sellin, Q. 8888.

weapon lest the temptation to use it in a tight corner should prove irresistible. These witnesses had no doubt that the existence of the death penalty was the main reason why lethal violence was not more often used and why criminals in this country do not usually carry firearms or other weapons. They thought that, if there were no capital punishment, criminals would take to using violence and carrying weapons; and the police, who are now unarmed, might be compelled to retaliate. It is in the nature of the case that little could be adduced in the way of specific evidence that criminals had been deterred by the death penalty. What an offender says on his arrest, probably some time after the commission of the crime, is not necessarily a valid indication of what was in his mind when he committed it; nor is it certain that a man who tells the police that he refrained from committing a murder because he might have to "swing for it" was in fact deterred wholly or mainly by that fear. Moreover we received no evidence that the abolition of capital punishment in other countries had in fact led to the consequences apprehended by our witnesses in this country; though it is fair to add that any comparison between Great Britain and most of these countries, with the exception of Belgium, is vitiated by the differences in social and industrial conditions and in density of population. But we cannot treat lightly the considered and unanimous views of these experienced witnesses, who have had many years of contact with criminals. Some of our most distinguished judicial witnesses—notably the Lord Chief Justice, Mr. Justice Humphreys and the Lord Justice General—felt no doubt that they were right.[12] It seems to us inherently probable that, if capital punishment has any unique value as a deterrent, it is here that its effect would be chiefly felt and here that its value to the community would be greatest. For the professional criminal imprisonment is a normal professional risk, of which the idea is familiar, if not the experience, and which for him carries no stigma. It is natural to suppose that for such people (except the rare gangster, who constantly risks his life in affrays with the police and other gangs) the death penalty comes into an entirely different category from other forms of punishment. The Commissioner of Police of the Metropolis told us[13] of a gang of armed shop-

12. Goddard, Q. 3109; Humphreys, p. 260 (2); Cooper, Q. 5370-1.
13. p. 148 (Appendix B). Extracts from the Commissioner's evidence about this case are printed in Appendix 6, paragraph 15.

breakers who continued their operations after one of their members had been sentenced to death for murder and reprieved, but broke up and disappeared when, on a later occasion, two others were convicted of another murder and hanged. He thought it "a reasonable inference" that this was evidence of the uniquely deterrent effect of the death penalty; and that was the opinion of the police officers who dealt with the gang. It is also contended that in the case of a violent prisoner undergoing a life sentence the death penalty may be the only effective deterrent against his making a murderous assault on a fellow prisoner or a member of the prison staff.

62. We must now turn to the statistical evidence. This has for the most part been assembled by those who would abolish the death penalty; their object has been to disprove the deterrent value claimed for that punishment. Supporters of the death penalty usually counter them by arguing that the figures are susceptible of a different interpretation, or that for one reason or another they are too unreliable and misleading to form a basis for valid argument. The question should be judged, they say, not on statistics but on such considerations as we have been examining in the preceding paragraphs.

63. The arguments drawn by the abolitionists from the statistics fall into two categories. The first, and by far the more important, seeks to prove the case by showing that the abolition of capital punishment in other countries has not led to an increase of murder or of homicidal crime. This may be attempted either by comparing the homicide statistics of countries where capital punishment has been abolished with the statistics for the same period of countries where it has been retained, or by comparing the statistics of a single country, in which capital punishment has been abolished, for periods before and after abolition. The second category is of arguments drawn from a comparison of the number of executions in a country in particular years with the murder or homicide rate in the years immediately succeeding.

64. An initial difficulty is that it is almost impossible to draw valid comparisons between different countries. Any attempt to do so, except within very narrow limits, may always be misleading. Some of the reasons why this is so are more fully developed in Appendix 6.[14] Briefly they amount to this: that owing to differences in the legal

14. See paragraph 24.

definitions of crimes, in the practice of the prosecuting authorities and the courts, in the methods of compiling criminal statistics, in moral standards and customary behavior, and in political, social and economic conditions, it is extremely difficult to compare like with like, and little confidence can be felt in the soundness of the inferences drawn from such comparisons. An exception may legitimately be made where it is possible to find a small group of countries or States, preferably contiguous, and closely similar in composition of population and social and economic conditions generally, in some of which capital punishment has been abolished and in others not. These conditions are satisfied, we think, by certain groups of States in the United States of America, about which we heard evidence from Professor Thorsten Sellin, and perhaps also by New Zealand and the Australian States. In Appendix 6 [15] we print a selection from the relevant material. If we take any of these groups we find that the fluctuations in the homicide rate of each of its component members exhibit a striking similarity. We agree with Professor Sellin that the only conclusion which can be drawn from the figures is that there is no clear evidence of any influence of the death penalty on the homicide rates of these States, and that, "whether the death penalty is used or not and whether executions are frequent or not, both death-penalty States and abolition States show rates which suggest that these rates are conditioned by other factors than the death penalty." [16]

65. A firmer basis for argument is afforded by the trend of the homicide rate in a country before and after the abolition of capital punishment, and, in a few cases, its reintroduction. The nature of the statistics available differs from one country to another; in a few the number of homicides known to the police are available, but more often there are statistics only of prosecutions for murder or of convictions. The number of homicides known to the police clearly provides the most informative basis and the number of convictions the least: the ratio between crimes committed and convictions may vary widely owing to such factors as the efficiency of the police, the methods of recording crime and the attitude of the courts; moreover juries may sometimes be more ready to return a verdict of guilty when the death penalty has been abolished. But so long as a continuous series of

15. See paragraphs 32–36 and 51–54.   16. p. 650 (41, 44).

figures compiled on a uniform basis exists for the whole period under review, we think that the fluctuations in these figures can be taken as some index of fluctuations in the homicide rate. Whatever basis is chosen, interpretation of the relevant statistics involves elements of doubt and difficulty. In most countries where capital punishment has been abolished, statutory abolition has come after a long period when the death penalty was in abeyance, and this creates the problem of what date should be taken as the dividing line. Whatever date may be selected, it cannot safely be assumed that variations in the homicide rate after the abolition of capital punishment are in fact due to abolition, and not to other causes, or to a combination of abolition and other causes. There is some evidence [17] that abolition may be followed for a short time by an increase in homicides and crimes of violence, and a fortiori it might be thought likely that a temporary increase of this kind would occur if capital punishment were abolished in a country where it was not previously in abeyance but was regularly applied in practice; but it would appear that, as soon as a country has become accustomed to the new form of the extreme penalty, abolition will not in the long run lead to an increase of crime. The general conclusion which we have reached is that there is no clear evidence in any of the figures we have examined that the abolition of capital punishment has led to an increase in the homicide rate, or that its reintroduction has led to a fall.

66. We also review in Appendix 6 such evidence as has been submitted to us about the possible relation between the number of executions in particular years and the incidence of murder in succeeding years.[18] We need not here consider the evidence in detail; it is sufficient to say that we are satisfied that no such relationship can be established. (It was suggested to us by some Scottish witnesses that a fall in the number of murders and crimes of violence in Glasgow in 1946 was due, or mainly due, to the carrying out of three executions in that year after capital punishment had been in abeyance for 17 years, but the available evidence does not support this conclusion)[19]. We have suggested (paragraph 59) that any deterrent effect of capital punishment is likely to reside primarily in its long-term effect on the

17. See Appendix 6, paragraphs 69–73. 18. See Appendix 6, paragraphs 74–87.
19. See Appendix 6, paragraphs 78–80.

attitude of society to murder rather than in the conscious calculations of potential criminals. If this is so, it cannot be expected that variations in the number of executions from year to year would be directly reflected in a rise or fall of the murder rate, and a failure to find any such correlations cannot properly be used as an argument against the view that the death penalty is a unique deterrent.

67. The negative conclusion we draw from the figures does not of course imply a conclusion that the deterrent effect of the death penalty cannot be greater than that of any other punishment. It means only that the figures afford no reliable evidence one way or the other. It would no doubt be equally difficult to find statistical evidence of any direct relationship between the severity of any other punishment and the rise or fall of the crime to which it relates. Too many other factors come into the question. All we can say is that the deterrent value of punishment in general is probably liable to be exaggerated, and the effect of capital punishment specially so because of its drastic and sensational character. The conclusion of Professor Sellin, who has made a profound study of this subject, is summarised in the answers to four of the questions we put to him:

"*8916. We cannot conclude from your statistics . . . that capital punishment has no deterrent effect?—No, there is no such conclusion.*

8917. But can we not conclude that if it has a deterrent effect it must be rather small?—I can make no such conclusion, because I can find no answer one way or another in these data. . . . It is impossible to draw any inferences from the material that is in my possession, that there is any relationship . . . between a large number of executions, small number of executions, continuous executions, no executions, and what happens to the murder rates.

8918. . . . I think you have already agreed that capital punishment cannot, on the basis of your figures, be exercising an overwhelmingly deterrent effect?—That is correct.

8919. . . . But you would not like to go any further than that?—No. . . ."

68. We recognise that it is impossible to arrive confidently at firm conclusions about the deterrent effect of the death penalty, or indeed of any form of punishment. The general conclusion which we reach, after careful review of all the evidence we have been able to obtain

as to the deterrent effect of capital punishment, may be stated as follows. Prima facie the penalty of death is likely to have a stronger effect as a deterrent to normal human beings than any other form of punishment, and there is some evidence (though no convincing statistical evidence) that this is in fact so. But this effect does not operate universally or uniformly, and there are many offenders on whom it is limited and may often be negligible. It is accordingly important to view this question in a just perspective and not to base a penal policy in relation to murder on exaggerated estimates of the uniquely deterrent force of the death penalty.

Hon. Mr. Gilpin

Speech Against
Capital Punishment 1868 *

Capital Punishment within Prisons Bill—[Bill 36.]

(Mr. Secretary Gathorne Hardy, Mr. Walpole, Mr. Attorney General.)

COMMITTEE.

Order for Committee read.

Motion made, and Question proposed, "That Mr. Speaker do now leave the Chair."

Mr. Gilpin said, he rose to move the Amendment of which he had given notice—

"That, in the opinion of this House, it is expedient, instead of carrying out the punishment of death within prisons, that Capital Punishment should be abolished."

He felt some difficulty and hesitation in asking the attention of the House to the Motion of which he had given notice. In the first instance, he would express his extreme regret at the absence of his hon. Friend and Member for Dumfries (Mr. Ewart), whose name had been so closely connected with the amelioration of the criminal law, and who had done so much to abolish capital punishment. His reason for bringing forward this Motion now was, that he had a strong conviction that capital punishment was inexpedient and unnecessary; that it did not ensure the purposes for which it was enacted; that it was unjust in principle; that it involved not unfrequently the sacrifice of innocent human life; and further, that it afforded an escape for

---

* The Honorable Mr. Gilpin, "Parliamentary Debate on Capital Punishment Within Prisons Bill," in *Hansard's Parliamentary Debates*, 3rd series, April 21, 1868 (London: Hansard, 1868).

many guilty of atrocious crimes. Holding these opinions, he could not permit to pass an Act which proposed to reenact the punishment of death without entering his solemn protest against it, and submitting the reasons why he thought it inexpedient that capital punishment should be inflicted.. The late division on this question was no test whatever of the feeling of the House on the question of capital punishment. He was now asked. "Will you bring forward a Motion for the abolition of capital punishment in the face of the frequent murders, of the increase of the crime of murder—at a time when no doubt there are influences at work"—to which he would not particularly allude—"which aggravate the crime to an extent almost unprecedented?" He unhesitatingly replied, "Yes, I will bring it forward now, because, if my principle is good for anything, it is good at all times and under all circumstances." He would remind the House that the atrocious murders which were now being committed, and which they all so much deplored, were murders which were committed under the present law, and he believed would not be committed under the altered state of the law which he desired to introduce. The question he had to deal with was—by what means could they best stop the crime of murder? He disavowed emphatically any sympathy with crime—he disavowed any maudlin sentimentality with respect to this question. He was sure his right hon. Friend opposite (Mr. Gathorne Hardy) would agree with him that the question between them was, how best to prevent the crime of murder. He said, without fear of contradiction, that almost in every instance in which capital punishment had ceased to be inflicted for certain crimes those crimes had lessened in frequency and enormity since its abolition; yet, as regarded murder, where the punishment of death was still retained, the crime had increased not only in number but enormity. In proof of that allegation he might quote statistics; but the fact was well known, and he would not take up the time of the House by doing so. It was also not to be denied that this was a question upon which there had been a very considerable change in public opinion within a comparatively short period of time. Some of those who had the administration of the law in their hands, and some of those who had occupied the position of the right hon. Gentleman opposite (Mr. Gathorne Hardy), had come to the conclusion, at which he arrived many years ago, that capital punishment was undesirable—that it was unnecessary—and that the time had arrived when some other system ought to be adopted. Surely they were not succeeding in putting down murder. They had for centuries tried the *lex talionis*—the life for life principle—and they had miserably failed, and murder still stalked abroad. Earl Russell, in the introduction in the new edition of his work on the *English Constitution*, thus expressed himself as being favorable to the abolition of capital punishment—

"For my own part, I do not doubt for a moment either the right of a community to inflict the punishment of death, or the expediency of exercising that right in certain states of society. But when I turn from that abstract right and that abstract expediency to our own state of society—when I consider how difficult it is for any Judge to separate the case which requires inflexible justice from that which admits the force of mitigating circumstances—how invidious the task of the Secretary of State in dispensing the mercy of the Crown—how critical the comments made by the public—how soon the object of general horror becomes the theme of sympathy and pity—how narrow and how limited the examples given by this condign and awful punishment—how brutal the scene of execution—I come to the conclusion that nothing would be lost to justice, nothing lost in the preservation of innocent life, if the punishment of death were altogether abolished. In that case a sentence of a long term of separate confinement, followed by another term of hard labor and hard fare, would cease to be considered as an extension of mercy. If the sentence of the Judge were to that effect, there would scarcely ever be a petition for remission of punishment, in cases of murder, sent to the Home Office. The guilty, unpitied, would have time and opportunity to turn repentant to the Throne of Mercy."

Now, the first objection which he (Mr. Gilpin) had to the punishment of death was its essential injustice. They gave the same punishment to the crime of a Rush or a Manning as they did to that of a Samuel Wright, and other less guilty persons. They had, under the present law, constant occurrences in which the feeling, intellect, judgment, and Christianity of the public were against carrying out the extreme penalty, even in cases where the law was clear and unmistakable as to the matter and there was every reason to believe that it had been justly administered by the Judge who had condemned the criminal. Take, for instance, the case of the woman Charlotte Harris. She was sentenced to death, being *enceinte* at the time. According to custom she was reprieved until her babe was born, and then if the sentence of the law had taken its course she would have been hanged; but public opinion in the meantime had become so strong that the Home Office, even, he believed, in opposition to the judgment of the Secretary of State, had to give way, though the case was a fearful and atrocious one, and her life was spared. Richard Cobden, writing to him (Mr. Gilpin) with reference to this case, said—

"You are right. It is truly horrible to think of nursing a woman through her confinement, and then with her first returning strength to walk her to the scaffold! What is to become of the baby at its birth? Is it to lie upon the mother's breast until removed by the hand of Calcraft? Oh, horrible! horrible! Could you not have a meeting to shame the authorities."

Well, there were several meetings—one of 40,000 women, headed by Mary Howitt—and they petitioned the Throne for mercy, and mercy was extended. Then there was the case of Alice Holt. She, too, was pregnant; but the Home Office, having got wiser by this time, would not bring her to trial until after the birth of her child. Then they brought her to trial, sentenced her to death, and carried out the execution. Against the injustice of such a proceeding he had at the time most earnestly protested. A practical point most serious to the interests of society was this: numbers of criminals had escaped from the punishment due to their crimes, because of the unwillingness of juries to incur the possibility of convicting the innocent. He believed it was on this ground that Mr. Waddington, the former Under Secretary at the Home Office, came almost to the opinions that he (Mr. Gilpin) entertained. He knew it did not appear in his evidence before the Royal Commission; but Mr. Waddington told him though looking at the matter from a different standpoint and urged by different arguments, still he had very nearly come to his (Mr. Gilpin's) opinions that it would be desirable for the interests of society at large that the abolition of capital punishment should take place. He (Mr. Gilpin) believed it was not too much to say that there were men and women walking about red-handed amongst us—persons unquestionably guilty of the most atrocious murders—who, had the punishment for their crimes been other than capital, would be now immured in prison, utterly unable to repeat such crimes as those for which they had been already tried. This arose from the unwillingness of juries to convict—an unwillingness which did them honour—unless they had evidence positive and indisputable. It was right that evidence which would suffice to convict a man where the punishment would be fourteen years, or imprisonment for life, should be regarded as utterly insufficient to convict a man when the sentence would send him out of the world. Some twenty years ago Charles Dickens wrote a series of letters in *The Daily News* on the subject of capital punishment; and in one, headed "How Jurymen Feel," he said—

"Juries, like society, are not stricken foolish or motionless. They have, for the most part, an objection to the punishment of death; and they will, for the most part, assert it by such verdicts. As jurymen in the forgery cases (where jurors found a £10 note to be worth 39s., so as not to come under capital punishment) would probably reconcile their verdict to their consciences by calling to mind that the intrinsic value of a banknote was almost nothing; so jurymen, in cases of murder, probably argue that grave doctors have said all men are more or less mad, and therefore they believe the prisoner mad. This is a great wrong to society; but it arises out of the punishment of death. And the question will always suggest itself in jurors' minds, however earnestly the learned Judge presiding may discharge his duty—which is the greater wrong to society?—to give this man the benefit of the possibility of his being mad, or to have another public execution, with all its depraving and hardening influences? Imagining myself a juror, in a case of life or death, and supposing that the evidence had forced me from every other ground of opposition to this punishment in the particular case than a possibility of immediate mistake or otherwise, I would go over it again on this ground, and, if I could by any reasonable special pleading with myself find him mad rather than hang him, I think I would."

He had alluded to the numbers of persons who had escaped justice altogether, because juries could not make up their minds to convict under such circumstances; but there was another view of the case, and that was the execution of innocent persons, and when he said innocent persons, he meant persons innocent of the crimes with which they were charged. He would not delay the House by quoting what he quoted on a former occasion—the evidence of Daniel O'Connell, or the evidence of the present Lord Chief Baron, as to the frequency of the execution of innocent persons. But he would call the attention of the House to a case which occurred in 1865—that was the Italian Pollizzioni, who was tried for the Saffron Hill murder, when one of the most humane of our Judges expressed his entire belief that the conviction was right. Pollizioni was sentenced, and was within a few days of being hanged. Law had done its best and its worst, when Mr. Negretti—of the firm of Negretti and Zambra—heard of the case, and became convinced that the man was innocent. He busied himself in getting evidence, which at last satisfied the Home Secretary, not that the prisoner deserved secondary punishment, but that he was absolutely innocent, and then he was taken out of the condemned cell. But for the interference of a private individual this man would have been hanged. It might be said that a case like this was very exceptional, and God forbid that it should be frequent; but within a few months there was the case of another man at Swansea, Giardinieri—oddly enough, also an Italian—who was sentenced to death, and was within a short time of being hanged. Evidence was, however, procured which showed him to be innocent. These were solemn facts. Charles Dickens said—

"I entreat all who may chance to read this letter to pause for an instant, and ask themselves whether they can remember any occasion on which they have in the broad day, and under circumstances the most favorable to recognition, mistaken one person for another, and believed that in a perfect stranger they have seen going away from them, or coming towards them, a familiar friend."

Hence there should be a reasonable hesitation as to an irrevocable verdict. The frequency of cases of mistaken identity were notorious. Mr. Visschers, who held a high position in the Government of the King of the Belgians, stated that in his experience three men convicted of murder appealed to the Court of Cassation, when the conviction was confirmed. The King, however, commuted their sentence into one of perpetual imprisonment; but their innocence being afterwards established, they were liberated, and granted annuities for life. Mr. Serjeant Parry stated, in reply to a Question by Mr. Waddington—

"*I could mention six or eight instances within my own knowledge in which men have been acquitted, purely upon the ground that the punishment was capital.*"

And in reply to Mr. Bright, the learned gentleman said—

"*I know that juries have acquitted men clearly and beyond all doubt guilty of murder, and some of the very worst murders that have ever been committed in this country, and have done so simply because the punishment has been the punishment of death. They would have convicted if the punishment had been imprisonment for life, or any punishment short of taking the life of the man, and they have seized hold of any excuse rather than be agents in putting capital punishment into operation.*"

This was not unreasonable; because a man, if wrongly transported, as in the case of Mr. Barber, the solicitor, could have compensation made to him, but not so if wrongly hanged. Many years ago Sir James Mackintosh stated before a Committee on the Criminal Laws that during a long cycle of years an average of one person was executed every three years whose innocence was afterwards proved. And Sir Fitz Roy Kelly stated, in 1839, that there were no less than fourteen innocent persons within the first forty years of this century who had been convicted, and whose innocence since their death had been fully established. And doubtless the average of one innocent person every three years was much too low, because it should be remembered that after the person was executed there was no motive to discover whether he or she was innocent or not. It was only necessary again to refer to the well-known case of Samuel Wright, a working carpenter in Southwark, to show the inequality of the law, and that, too, resulting simply from the character of the punishment. He believed no jury would have found Wright guilty on the charge of murder, and that no Judge but one would have left him for execution. The prisoner, it was true, pleaded guilty to the crime, and neither the counsel nor the Court could induce him to retract the plea; but it was clear from the facts of the case that this was not a case of wilful murder. The man was awoke in the night, and was dragged out of bed by a violent woman with whom he lived. He struggled with her, and seizing his razor, which was lying in his way, without premeditation he killed her. He was brought up for trial, and he pleaded guilty. They could not expect a carpenter to be trained to the niceties of the law, and it could not be wondered at that he, a conscientious man, determined to plead guilty. Almost at the last moment a very large body of his fellow working men came up to the Home Office to plead that his life might be spared. The present Government was not then in office. [Mr. BUXTON: Who was the Home Secretary?] His right hon. Friend the Member for Morpeth (Sir George Grey). It was thought, most unwisely in his opinion, that the appearance of so large a body of working men on such a subject was an attempt to terrorise the Home Office, and a deaf ear was turned to their pleadings, which might wisely have been granted. Samuel Wright was executed, and that in the face of Charlotte Windsor, the hired murderess of babies, who, to solve some of the subtleties of law, was brought from one part of England to another, and after all was only imprisoned for life. He could never forget the morning of that execution. The people in the neighbourhood, instead of rushing to see the execution, had their blinds drawn down. It was a case which it would take a long time to wipe out from the memories of the people of that neighbourhood. That happened about the time that Townley, another murderer, was acquitted on the ground of insanity—a plea which his subsequent suicide showed to be true. But the question of insanity was one of the most uncertain character; the dividing line was disputed by doctors, and even by doctors in divinity; and the result was that in the case of men who were executed no time was allowed to show whether the crime was the result of a diseased brain, or of that moral obliquity which was rightly the subject of punishment. He felt grateful to the House for the indulgence they had shown him on a subject which had occupied his attention for twenty years. Now, he would ask, what was capital punishment? The punishment of death? No, it was not that. The sentence of death was decreed upon all of us by a higher than a mortal Judge. We but antedated the sentence, and by how much this was done no man could know. A man might be sent to the gallows who, according to medical opinion, could not live three months —and, in fact, a man had been recently executed, of whom the medical man said he could not live three months if he died in course of nature, and another man with a prospect of a long life. But what was the punishment? It was not death; it was antedating the sentence passed upon us all by the Most High. From ten thousand pulpits in the land, they were told, and rightly told, that for the repentant sinner the gates of Heaven were open, whether his death was a violent one or not; and yet in the face of those sermons they said—he did not mean that the Judges say it in so many words—"Your crime is so great that there can be no forgiveness with man; but appeal unto God and he may forgive you if you appeal in the right way and pay due attention to your religious advisers." We told the criminal in one breath that his crime was too great for man to forgive—that he was not fit to live on earth, but we commended him to the mercy of the Highest. We said, in effect, that those feet "which would leave no stain on the pure pavements of the New Jerusalem would leave the polluting mark of blood upon the ground that mortals tread." He knew not how to escape from this argument. If criminals were fit to die the time of their going to Heaven was hastened; and if not fit to die, they were allowed to go with all their unexpiated crimes on their heads before their final Judge. If we believed that faith which we professed, then the greater the sin the greater the need for repentance; and it was something monstrous that we should set ourselves up to decide that a fortnight from the date of his sentence was enough time for the worst murderer to make his peace with God. If we believed there was need for that peacemaking, let us give the murderer the time which God would give him to make his peace with Him. If we wanted to teach mercy, let us set an example of that mercy, and at all events stop short of shedding human blood. And if we would teach reverence for human life, let us not attempt to teach it by showing how it may be speedily taken away. He therefore moved the Amendment of which he had given notice, convinced that by the entire abolition of capital punishment, and the removal from their criminal code of the principle of revenge—the life for life principle—they would inaugurate an era in which the sanctity of human life would be regarded more highly than it had hitherto been, and in which the sense of that sanctity, permeating through society, would result in a great lessening of the crime of murder, and consequently in increased security to the public of this country.

John Stuart Mill

Speech In Favor of
Capital Punishment 1868 *

. . . It would be a great satisfaction to me if I were able to support this Motion. It is always a matter of regret to me to find myself, on a public question, opposed to those who are called—sometimes in the way of honour, and sometimes in what is intended for ridicule— the philanthropists. Of all persons who take part in public affairs, they are those for whom, on the whole, I feel the greatest amount of respect; for their characteristic is, that they devote their time, their labour, and much of their money to objects purely public, with a less admixture of either personal or class selfishness, than any other class of politicians whatever. On almost all the great questions, scarcely any politicians are so steadily and almost uniformly to be found on the side of right; and they seldom err, but by an exaggerated application of some just and highly important principle. On the very subject that is now occupying us we all know what signal service they have rendered. It is through their efforts that our criminal laws—which within my memory hanged people for stealing in a dwelling house to the value of 40s.—laws by virtue of which rows of human beings might be seen suspended in front of Newgate by those who ascended or descended Ludgate Hill—have so greatly relaxed their most revolting and most impolitic ferocity, that aggravated murder is now practically the only crime which is punished with death by any of our lawful tribunals; and we are even now deliberating whether the extreme penalty should be retained in that solitary case. This vast gain, not only to humanity, but to the ends of penal justice, we owe to the philanthropists; and if they are mistaken, as I cannot but think

* John Stuart Mill, "Parliamentary Debate on Capital Punishment Within Prisons Bill," in *Hansard's Parlimentary Debates*, 3rd series, April 21, 1868 (London: Hansard, 1868).

they are, in the present instance, it is only in not perceiving the right time and place for stopping in a career hitherto so eminently beneficial. Sir, there is a point at which, I conceive, that career ought to stop. When there has been brought home to any one, by conclusive evidence, the greatest crime known to the law; and when the attendant circumstances suggest no palliation of the guilt, no hope that the culprit may even yet not be unworthy to live among mankind, nothing to make it probable that the crime was an exception to his general character rather than a consequence of it, then I confess it appears to me that to deprive the criminal of the life of which he has proved himself to be unworthy—solemnly to blot him out from the fellowship of mankind and from the catalogue of the living—is the most appropriate, as it is certainly the most impressive, mode in which society can attach to so great a crime the penal consequences which for the security of life it is indispensable to annex to it. I defend this penalty, when confined to atrocious cases, on the very ground on which it is commonly attacked—on that of humanity to the criminal; as beyond comparison the least cruel mode in which it is possible adequately to deter from the crime. If, in our horror of inflicting death, we endeavour to devise some punishment for the living criminal which shall act on the human mind with a deterrent force at all comparable to that of death, we are driven to inflictions less severe indeed in appearance, and therefore less efficacious, but far more cruel in reality. Few, I think, would venture to propose, as a punishment for aggravated murder, less than imprisonment with hard labor for life; that is the fate to which a murderer would be consigned by the mercy which shrinks from putting him to death. But has it been sufficiently considered what sort of a mercy this is, and what kind of life it leaves to him? If, indeed, the punishment is not really inflicted —if it becomes the sham which a few years ago such punishments were rapidly becoming—then, indeed, its adoption would be almost tantamount to giving up the attempt to repress murder altogether. But if it really is what it professes to be, and if it is realized in all its rigour by the popular imagination, as it very probably would not be, but as it must be if it is to be efficacious, it will be so shocking that when the memory of the crime is no longer fresh, there will be almost insuperable difficulty in executing it. What comparison can there really be, in point of severity, between consigning a man to the short pang of a rapid death, and immuring him in a living tomb, there to linger out what may be a long life in the hardest and most monotonous toil, without any of its alleviations or rewards—debarred from all pleasant sights and sounds, and cut off from all earthly hope, except a slight mitigation of bodily restraint, or a small improvement of diet? Yet even such a lot as this, because there is no one moment at which the suffering is of terrifying intensity, and, above all, because it does not contain the element, so imposing to the imagination, of the unknown, is universally reputed a milder punishment than death —stands in all codes as a mitigation of the capital penalty, and is thankfully accepted as such. For it is characteristic of all punishments which depend on duration for their efficacy—all, therefore, which are not corporal or pecuniary—that they are more rigorous than they seem; while it is, on the contrary, one of the strongest recommendations a punishment can have, that it should seem more rigorous than it is; for its practical power depends far less on what it is than on what it seems. There is not, I should think, any human infliction which makes an impression on the imagination so entirely out of proportion to its real severity as the punishment of death. The punishment must be mild indeed which does not add more to the sum of human misery than is necessarily or directly added by the execution of a criminal. As my hon. Friend the Member for Northampton (Mr. Gilpin) has himself remarked, the most that human laws can do to anyone in the matter of death is to hasten it; the man would have died at any rate; not so very much later, and on the average, I fear, with a considerably greater amount of bodily suffering. Society is asked, then, to denude itself of an instrument of punishment which, in the grave cases to which alone it is suitable, effects its purposes at a less cost of human suffering than any other; which, while it inspires more terror, is less cruel in actual fact than any punishment that we should think of substituting for it. My hon. Friend says that it does not inspire terror, and that experience proves it to be a failure. But the influence of a punishment is not to be estimated by its effect on hardened criminals. Those whose habitual way of life keeps them, so to speak, at all times within sight of the gallows, do grow to care less about it; as, to compare good things with bad, an old soldier is not much affected by the chance of dying in battle. I can afford to admit all that is often said about the indifference of professional criminals to the gallows.

Though of that indifference one-third is probably bravado and another third confidence that they shall have the luck to escape, it is quite probable that the remaining third is real. But the efficacy of a punishment which acts principally through the imagination, is chiefly to be measured by the impression it makes on those who are still innocent; by the horror with which it surrounds the first promptings of guilt; the restraining influence it exercises over the beginning of the thought which, if indulged, would become a temptation; the check which it exerts over the graded declension towards the state—never suddenly attained—in which crime no longer revolts, and punishment no longer terrifies. As for what is called the failure of death punishment, who is able to judge of that? We partly know who those are whom it has not deterred; but who is there who knows whom it has deterred, or how many human beings it has saved who would have lived to be murderers if that awful association had not been thrown round the idea of murder from their earliest infancy? Let us not forget that the most imposing fact loses its power over the imagination if it is made too cheap. When a punishment fit only for the most atrocious crimes is lavished on small offences until human feeling recoils from it, then, indeed, it ceases to intimidate, because it ceases to be believed in. The failure of capital punishment in cases of theft is easily accounted for; the thief did not believe that it would be inflicted. He had learnt by experience that jurors would perjure themselves rather than find him guilty; that Judges would seize any excuse for not sentencing him to death, or for recommending him to mercy; and that if neither jurors nor Judges were merciful, there were still hopes from an authority above both. When things had come to this pass it was high time to give up the vain attempt. When it is impossible to inflict a punishment, or when its infliction becomes a public scandal, the idle threat cannot too soon disappear from the statute book. And in the case of the host of offences which were formerly capital, I heartily rejoice that it did become impracticable to execute the law. If the same state of public feeling comes to exist in the case of murder; if the time comes when jurors refuse to find a murderer guilty; when Judges will not sentence him to death, or will recommend him to mercy; or when, if juries and Judges do not flinch from their duty, Home Secretaries, under pressure of deputations and memorials, shrink from theirs, and the threat becomes, as it became

in the other cases, a mere *brutum fulmen;* then, indeed, it may become necessary to do in this case what has been done in those—to
abrogate the penalty. That time may come—my hon. Friend thinks
that it has nearly come. I hardly know whether he lamented it or
boasted of it; but he and his Friends are entitled to the boast; for if
it comes it will be their doing, and they will have gained what I cannot but call a fatal victory, for they will have achieved it by bringing
about, if they will forgive me for saying so, an enervation, an effemi-
nancy, in the general mind of the country. For what else than effem-
inancy is it to be so much more shocked by taking a man's life than
by depriving him of all that makes life desirable or valuable? Is death,
then, the greatest of all earthly ills? *Usque adeone mori miserum
est?* Is it, indeed, so dreadful a thing to die? Has it not been from of
old one chief part of a manly education to make us despise death—
teaching us to account it, if an evil at all, by no means high in the
list of evils; at all events, as an inevitable one, and to hold, as it were,
our lives in our hands, ready to be given or risked at any moment, for
a sufficiently worthy object? I am sure that my hon. Friends know
all this as well, and have as much of all these feelings as any of the
rest of us; possibly more. But I cannot think that this is likely to be
the effect of their teaching on the general mind. I cannot think that
the cultivating of a peculiar sensitiveness of conscience on this one
point, over and above what results from the general cultivation of the
moral sentiments, is permanently consistent with assigning in our
own minds to the fact of death no more than the degree of relative
importance which belongs to it among the other incidents of our humanity. The men of old cared too little about death, and gave their
own lives or took those of others with equal recklessness. Our danger
is of the opposite kind, lest we should be so much shocked by death,
in general and in the abstract, as to care too much about it in individual cases, both those of other people and our own, which call for its
being risked. And I am not putting things at the worst, for it is proved
by the experience of other countries that horror of the executioner by
no means necessarily implies horror of the assassin. The stronghold,
as we all know, of hired assassination in the 18th century was Italy;
yet it is said that in some of the Italian populations the infliction of
death by sentence of law was in the highest degree offensive and revolting to popular feeling. Much has been said of the sanctity of hu-

man life, and the absurdity of supposing that we can teach respect for life by ourselves destroying it. But I am surprised at the employment of this argument, for it is one which might be brought against any punishment whatever. It is not human life only, not human life as such, that ought to be sacred to us, but human feelings. The human capacity of suffering is what we should cause to be respected, not the mere capacity of existing. And we may imagine somebody asking how we can teach people not to inflict suffering by ourselves inflicting it? But to this I should answer—all of us would answer—that to deter by suffering from inflicting suffering is not only possible, but the very purpose of penal justice. Does fining a criminal show want of respect for property, or imprisoning him, for personal freedom? Just as unreasonable is it to think that to take the life of a man who has taken that of another is to show want of regard for human life. We show, on the contrary, most emphatically our regard for it, by the adoption of a rule that he who violates that right in another forfeits it for himself, and that while no other crime that he can commit deprives him of his right to live, this shall. There is one argument against capital punishment, even in extreme cases, which I cannot deny to have weight —on which my hon. Friend justly laid great stress, and which never can be entirely got rid of. It is this—that if by an error of justice an innocent person is put to death, the mistake can never be corrected; all compensation, all reparation for the wrong is impossible. This would be indeed a serious objection if these miserable mistakes— among the most tragical occurrences in the whole round of human affairs—could not be made extremely rare. The argument is invincible where the mode of criminal procedure is dangerous to the innocent, or where the Courts of Justice are not trusted. And this probably is the reason why the objection to an irreparable punishment began (as I believe it did) earlier, and is more intense and more widely diffused, in some parts of the Continent of Europe than it is here. There are on the Continent great and enlightened countries, in which the criminal procedure is not so favorable to innocence, does not afford the same security against erroneous conviction, as it does among us; countries where the Courts of Justice seem to think they fail in their duty unless they find somebody guilty; and in their really laudable desire to hunt guilt from its hiding places, expose themselves to a serious danger of condemning the innocent. If our own procedure and Courts of Justice afforded ground for similar apprehension, I should be the first to join in withdrawing the power of inflicting irreparable punishment from such tribunals. But we all know that the defects of our procedure are the very opposite. Our rules of evidence are even too favorable to the prisoner; and juries and Judges carry out the maxim, "It is better that ten guilty should escape than that one innocent person should suffer," not only to the letter, but beyond the letter. Judges are most anxious to point out, and juries to allow for, the barest possibility of the prisoner's innocence. No human judgment is infallible; such sad cases as my hon. Friend cited will sometimes occur; but in so grave a case as that of murder, the accused, in our system, has always the benefit of the merest shadow of a doubt. And this suggests another consideration very germane to the question. The very fact that death punishment is more shocking than any other to the imagination, necessarily renders the Courts of Justice more scrupulous in requiring the fullest evidence of guilt. Even that which is the greatest objection to capital punishment, the impossibility of correcting an error once committed, must make, and does make, juries and Judges more careful in forming their opinion, and more jealous in their scrutiny of the evidence. If the substitution of penal servitude for death in cases of murder should cause any declaration in this conscientious scrupulosity, there would be a great evil to set against the real, but I hope rare, advantage of being able to make reparation to a condemned person who was afterwards discovered to be innocent. In order that the possibility of correction may be kept open wherever the chance of this sad contingency is more than infinitesimal, it is quite right that the Judge should recommend to the Crown a commutation of the sentence, not solely when the proof of guilt is open to the smallest suspicion, but whenever there remains anything unexplained and mysterious in the case, raising a desire for more light, or making it likely that further information may at some future time be obtained. I would also suggest that whenever the sentence is commuted the grounds of the commutation should, in some authentic form, be made known to the public. Thus much I willingly concede to my hon. Friend; but on the question of total abolition I am inclined to hope that the feeling of the country is not with him, and that the limitation of death punishment to the cases referred to in the Bill of last year will be generally considered sufficient. The mania which existed a short time ago for paring down all our punishments seems to have reached its limits, and not before it was time. We were in danger of being left without any effectual punishment, except for small offences. What was formerly our chief secondary punishment—transportation—before it was abolished, had become almost a reward. Penal servitude, the substitute for it, was becoming, to the classes who were principally subject to it, almost nominal, so comfortable did we make our prisons, and so easy had it become to get quickly out of them. Flogging—a most objectionable punishment in ordinary cases, but a particularly appropriate one for crimes of brutality, especially crimes against women—we would not hear of, except, to be sure, in the case of garotters, for whose peculiar benefit we reestablished it in a hurry, immediately after a Member of Parliament had been garrotted. With this exception, offences, even of an atrocious kind, against the person, as my hon. and learned Friend the Member for Oxford (Mr. Neate) well remarked, not only were, but still are, visited with penalties so ludicrously inadequate, as to be almost an encouragement to the crime. I think, Sir, that in the case of most offences, except those against property, there is more need of strengthening our punishments than of weakening them; and that severer sentences, with an apportionment of them to the different kinds of offences which shall approve itself better than at present to the moral sentiments of the community, are the kind of reform of which our penal system now stands in need. I shall therefore vote against the Amendment.

Chapter Five

Alternatives to Punishment

Bernard Shaw	Imprisonment
Samuel Butler	Erewhon and Erewhon Revisited
R. Martinson	The Paradox of Prison Reform
R. Wasserstrom	Why Punish the Guilty
J. Andenaes	Does Punishment Deter Crime?
Karl Marx	Punishment and Society
Clarence Darrow	The Holdup Man

Bernard Shaw

Imprisonment *

The spirit in which to read this essay

Imprisonment as it exists today is a worst crime than any of those committed by its victims; for no single criminal can be as powerful for evil, or as unrestrained in its exercise, as an organized nation. Therefore, if any person is addressing himself to the perusal of this dreadful subject in the spirit of a philanthropist bent on reforming a necessary and beneficent public institution, I beg him to put it down and go about some other business. It is just such reformers who have in the past made the neglect, oppression, corruption, and physical torture of the old common gaol the pretext for transforming it into that diabolical den of torment, mischief, and damnation, the modern model prison.

If, on the contrary, the reader comes as a repentant sinner, let him read on.

The obstacle of vindictiveness

The difficulty in finding repentant sinners when this crime is in question has two roots. The first is that we are all brought up to believe that we may inflict injuries on anyone against whom we can make out a case of moral inferiority. We have this thrashed into us in our childhood by the infliction on ourselves of such injuries by our parents and teachers, or indeed by any elder who happens to be in charge

* George Bernard Shaw, "Imprisonment," preface to S. and B. Webb, *English Prisons Under Local Government* (London: Longmans Green, 1922), reprinted by permission of the Society of Authors, on behalf of the Bernard Shaw Estate.

of us. The second is that we are all now brought up to believe, not that the king can do no wrong, because kings have been unable to keep up that pretence, but that Society can do no wrong. Now not only does Society commit more frightful crimes than any individual, king or commoner: it legalizes its crimes, and forges certificates of righteousness for them, besides torturing anyone who dares expose their true character. A society like ours, which will, without remorse, ruin a boy body and soul for life for trying to sell newspapers in a railway station, is not likely to be very tender to people who venture to tell it that its laws would shock the Prince of Darkness himself if he had not been taught from his earliest childhood to respect as well as fear them.

Consequently we have a desperately sophisticated public, as well as a quite frankly vindictive one. Judges spend their lives consigning their fellow creatures to prison; and when some whisper reaches them that prisons are horribly cruel and destructive places, and that no creature fit to live should be sent there, they only remark calmly that prisons are not meant to be comfortable, which is no doubt the consideration that reconciled Pontius Pilate to the practice of crucifixion.

The obstacle of stupidity

Another difficulty is the sort of stupidity that comes from lack of imagination. When I tell people that I have seen with these eyes a man (no less a man than Richard Wagner, by the way) who once met a crowd going to see a soldier broken on the wheel by the crueller of the two legalized methods of carrying out that hideous sentence, they shudder, and are amazed to hear that what they call medieval torture was used in civilized Europe so recently. They forget that the punishment of half-hanging, unmentionably mutilating, drawing and quartering, was on the British statute book within my own memory. The same people will read of a burglar being sentenced to ten years' penal servitude without turning a hair. They are like Ibsen's Peer Gynt, who was greatly reassured when he was told that the pains of hell are mental: he thought they cannot be so very bad if there is no actual burning brimstone. When such people are terrified by an outburst of robbery with violence, or sadistically excited by reports of the white slave traffic, they clamor to have sentences of two years hard labor supplemented by a flogging, which is a joke by comparison. They will try to lynch a criminal who illtreats a child in some sensationally cruel manner; but on the most trifling provocation they will inflict on the child the prison demoralization and the prison stigma which condemn it for the rest of its life to crime as the only employment open to a prison child. The public conscience would be far more active if the punishment of imprisonment were abolished, and we went back to the rack, the stake, the pillory, and the lash at the cart's tail.

Blood sports disguised as punishment are less cruel than imprisonment but more demoralizing to the public

The objection to retrogression is not that such punishments are more cruel than imprisonment. They are less cruel, and far less permanently injurious. The decisive objection to them is that they are sports in disguise. The pleasure to the spectators, and not the pain to the criminal, condemns them. People will go to see Titus Oates flogged or Joan of Arc burnt with equal zest as an entertainment. They will pay high prices for a good view. They will reluctantly admit that they must not torture one another as long as certain rules are observed; but they will hail a breach of the rules with delight as an excuse for a bout of cruelty. Yet they can be shamed at last into recognizing that such exhibitions are degrading and demoralizing; that the executioner is a wretch whose hand no decent person cares to take; and that the enjoyment of the spectators is fiendish. We have then to find some form of torment which can give no sensual satisfaction to the tormentor, and which is hidden from public view. That is how imprisonment, being just such a torment, became the normal penalty. The fact that it may be worse for the criminal is not taken into account. The public is seeking its own salvation, not that of the lawbreaker. For him it would be far better to suffer in the public eye; for among the crowd of sightseers there might be a Victor Hugo or a Dickens, able and willing to make the sightseers think of what they are doing and ashamed of it. The prisoner has no such chance. He envies the unfortunate animals in the zoo, watched daily by thousands of disinterested observers who never try to convert a tiger into a Quaker by solitary confinement, and would set up a resounding agitation in the papers if even the most ferocious man-eater were made to suffer what the most docile convict suffers. Not only has the convict no such protection: the secrecy of his prison makes it hard to convince the public that he is suffering at all.

How we all become inured to imprisonment

There is another reason for this incredulity. The vast majority of our city populations are inured to imprisonment from their childhood. The school is a prison. The office and the factory are prisons. The home is a prison. To the young who have the misfortune to be what is called well brought up it is sometimes a prison of inhuman severity. The children of John Howard, as far as their liberty was concerned, were treated very much as he insisted criminals should be treated, with the result that his children were morally disabled, like criminals. This imprisonment in the home, the school, the office, and the factory is kept up by browbeating, scolding, bullying, punishing, disbelief of the prisoner's statements and acceptance of those of the official, essentially as in a criminal prison. The freedom given by the adult's right to walk out of his prison is only a freedom to go into another or starve: he can choose the prison where he is best treated: that is all. On the other hand, the imprisoned criminal is free from care as to his board, lodging, and clothing: he pays no taxes, and has no responsibilities. Nobody expects him to work as an unconvicted man must work if he is to keep his job: nobody expects him to do his work well, or cares twopence whether it is well done or not.

Under such circumstances it is very hard to convince the ordinary citizen that the criminal is not better off than he deserves to be, and indeed on the verge of being positively pampered. Judges, magistrates, and Home Secretaries are so commonly under the same delusion that people who have ascertained the truth about prisons have been driven to declare that the most urgent necessity of the situation is that every judge, magistrate, and Home Secretary should serve a six months' sentence incognito; so that when he is dealing out and enforcing sentences he should at least know what he is doing.

Competition in evil between prison and slum

When we get down to the poorest and most oppressed of our population we find the conditions of their life so wretched that it would be impossible to conduct a prison humanely without making the lot of the criminal more eligible than that of many free citizens. If the prison does not underbid the slum in human misery, the slum will empty and the prison will fill. This does in fact take place to a small extent at present, because slum life at its worst is so atrocious that its victims, when they are intelligent enough to study alternatives instead of taking their lot blindly, conclude that prison is the most comfortable place to spend the winter in, and qualify themselves accordingly by committing an offence for which they will get six months. But this consideration affects only those people whose condition is not defended by any responsible publicist: the remedy is admittedly not to make the prison worse but the slum better. Unfortunately the admitted claims of the poor on life are pitifully modest. The moment the treatment of the criminal is decent and merciful enough to give him a chance of moral recovery, or, in incorrigible cases, to avoid making bad worse, the official descriptions of his lot become so rosy that a clamor arises against thieves and murderers being better off than honest and kindly men; for the official reports tell us only of the care that is taken of the prisoner and the advantages he enjoys, or can earn by good conduct, never of his sufferings; and the public is not imaginative or thoughtful enough to supply the deficiency.

What sane man, I ask the clamorers, would accept an offer of free board, lodging, clothing, waiters in attendance at a touch of the bell, medical treatment, spiritual advice, scientific ventilation and sanitation, technical instruction, liberal education, and the use of a carefully selected library, with regular exercise daily and sacred music at frequent intervals, even at the very best of the Ritz Hotels, if the conditions were that he should never leave the hotel, never speak, never sing, never laugh, never see a newspaper, and write only one sternly censored letter and have one miserable interview at long intervals through the bars of a cage under the eye of a warder? And when the prison is not the Ritz Hotel, when the lodging, the food, the bed, are all deliberately made so uncomfortable as to be instruments of torture, when the clothes are rags promiscuously worn by all your fellow prisoners in turn with yourself, when the exercise is that of a turnspit, when the ventilation and sanitation are noisome, when the instruction is a sham, the education a fraud, when the doctor is a bully to whom your ailments are all malingerings, and the chaplain a moral snob with no time for anything but the distribution of unreadable books, when the waiters are bound by penalties not to speak to you except to give you an order or a rebuke, and then to address you as you would not dream of addressing your dog, when the manager holds over your head a continual threat of starvation and confinement in a punishment cell (as if your own cell were not punishment enough), then what man in his senses would voluntarily exchange even the most harassed freedom for such a life, much less wallow luxuriously in it, as the *Punch* burglar always does on paper the moment anyone suggests the slightest alleviation of the pains of imprisonment?

Giving them Hell

Yet people cannot be brought to see this. They ask, first, what right the convict has to complain when he has brought it on himself by his own misconduct, and second, what he has to complain of. You reply that his grievances are silence, solitude, idleness, waste of time, and irresponsibility. The retort is, "Why call that torture, as if it were boiling oil or red hot irons or something like that? Why, I have taken a cottage in the country for the sake of silence and solitude; and I should be only too glad to get rid of my responsibilities and waste my time in idleness like a real gentleman. A jolly sight too well off, the fellows are. I should give them hell."

Thus imprisonment is at once the most cruel of punishments and the one that those who inflict it without having ever experienced it cannot believe to be cruel. A country gentleman with a big hunting stable will indignantly discharge a groom and refuse him a reference for cruelly thrashing a horse. But it never occurs to him that his stables are horse prisons, and the stall a cell in which it is quite unnatural for the horse to be immured. In my youth I saw the great Italian actress Ristori play Mary Stuart; and nothing in her performance remains more vividly with me than her representation of the relief of Mary at finding herself in the open air after months of imprisonment. When I first saw a stud of hunters turned out to grass, they reminded me so strongly of Ristori that I at once understood that they had been prisoners in their stables, a fact which, obvious as it was, I had not thought of before. And this sort of thoughtlessness, being continuous and unconscious, inflicts more suffering than all the malice and passion in the world. In prison you get one piled on the other: to the cruelty that is intended and contrived, that grudge you even the inevitable relief of sleep, and makes your nights miserable by plank beds and the like, is added the worse cruelty that is not intended as cruelty, and, when its perpetrators can be made conscious of it all, deludes them by a ghastly semblance of pampered indulgence.

The three official aims of imprisonment

And now comes a further complication. When people are at last compelled to think about what they are doing to our unfortunate convicts, they think so unsuccessfully and confusedly that they only make matters worse. Take for example the official list of the results aimed at by the Prison Commissioners. First, imprisonment must be "retributory" (the word vindictive is not in official use). Second, it must be deterrent. Third, it must be reformative.

The retribution muddle

Now, if you are to punish a man retributively, you must injure him. If you are to reform him, you must improve him. And men are not improved by injuries. To propose to punish and reform people by the same operation is exactly as if you were to take a man suffering from pneumonia, and attempt to combine punitive and curative treatment. Arguing that a man with pneumonia is a danger to the community, and that he need not catch it if he takes proper care of his health, you resolve that he shall have a severe lesson, both to punish him for his negligence and pulmonary weakness and to deter others from following his example. You therefore strip him naked, and in that condition stand him all night in the snow. But as you admit the duty of restoring him to health if possible, and discharging him with sound lungs, you engage a doctor to superintend the punishment and administer cough lozenges, made as unpleasant to the taste as possible so as not to pamper the culprit. A Board of Commissioners ordering such treatment would prove thereby that either they were imbeciles or else they were hotly in earnest about punishing the patient and not in the least in earnest about curing him.

When our Prison Commissioners pretend to combine punishment with moral reformation they are in the same dilemma. We are told that the reformation of the criminal is kept constantly in view; yet the destruction of the prisoner's self-respect by systematic humiliation is deliberately ordered and practised; and we learn from a chaplain that he "does not think it is good to give opportunity for the exercise of Christian and social virtues one towards another" among prisoners. The only consolation for such contradictions is their demonstration that, as the tormentors instinctively feel they must be liars and hypocrites on the subject, their consciences cannot be very easy about the torment. But the contradictions are obvious here only because I put them on the same page. The Prison Commissioners keep them a few pages apart; and the average reader's memory, it seems, is not long enough to span the gap when his personal interests are not at stake.

Plausibility of the Deterrence Delusion

Deterrence, which is the real object of the courts, has much more to be said for it, because it is neither simply and directly wicked like retribution, nor a false excuse for wickedness like reformation. It is an unquestionable fact that, by making rules and forcing those who break them to suffer so severely that others like them become afraid to break them, discipline can be maintained to a certain extent among creatures without sense enough to understand its necessity, or, if they do understand it, without conscience enough to refrain from violating it. This is the crude basis of all our disciplines: home discipline, school discipline, factory discipline, army and navy discipline, as well as of prison discipline, and of the whole fabric of criminal law. It is imposed not only by cruel rulers, but by unquestionably humane ones: the only difference being that the cruel rulers impose it with alacrity and gloat over its execution, and the humane rulers are driven to it reluctantly by the failure of their appeals to the consciences of people who have no conscience. Thus we find Mahomet, a conspicuously humane and conscientious Arab, keeping his fierce staff in order, not by unusual punishments, but by threats of a hell after death which he invented for the purpose in revolting detail of a kind which suggests that Mahomet had perhaps too much of the woman and the artist in him to know what would frighten a Bedouin most. Wellington, a general so humane that he sacrificed the exercise of a military genius of the first order to his moral horror of war and his freedom from its illusions, nevertheless hanged and flogged his soldiers mercilessly because he had learnt from experience that, as he put it, nothing is worse than impunity. All revolutions have been the work of men who, like Robespierre, were sentimental humanitarians and conscientious objectors to capital punishment and to the severities of military and prison discipline; yet all the revolutions have after a very brief practical experience been driven to Terrorism (the proper name of Deterrence) as ruthless as the Counter-Revolutionary Terror of Sulla, a late example being that of the Russian revolution of 1917. Whether it is Sulla, Robespierre, Trotsky, or the fighting mate of a sailing ship with a crew of loafers and wastrels, the result is the same: there are people to be dealt with who will not obey the law unless they are afraid to disobey it, and whose disobedience would mean disaster.

Crime cannot be killed by kindness

It is useless for humanitarians to shirk this hard fact, and proclaim their conviction that all lawbreakers can be reformed by kindness.

That may be true in many cases, provided you can find a very gifted practitioner to take the worst ones in hand, with unlimited time and means to treat them. But if these conditions are not available, and a policeman and an executioner who will disable the wrongdoer instantaneously are available, the police remedy is the only practicable one, even for rulers filled with the spirit of the Sermon on the Mount. The late G. V. Foote, President of the English National Secular Society, a strenuous humanitarian, once had to persuade a very intimate friend of his, a much smaller and weaker man, to allow himself to be taken to an asylum for lunatics. It took four hours of humanitarian persuasion to get the patient from the first floor of his house to the cab door. Foote told me that he had not only recognized at once that no asylum attendant, with several patients to attend to, could possibly spend four hours in getting each of them downstairs, but found his temper so intolerably strained by the unnatural tax on his patience that if the breaking point had been reached, as it certainly would have been in the case of a warder or asylum attendant, he would have been far more violent, not to say savage, than if he had resorted to force at once, and finished the job in five minutes.

From resorting to this rational and practically compulsory use of kindly physical coercion to making it so painful that the victim will be afraid to give any trouble next time is a pretty certain step. In prisons the warders have to protect themselves against violence from prisoners, of which there is a constant risk and very well founded dread, as there are always ungovernably savage criminals who have little more power of refraining from furious assaults than some animals, including quite carefully bred dogs and horses, have of refraining from biting and savaging. The official punishment is flogging and putting in irons for months. But the immediate rescue of the assaulted warder has to be effected by the whole body of warders within reach; and whoever supposes that the prisoner suffers nothing more at their hands than the minimum of force necessary to restrain him knows nothing of prison life and less of human nature.

Any criticism of the deterrent theory of our prison system which ignores the existence of ungovernable savages will be discredited by the citation of actual cases. I should be passed over as a sentimentalist if I lost sight of them for a moment. On any other subject I could dispose of the matter by reminding my critics that hard cases make bad law. On this subject I recognize that the hard cases are of such a nature that provision must be made for them. Indeed hard cases may be said to be the whole subject matter of criminal law; for the normal human case is not that of the criminal, but of the law-abiding person on whose collar the grip of the policeman never closes. Only, it does not follow that the hardest cases should dictate the treatment of the relatively soft ones.

The seamy side of deterrence

Let us now see what are the objections to the Deterrent or Terrorist system.

It necessarily leaves the interests of the victim wholly out of account. It injures and degrades him; destroys the reputation without which he cannot get employment; and when the punishment is imprisonment under our system, atrophies his powers of fending for himself in the world. Now this would not materially hurt anyone but himself if, when he had been duly made an example of, he were killed like a vivisected dog. But he is not killed. He is, at the expiration of his sentence, flung out of the prison into the streets to earn his living in a labor market where nobody will employ an ex-prisoner, betraying himself at every turn by his ignorance of the common news of the months or years he has passed without newspapers, lamed in speech, and terrified at the unaccustomed task of providing food and lodging for himself. There is only one lucrative occupation available for him; and that is crime. He has no compunction as to Society: why should he have any? Society having for its own selfiish protection done its worst to him, he has no feeling about it except a desire to get a bit of his own back. He seeks the only company in which he is welcome: the society of criminals; and sooner or later, according to his luck, he finds himself in prison again. The figures of recidivism show that the exceptions to this routine are so few as to be negligible for the purposes of our argument. The criminal, far from being deterred from crime, is forced into it; and the citizen whom his punishment was meant to protect suffers from his depredations.

Our plague of unrestrained crime

It is, in fact, admitted that the deterrent system does not deter the convicted criminal. Its real efficacy is sought in its deterrent effect on the free citizens who would commit crimes but for their fear of punishment. The Terrorist can point to the wide range of evil-doing which, not being punished by law, is rampant among us; for though a man can get himself hanged for a momentary lapse of self-control under intolerable provocation by a nagging woman, or into prison for putting the precepts of Christ above the orders of a Competent Military Authority, he can be a quite infernal scoundrel without breaking any penal law. If it be true, as it certainly is, that it is conscience and not the fear of punishment that makes civilized life possible, and that Dr. Johnson's

> How small, of all that human hearts endure
> That part that laws or kings can cause or cure!

is as applicable to crime as to human activity in general, it is none the less true that commercial civilization presents an appalling spectacle of pillage and parasitism, of corruption in the press and in the pulpit, of lying advertisements which make people buy rank poisons in the belief that they are health restorers, of traps to catch the provision made for the widow and the fatherless and divert it to the pockets of company promoting rogues, of villainous oppression of the poor and cruelty to the defenceless; and it is arguable that most of this could, like burglary and forgery, be kept within bearable bounds if its perpetrators were dealt with as burglars and forgers are dealt with today. It is, let us not forget, equally arguable that if we can afford to leave so much villainy unpunished we can afford to leave all villainy unpunished. Unfortunately, we cannot afford it: our toleration is threatening our civilization. The prosperity that consists in the wicked flourishing like a green bay tree, and the humble and contrite hearts being thoroughly despised, is a commercial delusion. Facts must be looked in the face, rascals told what they are, and all men called on to justify their ways to God and Man up to the point at which the full discharge of their social duties leaves them free to exercise their individual fancies. Restraint from evil-doing is within the rights as well as within the powers of organized society over its members;

and it cannot be denied that the exercise of these powers, as far as it could be made inevitable, would incidentally deter from crime a certain number of people with only marginal consciences or none at all, and that an extension of the penal code would create fresh social conscience by enlarging the list of things which law-abiding people make it a point of honor not to do, besides calling the attention of the community to grave matters in which they have hitherto erred through thoughtlessness.

Deterrence a function of certainty, not of severity

But there is all the difference in the world between deterrence as an incident of the operation of criminal law, and deterrence as its sole object and justification. In a purely deterrent system, for instance, it matters not a jot who is punished provided somebody is punished and the public persuaded that he is guilty. The effect of hanging or imprisoning the wrong man is as deterrent as hanging or imprisoning the right one. This is the fundamental explanation of the extreme and apparently fiendish reluctance of the Home Office to release a prisoner when, as in the Beck case, the evidence on which he was convicted has become discredited to a point at which no jury would maintain its verdict of guilty. The reluctance is not to confess that an innocent man is being punished, but to proclaim that a guilty man has escaped. For if escape is possible deterrence shrinks almost to nothing. There is no better established rule of criminology than that it is not the severity of punishment that deters, but its certainty. And the flaw in the case of Terrorism is that it is impossible to obtain enough certainty to deter. The police are compelled to confess every year, when they publish their statistics, that against the list of crimes reported to them they can set only a percentage of detections and convictions. And the list of reported crimes can form only a percentage, how large or small it is impossible to say, but probably small, of the crimes actually committed; for it is the greatest mistake to suppose that everyone who is robbed runs to the police: on the contrary, only foolish and ignorant or very angry people do so without very serious consideration and great reluctance. In most cases it costs nothing to let the thief off, and a good deal to prosecute him. The burglar in Heartbreak House, who makes his living by breaking into people's houses, and then blackmailing them by threatening to give himself up to the police and put them to the expense and discomfort of attending his trial and giving evidence after enduring all the worry of the police enquiries, is not a joke: he is a comic dramatization of a process that is going on every day. As to the black sheep of respectable families who blackmail them by offering them the alternative of making good their thefts and frauds, even to the extent of honoring their forged cheques, or having the family name disgraced, ask any experienced family solicitor.

Beside the chance of not being prosecuted, there are the chances of acquittal; but I doubt whether they count for much except with very attractive women. Still, it is worth mentioning that juries will snatch at the flimsiest pretexts for refusing to send people who engage their sympathy to the gallows or to penal servitude, even on evidence of murder or theft which would make short work of a repulsive person.

Some personal experiences

Take my own experience as probably common enough. Fifty years ago a friend of mine, hearing that a legacy had been left him, lent himself the expected sum out of his employers' cash; concealed the defalcation by falsifying his accounts; and was detected before he could repay. His employers angrily resented the fraud, and had certainly no desire to spare him. But a public exposure of the affair would have involved shock to their clients' sense of security, loss of time and consequently of money, an end to all hope of his ever making good the loss, and the unpleasantness of attendance in court at the trial. All this put any recourse to the police out of the question; and my friend obtained another post after a very brief interval during which he supported himself as a church organist. This, by the way, was a quite desirable conclusion, as he was for all ordinary practical purposes a sufficiently honest man. It would have been pure mischief to make him a criminal; but that is not the present point. He serves here as an illustration of the fact that our criminal law, far from inviting prosecution, attaches serious losses and inconveniences to it.

It may be said that whatever the losses and inconveniences may be, it is a public duty to prosecute. But is it? Is it not a Christian duty not to prosecute? A man stole £500 from me by a trick. He speculated in my character with subtlety and success; and yet he ran risks of detection which no quite sensible man would have ventured on. It was assumed that I would resort to the police. I asked why. The answer was that he should be punished to deter others from similar crimes. I naturally said, "You have been punishing people cruelly for more than a century for this kind of fraud; and the result is that I am robbed of £500. Evidently your deterrence does not deter. What it does do is to torment the swindler for years, and then throw him back upon society, a worse man in every respect, with no other employment open to him except that of fresh swindling. Besides, your elaborate arrangements to deter me from prosecuting are convincing and effective. I could earn £500 by useful work in the time it would take me to prosecute this man vindictively and worse than uselessly. So I wish him joy of his booty, and invite him to swindle me again if he can." Now this was not sentimentality. I am not a bit fonder of being swindled than other people; and if society would treat swindlers properly I should denounce them without the slightest remorse, and not grudge a reasonable expenditure of time and energy in the business. But to throw good money after bad in setting to work a wicked and mischievous routine of evil would be to stamp myself as a worse man than the swindler, who earned the money more energetically, and appropriated it no more unjustly, if less legally, than I earn and appropriate my dividends.

I must however warn our thieves that I can promise them no immunity from police pursuit if they rob me. Some time after the operation just recorded, an uninvited guest came to a luncheon party in my house. He (or she) got away with an overcoat and a pocketful of my wife's best table silver. But instead of selecting my overcoat, he took the best overcoat, which was that of one of my guests. My guest was insured against theft; the insurance company had to buy him a new overcoat; and the matter thus passed out of my hands into those of the police. But the result, as far as the thief was concerned, was the same. He was not captured; and he had the social satisfaction of providing employment for others in converting into a strongly fortified obstacle the flimsy gate through which he had effected an entrance, thereby giving my flat the appearance of a private madhouse.

On another occasion a drunken woman obtained admission by presenting an authentic letter from a soft hearted member of the House of Lords. I had no guests at the moment; and as she, too, wanted an overcoat, she took mine, and actually interviewed me with it most perfunctorily concealed under her jacket. When I called her attention to it she handed it back to me effusively, begged me to shake hands with her; and went her way.

Now these things occur by the dozen every day, in spite of the severity with which they are punished when the thief is dealt with by police. I daresay all my readers, if not too young to have completed a representative experience, could add two or three similar stories. What do they go to prove? Just that detection is so uncertain that its consequences have no really effective deterrence for the potential offender, whilst the unpleasant and expensive consequences of prosecution, being absolutely certain, have a very strong deterrent effect indeed on the prosecutor. In short, all the hideous cruelty practised by us for the sake of deterrence is wasted: we are damning our souls at great expense and trouble for nothing.

Judicial vengeance as an alternative to lynch law

Thus we see that of the three official objects of our prison system: vengeance, deterrence, and reformation of the criminal, only one is achieved; and that is the one which is nakedly abominable. But there is a plea for it which must be taken into account, and which brings us to the root of the matter in our own characters. It is said, and it is in a certain degree true, that if the Government does not lawfully organize and regulate popular vengeance, the populace will rise up and execute this vengeance lawlessly for itself. The standard defence of the Inquisition is that without it no heretic's life would have been safe. In Texas today the people are not satisfied with the prospect of knowing that a murderer or ravisher will be electrocuted inside a jail if a jury can resist the defence put up by his lawyer. They tear him from the hands of the sheriff; pour lamp oil over him; and burn him alive. Now the burning of human beings is not only an expression of outraged public morality: it is also a sport for which a taste can be acquired much more easily and rapidly than a taste for coursing hares, just as a taste for drink can be acquired from brandy and cocktails more easily and rapidly than from beer or sauterne. Lynching mobs begin with negro ravishers and murderers; but they presently go on to any sort of delinquent, provided he is black. Later on, as a white man will burn as amusingly as a black one, and a white woman react to tarring and feathering as thrillingly as a Negress, the color line is effaced by what professes to be a rising wave of virtuous indignation, but is in fact an epidemic of Sadism. The defenders of our penal systems take advantage of it to assure us that if they did not torment and ruin a boy guilty of sleeping in the open air, an indignant public would rise and tear that boy limb from limb.

Now the reply to such a plea, from the point of view of civilized law, cannot be too sweeping. The government which cannot restrain a mob from taking the law into its own hands is no government at all. If Landru could go to the guillotine unmolested in France, and his British prototype who drowned all his wives in their baths could be peaceably hanged in England, Texas can protest its criminals by simply bringing its civilization up to the French and British level. But indeed the besetting sin of the mob is a morbid hero worship of great criminals rather than a ferocious abhorrence of them. In any case nobody will have the effrontery to pretend that the number of criminals who excite popular feeling enough to provoke lynching is more than a negligible percentage of the whole. The theory that the problem of crime is only one of organizing, regulating, and executing the vengeance of the mob will not bear plain statement, much less discussion. It is only the retributive theory over again in its most impudent form.

The hard cases that make bad law

Having now disposed of all the official theories as the trash they are, let us return to the facts, and deal with the hard ones first. Everyone who has any extensive experience of domesticated animals, human or other, knows that there are negatively bad specimens who have no consciences, and positively bad ones who are incurably ferocious. The negative ones are often very agreeable and even charming companions; but they beg, borrow, steal, defraud and seduce almost by reflex action: they cannot resist the most trifling temptation. They are indulged and spared to the extreme limit of endurance; but in the end they have to be deprived of their liberty in some way. The positive ones enjoy no such tolerance. Unless they are physically restrained they break people's bones, knock out their eyes, rupture their organs, or kill them.

Then there are the cruel people, not necessarily unable to control their tempers, nor fraudulent, nor in any other way disqualified for ordinary social activity or liberty, possibly even with conspicuous virtues. But by a horrible involution, they lust after the spectacle of suffering, mental and physical, as normal men lust after love. Torture is to them a pleasure except when it is inflicted on themselves. In scores of ways, from the habitual utterance of wounding speeches, and the contriving of sly injuries and humiliations for which they cannot be brought to book legally, to thrashing their wives and children or, as bachelors, paying prostitutes of the hardier sort to submit to floggings, they seek the satisfaction of their desire wherever and however they can.

Possibilities of therapeutic treatment

Now in the present state of our knowledge it is folly to talk of reforming these people. By this I do not mean that even now they are all quite incurable. The cases of no conscience are sometimes, like Parsifal's when he shot the swan, cases of unawakened conscience. Violent and quarrelsome people are often only energetic people who are underworked: I have known a man cured of wife-beating by setting him to beat the drum in a village band; and the quarrels that make country life so very unarcadian are picked mostly because the quarrelers have not enough friction in their lives to keep them good humored.

Psychoanalysis, too, which is not all quackery and pornography, might conceivably cure a case of Sadism as it might cure any of the phobias. And psychoanalysis is a mere fancy compared to the knowledge we now pretend to concerning the function of our glands and their effect on our character and conduct. In the nineteenth century this knowledge was pursued barbarously by crude vivisectors whose notion of finding out what a gland was for was to cut it violently out and see what would happen to the victim, meanwhile trying to bribe the public to tolerate such horrors by promising to make old debauchees young again. This was rightly felt to be a villainous business; besides, who could suppose that the men who did these things would hesitate to lie about the results when there was plenty of money to be made by representing them as cures for dreaded diseases? But today we are not asked to infer that because something has happened to a violently multilated dog it must happen also to an unmultilated human being. We can now make authentic pictures of internal organs by means of rays to which flesh is transparent. This makes it possible to take a criminal and say authoritatively that he is a case, not of original sin, but of an inefficient, or excessively efficient, thyroid gland, or pituitary gland, or adrenal gland, as the case may be. This of course does not help the police in dealing with a criminal: they must apprehend and bring him to trial all the same. But if the prison doctor were able to say "Put some iodine in this man's skilly, and his character will change," then the notion of punishing instead of curing him would become ridiculous. Of course the matter is not so simple as that; and all this endocrinism, as it is called, may turn out to be only the latest addition to our already very extensive collection of pseudoscientific mares' nests; still, we cannot ignore the fact that a considerable case is being made out by eminent physiologists for at least a conjecture that many cases which are now incurable may be disposed of in the not very remote future by inducing the patient to produce more thyroxin or pituitrin or adrenalin or what not, or even administering them to him as thyroxin is at present administered in cases of myxedema. Yet the reports of the work of our prison medical officers suggest that hardly any of them has ever heard of these discoveries, or regards a convict as anything more interesting scientifically than a malingering rascal.

Samuel Butler

Erewhon and
Erewhon Revisited *

This is what I gathered. That in that country if a man falls into ill
health, or catches any disorder, or fails bodily in any way before he is
seventy years old, he is tried before a jury of his countrymen and if
convicted is held up to public scorn and sentenced more or less
severely as the case may be. There are subdivisions of illness into
crimes and misdemeanors as with offenses amongst ourselves—a man
being punished very heavily for serious illness, while failure of eyes
or hearing in one over sixty-five, who has had good health hitherto,
is dealt with by fine only, or imprisonment in default of payment.
But if a man forges a check, or sets his house on fire, or robs with
violence from the person, or does any other such things as are criminal in our own country, he is either taken to a hospital and most
carefully tended at the public expense, or if he is in good circumstances, he lets it be known to all his friends that he is suffering from
a severe fit of immorality, just as we do when we are ill, and they
come and visit him with great solicitude, and inquire with interest
how it all came about, what symptoms first showed themselves, and
so forth,—questions which he will answer with perfect unreserve; for
bad conduct, though considered no less deplorable than illness with
ourselves, and as unquestionably indicating something seriously
wrong with the individual who misbehaves, is nevertheless held to be
the result of either pre-natal or post-natal misfortune.

The strange part of the story, however, is that though they ascribe
moral defects to the effect of misfortune either in character or sur-
roundings, they will not listen to the plea of misfortune in cases
that in England meet with sympathy and commiseration only. Ill
luck of any kind, or even ill treatment at the hands of others, is con-

* Samuel Butler, *Erewhon and Erewhon Revisited*, intro. Lewis Mumford (New
York: Random House, 1927), pp. 88–101.

sidered an offense against society, inasmuch as it makes people uncomfortable to hear of it. Loss of fortune, therefore, or loss of some dear friend on whom another was much dependent, is punished hardly less severely than physical delinquency.

Foreign, indeed, as such ideas are to our own, traces of somewhat similar opinions can be found even in nineteenth-century England. If a person has an abscess, the medical man will say that it contains "peccant" matter, and people say that they have a "bad" arm or finger, or that they are very "bad" all over, when they only mean "diseased." Among foreign nations Erewhonian opinions may be still more clearly noted. The Mahommedans, for example, to this day, send their female prisoners to hospitals, and the New Zealand Maories visit any misfortune with forcible entry into the house of the offender, and the breaking up and burning of all his goods. The Italians, again, use the same word for "disgrace" and "misfortune." I once heard an Italian lady speak of a young friend whom she described as endowed with every virtue under heaven, "ma," she exclaimed, "povero disgraziato, ha ammazzato suo zio." ("Poor unfortunate fellow, he has murdered his uncle.")

On mentioning this, which I heard when taken to Italy as a boy by my father, the person to whom I told it showed no surprise. He said that he had been driven for two or three years in a certain city by a young Sicilian cabdriver of prepossessing manners and appearance, but then lost sight of him. On asking what had become of him, he was told that he was in prison for having shot at his father with intent to kill him—happily without serious results. Some years later my informant again found himself warmly accosted by the prepossessing young cabdriver. "Ah, caro signore," he exclaimed, "sono cinque anni che non lo vedo—tre anni di militare, e due anni di disgrazia," etc. ("My dear sir, it is five years since I saw you—three years of military service, and two of misfortune")—during which last the poor fellow had been in prison. Of moral sense he showed not so much as a trace. He and his father were now on excellent terms, and were likely to remain so unless either of them should again have the misfortune mortally to offend the other.

In the following chapter I will give a few examples of the way in which what we should call misfortune, hardship, or disease are dealt with by the Erewhonians, but for the moment will return to their treatment of cases that with us are criminal. As I have already said, these, though not judicially punishable, are recognized as requiring correction. Accordingly, there exists a class of men trained in soul-craft, whom they call straighteners, as nearly as I can translate a word which literally means "one who bends back the crooked." These men practice much as medical men in England, and receive a quasi-surreptitious fee on every visit. They are treated with the same unreserve, and obeyed as readily, as our own doctors—that is to say, on the whole sufficiently—because people know that it is their interest to get well as soon as they can, and that they will not be scouted as they would be if their bodies were out of order, even though they may have to undergo a very painful course of treatment.

When I say that they will not be scouted, I do not mean that an Erewhonian will suffer no social inconvenience in consequence, we will say, of having committed fraud. Friends will fall away from him because of his being less pleasant company, just as we ourselves are disinclined to make companions of those who are either poor or poorly. No one with any sense of self-respect will place himself on an equality in the matter of affection with those who are less lucky than himself in birth, health, money, good looks, capacity, or anything else. Indeed, that dislike and even disgust should be felt by the fortunate for the unfortunate, or at any rate for those who have been discovered to have met with any of the more serious and less familiar misfortunes, is not only natural, but desirable for any society, whether of man or brute.

The fact, therefore, that the Erewhonians attach none of that guilt to crime which they do to physical ailments, does not prevent the more selfish among them from neglecting a friend who has robbed a bank, for instance, till he has fully recovered; but it does prevent them from even thinking of treating criminals with that contemptuous tone which would seem to say, "I, if I were you, should be a better man than you are," a tone which is held quite reasonable in regard to physical ailment. Hence, though they conceal ill health by every cunning and hypocrisy and artifice which they can devise, they are quite open about the most flagrant mental diseases, should they happen to exist, which to do the people justice is not often. Indeed, there are some who are, so to speak, spiritual valetudinarians, and who make themselves exceedingly ridiculous by their nervous supposition that they are wicked, while they are very tolerable people all the time. This however is exceptional, and on the whole they use much the same reserve or unreserve about the state of their moral welfare as we do about our health.

Hence all the ordinary greetings among ourselves, such as, How do you do? and the like, are considered signs of gross ill-breeding; nor do the politer classes tolerate even such a common complimentary remark as telling a man that he is looking well. They salute each other with, "I hope you are good this morning;" or "I hope you have recovered from the snappishness from which you were suffering when I last saw you"; and if the person saluted has not been good, or is still snappish, he says so at once and is condoled with accordingly. Indeed, the straighteners have gone so far as to give names from the hypothetical language (as taught at the Colleges of Unreason), to all known forms of mental indisposition, and to classify them according to a system of their own, which, though I could not understand it, seemed to work well in practice; for they are always able to tell a man what is the matter with him as soon as they have heard his story, and their familiarity with the long names assures him that they thoroughly understand his case.

The reader will have no difficulty in believing that the laws regarding ill health were frequently evaded by the help of recognized fictions, which every one understood, but which it would be considered gross ill-breeding to even seem to understand. Thus, a day or two after my arrival at the Nosnibors', one of the many ladies who called on me made excuses for her husband's only sending his card, on the ground that when going through the public market-place that morning he had stolen a pair of socks. I had already been warned that I should never show surprise, so I merely expressed my sympathy, and said that though I had only been in the capital so short time, I had already had a very narrow escape from stealing a clothes-brush, and that though I had resisted temptation so far, I was sadly afraid that if I saw any object of special interest that was neither too hot nor too heavy, I should have to put myself in the straightener's hands.

Mrs. Nosnibor, who had been keeping an ear on all that I had been saying, praised me when the lady had gone. Nothing, she said, could have been more polite according to Erewhonian etiquette. She then explained that to have stolen a pair of socks, or "to have the socks" (in more colloquial language), was a recognized way of saying that the person in question was slightly indisposed.

In spite of all this they have a keen sense of the enjoyment consequent upon what they call being "well." They admire mental health and love it in other people, and take all the pains they can (consistently with their other duties) to secure it for themselves. They have an extreme dislike to marrying into what they consider unhealthy families. They send for the straightener at once whenever they have been guilty of anything seriously flagitious—often even if they think that they are on the point of committing it; and though his remedies are sometimes exceedingly painful, involving close confinement for weeks, and in some cases the most cruel physical tortures, I never heard of a reasonable Erewhonian refusing to do what his straightener told him, any more than of a reasonable Englishman refusing to undergo even the most frightful operation, if his doctors told him it was necessary.

We in England never shrink from telling our doctor what is the matter with us merely through the fear that he will hurt us. We let him do his worst upon us, and stand it without a murmur, because we are not scouted for being ill, and because we know that the doctor is doing his best to cure us, and that he can judge of our case better than we can; but we should conceal all illness if we were treated as the Erewhonians are when they have anything the matter with them; we should do the same as with moral and intellectual diseases,—we should feign health with the most consummate art, till we were found out, and should hate a single flogging given in the way of mere punishment more than the amputation of a limb, if it were kindly and courteously performed from a wish to help us out of our difficulty, and with the full consciousness on the part of the doctor that it was only by an accident of constitution that he was not in the like plight himself. So the Erewhonians take a flogging once a week, and a diet of bread and water for two or three months together, whenever their straightener recommends it.

I do not suppose that even my host, on having swindled a confiding widow out of the whole of her property, was put to more actual suffering than a man will readily undergo at the hands of an English doctor. And yet he must have had a very bad time of it. The sounds I heard were sufficient to show that his pain was exquisite, but he never shrank from undergoing it. He was quite sure that it did him good; and I think he was right. I cannot believe that that man will ever embezzle money again. He may—but it will be a long time before he does so.

During my confinement in prison, and on my journey, I had already discovered a great deal of the above; but it still seemed surpassingly strange, and I was in constant fear of committing some piece of rudeness, through my inability to look at things from the same standpoint as my neighbors; but after a few weeks' stay with the Nosnibors, I got to understand things better, especially on having heard all about my host's illness, of which he told me fully and repeatedly.

It seemed that he had been on the Stock Exchange of the city for many years and had amassed enormous wealth, without exceeding the limits of what was generally considered justifiable, or at any rate, permissible dealing; but at length on several occasions he had become aware of a desire to make money by fraudulent representations, and had actually dealt with two or three sums in a way which had made him rather uncomfortable. He had unfortunately made light of it and pooh-poohed the ailment, until circumstances eventually presented themselves which enabled him to cheat upon a very considerable scale;—he told me what they were, and they were about as bad as anything could be, but I need not detail them;—he seized the opportunity, and became aware, when it was too late, that he must be seriously out of order. He had neglected himself too long.

He drove home at once, broke the news to his wife and daughters as gently as he could, and sent off for one of the most celebrated straighteners of the kingdom to a consultation with the family practitioner, for the case was plainly serious. On the arrival of the straightener he told his story, and expressed his fear that his morals must be permanently impaired.

The eminent man reassured him with a few cheering words, and then proceeded to make a more careful diagnosis of the case. He inquired concerning Mr. Nosnibor's parents—had their moral health been good? He was answered that there had not been anything seriously amiss with them, but that his maternal grandfather, whom he was supposed to resemble somewhat in person, had been a consummate scoundrel and had ended his days in a hospital,—while a brother of his father's, after having led a most flagitious life for many years, had been at last cured by a philosopher of a new school, which as far as I could understand it bore much the same relation to the old as homoeopathy to allopathy. The straightener shook his head at this, and laughingly replied that the cure must have been due to nature. After a few more questions he wrote a prescription and departed.

I saw the prescription. It ordered a fine to the State of double the money embezzled; no food but bread and milk for six months, and a severe flogging once a month for twelve. I was surprised to see that no part of the fine was to be paid to the poor woman whose money had been embezzled, but on inquiry I learned that she would have been prosecuted in the Misplaced Confidence Court, if she had not escaped its clutches by dying shortly after she had discovered her loss.

As for Mr. Nosnibor, he had received his eleventh flogging on the day of my arrival. I saw him later on the same afternoon, and he was still twinged; but there had been no escape from following out the straightener's prescription, for the so-called sanitary laws of Erewhon are very rigorous, and unless the straightener was satisfied that his orders had been obeyed, the patient would have been taken to a hospital (as the poor are), and would have been much worse off. Such at least is the law, but it is never necessary to enforce it.

On a subsequent occasion I was present at an interview between Mr. Nosnibor and the family straightener, who was considered competent to watch the completion of the cure. I was struck with the delicacy with which he avoided even the remotest semblance of inquiry after the physical well-being of his patient, though there was a certain yellowness about my host's eyes which argued a bilious habit of body. To have taken notice of this would have been a gross breach of professional etiquette. I was told, however, that a straightener sometimes thinks it right to glance at the possibility of some slight physical disorder if he finds it important in order to assist him in his diagnosis; but the answers which he gets are generally untrue or evasive, and he forms his own conclusions upon the matter as well as he can. Sensible men have been known to say that the straightener should in strict confidence be told of every physical ailment that is likely to bear upon the case; but people are naturally shy of doing this, for they do not like lowering themselves in the opinion of the straightener, and his ignorance of medical science is supreme. I heard of one lady, indeed, who had the hardihood to confess that a furious outbreak of ill-humor and extravagant fancies for which she was seeking advice was possibly the result of indisposition. "You should resist that," said the straightener, in a kind, but grave voice; "we can do nothing for the bodies of our patients; such matters are beyond our province, and I desire that I may hear no further particulars." The lady burst into tears, and promised faithfully that she would never be unwell again.

But to return to Mr. Nosnibor. As the afternoon wore on many carriages drove up with callers to inquire how he had stood his flogging. It had been very severe, but the kind inquiries upon every side gave him great pleasure, and he assured me that he was almost tempted to do wrong again by the solicitude with which his friends had treated him during his recovery: in this I need hardly say that he was not serious.

During the remainder of my stay in the country Mr. Nosnibor was constantly attentive to his business, and largely increased his already great possessions; but I never heard a whisper to the effect of his having been indisposed a second time, or made money by other than the most strictly honorable means. I did hear afterwards in confidence that there had been reason to believe that his health had been not a little affected by the straightener's treatment, but his friends did not choose to be over-curious upon the subject, and on his return to his affairs it was by common consent passed over as hardly criminal in one who was otherwise so much afflicted. For they regard bodily ailments as the more venial in proportion as they have been produced by causes independent of the constitution. Thus if a person ruin his health by excessive indulgence at the table or by drinking, they count it to be almost a part of the mental disease which brought it about, and so it goes for little, but they have no mercy on such illnesses as fevers or catarrhs or lung diseases, which to us appear to be beyond the control of the individual. They are only more lenient towards the diseases of the young—such as measles, which they think to be like sowing one's wild oats—and look over them as pardonable indiscretions if they have not been too serious, and if they are atoned for by complete subsequent recovery.

It is hardly necessary to say that the office of straightener is one which requires long and special training. It stands to reason that he who would cure a moral ailment must be practically acquainted with it in all its bearings. The student for the profession of straightener is required to set apart certain seasons for the practice of each vice in turn as a religious duty. These seasons are called "fasts," and are continued by the student until he finds that he really can subdue all the more usual vices in his own person, and hence can advise his patients from the results of his own experience.

Those who intend to be specialists, rather than general practitioners, devote themselves more particularly to the branch in which their practice will mainly lie. Some students have been obliged to continue their exercises during their whole lives, and some devoted men have actually died as martyrs to the drink, or gluttony, or whatever branch of vice they may have chosen for their especial study. The greater number, however, take no harm by the excursions into the various departments of vice which it is incumbent upon them to study.

For the Erewhonians hold that unalloyed virtue is not a thing to be immoderately indulged in. I was shown more than one case in which the real or supposed virtues of parents were visited upon the children to the third and fourth generation. The straighteners say that the most that can be truly said for virtue is that there is a considerable balance in its favor, and that it is on the whole a good deal better to be on its side than against it; but they urge that there is much pseudovirtue going about, which is apt to let people in very badly before they find it out. Those men, they say, are best who are not remarkable either for vice or virtue. I told them about Hogarth's idle and industrious apprentices, but they did not seem to think that the industrious apprentice was a very nice person.

Robert Martinson

The Paradox of
Prison Reform *

The moment prisons were established they were found wanting, and their history is the story of unceasing attempts to improve them, apparently to no avail. The 19th and 20th century movements for prison reform have been as contradictory as the prison. When one asks what "prison reform" means, five traditions are discernable: 1) Prisons are for punishing offenders. (I will refer to these conservatives as the "hard-liners.") 2) Prisons are vicious instruments of revenge and should be abolished immediately. (I label this position "populist.") 3) Prisons are necessary to defend civilization but they should be improved to make them less punitive and more humane. (This is the mainstream tradition of the 19th and 20th century "humanitarian reform.") 4) Prisons should be transformed into effective instruments for the rehabilitation of offenders. (This is "correctional treatment.") 5) Prisons are necessary to some stages of civilization but can be replaced by milder forms of control to the degree permitted by democratic crime prevention. (The "social planning" view.) In what follows, I hope to document the disintegration of "correctional treatment" (number 4) in the hope of laying the basis for "social planning" (number 5).

I. Let us use the 1952–53 worldwide cycle of prison riots as a convenient benchmark. In the wake of those disturbances, John Bartlow Martin, a crime reporter with a gift for plain-talking, wrote a little book, *Break Down the Walls*, in which he denounced the "professional people" for having devised a dangerous myth—"myth because it is not true that prison can rehabilitate [treat] men, dangerous because their pretense that it can leads them to loose dangerous men

* Reprinted by permission of the *New Republic*, © 1972 Harrison Blaine of New Jersey.

upon society." He continued: "Rehabilitation [I prefer the term correctional treatment] in prison today is a pie-in-the-sky idea. . . . [We] appear to believe that if we provide the stainless-steel kitchen, the schools and shops and toilets, one day rehabilitation will descend upon the inmate, like manna. And it is not only wardens and penologists who believe this; it is inmates as well."

Mr. Martin wrote his critique at a watershed in American penology. He looked back upon a century of reform supported by uplift societies, trade union locals, ladies' clubs, probation lobbies and political groups from Populist to Socialist. The achievements were visible and uninterrupted: probation; parole; the juvenile court; prison classification systems, separate facilities for juveniles and females; abolition of the whip, the ball-and-chain, the striped clothes, bread-and-water (except as a punishment), and hard labor; the diagnostic clinic; a single state department of corrections; and civil service protections for guards. All that was in the past.

As the 20th century grew older, new professional groups in probation, parole, social welfare and psychiatry (in alliance with humanitarian reformers) began to introduce into prisons the chaplain, the teacher, the vocational instructor, the counsellor, the psychiatrist and the nonpolitical warden. The prison turnkey became professionalized as the correctional officer, and began to form trade unions. "Custody" and "treatment" jockeyed for power.

Sometimes treatment staff became unofficial spokesmen for prison rioters. They successfully convinced inmate leaders that disturbances should be moderate and limited to the improvement of treatment services or the inauguration of treatment programs. The '50s and '60s were to become the high point of the Age of Treatment. The myth of correctional treatment was co-opted by prison officials and enshrined in the Manual of Correctional Standards.

The new alliance between the professional people and the prison administrators was most firmly established in California after World War II. In 1943, Governor Earl Warren began reforms which changed the state's prison system from one of the most backward and crisis-ridden to one which gradually gained the reputation throughout the world as a model of correctional practice. The Warren reforms followed two decades of prison scandals. Relying on an informed and aroused public opinion, the governor appointed a treatment-oriented administrator, Mr. Richard McGee. New prisons (minimum and medium security) were built. Professionals were hired to man the diagnostic clinics and probation and parole were expanded. Prison record jackets bulged with new information about the inmate. Centralized control was combined with efficient classification. Individual wardens lost independence as central office staff monitored operations, transferred inmates, and lobbied directly with the governor and legislature.

For the first time, an entire prison system was permeated with the "dangerous myth" of corrections. Group counselling was introduced en masse, even in facilities as security-ridden as San Quentin and Folsom. Middle management was trained in group treatment techniques and custodial ranks were indoctrinated with the new perspective which came to be called the "correctional therepeutic community." New units called "Adjustment Centers" were built within the prisons, based on the principle of the indeterminate sentence and combining maximum security with individual treatment. A maximum security medical facility was opened at Vacaville. An outstanding research division was given wide powers to help plan experimental programs and evaluate their effects.

The progress of actuarial research made it possible to assign every California inmate a "base expectancy score" to predict his likelihood of returning to crime. "Good risk" inmates were released early from confinement and the savings used to underwrite the ten-year Special Intensive Parole Unit studies. Efficient classification made possible rapid transfer of inmates from one part of the far-flung system to another (called "bus therapy" by the insiders). An Army barracks in San Luis Obispo was turned into a minimum-security old men's home. Parole out-patient services were provided, and addicts were given the newly developed Nalline test four times a month (with one surprise visit) by state-hired doctors. Finally—to symbolize the coalescence of correctional administration and scientific method—a newly built medium-security prison (California Men's Colony—East) was opened to inmates using a research design randomly assigning newcomers to various quads of the prison.

I once questioned an older guard about the structure of his institution. "Structure?" he said ruefully, "structure is a dirty word around here." Prison officials get nervous when groups of inmates congregate, but in California the "large group" (about 50) was common. It was an unforgettable experience to see these men dressed in blue, sitting in a large circle sipping coffee and quietly putting one of their number on the "hot seat." When I was put on the hot seat the session broke up with whoops of glee, since I confessed I didn't know whether group treatment reduced recidivism—a favorite topic.

These group bull-sessions did break down barriers. There were few riots and no prison scandals in California during these years. Inmate disturbances were channeled toward passive and nonviolent forms of action—work stoppages, peaceful demonstrations, concerted mass cell lockups. The sessions, often led by crusty old maintenance workers— were sometimes hilarious. Inmates would present dramatic renditions of what they imagined to be the deep Freudian causes of their present sad state. The sophisticated young counsellors called this "shucking." They agreed that they were involved in a form of professional "shucking" when they permitted the men to explain things in this stereotyped way. One professional justification was that this mutual shucking could produce a more verbal offender who, hopefully, would turn to less violent and impulsive crimes when released.

Group sessions were called "correctional treatment" and were taken seriously by anyone who wished to rise in the ranks. Middling budget requests were expected to be prefaced by justifications linking new programs to treatment theory. It is difficult to argue—in the face of all this—that treatment has never been given a chance to work.

Struggle for Justice, a recent report prepared for the American Friends Service Committee, notes a number of gross effects. "From 1959 to 1969 the median time served [in California] has risen from 24 to 36 months, the longest in the country." [Also] "the number of persons incarcerated per 100,000 has continued to rise, from 65 in 1944 to 145 in 1965." Should we listen to a self-interested argument which asserts that the average California offender (in a state with a large in-migration) became more criminalistic in these years and that without treatment the length of stay would have scored even higher?

Prison reformers denounced the *brutality* of the prison regime (which was true enough), but they saw this brutality as the major cause of persistence in crime. So they deliberately reformed the prisons—only to produce a worse result. Why? The distinguished American criminologist, Edwin Sutherland, taught that younger offenders learn the ways of crime through "association" with criminal patterns combined with isolation from law-abiding patterns. On this view, the prison—no matter how improved—can still be regarded as a "crime school." Recent theories have done little to deepen this insight. Most theories have this in common—they look for the "causes" of recidivism in changes ("stigmatization," for example) presumably wrought in the offender through his interaction with official agencies. But were the reformers on the wrong track all the time? Could it be that the prison regime *as such* (brutality, food, inmate subculture, etc.) has little or nothing to do with the causes of repeated criminality?

Suppose (in the absence of firm data) that recidivism rates over the last 150 years were not affected by changes in the prison regime, that instead they simply reflect the *interruption of normal occupational progress*. Imagine what damage a five-year prison sentence would do to the chances for employment of a 20 year old apprentice in 1800 as compared to a 20 year old semi-skilled worker today. In 1800, the young apprentice could go on to a productive life despite his disadvantage; the semi-skilled worker of today might well give up the struggle. On this view (which is frankly speculative), the early prisons were brutal but not criminogenic. The released offender was needed in an expanding economy. He could take up a new life and did not leave the prison bereft of the minimum requirements—a strong back and a pair of willing hands. The reformers reduced the brutality of the prison, but society changed in the meantime. A relatively brief prison sojourn today may be more criminogenic than a much longer and more brutal sojourn a century ago.

The early prisons left physical and mental scars but did not inhibit the offender from productive work, marriage, family. Today, prisons produce invisible but ineffaceable damage however tenderly they treat the offender. To "make it" in the 1970s requires a more exacting sequence of moves—high school or college, marriage, first job, bank account, next job, and so forth. Let us say that interference with this sequence produces "life cycle damage." The damage is most intense (perhaps irreparable) at just the ages when crime peaks—from 15 to 25. One can now understand how the reformers could see a correlation between prison and further criminality and could come to the false conclusion that the highly visible prison *regime* was responsible. But the prison produces its paradoxical result—more recidivism as it is enriched and improved—not directly through anything it does or does not do to the offender, but simply by removing him from society.

On this view, society has outgrown the prison, and deprivation of liberty has come to be a self-defeating measure in a modern industrial economy. The myth of treatment is "dangerous" insofar as treatment systems—such as California's—which are based on the indefinite sentence, end up removing more offenders from society for longer periods of time.

II. Treatment has not worked—according to its apologists—because it is resisted by backward guards (who must be professionalized). Doubting Thomases (who will succumb to evangelical exhortation), ordinary citizens (permeated with racism and revenge), archaic judges (unacquainted with psychiatry), timid academics (who will not abandon theory for the work of reforming delinquents), and short-sighted legislators (interested in taxes, not in transforming prisons into hospitals).

If we took this view literally, research would be useless and evidence of success and failure irrelevant. If a study indicates that a particular treatment has no effect, there's no need to worry, for it means that *more* treatment is needed or more *intense* treatment. But what if all available forms of correctional treatment are found to be unsuccessful? For instance, there is a good deal of enthusiasm these days about work release for inmates. Ramsey Clark finds that ". . . the most discouraging thing [about it is the] timidity of the program and the opposition it arouses." But do we know that it works? My colleagues and I who have been examining the literature have found no study of work release that meets minimal scientific standards. Successful programs to divert offenders from prisons are needed, and I am anxious to look at the research design as well as Mr. Clark's interpretation of the findings. Mr. Clark asserts that "five percent failed" on work release. This is heartening since ". . . before the program was lauched 50 percent were failing when finally released." One does not come across such dramatic successes often. But then Mr. Clark tells us that prisoners for work release were "cautiously selected," and ". . . nearly every prisoner wanted work release." If one "cautiously selects" such "good risks" their rates would be low whatever program you placed them on—work release, standard parole, or running the wheel at Las Vegas. Prisons are filled with offenders who will never commit another crime. If the "expected" rate of recidivism for these men was in fact 50 percent, then the "observed" rate of 5 percent was an improvement and work release an astounding success. But was it?

Let me refer to one more study mentioned in *Crime in America* because Mr. Clark seems to be citing evidence from studies conducted by the California Youth Authority under the direction of Marguerite Warren—the Community Treatment Project. Young offenders were randomly designated as "experimentals" (those who receive the treatment) and "controls" (those who do not). Hence, comparisons between recidivism rates are interpretable. The failure rates cited are 54 percent for "controls," and only 30 percent for "experimentals."

Marguerite Warren's project evaluated community supervision in lieu of incarceration for juvenile offenders (male and female) ready for their first commitment to an institution. Experimental subjects, graded by "maturity level," were assigned to small caseloads (1_2) and given the type of supervision deemed best for the type of offender. The lowest maturity level delinquents (1_2) were given supportive help, the middle group (1_3) secure control, and the most mature group (1_4) "insight" supervision. "Controls" were incarcerated and then released on standard youth parole (about 50 to 70 in a caseload). What were the results?

Matching maturity level with type of supervision produced no significant difference in success rates. However, a significant difference in failure rates resulted for all but one of the maturity subgroups, the group called "Cultural Identifiers," which had a significantly *higher* failure rate than its controls; to be blunt, the treatment *harmed* them.

Why did "success" rates (measured by honorable discharges) and "failure" rates (by reconfinement) not mirror one another? This puzzle took months to unravel. My colleagues and I concluded that the experimental agents (who received special training) *tolerated more misbehavior* than the control agents. In short, *treatment may change the behavior of the agent rather than the behavior of the offender.* Finally, however, experimental offenders committed a larger number of offenses of all sorts than did controls and a larger number of more severe offenses.

Was the program a failure or a success?

Experimentals committed *more* offenses but were kept out of prison; controls committed *fewer* offenses under supervision of the regular agents but were returned to prison more often. How do you make a cost benefit analysis of that? What costs should be included? The experimental program had high costs for training these special agents and so forth. The control program included the higher costs of incarceration (about 10 times the cost of supervision in the community). But experimentals committed more offenses and these offenses involved victims. The property stolen from the victims might be included, but how is one rationally to include the cost of a violent offense or a rape?

Many hopes hang on the results of the Marguerite Warren studies, but they are difficult to interpret. To illustrate, one study in the Northern California Federal Probation district randomly assigned probationers to three types of supervision—15-man caseloads, standard 50-man caseloads, and "minimal" (no supervision). The study (Joseph Lohman, 1967) reported *no significant differences* in the new offense rates for these three types of supervision. However, the 15-man caseloads were associated with a *higher* rate of "technical" violation (that is, return to prison by action of the agent) than the other two levels of supervision.

The implications are immense. "No supervision" appears to do as well as standard probation supervision in 50-man caseloads, and more treatment (small caseloads) resulted in more probationers being sent to prison by their agents. Why? The reader will never know until this type of inquiry is guided by a theory of probation supervision. Instead of a theory (open to testing), we have the myth which asserts that probation officers "treat" probationers and that smaller caseloads must mean more "treatment."

If we are to Break Down the Walls, as John Bartlow Martin advised, we must provide alternatives to incarceration for large numbers of offenders. If small caseloads (intense supervision) damage the probationer, or standard probation supervision is fruitless, why waste the time and energies of trained probation personnel?[1] The caseload con-

1. Although the *supervision* given on standard probation may be fruitless, assignment to probation may be preferable for many offenders due to the "damage" caused by the prison sojourn. (Ed.)

cept (borrowed from social welfare) has somehow become the basis of an organization designed to control *criminal* behavior. Is "help" given to an offender by professionals who have the duty to return him to prison self-contradictory? Why has another study indicated that a factor called "adequacy" of supervision is more important than caseload size in determining recidivism rates? Could a properly organized probation and parole system combine genuine help and non-damaging deterrence or should these functions be completely separated?

The aim of research is knowledge not justification. Without more and better research, we will permit arrogant assertion to rule us. To bring scattered research together, my colleagues and I initiated a search in 1967 for all studies of correction treatment published since 1945. The search took six months and resulted in 231 accepted studies which generated 285 findings.

The conclusions will not come as a surprise to those engaged in correctional research, or to many practitioners who have long suspected that it is difficult to treat persons who do not wish to be treated. On the whole, the evidence from the survey indicated that the present array of correctional treatments has no appreciable effect —positive or negative—on the rates of recidivism of convicted offenders.

The present list of treatments is not lengthy. For example, Americans believe strongly in the value of education, so no self-respecting prison can be without formal classroom instruction. Or since many Americans find salvation in therapy groups why not try them on inmates? The list includes small caseloads in probation or parole which have no effect (with the interesting exception of *youthful* offenders given "intensive probation supervision). Group counselling or therapy has no effect, although "group" supervision reduces costs. Psychiatric treatment may actually be "harmful" if it is given to younger "nonamenable" offenders. Formal education increases reading and writing skills but those who benefit go on to recidivate at the same rate. Early release (90 days) does not increase recidivism for adult offenders and may decrease rates slightly for young people. Early release also saves money. The highly touted halfway houses actually *increased* recidivism slightly, probably because offenders perceived their stay as an additional period of deprivation of liberty, but there are only a handful of studies on this. The picture is little different for cosmetic surgery for facial defects (by itself), specialized caseloads for addicts or chronic drunks, job training (a little hope), prison vocational training, and for programs resembling these in the *intensity* of the treatment.

How can all this determined effort come to naught? Recently critics have suggested that the "individual treatment model" is faulty since it grants "broad discretionary powers" so that treatment agents may attend to "each offender's unique needs." But surely a humane society would do just this! In fact, there is little evidence in these studies of truly "individualized" help. And in all cases, treatment is forced and involves some degree of deprivation of liberty and therefore the strong probability of interference with what I have called "life cycle progress." To jettison real help for those who are faltering on the path is a counsel of despair. The "dangerous myth" permits professional experts to one-sidedly impose un-asked-for help, and to use "broad discretionary powers" to continue the process when the "help" does not help.

Taking a foreshortened view, these critics fail to see the central paradox—*deprivation of liberty is increasingly damaging in a society which fails to provide democratic opportunity, and yet demands skillful and uncoerced effort from its citizens.* In the long run, we must replace coerced treatment with real help.

III. The dungeons of American penology were built mostly in the 19th century and have always been vulnerable to convict disturbances. The state with the most fearsome "pen" hoped to deter crime into its neighbors' streets and fields. From this amiable competition there resulted a "big house" in each state, fed by county jails and city lock-ups.

Probation and parole, now standard, began as privileges given to the "Square John" type of offender. Parole authorities increasingly used parole as a "testing ground," releasing more offenders than could succeed, with the expectation that agents would return to prison those who began to mess up. The proportion under community supervision increased, filling the prisons with the most hardened cons and only a small leaven of stable offenders. Once completed, this system (less than 100 years old!) has undergone almost no change.

Our early prisons were unashamedly brutal and the frontier beckoned inmates who could escape. In pre-bureaucratic America, escape meant something: one could change his name, start a new life, no questions asked. Every prison disturbance implied mass escape, and convict unrest was met with deadly fury. Today, mass escape has disappeared and practically all individual escapes are walk-aways by minimum security inmates, similar to parole absconding. Hopelessness plus ingenuity may still provoke an attempt to "hit the wall" or dig a tunnel or hide in a garbage truck, but it is rare.

Once escape was cut off, inmate disturbances turned inward. The prison riot was a struggle for reform of prison rules and conditions or a struggle for power within the inmate body for the meager privileges available. True, the riot usually spent itself in a short time and dissolved into anarchy as inmates settled old grudges or refused to fall in behind any leadership. Inmate riot was often nicely calculated to provoke interference by the humanitarian reformers. Sometimes it led to changes in paroling practices, better food, less punishment for breaking prison rules or fewer rules.

During the twenties and thirties, many American prisons were run by a corrupt inmate leadership who maintained order (for a price) while preaching the "inmate code." Treatment was believed to be aimed at putting a stop to this, and its attempts to do so were partially responsible for the riots of 1952–53. In the larger state systems, "bus therapy" aided administrators in beheading incipient revolts. Group counseling was sold to the old-school wardens—along with the new title of superintendent—as one means of maintaining order. The fearful reaction of guards to the "large group" diminished as they learned that such groups were useful in draining energies into verbal attack. In the San Quentin Adjustment Center in 1967, therapy groups led by young counselors were used as a privilege to relieve monotony. The inmates dealt out unbelievable personal abuse, but I was told by the counselors that this was part of the job of "treating" these "problem cases."

The "dangerous myth" of treatment is now disintegrating. But the policy which this myth protects—the policy of the indeterminate sentence—has been successfully embodied in law, in the power of paroling authorities, in treatment specialties, in public opinion. The spokesmen for treatment favor the *extension* of the indeterminate sentence. Most hard-liners long ago accepted the idea, only adding mandatory minimum sentences in case paroling authorities became too lenient.

Until recently, the only motivation among inmates worth talking about was the desire to get out. They saw parole as a privilege, but they had to convince the harassed paroling authority to make the visible and politically sensitive decision to let them out. This naturally led to second-guessing "the board." In California, one formula —believed to be fool-proof by its inmate adherents—prescribed a short period of intense "messing up" on first entering prison followed by a mixture of one-half group therapy and one-half vocational training with a *gradual* reduction in prison misbehavior and a few carefully written letters to close kin.

Inmates have always detested the indeterminate sentence and have prefered fixed sentences and "good time" laws. But indeterminacy has a different meaning to the confined when real opportunities beckon than when parole appears to be a trap. (The main source of convict information about parole is from those who have been returned to prison after failing, as Jerome Skolnick has pointed out.) If escape is useless (where do you go? what do you do?), and parole is a "testing ground," offenders can come to see all of society as a web of indeterminacy. ("They will never get off your ass.")

The sentence, say, is one year to life. After years of confinement the parole authority fixes a date for release and a term of parole that can be extended up to the last moment on parole. The parolee commits an offense against the parole rules and is returned for technical violation "to finish term." The paroling authority, after a few more years, resets a release date and a new term on parole. The inmate messes-up in prison just prior to release, perhaps in fear of a new failure. He is remanded to the adjustment center for an indefinite period. After several weeks, he threatens the life of a correctional officer and is bused to the third floor of the Adjustment Center at Folsom as a "problem case." (We are talking about California where indeterminacy is the rule.) His mind may now begin to snap so he is moved to the second and then to the first floor. He babbles and annoys the guards and inmates with his incessant demands. They remove his clothes, glasses and belongings and place him in a "strip" cell at the rear of the first floor where the iron doors shut him off in darkness and quiet.

The federal courts have tried to set minimum physical conditions for these "quiet" cells. If the inmate smears the walls with excrement, this must be washed off, he must be observed by the guard every so often. And so forth. Courts cannot administer prisons. They can arrange for lawyers to be present at parole hearings, but how can they subject a decision-making process based on the myth of corrections to judicial scrutiny? The essence of the treatment position is that it requires *expert judgment* to make treatment decisions. Evidence that the inmate should be released from the adjustment center comes to the decision-maker through a variety of sources, including the correctional officers who are shut up daily with him and must listen to his babbling and his abuse, and must clean the excrement from his walls, put out the fires he sets or replace the toilets he smashes.

The California adjustment centers are the best example of a false position run riot. Inside every prison is a unit to hold those who "cannot manage the freedom of the yard." But the old maximum security unit was for punishment (say, 15 days) while the adjustment center uses the indeterminate sentence. In California this was the creation of Dr. Norman Fenton, a mild-mannered, kindly man who hated the "hole" and hoped to combine maximum security confinement with individual treatment. I found inmates who had spent almost four years in these "max-max" units. The new breed of militant black convict has made these places known throughout the world. An "end of the line" prison, like Attica, plays the role of adjustment center for a large system of prisons.

The 1972 Attica prison revolt reflected a growing disgust with what the inmates regarded as the hypocritical fakery of treatment. Convicts know that treatment spokesmen denounce "punishment," but advocate life on the installment plan, a terror described by Franz Kafka. As the myth of treatment has been coopted by correctional officials, it has ceased to grip anybody. Those closest to the offender —the correctional officers—tend to view it as a form of "brainwashing." It could be argued (and was) that if treatment didn't rehabilitate, at least it kept the lid on. And it did keep the lid on for almost two decades. Attica was a warning that it no longer can do so.

The *expressive mutiny* (as I think Attica might be called) is a new form of collective disturbance, not merely a temporary reflection of new-left influence among a group of politicized black convicts. It communicates the inmate's plight to the public so far as he understands it. The prison is used as an arena in which to stage dramatic renditions of inhumanity and rebellious gestures of inchoate despair and apocalypse.

IV. Today the corrections system is a self-contained bureaucracy subject to declining vision, inmate revolt, and popular discontent. As the incidence of crime has increased and the potential victim of crime has become more restive, a widespread "fear of crime" has surfaced. It has been exploited by politicians who offer little but denunciations and is partially intertwined with racial tensions. The fear, however, is genuine. Offenders—disciplined by the regime of the indeterminate sentence and taunted by promises of rehabilitation—have brought their suffering into the open, only to be cruelly used. No solution is possible which does not submit the correctional systems to democratic control through agencies that have the power and resources to introduce change. To work successfully, planning agencies must gain public support. But a new principle is required before the public will finally overthrow the myth of treatment, and the controversy between the "punitive" hard-liners and their "bleeding heart" treatment opponents needs clarification if that new principle is to come to the fore.

Contrary to what we hear, for the hard-liners punishment is not the goal of the postadjudicatory system. The goal is deterrence—individual and general deterrence—and the hard-liners assert that punishment is the appropriate means to this goal. They demand that the threat (of punishment) contained in every penal statute be carried out promptly, so that everyone will be assured that it is a credible threat: to legally convict and then punish an offender will "deter" him from further offending; it will also "deter" potential offenders from committing crime. The spokesmen for treatment, on the other hand, believe the goal should be rehabilitation and that treatment is the means of this goal. Do they believe that successful rehabilitation of an offender will have a chilling effect on potential offenders? No effect? The treatment argument is obscure at this point, primarily because treatment of offenders must go on within a punitive context —unless we decide to abolish the penal statute and reward offenders.

These two classical positions are not opposites. Each advocates a different mix of punishment and treatment. The hard-liners wish to strengthen the capacity of the state to strike fear into the hearts of potential offenders in order to maintain public order. Treatment is primarily concerned with changing the convicted offender into a law-abiding person. Both positions claim to "protect the public."

Must we choose between the two? Not if we shift attention from the offender (and the state) to the public and especially to the victim. The proximate goal of crime control policy as a whole (not merely corrections) would then be: *maximum protection to the public balanced against minimum harm to the offender.*

Both factions will oppose this formulation since it places the *victim* at the center of public policy. Treatment spokesmen seldom mention the victim except to warn that he may overthrow our system of justice in his thirst for vengeance. Hard-liners claim that the offense against the victim is "really" an offense against the state and that the victim's legitimate feelings of revenge are reconciled through legal punishment. I suggest it should be the aim of public policy to protect the public and to inhibit vengefulness by compensating the victim for the failure of the state to provide protection. Revenge wells up when the victim feels the state abandoned him; he has no place to turn for help. Then "fear of crime" is magnified out of all proportion to risk. Folk-justice is vengeful and subject to intolerable injustice, because the only gain is the momentary alleviation of feelings.

The maintenance of order in society takes place at the expense of a very small number of those who commit offenses. (About two percent of violent crime and 0.5 percent of property crime ends in conviction and imprisonment in America today.) But convicted offenders are *harmed* no matter with what care they are handled. A proper aim of public policy is to discover ways to reduce this harm to a minimum compatable with public safety.

As we become more productive, the income pyramid bulges in the middle. So although the victim of crime is still concentrated in the ghettos and inner-city areas, he is increasingly located in the middle layers of society, and he is not powerless. Of middle or well-to-do status, he is organized in small business associations, trade unions, citizen lobbies and political parties. Jurisprudence, public policy, administrative procedure must change to fit these facts.

Everyone suspects that we are now getting *minimum* protection for the public and *maximum* harm to the offender. To move beyond suspicion to knowledge requires research that combines the analytical skills of the economist, the jurisprudence of legal advocacy, the sociology of the life span, and the analysis of systems. Centers and institutes combining such skills could aid planning agencies in evaluating programs, allocating public funds, and undertaking basic crime research. To combine "organizational intelligence" and public disquiet to produce substantial change in criminal justice systems is ultimately a political problem. Many of the elements for change are present—concern over Attica, a growing determination to shut down prisons (San Quentin, juvenile institutions in Massachusetts), the creation of 50 state planning agencies, increasing judicial intervention, the disintegration of the myth of treatment, growing attacks on the principle of the indeterminate sentence.

There are four major solutions currently advocated; 1) decriminalization (reducing or abolishing penalties for certain behavior); 2) operational efficiency (reducing irrationality by improving agency functioning; 3) diversion (shifting offenders from confinement to other parts of corrections or to the community; 4) crime prevention.

These "solutions" reflect different estimates of the need for change, and different criteria for determining when success has been achieved. Let us look at each from the standpoint of the victim or potential victim.

Decriminalization asks the public to tolerate more deviant behavior and cease using the law to enforce moral conformity. It assumes lack of consensus in such areas as abortion, sexual behavior, drugs, vagrancy, public drunkenness, prostitution, obscenity, and so forth and simply removes the behavior from the penal codes and reduces penalties. People who live in high rise apartments with doormen, or in well-to-do suburbs may find this a cheap solution. Persons in small towns or from rural backgrounds may find it shocking. Many of those required to tolerate the behavior—urban dwellers, ghetto inhabitants, small business people—refuse to make nice distinctions. Unless decriminalization is combined with concrete protection against the most feared crimes—robbery, burglary, purse snatching, mugging—it will be a "solution" achieved at the expense of the public.

Some progress might be made through increasing the operational efficiency of existing agencies, especially the police, but only if they are regarded as parts of a larger "system" whose boundaries are not arbitrarily fixed to deal with "symptoms" and ignore "causes." The *potential* victim in precinct A is not enthusiastic if it turns out that increased police efficiency in precinct B has chased the offender into his backyard. Displacement of crime is part of the larger problem of deterrence. Five centuries of philosophical discussion ought to have prepared us to find out something about it. What kinds of activity, under what conditions, and with what amounts of public resources will inhibit what types of potential offenders from committing what kinds of offenses? In the absence of knowledge, planning agencies succumb to bureaucratic incrementalism: as Congress appropriates funds each criminal justice agency is given its added share.

A new strategy of *diversion* ("divert" offenders from confinement to community supervision) is growing among correctional insiders. This policy advocates bail reform, work release, weekend jail lockup, local supervision—any device that will reduce the contact between offender and the correctional system. Assuming that prison is always more damaging than probation or parole, diversion will reduce long-term criminal career costs. The potential victim wishes to know, however, whether this long-term saving is achieved by an increase in the probability of his being victimized. If he is given the facts, he may be willing to trade-off a short-term increase in risk for a less criminalistic society in the long run.

The strategy of diversion is not a panacea. All "contact" with the criminal justice system is not equally damaging to all offenders. I have argued that corrections cannot correct to the degree that its efforts —however well motivated—interfere with "life cycle progress" (the schedule of moves by which a person becomes a productive citizen). It is doubtful that probation or parole supervision are designed to minimize such interference and maximize help, especially if the treatment myth (smaller caseloads) continues to dominate public policy. Will a spectacular planned reduction in the median length of stay in California prisons under Governor Reagan be accompanied by a real *increase* in help to these released offenders (through job training, placement services, parole income, free psychiatric help, if requested), or will the philosophy of pinch-penny provide the public with neither short-run nor long-run protection? If deprivation of liberty as a punishment is becoming outmoded, it is not simply that incarceration is damaging but that liberty is *no longer so precious* for large numbers as it once was. Liberty is most precious when it is most useful. To offer offenders a hollow freedom is mockery, although they may prefer it to prison.

Finally, there is *crime prevention*. All the parts of criminal justice are in the public realm except the most important "part"—the social process that generates the criminal behavior and influences the police to select out the tiny number of persons to "process" from the mass of crime. The kinds of intervention covered over by the term "prevention" differ profoundly.

In an official report submitted by the Space-General Corporation to the state of California in 1966, the systems engineers gave us one version of the future. Their "Potential Offender Identification Program" included a "population planning program" aimed to "reduce the production of potential offenders." The report revealed that the crime problem was concentrated in the Negro and Mexican-American ethnic segments of the state. What a discovery! Yet the then governor, Pat Brown, heralded the report as real science and not mere sociology. It was a preventive version of the myth of treatment.

In the 1960s programs such as Mobilization for Youth were premised on crime prevention, and promised to provide information testing the "opportunity" theory—the idea that real expansions of economic opportunity will reduce crime. But these programs provided no research worth looking at. As a result, crime prevention— the intervention into social conditions immediately associated with crime—is still a slogan and a hope. Yet, if it is the lack of social opportunity in an affluent society rather than the brutality of prison which is responsible for soaring crime rates, crime prevention *is* the core of a solution. By removing offenders from society, the prison damages their capacity to take advantage of opportunities even if they were provided. If the planning perspective is to prosper, it must distinguish sharply between programs to stop the breeding of "potential" offenders and programs to expand opportunity in a democratic society.

The focus of social planning is the potential victim, not the offender. Social planning will not hesitate to properly allocate resources devoted to crime control. It will not hesitate to introduce radical changes in the present administration of justice aimed at reducing to a minimum the long-run damage done to convicted offenders. It will do this openly, through pragmatic experimentation, seeking to convince the public through *experience* that more deviant behavior can be tolerated, that a gradual reduction in crime is worth taking immediate risks for. But it will insist that risk must be shared equally through a national scheme for the compensation of victims. And, it will not taunt the convicted offender with promises of "treatment." Instead, it will squeeze the fat and the "rackets" out of corrections, and gradually close the noisome prisons.

Let me end with a coda. The long history of "prison reform" is over. On the whole the prisons have played out their allotted role. They cannot be reformed and must be gradually torn down. But let us give up the comforting myth that the remaining facilities (and they will be prisons) can be changed into hospitals. Prisons will be small and humane; anything else is treason to the human spirit. We shall be cleansed of the foreign element of forced treatment with its totalitarian overtones. Officials will no longer be asked to do what they cannot do; they would be relieved of the temptation to do what should not be done; further utilize the iron pressure chamber of prison life to change the offender.

Crime arises from social causes and can be controlled and reduced (but not eliminated) through social action. The myth of correctional treatment is now the main obstacle to progress; it has become the last line of defense of the prison system; it prevents the sound use of resources to balance public protection and inmate rights; and it diverts energy away from defending democracy through widening opportunity. It is time to awake from the dream.

Richard Wasserstrom

Why Punish the Guilty *

. . . While philosophers have been preoccupied with the problem of
punishing the innocent, some concerned lawyers, social scientists and
laymen have seen the central issue to be a quite different one, involving a decision whether to punish at all. Simply stated, they have seen
it as necessitating a choice between punishment and something else
variously called reform, rehabilitation or treatment. Typically, they
resolve the issues against the justifiability of punishment.

Although discussion of the subjects are often obscure and puzzling,
superficially, at least, the ultimate resolution seems to make good
sense. Punishment, it is said, is simply vindictiveness institutionalized.
To punish is to react naturally but irrationally toward one who has
harmed another. It is to return evil for evil instead of good for evil;
to focus on the offense, not the offender. If the evil of punishment is
so simply exposed, the benefit of treatment is no less obvious. For
what could be more humane, more civilized, more sensible and more
benevolent than directing society's efforts solely toward the end of
achieving the rehabilitation or cure of that social misfit who breaks
the law? Surely the reigning maxim should be: "Always treat the
offender; never punish the crime."

The plausibility of this stand—the question of whether it is right
to punish even the guilty—is the central issue which concerns me in
this paper. And if we are ever adequately to assess the challenge to
punishment made so explicit in recent legal writings, we must begin
by asking whether it makes sense to set up a dichotomy between
punishment and treatment. If it does, if there are real alternatives to
choose from, we must then clarify the respects in which punishment
and treatment differ from each other.

To put the problem of differentiation in concrete perspective, com-

* Richard Wasserstrom, "Why Punish the Guilty?" *Princeton University Magazine,* 20 (1964), pp. 14–19. Reprinted by permission of the author.

pare the case of a person discovered to have infectious, non-arrested tuberculosis who, because of this, is committed unwillingly to a State hospital for treatment, with that of an embezzler who has dissipated all the funds collected in the annual Easter Seal Campaign and been sentenced to five years in prison for his offense. How does punishment of the one differ from treatment of the other?

To begin with, a punishment must involve an unpleasantness imposed upon a person in virtue of the fact that he is believed to have done some blameworthy action for which he was responsible when he acted. A treatment, on the other hand, need not involve an unpleasantness (although it may, is in the case of the tuberculosis victim); and assessments of responsibility and blameworthiness are simply irrelevant.

Moreover, the nature and magnitude of a punishment must be selected (within some limits) comtemporaneously with the decision to punish; at the time of the trial (whether or not the person is still a threat to society) rather than at the time of the presumed misbehavior. Treatment, however, must be believed capable of improving a *present* condition: it would make no sense to treat someone for a past ailment by which he was no longer afflicted. Thus, unlike punishment, the question of the appropriateness of any particular treatment can be answered only by referring to the state or condition of the person at the time the question is asked.

Having made these distinctions with some degree of confidence, a caveat is no doubt in order. My differentiations are not wholly satisfactory: they are vague, and not entirely accurate. We do, for example, sometimes punish people for their present status or condition rather than for past actions—as when, in California, we convict and imprison a person for the crime of being a common prostitute, or a narcotics addict. Nonetheless, the distinctions I have drawn are more than sufficiently accurate for my purposes. We can now examine and evaluate some of the reasons which have been or might be advanced to support either treatment or punishment of the guilty.

There are at least two quite different arguments commonly advanced to support the claim that treatment ought always to be substituted for punishment, and a good deal of confusion (particularly in nonphilosophical discussions of the evils of punishment and virtues of treatment) results from a failure to get them clear and keep them separate. The first is superficially the more attractive, though ultimately the less plausible. There is no standard or correct way to state it, but one version might be this:

Everyone would agree that it is wrong to punish someone for something which he could not help; furthermore, no one can help being sick. Therefore, no one ought ever be punished for being sick. In the words of the Supreme Court of the United States: "Even one day in prison would be cruel and unusual punishment for the 'crime' of having a common cold." It just so happens to be the case that everyone who commits a crime is sick. Hence, it is morally wrong to punish anyone who commits a crime.

This—or something like it—is the argument. Although I have stated it in a somewhat outrageous fashion, I doubt that either a more circumspect or a more lengthy statement could save it. But before showing why I think this to be the case, I want to make three preliminary points. First, I shall seek neither to call into question nor to justify the claim that a person ought never be punished (or, for that matter, blamed) for something which he could not, in some meaningful sense, have helped. Rather, I shall assume that this is sound, and shall, therefore, seek to call into question only the remainder of the argument. Second, as I shall interpret it, the argument in no way depends on the truth of determinism. As I construe it, the argument depends upon establishing certain relationships between sickness, crime and the wrongness of punishment, not upon a special relationship between all events. And third, although the fact is not always noted, this argument is not to be interpreted as purporting to demonstrate that it is always wrong to punish people. For, at least as I have stated it, the argument is restricted to the claim that it is always wrong to punish criminals—those who break the law. Thus, someone might think that it is sometimes right to punish people—children or friends for instance—and still consistently maintain that punishment ought never follow the commission of a crime. A fortiori a person need not hold that no one is ever responsible or blameworthy—only that no criminal is responsible or blameworthy.

Turning now to my statement of the argument itself, the first thing that is apparent is that the relevance of sickness to the rightness of the punishment of offenders is anything but certain. Indeed, one is very tempted to argue that the entire argument is a non sequitur just because we seldom, if ever seek to punish people for being sick. Instead we punish them for the actions they perform. On the surface, at least, it would seem that even if someone is sick, and even if he cannot help being sick, this in no way implies that none of his actions could have been other than what it was. Thus, if the argument against ever punishing the guilty criminal is to be at all persuasive, it must be shown that for one reason or another, the sickness which afflicts all criminals must affect their actions in such a way that they are thereby prevented ever from acting differently. Construed in this fashion, the argument is at least coherent and responsive. Unfortunately there is now no reason to be persuaded by it.

It might be persuasive were there any reason to believe that all criminal acts were, for example, instances of compulsive behavior; if, that is, we thought it likely to be true that all criminals were in some obvious and distinguishable sense afflicted by or subjected to irresistible impulses which compelled them to break the law. For there are people who do seem to be subjected to irresistible impulses and who are thereby unable to keep themselves from, among other things, committing crimes. And it is surely monstrous ever to punish them for these actions. Thus, the kleptomaniac or the person who is truly already addicted to narcotics does seem to be suffering from something resembling a sickness and, moreover, to be suffering from something which makes it very difficut if not impossible for him to control his actions. He deserves pity, not blame; treatment, not punishment.

Now, the notion of compulsive behavior is not without difficulties of its own. How strong, for instance, does a compulsion have to be before it cannot be resisted? Would someone be a kleptomaniac only if he went up and stole an object even though a policeman was known by him to be present and observing his every move? Is there anything more that is meant by compulsive behavior than the fact that it is behavior which is inexplicable or unaccountable in terms of the motives and purposes people generally have? More importantly, perhaps, why do we and why should we suppose that the apparently "motiveless" behavior must be the product of compulsions which are less resistible than those to which we all are at times subjected. In particular, as Barbara Wooton has observed, " . . . it is by no means self-evident that (a wealthy) person's yearnings for valueless (items) are inevitably stronger or more nearly irresistible than the poor man's hunger for a square meal or for a pack of cigarettes." (*Social Science and Social Pathology*, p. 235.)

But while these are all problems, the more basic one is simply that there is no reason at all to believe that all criminal acts are instances of compulsive behavior. Even if we are persuaded that there are people who are victims of irresistible impulses, and even if we do concede that we ought always to treat and never to punish such people, it surely does not follow that everyone who commits a crime is doing a compulsive act. And because this is so, it cannot be claimed that all criminals ought to be exempted from punishment—treated instead—because they have this sickness.

It might be argued, though, that while compulsive behavior accounts for only some criminal acts, there are other sicknesses which account for the remainder. At this juncture, the most ready candidate to absorb the remaining cases is that of insanity. The law, for example, has always been willing to concede that a person ought never be punished if he was so sick or so constituted that he did not know the nature or quality of his act, or if he did know this, that he did not know that what he was doing was wrong. And more recently, attempts have been made, sometimes successfully, to expand this exemption to include any person whose criminal action was substantially the product of mental defect or disease.

Once again, though, the crucial point for my purposes is not the formulation of the most appropriate test for insanity, but the fact that it is far from evident, even under the most "liberal" test imaginable, that it would be true that everyone who commits a crime would be found to be sick and would be found to have been afflicted with a sickness which in some sense rendered the action in question unavoidable. Given all of our present knowledge, there is simply every reason to suppose that some of the people who do commit crimes are neither subject to irresistible impulses, incapable of knowing what they are doing, nor suffering from some other definite mental disease. And, if this is so, then it is a mistake to suppose that the treatment of criminals is on this ground always to be preferred to their punishment.

There is, however, one final version of the claim that every criminal action is excusable on grounds of the sickness of the actor. And this version does succeed in bringing all the remaining instances of criminality, not otherwise excusable, within the category of sickness. It does so only by making the defining characteristic or symptom of mental illness the intentional commission of an illegal act. All criminals, so this argument goes, who are not insane or subject to irresistible impulses are sociopaths or psychopaths—people afflicted with that mental illness which manifests itself exclusively through the commission of antisocial acts. This sickness, like any other sickness, must be treated rather than punished.

Once this stage of the discussion is reached, it is terribly important that we be aware of what has happened. In particular, we are no longer confronted with the evidentiary claim that all criminal acts are caused by some sickness. We are faced instead with the bare assertion that this must be so—an assertion, moreover, of a somewhat deceptive character. The illness which afflicts these criminals *is simply the criminal behavior itself*. The disease which is the reason for not punishing the action is identical with the action itself. At this point any attempt to substantiate or disprove the existence of a relationship between sickness and crime is ruled out of order. The presence of mental illnesses of these kinds cannot be reasons for not punishing, or for anything else.

Thus, I would insist that even if it is true that we ought never to punish and that we ought always to treat someone whose criminal action was unavoidable because the product of some mental or physical disease—even if we concede all this—it has yet to be demonstrated, without begging the question, that all persons who commit crimes are afflicted with some disease or sickness of this kind. And, therefore, if it is always wrong to punish people, or if it is always preferable to treat them, then an argument of a different sort must be forthcoming. It is this argument to which I now turn.

The argument goes like this. Let us concede that not all people, and not even all criminals, are sick. Let us grant that there are some and perhaps many persons who are responsible at the time they perform actions which violate the law and who are blameworthy for so acting. It does not follow from this fact alone, so the argument goes, that punishing anyone is ever morally justified. Even if a person was responsible when he acted and blameworthy for having so acted, this does not preclude the possibility that we ought to behave toward him just as we behave toward those who are sick—that we ought to do something very much like treating him. Surely, this makes more sense than punishing him. The point is not that it is wrong to punish people because they are sick; rather, it is that it is simply more humane and more rational always to concern ourselves solely with the question of how best to effect the most rapid and complete rehabilitation or treatment of the offender. The argument is not that no one is responsible or blameworthy; instead, it is that these descriptions are simply irrelevant to what, on moral grounds, ought to be the only significant considerations: namely, what mode of behavior toward the offender is most apt to maximize the likelihood that he will not in the future commit those obnoxious or dangerous acts which are proscribed by the law. In short, the claim is that we would gain much and lose little were we to abolish the practice of punishing offences and substitute the practice of treating offenders.

There are at least three arguments which can be made in support of such a proposal. Briefly, they are as follows:

First, by making irrelevant the question of whether the actor was responsible when he acted, we can simplify greatly the operation of the criminal law. More specifically, by "eliminating" the issue of responsibility we thereby necessarily eliminate the requirement that the law continue to attempt to make those terribly difficult judgments of legal responsibility which any definite system of punishment requires to be made. And, as a practical matter at least, this is no small consideration. For surely there is no area in which the techniques of legal adjudication have functioned less satisfactorily than in that of determining the actor's legal responsibility as of the time he violated the law. The attempts to formulate and articulate satisfactory and meaningful criteria of responsibility; the struggles to develop and then isolate specialists who can meaningfully and impartially relate these criteria to the relevant medical concepts and evidence; and the difficulties encountered in requiring the traditional legal fact finding mechanism—the jury—ultimately to resolve these issues: all of these bear impressive witness for the case for ceasing to make the effort.

Second, I think it fair to say that most people do not like to punish others. They may, indeed, have no objection to the punishment of others; but the actual task of inflicting and overseeing the infliction of an organized set of punishments is, I am sure, distasteful to most. It is all too easy, therefore, and all too typical, for society to entrust the administration of punishments to those who, if they do not actually enjoy it, at least do not find it unpleasant. Just as there is no necessary reason for punishment ever to be needlessly severe, so there is no necessary reason for those who are charged with the duty of punishing to be brutal or unkind. Nonetheless, it is simply a fact that it is difficult, if not impossible, to attract sensitive, kindly or compassionate persons to assure this charge. No such analogous problem attends the call for treatment.

These are both serious and real practical objections to punishment. There is in addition a more sweeping theoretical objection. It is this. If there is one thing which serves to differentiate the techniques of punishment from that of treatment it is that punishment necessarily permits the possibility and even the desirability that punishment will be imposed upon an offender even though he is fully "cured"—even though there is no significant likelihood that he will behave improperly in the future. And, in every such case in which a person is punished—in every case in which the infliction of the punishment will help the offender not at all (and may in fact harm him immeasurably)—the act of punishment is, on moral grounds, seriously offensive. Even if it were true that some of the people who commit crimes are responsible and blameworthy, and even if it were the case that we had meaningful techniques at our disposal for distinguishing those who are responsible from those who are not—still, every time we inflict a punishment on someone who will not himself be benefited by it, we commit a seriously immoral act. This claim, or something like it, lies, I think, at the base of the case which can be made against the punishment of the guilty. Any system of social punishment must permit, and probably must require, that people be made to suffer even though the suffering will help the sufferer not at all. It is this which the analogue to a system of treatment expressly prevents, and it is in virtue of this that a system of treatment is clearly preferable.

There are, of course, a variety of objections to this proposal and to the premises upon which it rests; and there are, correspondingly, a number of arguments which might be advanced in favor of punishing the guilty. I wish to consider four.

The first is this. It is important to recognize (especially because it is all too often overlooked) that treatment as an alternative to punishment may itself have certain undesirable features. In particular, any system of treatment would necessarily permit of the possibility that the treatment deemed to be required might be more unpleasant than the corresponding punishment. To take just one example, at present we typically punish the offense of indecent exposure by a maximum term of six months—at least for the first few offenses. Now it is also the case that, as yet, there is no "cure" for indecent exposure. Psychiatrists know of no simple way to treat someone who does expose himself so as to "cure" him of doing so. Under these circumstances, so the argument might go, treatment would be more unpleasant than punishment.

The point is that punishments are of a fixed maximum extent—they always have a definite point of termination, set in advance. Treatment, on the other hand, ends at the moment of cure, be that moment imminent or distant. Thus, given an offense whose punishment is relatively minor and whose treatment is as yet undiscovered, the punishment of this offense will involve a lesser interference with the actor's freedom than would his indefinite confinement under a program of treatment.

In a sense, this is a special case of a still more general objection. Treatments, no less than punishments, are capable of giving rise to serious moral problems. If, for instance, a person can be treated effectively only by performing a prefrontal lobotomy or by altering in some other more sophisticated fashion, his basic personality or identity, it might well be that punishment would have the virtue (and it is no small one) of leaving the individual intact. Imprisonment may be a poor way to induce a person to behave differently in the future, but imprisonment may, nonetheless, permit him to remain the same person throughout. In short, treatments as well as punishments may involve serious interferences with the most significant moral claims an individual can assert. Like punishments, treatments of the type contemplated will doubtless be imposed without the actor's consent. The substitution of treatment for punishment could never, therefore, absolve us from involvement in that difficult but unavoidable task of assessing and resolving the competing claims of society and the individual.

Correspondingly, as a practical matter, a system of treatments is clearly capable of encouraging attitudes which, if they predominated, could only be viewed with alarm. In deeming irrelevant all questions of responsibility and blameworthiness, such a system might well encourage a neglect of just those features which distinguish adult human beings from children. Such a system might thereby all too easily induce a blurring of the differences between the moral claims of responsible adults and those of persons who are not responsible. If a society which punishes offenders always runs the risk of being needlessly cruel and lacking in compassion, one which treats offenders runs the risk of being stiflingly paternalistic and insensitively manipulative.

Neither of these objections is, of course, decisive. A system of treatment need not be attended by these defects. Within such a system certain treatments might be deemed impermissible for the same reasons that some punishments are presently proscribed. Modes of undesirable but untreatable behavior might be tolerated just because the alternatives were less desirable still. At best, the two objections advanced so far are persuasive only as reminders that the substitution of treatment for punishment would be no panacea for the ills of social disorder and offense.

There are, however, two affirmative arguments for punishing the guilty. The first is, I think, not an argument but merely an assertion— the assertion that the guilty ought to be punished because they deserve it. Bradley's claim, for instance, that there is a necessary connection between punishment and guilt, that "we pay the penalty because we owe it, and for no other reason," * is surely as susceptible of this interpretation as any other. Yet as it stands, the assertion is manifestly unsatisfying. Punishment is an evil, an unpleasantness; it requires that someone suffer. Its infliction demands justification. What does it mean, therefore, to say that the guilty deserve punishment? Why do they deserve anything even though they are guilty? And, more importantly, why do they deserve to suffer, to be punished? These are questions which must be answered before we would be entitled to be persuaded that punishing even the guilty is morally permissible.

There is, however, an argument of sorts which can be made. It

* F. H. Bradley, *Ethical Studies* (2nd Ed.), pp. 26–27.

focuses on the fact that to say of anyone that he is guilty is to imply that he was responsible at the time he acted, that he chose freely to perform that action rather than others which were open to him. And, it insists, it is this fact that the action was the outcome of the actor's free choice which makes punishment permissible (if not deserved or required.) Punishment of the guilty is not immoral, because the actor had a fair opportunity to choose between obeying the law or being punished.

It is easy, I think, to make too much of this argument. It is true, of course, that the punishment of the guilty—in this sense of guilty—is less undesirable than the punishment of those who are not responsible; or of those who are innocent. But this is not the same as showing that punishment is justifiable. More specifically, the precise import of the presence of free choice remains far from clear. Criminals, even the most hardened ones, do not choose to be punished. In punishing them we are not giving them what they asked for or requested. We are not fulfilling their desires. (If we were, oddly, we would think they were not responsible and hence not properly subject to punishment.) Still, you might say, they knew what to expect, they could have avoided the punishment by obeying the law. This certainly is true, but not yet wholly satisfactory by any means. Should it not be relevant, for example, whether the offender had an opportunity to choose that the laws would be such that they would present him with these choices. Does the ostensibly general case for punishing the guilty depend on the existence of democracy? If so, no one has suggested such a restriction before.

This and similar objections aside, the more basic point is that showing that the commission of the offense was avoidable does not indicate, at least to me, why the offender ought to be made to suffer.

At this point, of course, we must consider the final argument for punishing the guilty—the argument that punishment deters others from the commission of comparable offenses, and that treatment would not. H.L.A. Hart has put the argument this way: It is paradoxical to suppose that the main purpose of "providing punishment for murder was to reform the murderer, not to prevent murder. And the paradox is greater where the legal offense is not a serious one, e.g. infringing a state monopoly of transport. Reform foregoes the hope of influencing those who have not broken the law, but who may, in favor of those have broken it." ("Prolegomenon to the Principles of Punishment," *Proceedings, Aristotelian Society*; 1959–60; p. 25.)

Competing claims concerning the efficacy of punishment as a deterrent abound in the literature. For obvious methodological reasons it is virtually impossible to accumulate reliable empirical evidence bearing on this question, and I pretend no thorough acquaintance with those empirical inquiries which have been undertaken. (Many, by the way, focus upon the evidence which is thought to show that the threat of capital punishment does not deter. Nothing, of course, follows from this data as to the efficacy of threats of unpleasantness of other kinds.) For the purposes of argument, therefore, I shall assume that the threat of punishment can in some circumstances deter people from acting in certain ways. And I shall look, instead, at the position which holds that, given the deterrent effect of punishment, the punishment of the guilty is clearly and conclusively shown to be justifiable. There are only two points I wish to make.

First, in discussing or accepting this position it is very easy to confuse two quite different propositions. One is that the only persons who will be capable of being deterred by the threat of punishment are those who are capable of exercising freedom of choice. This proposition is doubtless true. Unless a person has the ability to guide and control his actions, he cannot be influenced effectively by the fear or dislike he has of the sanctions which he believes will be visited upon him if he behaves in certain ways.

The other proposition is that in order to deter others it is proper to punish those persons who are capable of exercising freedom of choice and who, in so doing, violate the law. The two propositions are distinguishable. The first makes a statement about the class of persons *who are deterrable;* the second makes an assertion about the class of persons *whom it is right to punish.* Furthermore, it is important to see what the connection between these two propositions is. The argument presently under consideration is not that punishment will have a desirable effect upon the guilty offender, that punishing him will have a beneficial effect upon his future conduct. Rather, it is that the punishment of the guilty offender will have an influence upon the present and future decisions of others. The case for punishing the guilty is that by punishing them we most effectively bring home to other members of the class of responsible persons the undesirability of engaging in similar conduct. The point I wish to make is this: If there were *some other* way by which we could make all potential, responsible offenders believe that they would be punished were they to break the law, the punishment of the guilty would be unnecessary. It is the *belief that they will be punished*, and that punishment is to be avoided because it is so unpleasant, which deters people from breaking the law. The punishment of the guilty must, on this view, be justifiable only because it appears to be the most available means by which to inculcate *that belief*—and not because there is anything especially fitting about punishing the guilty.

And this leads directly into my final point. I began by referring to recent philosophical concern about the punishment of an innocent person, known to be such, whenever the consequences of punishing him would be justifiable on utilitarian grounds (such as those argued in "Judgment at Nuremberg"). And this is wrong, it is insisted, because it is wrong to use a person simply as a means by which to bring it about that others will be benefited. In an extreme enough case we might think it justifiable to punish an innocent man, but, in H.L.A. Hart's words, "we should do so with the sense of sacrificing an important principle. We should be conscious of choosing the lesser of two evils, and this would be inexplicable if the principle sacrificed to utility were itself only a requirement of utility." (p. 169)

Now my point is simply this. If I am right in thinking that the case for punishing the guilty must be made utimately on the claim that such is justifiable as the only realistic means by which to deter potential offenders, then those who are so horrified by the presence of the bare possibility of the punishment of the innocent ought to be far more concerned than they are over the punishment of the guilty. If I am even partly right, it is paradoxical, to say the least, that those who worry so much about the punishment of the innocent fail even to consider that the punishment of the guilty may be offensive for precisely those same reasons which they are so ready to regard as decisive whenever the possibility of the punishment of the innocent is raised. In both cases the objection is identical: a person is used as a means to benefit others—whether through deterrence in punishing the guilty; or some other real or presumed benefit to others, in punishing the innocent.

If it is correct, as I think it is, that any instance of the punishment of an innocent person would, at a minimum, involve the sacrifice of important moral principles, then it is also correct that every time a guilty person is punished in order to deter others, some of these same principles are correspondingly denigrated.

And such a conclusion is not without important social consequences. It requires, for one thing, that we scrutinize with excessive care the claim that the punishment of some will deter others. It suggests, for another, that we search with appreciably more zeal than we have in the past for alternative methods of achieving this same end of deterrence. It suggests too, that we strive more earnestly than we have to date to eliminate those all too prevalent conditions which make criminal behavior—even when punishment is a real and immediate threat—the most plausible means by which to obtain needed, though relatively minimal, satisfactions. And it demands, finally, a change in our attitude toward every instance of punishment, for it demands that we never view a punishment as something which is the obviously fitting, appropriate or deserved reaction to an offense: that we see it as, at best, a needed but nonetheless lamentable form of societal control.

Johannes Andenaes

Does Punishment Deter Crime? *

I

I spent the Spring of 1968 in Chicago—a city with a long-standing reputation as a high crime area, and thus a fitting place for one who is concerned with the study of crime and punishment.

I visited the Chicago Police Headquarters, had an interesting conversation with the Superintendent and was shown around. The Police Department has very impressive technical machinery. Especially impressive is the communications system which is set up to make it possible for the Headquarters to have contact with the hundreds of police cars which patrol the streets at any one time, and to direct them instantly to the spot where trouble has been reported. It takes 300 people to man the communications system alone—rows of operators watching large maps of the city, with lamps indicating the position of the patrol cars. Lamps flash, reports come in, orders are given: the whole system seems to work with smooth efficiency. Further, the Police Department has impressive laboratories, electronic computors for processing the information, and so on. The Chicago Police Department is very proud of its equipment and justly so. It has cost millions of dollars, and is said to be the most highly developed in the world.

What struck me, when reflecting on the visit on my way home, was the discrepancy between the high investment of technical insight and skill in a law enforcement agency such as the Chicago Police, and our lack of basic knowledge about the effects of criminal law and enforcement. Not only is there a lack of insight, but also a lack of real effort to acquire such insight. In recent years considerable effort has been

* Johannes Andenaes, "Does Punishment Deter Crime," *Criminal Law Quarterly*, 11 (1968), pp. 76–93. Reprinted by permission of the author and the publisher.

made to compare the effect of different kinds of treatment of offenders by scientific methods, but research into the general deterrent effects of criminal law has been neglected. To deter people from conduct considered anti-social is traditionally considered a major aim, perhaps the major aim of criminal law. But our knowledge of how this works is dim and fragmentary and very little is being done to make up for this deficiency. Research in the field is almost non-existent. What knowledge we have is based mostly on chance observations and commonsense psychological reasoning. On several occasions, I have made a plea for research in this area. Small beginnings have been made, but on a wholly unsatisfactory scale.

The subject on which I am going to speak today is a most controversial one. An American author said some time ago, somewhat ironically, that one of the basic principles learned by every student of criminology is that "punishment does not deter." [1] On the other hand a large part of the general public, politicians, police authorities and judges seem to think very highly of the deterrent potentialities of criminal law. When I first wrote about the deterrent effects of criminal law 16 years ago it was under the heading: "General Prevention—Illusion or Reality?" [2] When I returned to the subject many years later, in a General Report to the International Congress of Criminology in Montreal in 1965, I had become somewhat bolder. I ventured to drop the question-mark, and in the Summary of my report I stated that "the problem is not one of determining whether such effects exist; it is one of determining the conditions under which they occur and the degree to which they occur." [3]

Against this background you will not expect me to answer the question "Does punishment deter crime?" with a simple "yes" or "no". Instead I shall try, very briefly, to analyze some aspects of this highly complex subject. I shall restrict myself to the empirical problems which the question poses. Thus, I am not going to make any

1. C. R. Jeffery, "Criminal Behavior and Learning Theory", 56 Jo. of Cr. L., Crim. & P.S. 294 (1965).

2. 43 Jo. of Cr. L., Crim. & P.S. 176 (1952).

3. The proceedings of the Congress are not published, but my report appears, in a somewhat revised version, in 114 U. of Pa. L. Rev. 949 (1966), as "The General Preventive Effects of Punishment"; it is also printed in French in 55 Themis 159 (1965).

recommendations concerning the role which deterrence *ought* to play in the policies of legislatures, courts and the prosecution.

In an analysis of the deterrent effects of punishment it is first necessary to make a distinction between the effects of a *threat of punishment* and the effects of *actual punishment* on the punished individual.

The threat of punishment is directed to all members of society. It is pronounced in the criminal law and is demonstrated and made real by the activities of police, prosecution, courts and prisons. The law must always be seen in connection with the machinery of justice which makes it operate. In so far as this threat of punishment has a restraining effect with regard to criminal conduct, we speak of *general deterrence*. It is this aspect of deterrence which has been my special field of interest.

When a person is actually punished he is, in his future conduct, still under the threat of the law but his motivation is a more complex one than before. He knows what it is like to be prosecuted and punished and this may influence him in various ways. The threat of the law alone was not sufficient to make him conform previously. If he is now deterred by the actual experience of punishment we speak of *special deterrence*.

In the case of serious crimes, such as murder, rape or armed robbery, the number of convicted and punished offenders will be very small in comparison with the bulk of the population. The experience of "special deterrence" will be an experience for the few. In the case of minor offences, for example traffic offences, this is different. Traffic law violations have been characterized as "a folk crime." [4] "Few drivers (and increasingly this means few adults) have never in their lives received a traffic summons and even fewer can claim that they have never violated the law." [5]

4. H. Lawrence Ross, "Traffic Law Violation: A Folk Crime", *Social Problems* (Winter 1960–61), 8:3:231 (Reprinted in Haddon et al., *Accident Research*, p. 497.)
5. William Haddon et al., *Accident Research* (Harper and Row, 1964), p. 496.

II

We shall return to the deterrent effect of actual punishment later. First I shall concentrate on general deterrence: the effect of the *threat of punishment.*

Two extreme positions often emerge from the literature on the subject. One is the position of Jeremy Bentham, who considered man to be a rational being who chooses between possible modes of action on the basis of a calculation of risks of pain and pleasure. The consequence of this model is clear enough: If we make the risk of punishment sufficient to outweigh the prospect of gain, the potential lawbreaker will, as a rational man, choose to stay within the limits of the law.

The other extreme, often represented by psychiatrists, discards this model as unrealistic. When people remain lawabiding, they maintain, it is not because of fear of the criminal law, but because of moral inhibitions, internalized norms. If this internal restraint is lacking, the threat of punishment does not make much difference since criminals do not make rational choices, calculating gain against the risk of punishment; they act out of emotional instability, lack of self-control or because they have acquired the system of values of a criminal subculture. For the sake of convenience I shall speak of this as the psychiatric model although not all psychiatrists would agree with it. The extreme representatives of this way of thinking tend to look upon the idea of general deterrence as a kind of superstition, used by lawyers to defend their outmoded system of criminal law or as a cloak to conceal and rationalize their retributive feelings.

In my opinion both extremes are equally mistaken— or to put it in a more friendly way—they each represent but a part of the truth. I should like to make three points:

1. The first concerns the *danger of generalization.* It is necessary to distinguish carefully between different kinds of offences: murder, incest, abortion, shoplifting, tax-dodging, drunk driving and so on. They vary so immensely in motivation, that it is obvious that the role of the criminal law in upholding norms of conduct is very different in each of these offences. Any realistic discussion of general deterrence must be based on distinctions between various types of norms and on an analysis of the circumstances motivating transgression in each parti-

cular type. In one of my previous papers I have analyzed this in some detail. In general terms it can only be stated that general deterrence works well in some fields and works poorly or not at all in other fields.

2. *People react differently.* I stated at the outset that the threat of punishment is directed to all of us. But it affects us differently. There is no uniform response to the threat of the law. In a very general way we may say that with regard to a certain kind of criminal conduct the population could be divided into three groups: (a) the good, law-abiding citizen who does not need the threat of the law to keep him on the right path; (b) the criminal group—individuals who may well fear the law, but not sufficiently to keep them from breaking it; (c) the potential criminal, who would have broken the law if it had not been for the threat of punishment. It is in this intermediate group, the potential criminal, that the threat of punishment is at work.

We do not know the proportions of persons in these categories but they will obviously vary from offence to offence and from one geographical area to another. Nor do we have any easy means of identifying the citizens who belong to the different groups. Moreover, the groups are not static, but change with changing conditions. Under exceptional conditions, e.g., war or other serious crises, the number of actual as well as potential offenders may increase many times.

3. My third point refers to what is generally called the *moral* or *educative* effect of the criminal law. Both the Bentham model and the psychiatric model restrict themselves to the direct deterrent effects of the law. This is, in my view, a too narrow approach. Punishment is not only the artificial creation of a risk of unpleasant consequences, it is a means of expressing *social disapproval.* The act is branded as reprehensible by authorized organs of society, and this official branding of the conduct may influence attitudes quite apart from the fear of sanctions. The term general *deterrence* is, in fact, too narrow in so far as it seems to exclude this moral or educative influence. I prefer the Continental tradition of speaking of *general preventive effects* of punishment.

There may be conflicting views on how important this moral or educative aspect is. In Continental legal literature the moral or educative influence of the criminal law is generally taken for granted and regarded as being of high importance. In fact, it is sometimes considered more important than the direct deterrent influence. The German criminologist, Hellmuth Mayer, thus asserts that "the basic general preventive effect of criminal law does not at all stem from its deterrent but from its morality-shaping force . . . Nothing is so convincing to man as power, provided it appears as expression of a moral order." [6] In the same vein the Canadian Professor, J. S. Morton, professes as his theory that "the most important function of the criminal law is that of education or conditioning." [7] In the United States the idea seems less acceptable, and this may tell us something about attitudes to law and authority in American society. European observers of American society have often remarked that respect for legislation is less in the United States than in most European countries. As the Swedish criminologist Kinberg put it after a stay in the United States in the thirties: "The legislative mill grinds as it does in European countries, but the average American cares little for what comes out of it." [8] I do not know whether this holds true as a general proposition. But it seems obvious that the young, underprivileged ghetto Negro is not likely to accept law and law enforcement as authoritative statements of moral values. On the contrary, law and law enforcement seem rather to be the targets of his aggression. In the recent Report of the President's National Advisory Commission on Civil Disorders, the deep hostility between the police and the ghetto community is cited as a primary cause of the disorders of 1967. And it is pointed out that this aggression is directed against the police as symbols of the entire system of law and criminal justice.[9] These observations may serve as a renewed warning against all sweeping generalizations. The workings of the criminal law must always be seen in its full cultural context. There is certainly a complicated interplay between the law and the multitude of other factors which shape our attitudes and behavior.

6. Hellmuth Mayer, *Das Strafrecht des deutshen Volkes* (Stuttgart, 1936), pp. 26 and 32. Similar viewpoints are put forward by Swedish authors such as Lundstedt, Stjernberg and Wetter.

7. J. D. Morton, *The Function of Criminal Law* (Canadian Broadcasting Corporation, Toronto, 1962), pp. 43 and 46.

8. Olaf Kinberg, *Basic Problems of Criminology* (1935), pp. 168–9.

9. *Report of the National Advisory Commission on Civil Disorders* (Bantam Book Paperback Edition, 1968), p. 299.

So far I have only given an outline of a kind of theoretical structure. Instead of trying to cover a wide field of practical application, I shall concentrate on two subjects: the death penalty for murder, and legislation on drunk driving.

The question of the importance of the severity of the penalty has been discussed in great detail with reference to the death penalty. The rate of murder in states which employ capital punishment has been compared with the murder rate in states which have abolished it. And in abolitionist states comparisons have been made between the frequency of murder before and after abolition. There are many methodological difficulties involved in such comparisons, but without going into details I think it can be confidently stated that capital punishment has had no appreciable influence on the murder rate in the states which have been investigated. Some people tend to jump to the conclusion that since the severity of punishment has no effect on murder rates, the same applies to other crimes. It may be necessary, therefore, to stress the limitations of these findings. They do not say that the severity of punishment for murder is without any deterrent effect, they only say that the choice between the death penalty and the alternative, life imprisonment, does not seem to make a difference as to deterrent effect. It may well be that a radical reduction of sentences, e.g., to three or four years of imprisonment, would make a great difference. Further, the research is concerned only with murder, which in our culture is a crime of a rather special kind, surrounded by feelings of strong moral condemnation. It is conceivable that capital punishment for other crimes, e.g., espionage or war crimes, at least under certain conditions, may have a superior deterrent effect than would lesser penalties. Finally, the research only tells us about the lack of deterrent effect of capital punishment as it has been applied in our part of the world during recent generations, an application which has on the whole been both slow, sparing and haphazard. It cannot be said to be proved that a quick and consistent application of capital punishment in all cases of murder would be without effect. I do not assert that it *would* have such an effect, still less do I advocate such a solution. What I am saying is that the possibility of such a deterrent effect is not disproved.

I now move to the question of drunk driving, or rather driving under the influence of alcohol. This is a field where great differences in legislation and enforcement exist in different countries.

The Scandinavian states have for a long time had very strict legislation against driving under the influence of alcohol, and strict enforcement as well. In Norway, for example, the law prohibits the driving of motor cars when a driver's blood alcohol level exceeds .05%. A driver suspected of violation of this provision must consent to a blood test; the consistent policy of the courts has been to give prison sentences, and in addition the loss of the driver's license for at least one year is automatic. It has been felt that this strict policy has had a considerable effect on the attitudes of drivers with regard to driving under the influence of alcohol, and alcohol seems to be responsible only for a very small proportion of road traffic accidents.[10] But as this legislation has been in force for a very long time and was introduced at a time when motor traffic was slight and motor traffic accidents few in comparison with the situation today, it is impossible to show statistically the impact of the legislation.

This case is different with the new British legislation (Road Safety Act 1967, 1967 (U.K.), c. 30), which went into effect on October 9, 1967. In addition to the old provisions on drunk driving, which only led to conviction in cases with a high degree of intoxication, the law created a new offence, driving with an undue proportion of alcohol in the blood. The prescribed limit is defined as 80 milligrammes of alcohol in 100 millilitres of blood (.08%). The police may ask for a breath test if the constable has reasonable cause to suspect the driver of having alcohol in his body or of having committed a traffic offence while the vehicle was in motion. Even without such case for suspicion the police may ask for a breath test if the driver has been involved in an accident.[11] If the breath test indicates that the driver is probably above the legal limit, he may be arrested and taken to a police station. In the police station he will be asked to submit to a blood test, or if he refuses, to provide two specimens of urine for analysis. A failure to co-operate at this stage renders the driver liable to the same penalties as if the sample had been taken, analyzed and found to be above the limit. Drivers convicted of the new offence are liable to a fine of £100

10. See Andenaes, "The General Preventive Effects of Punishment", 114 U. Pa. L. Rev., at pp. 968–969.

11. The proposal in the Government's White Paper, "Road Safety Legislation 1965–66", to give the police the power to make random tests did not receive the approval of Parliament.

or four months' imprisonment or both. Disqualification from driving for a minimum of one year is automatic, except in the most special circumstances. The new law was accompanied by a large publicity campaign, beginning two weeks before the new law came into force and running until the end of the year. The campaign, which was estimated to cost nearly £350,000, was particularly intensive at the beginning and during the Christmas/New Year period.

Statistics of road accidents were carefully compiled to gauge the effect of the new legislation. Actually, this is one of the very few examples where a real effort has been made to establish a continuous assessment of the effects of a new policy. According to the official figures given by the Ministry of Transport a substantial decrease in road traffic accidents took place after the new statute came into effect.[12] The following table is compiled from these reports. The figures for the month of October refer to the period after the coming into force of the new law, figures in brackets refer to the first eight days of the month.

Road Casualties in Great Britain, Oct. to Dec. 1967
Decrease in percentage compared with previous year

		Oct.	Nov.	Dec.	Oct.–Dec.	Christmas
Killed	(1)	17	20	33	23	36
Seriously Injured	(2)	15	15	22	17	30
Slightly Injured	(2)	11	13	20	15	

In the first nine months of 1967 there was no consistent trend in total road accidents, some months being worse than the previous year and some being better; overall there was a two percent decrease in casualties as compared with 1966. Overall traffic compared with the previous year was estimated to have increased by 5 percent in October, two percent in November, and to have decreased one percent in December.

That the reduction is greater for serious accidents than for the less

12. Ministry of Transport, Press Notices No. 892 of December 19, 1967, No. 78 of February 8, 1968, and No. 157 of March 21, 1968.

serious is in harmony with the findings of previous traffic research which shows that when drivers with blood alcohol levels over .08 percent have accidents they tend to be more severe than the average accident.

A striking pattern emerges if the accidents are related to the hourly period when they took place. During working hours (8 a.m. to 6 p.m.) the reduction is slight (2 percent of fatal and serious accidents in October and November, 7 percent in December). Between 8 p.m. and 4 a.m. the figures were 36, 38 and 41 respectively; for the hours after midnight they were still higher. The conclusion is inevitable: In this socially very important area it has proved possible, through new legislation, to influence people's conduct to a considerable degree, at least temporarily.

If we compare the figures for reduction of traffic casualties under the new British law with previous research on the role of alcohol in traffic accidents, it would seem that the new law has reduced alcohol from a major cause of accidents to a rather insignificant one. I shall make no attempt to assess *what part* of the new legislation has been most important in bringing about this effect. This would require a thorough study, with comparisons to other countries where legislation of a more or less similar kind has been introduced.

It remains to be seen whether the reduction in accident rates will continue on the same level. It may be possible that the introduction of the new legislation with its accompanying publicity campaign has had a shock impact which may gradually wane as the publicity campaign subsides and many drivers come to realize that perhaps the risk of detection is not as great as they had imagined. On the other hand it is possible that new habits related to alcohol consumption and driving may survive even though it is understood that the risk for detection is not as great as originally thought. The initial success of the law may also have some effect in convincing drivers of the reasonableness of the restrictions on driving when under the influence of alcohol. Only time can answer these questions.

Statistical evidence of the general preventive effects of punishment is scarce. What conclusions of a more general kind can be drawn from the British experience? Why does it happen that in this case statistics yield the unequivocal results which are otherwise so difficult to obtain?

First, the situation is different from traditional crime in that conduct which was previously not criminalized, namely driving under the influence of alcohol not reaching the high level which in practice was required for conviction under the previous law, has been made a criminal offence. We therefore have the possibility of measuring the *total impact* of the law. Crimes such as murder, robbery, rape and burglary remain, in substance, the same from one generation to another. The changes which occur, normally relate either to the level of penalties or to the level of enforcement. Instead of measuring the total impact of the criminal provision we face the much more difficult task of measuring the marginal effect of a change in penalties or enforcement.

Second, we possess in this case an *independent measure* of the forbidden conduct in the statistics of road accidents. We thus avoid many of the difficulties involved in directly measuring the extent of violations. It should be added that we cannot take for granted that the number of traffic casualties due to alcohol consumption is in simple proportion to the number of violations of the provisions on driving under the influence of alcohol. The effect of the law may, in many cases, be that the driver reduces his consumption in order to reduce the risk of detection, although he remains above the limit fixed by the law. Since the accident risk increases with the amount of alcohol, such a reduction may be highly important in regard to the aims of the law. If the limit of the law is low, a high rate of fringe violators may be of minor importance for road safety. Since the aim of the law is to promote road safety it can be said that the influence of the law on road accidents is in fact a better measure of its efficacy than would be the number of drivers who drive in excess of the prescribed limit before and after the law came into effect.

The two points so far mentioned refer to the problem of measuring impact. It is not my intention, however, to contend or imply that we would find similar general preventive effects in other fields if we only had the methods to measure them. Here, as elsewhere, I would warn against rash generalizations. Driving under the influence of alcohol is a kind of behavior which is not restricted to a criminal sub-culture, but is rather widespread in the population, and it is not surrounded by much feeling of moral condemnation. Further, it is behavior which is not normally the outcome of strong emotions or triggered off on the spur of the moment. The decision to drink or not to drink can in most cases be made deliberately, as a rational choice. And the motivation for committing the act is not a terribly strong one. The law interferes with personal liberty, but not very much. It does not ask the man to stop drinking, nor does it ask him to stop driving, it only prohibits the combination of the two. In short, it is a situation where risk of punishment on commonsense grounds can be expected to be given more weight than in many other offences.

III

I now return to the effects of actual punishment. The problem is usually discussed in terms of *reform* and *rehabilitation*. For a moment I shall concentrate upon the *deterrent* aspect. How does the experience of actual punishment influence the deterrent effect of the threat —a deterrent effect which has proved, in this case, insufficient to prevent the offence.

Prima facie it seems natural to expect that the experience of punishment would normally tend to strengthen fear. The abstract threat of the law has come to life, and the offender visualizes the consequences more clearly than he did before. In her book on department store shop-lifting, Mary Owen Cameron vividly describes this mechanism in the arrested amateur shoplifter ("the snitch").[13] The investigation procedure of the store makes it increasingly clear to the pilferer that he is considered a thief and is in imminent danger of being hauled into court and publicly exhibited as such. This realization is often accompanied by a dramatic change in attitudes and by severe emotional disturbance. "This is a nightmare," said one woman pilferer who had been formally charged with stealing an expensive handbag. "It can't be happening to me. Why, oh, why can't I wake up and find that it isn't so," she cried later as she waited at a store exit, accompanied by a city and a store policeman, for the city police van to arrive. The professional shoplifter who has been arrested behaves

13. Mary Owen Cameron, "The Booster and the Snitch," *The Free Press of Glencoe* (1964). See pp. 161–164.

quite differently. "He does, of course, make every effort possible to talk his way out of the situation. But once he finds that this is impossible, he accepts jail and its inconveniences as a normal hazard of the trade."

This description highlights several important points. It shows how the actual experience is much stronger than the theoretical knowledge. It further shows not only how fear might influence the future behavior of the shoplifter but also that because of apprehension he now realizes more clearly than before that he has committed a criminal and shameful act. The experience acts as a "moral eye-opener." Before arrest most shoplifters do not think of themselves as thieves, but this is brought home to them through arrest and investigtion. Further, the description illustrates what a serious shock detection and arrest can be even if no prosecution, conviction and sentence follow. "Among pilferers who are apprehended and interrogated by the store police but set free without formal charge there is *very little or no recidivism.*" [14] Whereas the threat of the law has not had a sufficient deterrent or moral effect, the actual experience of being caught has. The special preventive effects are, in this situation, not due to legal punishment. But the institution of legal punishment looms in the background, gives the apprehension and investigation its dramatic impact, and defines the risk connected with repetition of the crime.

The experience of being caught may also lead the offender to perceive the *risk* of detection and apprehension as greater than he did previously. In a study of drunk driving in Sweden, Klette asked a sample of automobile owners about their estimate of the risk for a drunk driver to be arrested under various circumstances.[15] The result was that drivers who had themselves been arrested for drunk driving had an estimate of risk many times higher than other drivers. This may be due to the common tendency to generalize from personal experience, and thus hold true also for other kinds of offences.

We cannot, however, take for granted that the experience of punishment always tends to strengthen the offender's fear of the law. It may work the other way. It is conceivable that he has had exaggerated

14. *Op. cit.*, p. 151.
15. Hans Klette, "On the Functioning of the Swedish Legislation Concerning Drunken Driving," p. 7 (mimeographed).

ideas of the consequences of being caught and now draws the con-clusion that it was not as bad as he had imagined. More important, probably, is the fact that if a person has been convicted of a some-what more serious crime, and especially if he is sentenced to im-prisonment, he will have less to fear from a new conviction, since his reputaton is already tarnished. In penological literature it is often asserted that the offender's fear of imprisonment is much reduced once he has become acquainted with it, but there does not seem to be any systematic research which could prove or disprove such assertions.

To complete the picture, it is necessary to mention the effect which, in psychological terminology, is called "reinforcement." When a person commits a crime this will change his perception of the threat of punishment whether he is detected or prosecuted or not. If the criminal act leads to the envisaged goal and is not followed by un-pleasant consequences this will normally reinforce his tendency to repeat the act. The psychological barrier which the fear of punish-ment represented will be weakened. If the act is repeated with the same result, further reinforcement will take place and a criminal habit can be formed. The teller who once has started to embezzle or the warehouseman who has started to steal from the stock, will tend to continue his activity until he is detected. This mechanism of reinforcement is probably especially strong if the crimes are com-mitted in company with others who share the experience and give each other mutual support.

There is every reason to believe that detection and punishment have a deterrent effect in the majority of cases as compared with the alternative no detection and punishment. And, common-sense would indicate that the deterrent effect increases in strength with the severity of punishment.

But, of course, to deal with the effects of actual punishment under the aspect of deterrence alone, is a too narrow perspective. The punishment may change the offender for better or worse, quite apart from its deterrent or nondeterrent effects. The situation is very dif-ferent for the various penalties. As far as the fine is concerned there will not be much other effect than a more or less pronounced deter-rence. Much the same is the case with the short prison sentence. A radical personality change cannot be expected to take place through this kind of punishment. Whatever positive effect it may have, apart from the moral eye opener effect described in the shoplifting example, is primarily as a deterrent.

The case is different and more complex with long-term imprisonment. The prison staff tries to train and reform the offender in order to release him from the prison as a better man than he was on his arrival. Both the day to day experience of the prison staff and sociological prison research in recent years show how the influence of fellow inmates often works in the opposite direction. The prisoner may leave prison as a worse man than when he entered, more deeply entrenched in a criminal culture, more hostile to society and its values, and less fit to meet the problems of a life in free society. Which of these opposite forces are, on the whole, the stronger? Although it has for generations been dogma in penology that short prison sentences represent a bad solution, since they do not give real opportunities for rehabilitative work, there is little evidence that longer prison sentences give better results than short ones. Since a long sentence ought to have a stronger *deterrent* value than a short one, this seems to indicate that the negative influences during a prolonged stay in prison outweigh or at least neutralize the rehabilitative efforts of the staff. If this is correct, whatever positive effect the prison may have on the prisoner's future conduct would, also in these cases, be primarily the result of deterrence.

The situation is further complicated by the effect which conviction and sentence may have on the social status of the offender. The stigma attached to conviction and sentence may reduce his chances of getting work or being accepted in his previous social circle. The stigmatization which serves a useful social function in the process of general prevention, is harmful as far as special prevention is concerned.

In practice it will be difficult or impossible to isolate the deterrent effects of the prison experience from other effects. Research into attitudes and motivation may give some clues, but does not permit any statistical evaluation of the relative importance of various influences. If the prisoner does not relapse into crime we will not be able to tell whether this is due to a deterrent or a reformative effect of the prison, or if it might not have happened if no prison sentence had been imposed. What we can measure is how offenders perform after punishment, expressed in figures of recidivism. And here three main features stand out clearly.

1. If we look merely at recidivism rates after various kinds of treatment, the dominant pattern is: the more lenient the treatment the better the results. Fines or probation give better results than prison sentences, and short sentences give better results than long ones. But then the composition of these groups is different in regard to personal characteristics and criminality. The less severe cases receive the most lenient sentences, which is a different way of saying that the group with lenient sentences represents the better risks.

2. If we correct for these differences and use modern prediction techniques to compare groups which can be considered equally good or bad risks, the dominant feature of the results is that the overall differences between the various methods of treatment are small or nonexistent. It seems as if the personality of the offender and the social environment to which he is returning, are of much greater significance for his future conduct than the differential effects of our various kinds of treatment. It is not easy to change people, at least where treatment is carried out against their will. From the point of view of the prison administrator this may seem a pessimistic and depressing fact. In a broader, political perspective, it is a fact which also has its positive aspects.

3. First offenders, that is offenders who have only one conviction and sentence, have a rather low rate of recidivism irrespective of sentence, but the recidivism rate increases sharply with the number of previous convictions. It thus seems as though the majority of offenders react positively to punishment but that there remains a hard core of offenders who are neither reformed nor deterred. In these cases punishment fails. So, on the whole, do other methods of treatment.

Karl Marx

Punishment and Society *

. . . Punishment in general has been defended as a means either of ameliorating or of intimidating. Now what right have you to punish me for the amelioration or intimidation of others? And besides, there is history—there is such a thing as statistics—which prove with the most complete evidence that since Cain the world has been neither intimidated nor ameliorated by punishment. Quite the contrary. From the point of view of abstract right, there is only one theory of punishment which recognizes human dignity in the abstract, and that is the theory of Kant, especially in the more rigid formula given to it by Hegel. Hegel says:

Punishment is the right of the criminal. It is an act of his own will. The violation of right has been proclaimed by the criminal as his own right. His crime is the negation of right. Punishment is the negation of this negation, and consequently an affirmation of right, solicited and forced upon the criminal by himself.

There is no doubt something specious in this formula, inasmuch as Hegel, instead of looking upon the criminal as the mere object, the slave of justice, elevates him to the position of a free and self-determined being. Looking, however, more closely into the matter, we discover that German idealism here, as in most other instances, has but given a transcendental sanction to the rules of existing society. Is it not a delusion to substitute for the individual with his real motives, with multifarious social circumstances pressing upon him, the abstraction of "free will"—one among the many qualities of man for man himself? This theory, considering punishment as the result of the criminal's own will, is only a metaphysical expression for the old *jus talionis*; eye against eye, tooth against tooth, blood against blood. Plainly speaking, and dispensing with all paraphrases, punishment is

* Karl Marx, "Capital Punishment," in *Marx and Engels: Basic Writings on Politics and Philosophy*, ed. L. Feuer (Garden City: Anchor Books, 1959), pp. 487–89.

nothing but a means of society to defend itself against the infraction of its vital conditions, whatever may be their character. Now what a state of society is that which knows of no better instrument for its own defense than the hangman, and which proclaims, through the "leading journal of the world," its own brutality as eternal law?

Mr. A. Quételet, in his excellent and learned work *L'Homme et ses Facultés*, says:

There is a budget which we pay with frightful regularity—it is that of prisons, dungeons, and scaffolds. . . . We might even predict how many individuals will stain their hands with the blood of their fellow men, how many will be forgers, how many will deal in poison, pretty nearly the same way as we may foretell the annual births and deaths.

And Mr. Quételet, in a calculation of the probabilities of crime published in 1829, actually predicted with astonishing certainty not only the amount but all the different kinds of crimes committed in France in 1830. That it is not so much the particular political institutions of a country as the fundamental conditions of modern *bourgeois* society in general which produce an average amount of crime in a given national fraction of society may be seen from the following table, communicated by Quételet, for the years 1822–24. We find in a number of one hundred condemned criminals in America and France:

Age	Philadelphia	France
Under twenty-one years	19	19
Twenty-one to thirty	44	35
Thirty to forty	23	23
Above forty	14	23
	—	—
Total	100	100

Now, if crimes observed on a great scale thus show, in their amount and their classification, the regularity of physical phenomena—if, as Mr. Quételet remarks: "It would be difficult to decide in respect to which of the two [the physical world and the social system] the acting causes produce their effect with the utmost regularity"— is there not a necessity for deeply reflecting upon an alteration of the system that breeds these crimes, instead of glorifying the hangman who executes a lot of criminals to make room only for the supply of new ones?

Clarence Darrow

The Holdup Man *

The season of the "holdup man" and the "anti-holdup man" is once more at hand. This period comes annually at the same time of year, just after the flower show, the horse show, and along with the college football games. It begins with the season of gaiety, when the days grow short and the nights grow long, when the first sharp, tingling frost of winter drives the people off the streets and huddles them around the fires, and when the price of coal goes up.

The season of the "holdup man" will wane as the winter gaieties fade away—soon after Lent—when the nights again grow short and the days grow long, when the price of coal goes down and the sun comes back once more and warms the poor and homeless, without money and without price.

Lawyers, mayors, doctors and policemen freely give their advice as to the best way to treat the "holdup man." There is scarcely a topic of the day in which all classes of society so generally agree—one remedy is prescribed by all—more police, more revolvers, more clubs, more jails—this is the remedy for the "holdup man." One able lawyer advises every citizen to carry a revolver and to shoot at every suspected holdup—to aim at the abdomen, presumably the most fatal spot. Why the "holdup man" should be treated differently from other men who transgress the moral law is not quite clear. If all sinners were to be shot at sight few would be left to bury the dead. A doctor, generally humane and wise, declares that the mayor is responsible for all the holdup men, that there is no excuse for a burglary on "Maple Street," and some other street. What the residents of these streets have done to exempt them from the holdup man is not made clear.

It has not occurred to any of these eminent people to find the cause

* Clarence Darrow, "The Holdup Man," *The International Socialist Review* (1909), reprinted in *Verdicts Out of Court* (1963), pp. 220–24.

for the "holdup man," and yet most of them know that nothing in this world exists without a cause.

Of course no one but a crank or a fanatic could find any necessary connection between the brilliant costumes of the horse show, the cold blasts of winter, the price of coal and the holdup man; yet after all, many men whom the world has called wise—and even orthodox— have associated these causes and brought not only arguments but long tables of figures to show that there is a law which governs even the actions of the holdup man and relates him to every other living thing upon the earth.

There are many other facts that students have learned while policemen were wielding their brutal clubs.

The number of homeless girls who patrol the streets of our large cities grows greater, they walk more briskly and waste less time negotiating with the prospective customer as the nights grow long and cold—to most people this is an accident like all other things on earth. There are those who know that the rooms where these girls are poor, that they are not all heated with steam, that most of them are cold, and that to say nothing of food, these wanderers must do something to keep warm.

There are other facts, too, which the "crank" and sentimentalist has found out. Our jails and police stations are fuller in winter than in summer. The Salvation Army and other bodies of evangelists who have warm rooms and nice bowls of hot soup make many more converts in winter than in summer. The winter "Christian" is known to all who do this sort of work. Our poorhouses, wood yards, orphan asylums, and even art galleries and public reading rooms are well patronized in winter. This last would teach some profound thinkers that cold weather conduces to literature and art. Pawnshops and second hand furniture men get better bargains in winter than in summer—but still, what of it?—do not lawyers, doctors, policemen and clergymen all say that the panacea for all ills is the policeman's club?

There are other facts which dreamers and visionists are wont to note—those people have so little to do with the practical side of life that they must needs dream. In good times tramps are scarce, jails are empty, criminal courts not over busy, streetwalkers few, holdup men very rare.

The early winter is the time that frugal men and frugal beasts lay up their stores for the cold days and nights coming on. The thrifty mine owners lay in their stocks by marking up the price of the coal which the Lord placed in the earth long ages since; the lawyer and merchant telephones his dealer to put twenty tons of coal in his cellar to feed his furnace through the winter months—the poor seamstress works farther into the black night to buy a few bushels to keep her fingers from growing stiff. Old, bent, haggard women take huge sacks upon their shoulders and wander up and down the railroad tracks for the stray lumps that may drive away a portion of the frost, and lean, dirty little boys pull their carts through the streets and sweep up what the rich man leaves; and the holdup man, he, too, goes out to lay in his winter stock against the ice and cold.

The holdup men are not the ones who mark up the price of coal and gas and beef—these would take no such chances as fall to the lot of the holdup man. The holdup man comes from the home of the wretched and the poor. Who think you is this holdup man—was he born this way If so, don't fire as you meet him on the street, but turn your gun on God Almighty who made him as he is. But he was not born—he was made—he might have been an unsuccessful merchant who could not compete with the department store—or a railroad man whose name is on the black-list because he dared to strike. He grew more and more desperate year after year until he became a "holdup man."

It is fifty years since the great philosopher and historian Buckle gave his monumental work to the world. In this work he showed not alone by reason and logic, but by statistics covering long periods of time, that the suicides, the defalcations, and the crimes of all kinds increased and decreased in England, and have for years, exactly as the price of bread went up and down. This was not new when Buckle wrote it down; it was known before and has been shown by almost every good economist since then.

There are many other facts that cranks often cite. Australia was settled by exported criminals, but they went to a country where land was cheap and opportunity great, and became industrious, hard-working men; the next generation became respected, high-toned citizens. Take a thousand of our low-class crooks and a thousand of our commonest prostitutes, and put them on an island where land is cheap and opportunity great, and in the third generation their descendants will be civilized, well-mannered citizens, with houses and barns, books and pictures, churches, policemen and jails.

The holdup man of today is the same man who lurked around the mansions of the rich in Rome fifteen hundred years ago. He was sent to jail, but he battered away at the civilization of Rome until the rich and poor went down in common ruin and despair. He is the same holdup man that Louis XV and Louis XVI were wont to club and kill in France a hundred years ago, but one day all the disinherited holdup men crept out from the alleys and caverns and marched on the king's palace and took possession of the state. Then these men made the rules of the game, and the nobles and princes went into the back alleys and took the place of the holdup men—that is, those who did not move to the catacombs.

Every increase in the price of coal makes "holdup men." Every time the price of meat goes up, some women go upon the streets, and some men get burglars' tools. Every extortionate penny taken by the gas trust makes holdup men. In their last analysis these despised criminals are men whom our social system has frozen out—who cannot live—who have no place upon the earth. Even the prostitute who plies her trade for the love of the trade, and the criminal who loves crime (if any such there be) have come to their present place through years of misfortune or hard environment, and would surely disappear under fairer conditions and with anything like a decent chance.

The rescue missions save many girls from prostitutes' lives, but they only make room for some other girl whom society is starving and freezing until she takes her place. So you may kill all the holdup men, but back of these are a long line of other men standing on the border, waiting for a chance to take their place.

Chicago is fairly well-to-do for jails and lockups. We have just built a fine, large addition to our county jail—the building has steam heat and electric lights and many boarders are found therein, especially in winter time, but has crime decreased as the jail increased in size? No one seems to expect this—it is taken for granted that this will grow as fast as any other institution of the town. If a pestilence of typhoid fever should break out in town the wise, humane doctors would advise us to build more hospitals—the cranks and visionists would tell us to boil the drinking water and stop the scourge. Thank God, the practical man has always ruled the world—with clubs!

With a small handful of men controlling all the earth and every opportunity for life, and the great mass forced into hopeless want, it will take more jails, policemen and clubs to keep the disinherited at bay. There is one way, and only one, to treat the holdup men—feed them, or rather let them feed themselves.

But more grim and farcical still than the senseless talk about the holdup man is one other fact. Chicago has hundreds of Christian churches—we are a Christian people. It is nineteen hundred years since Christ's teachings were given to the world—we profess to be the disciples of that lowly man who believed in no jails or clubs—who taught infinite love and infinite mercy—who said if a man asked for your coat, give him also your cloak—and yet today we know nothing better than hatred, repression, brute force, jails and clubs. We single out a considerable class of our fellow men to shoot on sight. Of course, the world will continue to treat its so called criminals in this enlightened human way. Therefore would it not be well to rechristen our churches, and stop calling them after Christ?

Bibliography

GENERAL

Beccaria, C. *On Crimes and Punishment*, trans. H. Paolucci, Indianapolis: Bobbs-Merrill, 1963.

Benn, S. "Punishment," in P. Edwards (ed.), *The Encyclopedia of Philosophy*. New York: Macmillan, 1967.

Bentham, J. *The Rationale of Punishment*, in J. Bowring (ed.), *The Works of Jeremy Bentham*. Edinburgh: W. Tait, 1843.

Bentham, J. *An Introduction to the Principles of Morals and Legislation*. Oxford: Basil Blackwell, 1948 (1789).

Durkheim, E. *The Division of Labor in Society*, trans. G. Simpson. New York: Free Press, 1965.

Ewing, A. *The Morality of Punishment*. London: K. Paul, Trench, Trubner and Co. Ltd., 1929.

Fitzgerald, P. *Criminal Law and Punishment*. Oxford: Clarendon Press, 1962.

Fuller, L. "The Case of the Speluncean Explorers," *Harvard Law Review*, 62(1949).

Gerber, J. and P. McAnany (eds.) *Contemporary Punishment, Views, Explanations and Justifications*. South Bend: University of Notre Dame, 1972.

Hall, J. *General Principles of Criminal Law*, 2d ed. Indianapolis: Bobbs-Merrill, 1960.

Hart, H. L. *Punishment and Responsibility*. Oxford: Clarendon Press, 1968.

Hart, H. L. *Law, Liberty and Morality*. New York: Random House, 1963.

Hawkins, G. "Punishment and Deterrence: The Educative, Moralizing and Habituative Effects," *Wisconsin Law Review* (1969).

Hentig, H. *Punishment: Its Origin, Purpose and Psychology*. London: W. Hodge and Co. Ltd., 1937.

Honderich, T. *Punishment, Its Supposed Justifications*. New York: Harcourt, Brace and World, 1970.

Michael, J. and H. Wechsler, "A Rationale of the Law of Homicide,"
Columbia Law Review, 37(1937).

Michael, J. and H. Wechsler, Criminal Law and Its Administration.
Brooklyn: Foundation Press, 1940.

Model Penal Code. Philadelphia: American Law Institute, 1962.

Morris, H. (ed.). Freedom and Responsibility. Stanford: Stanford
University Press, 1961. Chapter X.

Parkenham, F. The Idea of Punishment. London: Geoffrey Chap-
man, 1961.

Pincoffs, E. The Rationale of Legal Punishment. New York: Humanities Press, 1966.

Radzinowicz, L. and J. Turner (eds.). The Modern Approach to
Criminal Law. London: Macmillan, 1948.

Stephen, J. A History of the Criminal Law in England. London: Macmillan, 1883.

Tarde, G. Penal Philosophy. Boston: Little, Brown and Co., 1912.

Williams, G. Criminal Law: The General Part. London: Stevens and
Sons Ltd., 1953.

CHAPTER I: THE CONCEPT OF PUNISHMENT

Benn, S. and R. Peters. Social Principles and the Democratic State.
London: George Allen and Unwin Ltd., 1959, pp. 182–3.

Bentham, J. The Rationale of Punishment, in J. Bowring (ed.), The
Works of Jeremy Bentham. Edinburgh: W. Tait, 1843, Chapter I.

Bobbio, N. "Law and Force," The Monist, 49(1965).

Durkheim, E. The Division of Labor in Society, trans. G. Simpson.
New York: Free Press, 1965. Chapter II.

Flew, A. "The Justification of Punishment," Philosophy, 29(1954).

Gahringer, R. "Punishment and Responsibility," Journal of Philosophy, 66(1969).

Hart, H. L. "Prolegomenon to the Principles of Punishment," Proceedings of the Aristotelian Society, 60(1959–60). Reprinted
in Hart, Punishment and Responsibility.

Hart, H. M. "The Aims of the Criminal Law," Law and Contemporary Problems, 23(1958).

Honderich, T. *Punishment: The Supposed Justifications*. New York: Harcourt, Brace and World, 1970. Chapter III.

Kasachkoff, T. "Analysing 'Punishment,' " *Canadian Journal of Philosophy*, 2(1972).

Kaufman, A. "Anthony Quinton on Punishment," *Analysis*, 20(1959).

Lasswell, H. and R. Donnelly. "The Continuing Debate Over Responsibility: An Introduction to Isolating the Condemnation Sanction," *Yale Law Journal*, 68(1959).

McCloskey, H. "The Complexity of the Concepts of Punishment," *Philosophy*, 37(1962).

McPherson, T. "Punishment: Definition and Justification," *Analysis*, 28(1967).

Strömberg, T. "Some Reflections on the Concept of Punishment," *Theoria*, 23(1957).

CHAPTER II: THE JUSTIFICATION OF PUNISHMENT

Aquinas, T. "Of the Debt of Punishment," in *Summa Theologica*. New York: Benziger Brothers, 1947. Question 87, Articles 1–8.

Aristotle. *Nicomachean Ethics*, trans. W. Ross, in *The Works of Aristotle*. Oxford: Clarendon Press, 1938. 1104b, 15–19.

Beccaria, C. *On Crimes and Punishment*, trans. H. Paolucci. Indianapolis: Bobbs-Merrill, 1963.

Benn, S. "An Approach to the Problems of Punishment," *Philosophy*, 33(1958).

Bentham, J. *An Introduction to the Principles of Morals and Legislation*. Oxford: Basil Blackwell, 1948.

Bentham, J. *Theory of Legislation*. London: Routledge and Kegan Paul Ltd., 1950.

Bentham, J. *The Rationale of Punishment*, in J. Bowring (ed.), *The Works of Jeremy Bentham*. Edinburgh: W. Tait, 1843.

Bentham, J. *Of Laws in General*, in H. L. Hart (ed.), *Collected Works of Jeremy Bentham*. London: Athlone Press, 1970. Chapter XI.

Bosanquet, B. *The Philosophical Theory of the State*, 4th ed. London: Macmillan, 1966.

Bradley, F. *Ethical Studies*, 2d ed. London: Oxford University Press, 1927. Essay I.

Bradley, F. "Some Remarks on Punishment," *International Journal of Ethics*, 4(1894).

Brandt, R. *Ethical Theory*. Englewood Cliffs: Prentice-Hall, 1959. Chapter 19.

Brentano, F. *The Origin of Our Knowledge of Right and Wrong*, English edition, ed. R. Chisholm. London: Routledge and Kegan Paul Ltd., 1969, pp. 118–122.

Carritt, E. *Ethical and Political Thinking*. Oxford: Clarendon Press, 1947. Chapter V.

Carritt, E. *The Theory of Morals*. London: Oxford University Press, 1952. Chapter XII.

Cohen, M. *Reason and Law*. Glencoe: Free Press, 1950. Chapter II.

Darrow, C. *Crime: Its Cause and Treatment*. New York: Crowell, 1922.

Dewey, J. *Human Nature and Conduct*. New York: Modern Library, 1930, pp. 17–19.

Feinberg, J. "On Justifying Legal Punishment," in C. Friedrich (ed.), *Responsibility*. New York: Liberal Arts Press, 1960.

Finnis, J. "Punishment and Pedagogy," *Oxford Review*, 1967.

Gahringer, R. "Punishment and Responsibility," *Journal of Philosophy*, 66(1969).

Gallie, W. "The Lords' Debate on Hanging, July 1956: Interpretation and Comment," *Philosophy*, 32(1957).

Gendin, S. "A Plausible Theory of Retribution," *Journal of Value Inquiry*, 6(1972).

Glover, J. *Responsibility*. New York: Humanities Press, 1970. Chapter 8.

Goldinger, M. "Punishment, Justice and the Separation of Issues," *The Monist*, 49(1965).

Goldinger, M. "Rule-utilitarianism and Criminal Reform," *Southern Journal of Philosophy*, 5(1967).

Grotius, H. *On the Rights of War and Peace*, trans. W. Whewell. London: John W. Parker, 1853. Chapter XX.

Hart, H. L. "Prolegomenon to the Principles of Punishment," *Proceedings of the Aristotelian Society*, 60(1959–60). Reprinted in Hart, *Punishment and Responsibility*.

Hegel, G. *Philosophy of Right*, trans. T. Knox. London: Oxford University Press, 1969. Section 100.

Hobbes, T. *A Dialogue Between a Philosopher and a Student of the Common Laws of England*, ed. and intro. J. Cropsey. Chicago: University of Chicago Press, 1971.

Kant, I. *Critique of Practical Reason*, trans. L. Beck. New York: Liberal Arts Press, 1956. Part I, Book I, Chapter 2.

Kant, I. *The Philosophy of Law*, trans. W. Hastie. Edinburgh: T. T. Clark, 1887. Part II.

Kaufman, A. "The Reform Theory of Punishment," *Ethics*, 71(1960).

Leibniz, G. *Theodicy*, ed. A. Farrer. New Haven: Yale University Press, 1962. Part I, Sections 73–5.

Lewis, C. "Humanitarian Theory of Punishment," *Res Judicatae*, 6(1953).

MacLaglan, W. "Punishment and Retribution," *Philosophy*, 14(1939).

Maimonides. *The Guide for the Perplexed*. London: Routledge and Kegan Paul, 1904.

Mill, J. *An Examination of Sir William Hamilton's Philosophy*. New York: H. Holt, 1884. Chapter XXVI.

Morris, H. "Punishment for Thoughts," *The Monist*, 49(1965).

Mundle, C. "Punishment and Desert," *Philosophical Quarterly*. 4(1954).

Paley, W. *The Principles of Moral and Political Philosophy*, 13th ed. London: R. Faulder, 1801. Chapters I, X.

Plamenatz, J. "Responsibility, Blame and Punishment," in *Philosophy, Politics and Society*, 3rd series, ed. P. Laslett and W. G. Runciman. Oxford: Basil Blackwell, 1967.

Price, R. *A Review of the Principal Questions in Morals*, ed. D. Raphael. London: Oxford University Press, 1948.

Raphael, D. *Moral Judgement*. London: George Allen and Unwin Ltd., 1955. Chapter V.

Rashdall, H. *Theory of Good and Evil*, 2d ed. Oxford: Clarendon Press, 1924. Vol. I, Chapter 9.

Rawls, J. "Two Concepts of Rules," *Philosophical Review*, 64(1955).

Ross, W. "The Ethics of Punishment," *Philosophy*, 4(1925).

Sidgwick, H. *The Methods of Ethics*, 7th ed. Chicago: University of Chicago Press, 1962. Book III, Chapter V.

Smith, A. *The Theory of Moral Sentiments*. Philadelphia: Finley, 1817. Part II, Section 3, Chapters 1, 2.

Strawson, P. "Freedom and Resentment," in *Studies in the Philosophy of Thought and Action*. London: Oxford University Press, 1968.

Strong, E. "Justification of Juridical Punishment," *Ethics*, 79(1969).

Thompson, D. "Retribution and the Distribution of Punishment," *Philosophical Quarterly*, 16(1966).

CHAPTER III: STRICT LIABILITY

Austin, J. *Lectures on Jurisprudence*, 5th ed., ed. R. Cambell. London: J. Murray, 1911.

Bentham, J. *An Introduction to the Principles of Morals and Legislation*. Oxford: Basil Blackwell, 1948. Chapter XIII.

Brandt, R. "A Utilitarian Theory of Excuses," *Philosophical Review*, 78(1969).

Braybrooke, D. "Professor Stevenson, Voltaire and the Case of Admiral Byng," *Journal of Philosophy*, 53(1956).

Edwards, J. *Mens Rea in Statutory Offences*. London: Macmillan, 1955, p. 247.

Edwards, J. *Strict Liability in Statutory Offences*. London: Macmillan, 1950.

Glover, J. *Responsibility*. New York. Humanities Press, 1970: Chapter 3.

Hall, J. *General Principles of Criminal Law*, 2d ed. Indianapolis: Bobbs-Merrill, 1960. Chapter 10.

Hart, H. L. "Legal Responsibility and Excuses," in S. Hook (ed.), *Determinism and Freedom in the Age of Modern Science*. New York: New York University Press, 1958.

Holmes, O. *The Common Law*. Boston: Little, Brown and Co., 1881.

Howard, C. *Strict Responsibility*. London: Sweet, 1963.

Kneale, W. "The Responsibility of Criminals," in J. Rachels (ed.), *Moral Problems*. New York: Harper and Row, 1971.

Lyons, D. "On Sanctioning Excuses," *Journal of Philosophy*, 66(1969).

Morris, N. and C. Howard. *Studies in the Criminal Law.* Oxford: Clarendon Press, 1964.

Mueller, G. "On Common Law Mens Rea," *Minnesota Law Review*, 42(1958).

Packer, H. "Mens Rea and the Supreme Court," *Supreme Court Review*, 107(1962).

Sayre, F. "Public Welfare Offenses," *Columbia Law Review*, 33(1933).

Stern, L. "Deserved Punishment, Deserved Harm and Deserved Blame," *Philosophy*, 45(1970).

Thayer, E. "Liability Without Fault," *Harvard Law Review*, 29(1916).

Walker, O. "Why Should Irresponsible Offenders be Excused?" *Journal of Philosophy*, 66(1969).

Wasserstrom, R. "Strict Liability in the Criminal Law," *Stanford Law Review*, 12(1959–60).

Williams, G. *Criminal Law: The General Part*, 2d ed. London: Stevens and Sons Ltd., 1961. Chapters 6, 7.

Wootton, B. *Crime and the Criminal Law.* London: Stevens and Sons Ltd., 1963.

Wootton, B. "Diminished Responsibility: A Layman's View," *Law Quarterly Review*, 76(1960).

Wootton, B. *Social Science and Social Pathology.* London: George Allen and Unwin Ltd., 1959.

CHAPTER IV: THE DEATH PENALTY

Beccaria, C. *On Crimes and Punishment*, trans. H. Paolucci, Indianapolis: Bobbs-Merrill, 1963.

Bedau, H. "A Social Philosopher Looks at the Death Penalty," *American Journal of Psychiatry*, 123(1967).

Bedau, H. "Deterrence and the Death Penalty: A Reconsideration," *Journal of Criminal Law, Criminology and Police Science*, 61(1971).

Bedau, H. "The Courts, the Constitution and Capital Punishment," *Utah Law Review*, 1968.

Bedau, H. (ed.). *The Death Penalty in America*. Garden City: Doubleday, 1964.

Bentham, J. *The Rationale of Punishment*, in J. Bowring (ed.), *The Works of Jeremy Bentham*. Edinburgh: W. Tait, 1843. Chapters XI, XII.

Camus, A. "Reflections on the Guillotine," *Evergreen Review*, 1(1957), No. 3.

Capital Punishment. Staff Research Report, No. 46. Legislative Service Commission. Columbus: State of Ohio, 1961.

Capital Punishment. Department of Economic and Social Affairs. New York: United Nations, 1962.

Capital Punishment: Material Relating to Its Purpose and Value. Ottawa: Queen's Printer, 1965.

DiSalle, M. and L. Blochman. *The Power of Life or Death*. New York: Random House, 1965.

Ehrmann, H. *The Untried Case: The Sacco-Vanzetti Case and the Morelli Gang*, 2d ed. New York: Vanguard Press, 1960.

Ehrmann, H. *The Case That Will Not Die: Commonwealth vs. Sacco and Vanzetti*. Boston: Little, Brown and Co., 1969.

Gahringer, R. "Punishment and Responsibility," *Journal of Philosophy*, 66(1969).

Gottlieb, G. *Capital Punishment*. Santa Barbara: Center for the Study of Democratic Institutions, 1967.

Hart, H. L. "Murder and the Principles of Punishment: England and the United States," *Northwestern Law Review*, 52(1958).

Johnson, J. (ed.). *Capital Punishment*. New York: H. W. Wilson Co., 1939.

Koestler, A. and C. Rolph. *Hanged by the Neck*. Harmondsworth: Penguin Books, 1961.

Lawes, L. "Capital Punishment," in *Encyclopedia Americana*. New York: Americana Corp., 1966.

Lawrence, J. *A History of Capital Punishment*, 2d ed. New York: Citadel Press, 1960.

McClellan, G. (ed.). *Capital Punishment*. New York: H. W. Wilson Co., 1961.

Marx, K. "Capital Punishment," in L. Feuer (ed.), *Marx and Engels: Basic Writings on Politics and Philosophy*. Garden City: Anchor Books, 1959.

Parliamentary Debate on Capital Punishment Within Prisons Bill. *Hansard's Parliamentary Debates*, 3d series. London: Hansard, 1868.

Rousseau, J. *The Social Contract*, intro. C. Frankel, New York: Hafner, 1949. Book II, Chapter V.

Royal Commission on Capital Punishment 1949–1953 Report. London: Her Majesty's Printing Office, 1953.

Rush,, B. "Considerations of the Injustice and Impolicy of Punishing Murder by Death," *American Museum*, 1792. Reprinted in D. Runes (ed.), *The Selected Writings of Benjamin Rush*.

Schneir, W. and M. Schneir. *Invitation to an Inquest*. Garden City, Doubleday and Co., 1965.

Scott, G. *The History of Capital Punishment*. London: Torchstream Books, 1950.

Sellin, T. (ed.). *Capital Punishment*. New York: Harper and Row, 1967.

Sellin, T. (ed.) "Murder and the Death Penalty," in *The Annals of the American Academy of Political and Social Science*, 284(1952).

Sellin, T. *The Death Penalty*. Tentative Draft No. 9, Model Penal Code. Philadelphia: American Law Institute, 1959.

Van den Haag, E. "On Deterrence and the Death Penalty," *Ethics*, 78(1968).

Van den Haag, E. "On Deterrence and the Death Penalty," *Journal of Criminal Law, Criminology and Police Science*, 60(1969).

CHAPTER V: ALTERNATIVES TO PUNISHMENT

Abrahamsen, D. *Crime and the Human Mind*. Montclair: Patterson Smith, 1969 (1944).

Alexander, F. and H. Staub. *The Criminal, the Judge and the Public*, rev. ed. Glencoe: Free Press, 1956.

Andenaes, J. "The General Preventive Effects of Punishment," *University of Pennsylvania Law Review*, 114(1966).

Andenaes, J. "General Prevention—Illusion or Reality?" *Journal of Criminal Law, Criminology and Police Science*, 43(1952).

Ball, J. "The Deterrence Concept in Criminology and Law," *Journal of Criminal Law, Criminology and Police Science*, 46(1955).

Barnes, H. and N. Teeters. *New Horizons on Criminology*, rev. ed. New York: Prentice-Hall, 1950.

Birnbaum, M. "The Right to Medical Treatment," *American Bar Association Journal*, 46(1960).

Bixby, F. "Treating the Prisoner: A Lesson from Europe," *Federal Probation*, 25(1961).

Bromberg, W. *Crime and the Mind*. Philadelphia: J. B. Lippincott Co., 1948.

Christie, *Research Into Methods of Crime Prevention*. Report to the European Council No. DPC-CDIR 10, 1964.

Conrad, J. *Crime and Its Correction*. Berkeley: University of California Press, 1965.

Conrad, J. *The Future of Corrections*, in *The Annals of the American Academy of Political and Social Science*, 381(1969).

Correction. Task Force Report. Washington: President's Commission on Law Enforcement and the Administration of Justice, 1967.

DeGrazia, E. "Crime Without Punishment: A Psychiatric Conundrum," *Columbia Law Review*, 52(1952)

Dershowitz, A. "The Psychiatrist's Power in Civil Commitment: A Knife That Cuts Both Ways." *Psychology Today*, 3(1969).

Ellingston, J. *Protecting Our Children From Criminal Careers*. New York: Prentice-Hall, Inc., 1948.

Elliot, M. *Conflicting Penal Theories in Statutory Criminal Law*. Chicago: University of Chicago Press, 1931.

Empey, L. *Alternatives to Incarceration*. Washington: Office of Juvenile Delinquency, 1967.

Feinberg, J. "What is So Special About Mental Illness?" in *Doing and Deserving: Essays in the Theory of Responsibility*. Princeton: Princeton University Press, 1970.

Ferenczi, S. "Psycho-Analysis and Criminology," in *Further Contributions to the Theory and Technique of Psycho-Analysis*, trans. J. Suttie and others. London: Hogarth Press Ltd., 1950.

Freud, S. "Psycho-Analysis and the Establishment of the Facts in Legal Proceedings," in J. Strachey (ed.), *The Standard Edition of the Complete Psychological Works of Sigmund Freud*. London: Hogarth Press, 1959, pp. 97–114. Volume 9.

Gibbons, D. *Changing the Lawbreaker: The Treatment of Delinquents and Criminals.* Englewood Cliffs: Prentice-Hall, 1965.

Glaser, D. *The Effectiveness of a Prison and Parole System,* abridged ed. Indianapolis: Bobbs-Merrill, 1969.

Hakeem, M. "A Critique of the Psychiatric Approach to Crime and Correction," *Law and Contemporary Problems,* 23(1958).

Hall, J. *General Principles of Criminal Law,* 2d ed. Indianapolis: Bobbs-Merrill, 1960. Chapter 13.

Hess, A. *The Young Adult Offender: A Review of Current Practices and Programs in Prevention and Treatment.* New York: United Nations Department of Economic and Social Affairs, 1965.

Hood, *Research on the Effectiveness of Punishment.* Report to the European Council No. DPC/CDIR 9, 1964.

Karpman, B. "Criminality, Insanity and the Law," *Journal of Criminal Law, Criminology and Police Science,* 39(1949).

Kassenbaum, G., D. Ward and D. Wilner. *Prison Treatment and Parole Survival: An Empirical Assessment,* in press.

Kinberg, O. *Basic Problems of Criminology.* London: William Heinemann, Ltd. 1935.

Klare, H. (ed.). *Changing Concepts of Crime and Its Treatment.* London: Pergamon Press, 1966.

Landis, P. *Social Policies in the Making.* New York: D. C. Heath and Co., 1952.

Lipton, D., R. Martinson and J. Wilks. *The Treatment Evaluation Survey,* to appear.

Manual of Correctional Standards. Washington: American Correctional Association, 1966.

Maudsley, H. *Responsibility in Mental Disease.* New York: Appleton, 1896.

Menniger, K. *The Crime of Punishment.* New York: Viking Press, 1968.

Menniger, K. "The Psychiatrist in Relation to Crime," *Reports of the American Bar Association,* 51(1926).

Middendorf, W. *The Effectiveness of Punishment.* South Hackensack: Fred B. Rothman, 1968.

Morris, N. *The Habitual Criminal.* Cambridge: Harvard University Press, 1951.

Owen, R. *Essays on the Formation of the Human Character.* Manchester: Heywood, 1837.

Packer, H. *The Limits of the Criminal Sanction*. Stanford: Stanford University Press, 1968.

Powers, E. and H. Witmer. *An Experiment in the Prevention of Delinquency: The Cambridge-Somerville Youth Study*. New York: Columbia University Press, 1951.

Ross, A. "The Campaign Against Punishment," *Scandinavian Studies in Law*, 14(1970).

Russell, B. *Roads to Freedom*, 3d ed. London: Allen and Unwin Ltd., 1966, pp. 124–28.

Saleebey, G., H. Bradley, G. Smith and W. Salstrom. *The Non-Prison: A New Approach to Treating Youthful Offenders*. St. Paul: Bruce Publishing Co., 1970.

Scarborough, D. and A. Novick (eds.). *Institutional Rehabilitation of Delinquent Youth*. Albany: National Conference of Superintendents of Training Schools and Reformatories, 1962.

Schwartz, L. (ed.). *Crime and the American Penal System*, in *The Annals of the American Academy of Political and Social Science*, 339(1962).

Shoham, S. *Crime and Social Deviation*. Henry Regnery Co., Chicago, 1966.

Slavson, S. *Reclaiming the Delinquent: New Tools for Group Treatment*. New York Free Press, 1965.

Street, D., R. Vinter and C. Perrow. *Organization for Treatment: A Comparative Study of Institutions for Delinquents*. New York: Free Press, 1966.

Studt, E., S. Messinger and T. Wilson. *C-Unit: Search for Community in Prison*. New York: Russell Sage Foundation, 1968.

Sturop, G. *Treating the Untreatable*. Baltimore: Johns Hopkins University Press, 1968.

Toby, J. "Is Punishment Necessary?" *Journal of Criminal Law, Criminology and Police Science*, 55(1964).

White, W. *Crimes and Criminals*. New York: Farrar and Rinehart, Inc., 1933. Chapter XI.

Wilkins, L. *Evaluation of Penal Measures*. New York: Random House, 1969.

Wilkins, L. "Criminology: An Operational Research Approach," in A. Welford (ed.), *Society: Problems and Methods of Study*. London: Routledge and Paul, 1962.

Wiseman, F. "Psychiatry and Law: Use and Abuse of Psychiatry in a Murder Case," *American Journal of Psychiatry*, 118(1961).

Zilboorg, G. *The Psychology of the Criminal Act and Punishment.* New York: Harcourt Brace, 1954, p. 80.

Zimring, F. *Perspectives on Deterrence.* Washington: U.S. Government Printing Office, 1971.